WHAT CAN THIS BOOK DO FOR YOU?

Within a few years, your high school experience will lead you into the work world of adults. This book is designed to give you guidance, ideas, and answers about the many options life offers and the steps you will need to take for each.

WHAT FIRST?

Take a few minutes to claim ownership of this book. Write your name in it. In pencil, lay out your career and life goals as you see them today. Consider the obstacles you may have to overcome in order to achieve your goals. If you don't have a formal plan, that's OK. Answering these questions will spark your imagination and help you make one. The first steps might not be easy, but there are no right or wrong answers. As you continue working through this book, refer to these goals and feel free to fill in any blanks you left or to change your ideas.

WHAT NEXT?

Your needs, goals, ideas, and talents are unique to you. What is right for you may not be right for others. But the steps in the process of choosing a career direction (and understanding what education you might need to get there) are the same whether you aspire to repair car engines or design the next generation of space shuttles.

THINK OF THIS BOOK AS A ROAD MAP

Knowing where you want to go and what roads will lead you there is the first step in the process. You can always change your destination and chart a new course. We're providing the map. The rest is up to you.

GET THE SUCCESS

Name _____
Age _____
Grade _____
Date Started _____

My current goal after I graduate from high school is to:
_____
_____

At school, to reach my goal I'll need:
Curriculum planning:
_____
_____

Clubs, teams, associations:
_____
_____

Career research:
_____
_____

Outside of school, to reach my goal I'll need:
Volunteer work:
_____
_____

Shadowing/mentor program:
_____
_____

Job experience:
_____
_____

Extracurricular activities:
_____
_____

Challenges my goal presents:
_____
_____

Ideas to overcome these challenges:
_____

PETERSON'S
A nelnet COMPANY

About Peterson's, a Nelnet company
Peterson's (www.petersons.com) is a leading provider of education information and advice, with books and online resources focusing on education search, test preparation, and financial aid. Its Web site offers searchable databases and interactive tools for contacting educational institutions, online practice tests and instruction, and planning tools for securing financial aid. Peterson's serves 110 million education consumers annually.

For more information, contact Peterson's, 2000 Lenox Drive, Lawrenceville, NJ 08648; 800-338-3282; or find us on the World Wide Web at www.petersons.com/about.

© 2007 Peterson's, a Nelnet company

Previous editions © 1999, 2000, 2001, 2002, 2003, 2004, 2005, 2006

Editor: Linda Seghers; Production Editor: Bernadette Webster; Manufacturing Manager: Ray Golaszewski; Composition Manager: Linda M. Williams

ALL RIGHTS RESERVED. No part of this work covered by the copyright herein may be reproduced or used in any form or by any means—graphic, electronic, or mechanical, including photocopying, recording, taping, Web distribution, or information storage and retrieval systems—without the prior written permission of the publisher.

For permission to use material from this text or product, complete the Permission Request Form at http://www.petersons.com/permissions.

ISBN-13: 978-0-7689-2450-3 (Middle Atlantic)
ISBN-10: 0-7689-2450-2 (Middle Atlantic)

ISBN-13: 978-0-7689-2451-0 (Midwest)
ISBN-10: 0-7689-2451-0 (Midwest)

ISBN-13: 978-0-7689-2452-7 (New England)
ISBN-10: 0-7689-2452-9 (New England)

ISBN-13: 978-0-7689-2453-4 (South)
ISBN-10: 0-7689-2453-7 (South)

ISBN-13: 978-0-7689-2454-1 (Texas)
ISBN-10: 0-7689-2454-5 (Texas)

ISBN-13: 978-0-7689-2455-8 (West)
ISBN-10: 0-7689-2455-3 (West)

Printed in the United States of America

10 9 8 7 6 5 4 3 2 1   09 08 07

Ninth Edition

Dear Student:

Whether graduation seems light-years away or alarmingly close, it's never too early—or too late—to think about what comes after high school. Do you know what your next step will be?

Peterson's Get a Jump! can help you figure that out. This book is designed to help you launch your career, whether this means going on for more education or directly entering the workforce. You have a multitude of options and some crucial choices to make. In the pages that follow, we have tried to give you a jump-start on planning the future that's right for you.

The book is arranged in five parts. Part 1 has all the guidance you'll need to make the transition to high school. Part 2 provides general introductory information about your options after high school and how to use your high school education to plan for the next phase of your life. Part 3 offers more detailed information about postsecondary education, whether you choose a two-year, four-year, vocational/career college, or the military. Part 4 provides useful information about the workplace and how to handle stress, peer pressure, conflict, and other obstacles you may encounter. Finally, Part 5 contains appendices for each state in your geographic region of the United States, including valuable information on two- and four-year colleges and universities in your area and your state's high school graduation requirements, scholarship and financial aid programs, summer programs, and vocational and career colleges.

We hope you find this publication helpful as you begin thinking about the rest of your life. If you have questions or feedback on *Peterson's Get a Jump!*, please contact us at: Editor—Get a Jump!
   Peterson's, a Nelnet company
   2000 Lenox Drive
   Lawrenceville, NJ 08648

Sincerely,
Peterson's Editorial Staff

Contents

PART 1: YOU'RE GOING TO BE A FRESHMAN . . .

Chapter 1: The Big Jump to High School 5
The Differences: Middle School vs. High School 6
There's So Much to Do! 7
Honors or Nonhonors: Choosing Classes 8
What in the World Is a GPA and What the Heck Is a Transcript? 10
Tips for a Smooth Start 14
Top 10 Mistakes 17

PART 2: JUMP-START YOUR FUTURE

Chapter 2: A Look at Yourself 21
Ready to Fly 21
The Top 10 Reasons to Continue Your Education 22
Choosing a Career You'll Be Happy With 24
On the Hunt for Information 25

Chapter 3: The First Steps to a Career 28
The Vocational/Career Education Path 28
The Tech-Prep Path 29
Using the Summer to Your Advantage 29
Flip Burgers and Learn About Life 30
Try Your Hand at an Internship 31
Volunteering in Your Community 32

PART 3: THE ROAD TO MORE EDUCATION

Chapter 4: Planning Your Education While in High School 35
Your Education Timeline 35
Classes to Take If You're Going to College 41

Chapter 5: Tackling the Tests 44
A Few Facts About the Major Tests 44
The ACT 44
The SAT 45
The PSAT/NMSQT 46
SAT Subject Tests 47
The TOEFL Internet-Based Test (iBT) 47
What Other Tests Should I Know About? 47
What Can I Do to Prepare for These Tests? 48

Chapter 6: The College Search 50
The Best Resources 50
Online Help 51
Campus Visits 52
The College Interview 53
Should You Head for the Ivy League? 57
Minority Students 58
Students with Disabilities Go to College 61

Chapter 7: Applying to College 64
What Schools Look for in Prospective Students 64
Admission Procedures 65
More Mumbo Jumbo 67
The Complete Application Package 68
Special Information for Athletes 75
Auditions and Portfolios 77
The Gap-Year Option 80

Chapter 8: Financial Aid Dollars and Sense . . 82
A Bird's-Eye View of Financial Aid 82
Types of Financial Aid 84
Federal Grants 85
Federal Scholarships 86
Federal Loans 87
Thinking Ahead to Paying Back Your Student Loan 88
Other Federal Programs 89
Families' Guide to Tax Cuts for Education 90
Applying for Financial Aid 91
National, Statewide, and Local Scholarships 92
Scholarships for Minority Students 93
Applying for Scholarships 93
What You Need to Know About Athletic Scholarships . . . 94

Contents

Myths About Scholarships and Financial Aid 95
Scholarship Scams.................................. 96
Financial Aid on the Web 98

Chapter 9: What to Expect in College 100
Choosing Your Classes............................. 100
Choosing Your Major 100
The Other Side of College: Having Fun!............. 108
Roommates 110
Commuting from Home 111
What If You Don't Like the College You Pick? 112

Chapter 10: Other Options After High School 113
Distance Learning 113
Community Colleges 116
Vocational/Career Colleges 118
Financial Aid Options for Career and
  Community Colleges 119
Apprenticeships 120

Chapter 11: The Military Option 123
Should I or Shouldn't I Work for the Largest Employer
  in the United States?........................... 123
Choosing Which Branch to Join 124
The ASVAB 126
Basic Training: What Have I Gotten Myself Into? 128
Paying for College Through the Armed Services....... 129

PART 4: YOU AND THE WORKPLACE

Chapter 12: Jump into Work 135
The College/Career Timeline 135
Writing Your Resume 136
Job Hunting 101 141
The Job Interview................................. 142
What Employers Expect from Employees 144
Jumping on the Salary Fast-Track.................. 145
On the Job.. 146

Chapter 13: Survival Skills 148
Skills to Make You Stress-Hardy 148
Winning the Time Management Game............. 150
Moving Out on Your Own?........................ 151
Drugs and Alcohol: Are You at Risk?................ 152
Conflict: How to Avoid It or Defuse It 154
The Lowdown on Sexual Harassment 155
Staying Healthy in Spite of Yourself................. 157

PART 5: APPENDICES

High School Diploma Test Requirements
Four-Year Colleges and Universities
Two-Year Colleges
Vocational/Career Colleges
Scholarships and Financial Aid
Summer Programs

YOU'RE GOING TO BE A FRESHMAN...

YOU KNOW WHAT IT'S SUPPOSED TO BE LIKE—being in high school should be COOL. But what will it REALLY be like? Will you be able to figure it all out? Of course you will . . . especially since you are reading this! Your high school years will be like nothing else you have experienced, and as a freshman you are going to have questions about everything. Luckily, it's right here that you will be able to get answers. Whether you're wondering about how to keep your "stuff" organized, choosing your classes, or what a GPA is, we are here to help! So, come on, jump in—you're going to be a FRESHMAN!

To Students, Parents, and Counselors:

It was my pleasure to experiment with using **Peterson's Get a Jump!** in selected high schools and elementary schools in Chicago. While the logistics of how high school students are scheduled and how they move from class to class made the job of getting the material to them and guiding them through it very challenging, the material was well received by the high schools, and those students who were exposed to the book were excited by all of the information it provided.

Conversely, the elementary school (which in Chicago means K-8) students, especially the sixth to eighth graders, were a captive audience and, with assistance from a teacher, were much easier to get together in presentation groups on a grade-by-grade and class-by-class basis. These students were so attentive and curious about high school and what happens there, and I was more than surprised that the students at both the high schools and elementary schools lacked knowledge about such things as: What is a transcript? What is a GPA? What are class ranks? What are honors classes and AP classes?

When I relayed these "discoveries" back to Peterson's, the idea of adding a special chapter on just these types of questions and issues facing the middle school student getting ready to make the transition to high school was a natural evolution. "The Big Jump to High School" gives parents, guidance counselors, and, most importantly, students the information they need to successfully make that transition—answering not only the questions about transcripts, GPAs, class ranks, and honors and AP classes, but also giving advice on participation in extracurricular activities, how to deal with the differences between middle school and high school, setting goals, staying organized, and how to study. And this advice comes not just from Peterson's, but also from guidance counselors, parents, and students all over the country!

Finally, as a college administrator who has worked with high schools, elementary schools, and middle schools for more than thirty years, I find **Peterson's Get a Jump!** to be a book that has been long overdue. It is an excellent vehicle for young people who seek guidance in planning their educational futures! Best of luck to all of you!

Nathaniel Thomas, Ph.D.

THE BIG JUMP TO HIGH SCHOOL

Even if you've never said anything to anyone else, chances are the thought of your first year of high school is totally scary, especially with all these questions whirling around in your head:

Who will I sit with at lunch **What if my best friends don't have lunch when I do WHERE IS THE VENDING MACHINE** How will I find my way around the halls What will I do when I have only four minutes to get to my next class What happens if I get lost *Will I remember my locker combination* WHAT HAPPENS IF I CAN'T OPEN MY LOCKER **What happens if there aren't any lockers** How will I carry all those books around in my backpack What if my best friend isn't in the same classes as me What if I don't know anyone in my classes What if I don't know where the bathroom is WHAT HAPPENS IF I FORGET WHERE TO GO FOR MY CLASS WHAT IF, WHAT IF, WHAT IF THE SENIORS ARE MEAN TO ME AND TREAT ME LIKE DIRT?????

Part 1: You're Going to be a Freshman . . .

IN MIDDLE SCHOOL, you knew where everything was. You knew exactly who would be sitting next to you at lunch. You knew all the teachers. All the teachers knew you. You were at the top of the heap. Now you're starting all over again.

First of all, take a deep breath, sit back, and realize that it's okay to have the ups and downs, the doubts, and the feelings that zip back and forth between "I can't wait to get into high school" to "I'm hiding under my bed and never coming out." The first few weeks of high school, you're surrounded by a lot of kids who are bigger, who seem to know an awful lot more than you do, and who know exactly where to go. You'll wonder what it will be like, trying out for sports teams or shows and activities with the tenth, eleventh, and twelfth graders.

FROM THE GUIDANCE OFFICE

"Freshmen are afraid the upper class students will pick on them, but honestly, that's not true. Upper class students are not the least bit interested in freshmen."

Helen Erbe
Guidance Counselor
Jackson Memorial High School
Jackson, New Jersey

Second, the friend of a friend's brother who told you he hated ninth grade isn't you. Everyone adjusts to high school in different ways and at different speeds. For some kids, the transition from junior high school/middle school to high school takes a short time, like days or weeks. For others, the adjustment takes longer, especially if they're not admitting to themselves and others what their feelings are and letting others help them get over their insecurities.

ADVICE FROM A SENIOR

Sometimes freshmen give older students too much power. My advice is don't be afraid to be yourself.

Kristen Seghers, Senior
West Windsor-Plainsboro High School South
Princeton Junction, New Jersey

Third, you are not alone. All those big kids ahead of you have gone through the same fears and have had the same feelings, too. They made it through, and you will too. It's most likely that the sophomores, juniors, and seniors are too busy dealing with the problems of being sophomores, juniors, and seniors to be concerned if you forgot your locker combination and have to go slinking off to the school office to find out what it is.

PARENT PERSPECTIVE

"Stephen was nervous about starting ninth grade. It took him only about two to three days to catch on."

Sharon Blumenthal
Parent to Stephen, who is going into the tenth grade.

THE DIFFERENCES: MIDDLE SCHOOL VS. HIGH SCHOOL

There's no getting around it. High school is a different ball game. It's like you're used to playing soccer and all of a sudden in order to score, you're expected to throw the ball, not kick it. Some of the major differences between middle school and high school are:

You are more independent. In middle school, you were part of a group. You did the same things together—ate lunch, took the same classes, goofed off. Same teachers, same schedule. It's a big adjustment to realize that you will have your own schedule of classes that could be very different from your best friend's. You will be in classes with people you don't know because there are different levels of classes. You could be in the middle level of a math class and your friend in the upper-level class.

ADVICE FROM A JUNIOR

"When I was a freshman, I got into band camp and got to know kids in the band. Then when I was walking through the halls I knew more people other than just the freshmen. If you know people around you then you'll feel comfortable. If you feel comfortable then you'll be more willing to do new things. My high school is a huge high school. The idea is to make as many friends as you can. So talk to everybody."

Matt Wolf, Junior
Doherty High School
Colorado Springs, Colorado

You have to take more responsibility. In middle school you probably had fewer choices about which classes you could take. In high school, there are many more choices about your education, especially as you go into your sophomore year. You'll get to choose some classes, or electives as they're called. As a freshman, the choices you have of electives are limited. Most freshmen can choose only one elective. Sophomores only two. At the junior and senior levels, you'll have more and more choices to make, depending on your goals and interests.

The way you are graded is different in high school. Your teachers in junior high school were probably a lot more lenient when it came to late homework. They were more likely to look at your past record and give you a little leeway. Teachers in high school aren't as likely to accept excuses. "I forgot" won't work. In high school, your grades are based on numbers. Some teachers will deduct two points if you don't get your homework done and turned in on time.

You have to speak up for yourself. In middle school, your parents probably helped you if you got into a tough situation, say with a teacher. They were the ones making the phone call or visiting the teacher. In high school, there will be times when you will have to deal with situations on your own, such as speaking with a teacher about homework, or getting your voice heard in clubs and activities even though you're the youngest one there. In high school, you have to develop the ability to get advice from your parents and counselors, figure out how to solve the problem, and then take action.

ADVICE FROM A SENIOR

"Speak up if you have a good idea. In sports or clubs, sometimes younger people have good ideas or strategies and ways to help out, but they don't want to say anything."

Kristen Seghers, Senior
West Windsor-Plainsboro High School South
Princeton Junction, New Jersey

THERE'S SO MUCH TO DO!

Your freshman year is a time for you to explore your interests—what's it like being a crime scene investigator, a computer graphics designer, a veterinarian, etc.

Explore your interests via elective classes. One of the main purposes of high school electives is to allow you to investigate career interests. Though you will be required to take a variety of basic classes like math, English, history, and science, your choice of electives can point you in the direction of a future college major. It could very well be that something you enjoy doing as a freshman could end up being the start of your career.

You can take electives in areas like computers, art, accounting, or music. Say you think you'd like to be in business some day, sitting in an office overlooking the city. You can begin to realize that dream by taking accounting as an elective. You may find out you really like working with numbers. Or, you may find out you'd rather be building high-rises instead of sitting in them.

Explore your interests via clubs and activities. In addition to sports, high school offers many clubs and activities outside of what you'll learn in the

Part 1: You're Going to be a Freshman . . .

> **FROM THE GUIDANCE OFFICE**
>
> "Some kids that I counsel know what they want to be. Others don't have a clue, and some have an inkling. Your high school courses can help you reach that goal and, if you don't have a goal, can help you explore what you want to do."
>
> Madeleine Wyckoff
> Director of Guidance
> Port Charlotte High School
> Port Charlotte, Florida

classroom. You may think these activities are there just so you can have some fun. While that's true, they also give you the opportunity to find out what your interests are. Extracurricular activities can help you find what goals you want to set and then how to reach them.

ADVICE FROM A JUNIOR

I would have definitely joined more clubs and done more activities in my freshman year. Say if you join a drama club as a freshman, you can be at the top when you get to be a junior or senior. If you wait to join when you're a junior, you'll be at the bottom end. Colleges want you to be a leader so you have to start going for the top of activities when you're a freshman.

Matt Wolf, Junior
Doherty High School
Colorado Springs, Colorado

Here's a sample list of clubs and activities in which you can participate. Every school is different, so you'll have to find out what your high school offers, but this list will give you an idea of what you can expect.

- Auto club
- Band
- Bowling club
- Cheerleading
- Choir
- Forensics club
- Math club
- Mock Trial
- Newspaper
- Science club

Explore your interests via volunteer work. High schools often offer opportunities for you to do volunteer work. Are you interested in working with younger kids? In being a lawyer? In helping those who are sick? You can volunteer to help out in a hospital or law office, for instance. By volunteering and working alongside people who are doing the things you may like to do, you can quickly judge if you really do like hospitals or law offices.

HONORS OR NONHONORS: CHOOSING CLASSES

One of the most critical decisions you're going to have to make in your first year of high school is whether to take classes on a regular level or on an honors level. You may have heard about AP classes, or Advanced Placement classes. You can't take those until your junior or senior year, but the time to start planning for this high academic level is actually in your freshman year. If your goal is to take college-level courses in high school (that's what AP classes are), you should start in the ninth grade by taking honors classes. AP classes are very competitive with little wiggle room for poor grades or performance as you move from freshman, to sophomore, to junior.

But first you need to know the difference between "regular," honors, and AP classes.

Classes at the "Regular" Level

Different high schools may have different labels for this level, but basically, if you're in a "regular" level class, you're getting what you need in that subject area to meet the requirements to graduate from high school in four years and go on to college. Do the work expected of you, turn in all your homework, do well on the tests, and you'll get that piece of paper in four years that says you've completed the necessary subjects to become a high school graduate.

Classes at the Honors Level

Honors-level classes require more from you. You'll do more reading and writing that demands more in-depth understanding of the subject matter. Classes at this level develop critical-thinking skills by asking you to interpret situations and events. Honors classes are designed to provide you with an in-depth investigation into a subject.

Teachers will expect you to participate in class discussions. You will learn to feel comfortable with a subject so you'll be able to talk about it. For instance, when studying the civil war in an honors class, you'll delve deeper into the conditions that brought the war about, in addition to dates, geographic locations, and famous names. Then you'll look at how the war affected history and learn something about the social and political issues that followed.

Some Things to Consider before Taking the Honors Plunge

Many students do well in honors classes. Others struggle, whereas they may have done very well starting off in a "regular" level class. Then, once they've become familiar with the different way classes are taught and what's expected academically of high school students, they may be able to handle an honors class with ease.

You must be honest with yourself and with your parents. Sometimes parents see their kids through rosy glasses and think their sons and daughters are geniuses. Meanwhile, the son or daughter is struggling to cope with the whole change from junior high school to high school, and falls behind. Your mindset has a lot to do with how well you'll do in high school, so it's much better to begin high school at a level that fits you.

If you are terrible at writing, but love science, that's your clue about which honors classes to take and in which sequence. You may take a science honors class your first semester. See how you do. Then you can add an English honors course the second semester.

If you're not confident about your study habits or organizational skills, the first semester of high school is a time to slowly dip your tootsies in the honors pool. Feel the temperature of the water by doing well in a "regular" class, flex your mind muscles, and then dive into honors. The goal is to excel in what you do well and then take the classes that challenge you.

The WORST mistake you can make is to select an honors class because your best friend decided to take it. How well you do in high school determines if many of the doors to your future plans will be open. If you do poorly, you begin to close doors even in your freshman year.

Classes at the AP (Advanced Placement) Level

In AP classes, you're actually learning at the college level. You are expected to do the assignments and perform on the tests as you would if you were in college. No wonder you can't take AP classes until your junior and senior year. In order to even get into an AP class, you must be a high achiever.

While the hurdles to getting into an AP class are high, the advantages for those who do well in AP classes are huge. The AP exams are given to students across the United States in May and are scored on a level from 1–5, with 5 being tops. If you get a 3, 4, or 5 in the exam of a particular class, you may be able to waive the introductory level of that class in college. Some colleges may even award you college credit! Not only will this save you time and money, but you'll also impress college admissions offices with the fact that you're taking AP classes. Colleges look favorably on students who worked hard in high school and did well in difficult subjects.

During the college admission process, some colleges "weight" the different levels of classes you take. For instance, they'll give you more points for an A in an honors or AP class than they would for an A in a "regular" class. An A in a class at a regular level may count as a 4, while an A in an honors or AP class would count as a 5 and a B in an honors or AP class would count as a 4.

What If You Want to Be a Chef and Your Parents Are Determined for You to Go to Harvard?

That's a tough situation and the above example is a little on the exaggerated side, but as a freshman, now is the time to address a difference of opinion about your future plans with your parents. So, say you do want to be a chef. You know that honors classes demand a lot more studying and time and that to get into culinary schools or other vocational tracks, you don't need to get As in honors classes. However, your parents know you could get As without too much effort. High school counselors will probably encourage you to take the honors classes. Why not leave your options open? As a freshman, your plans can change a lot before you graduate. If you start out with the plan to be a chef set in concrete and leave no room for change, you could get to your junior year and decide that you hate the smell of burning food. You would rather get a degree in business from a top college. If you'd taken honors classes, you'd be in a good position to go to the university of your choice.

ADVICE FROM A SENIOR

"When you're a freshman, it's hard to see the big picture of your future. I couldn't see it and probably could have done better than I did if I'd talked to some older people or taken a peek at college stuff and seen how important things are."

Kristen Seghers, Senior
West Windsor-Plainsboro High School South
Princeton Junction, New Jersey

Advice for Parents

Make sure your child can do well in the honors or AP classes before you start pushing for all As at that level. Each child has different skills. Let's imagine your child takes honors classes in everything that's offered that first year. The child works extremely hard and comes home with a C in biology. You're devastated. Your child is devastated. You've never seen a C on a report card. To help your child make the right decisions about honors and AP classes, talk with your child and your child's guidance counselor.

WHAT IN THE WORLD IS A GPA AND WHAT THE HECK IS A TRANSCRIPT?

Your GPA (Grade Point Average). If you haven't already heard about the GPA, those three letters—G, P, and A—are going to mean a lot as you move from freshman to senior. There's no getting around the fact that the GPA is important to your future: what college you can attend, what kind of upper-level high school classes you can take (such as those AP classes), what academic and athletic scholarships you may get, or for what special programs you may qualify.

In short, the GPA is the average of all your grades starting from your freshman year. A little planning in your freshman year can go a long way toward a better GPA when you graduate. If you know the impact a GPA can have, you may do things a little differently in your freshman year.

It's good to know how your GPA is computed. Different schools have their own ways to total up a GPA, but this will give you the basic idea.

In general, schools score letter grades as follows:

A = 4 points

B = 3 points

C = 2 points

D = 1 point

F = 0 points

Some schools give higher points for grades earned in honors courses. That's something you would need to check out in the school office. So, let's take a hypothetical student's grades for one semester:

English	A	4 points
History	B	3 points
Music	A	4 points
Math	C	2 points
Spanish	B	3 points
Physical Education	A	4 points

The points total 20 points. Divide that by the number of classes, which is 6, and you get a GPA of 3.33 for one semester.

Let's take the next semester and see how our student did.

English	A	4 points
History	A	4 points
Music	A	4 points
Math	B	3 points
Spanish	C	2 points
Physical Education	A	4 points

That totals 21 points divided by 6, which equals a 3.5 GPA. Now, add the total number of points over these last two semesters, which is 41 and divide by the number of classes (12) and you get a 3.42 GPA.

This is a simplified version of how schools score GPAs because some high schools give different points to each class level. For instance, an A in English may be worth more points than an A in physical education.

Your transcript. A transcript goes with you through high school and shows the final grade you received in each of your courses. Your transcript is a history of the classes you took and what grade you achieved in that class. It's what colleges ask for to assess what kind of a student you are.

As a freshman, you need to lay a good foundation academically. Competitive colleges that attract thousands of applications look carefully at your transcript. They're not only looking at your final GPA. They're also looking at how you challenged yourself during your high school years. Did you take courses that stretched you academically, like honors and AP classes, or did you take only those classes you were required to take?

Some Important Things to Know About Transcripts

Transcripts differ from school to school. You need to find out what your school records on your transcript. For example, say you got good grades but missed a lot of classes because you just didn't feel like showing up. If your transcript shows the number of times you were not in class, and you're going for a top college or university, your good grades (and high GPA) won't look so good.

- Some schools show how many absences you had for each class.
- Some schools are on the trimester system, which means you'll have three sets of grades for each year.
- Some schools show plus and minus grades, such as a B+ or an A–, and some don't.
- Some schools don't count the freshman year when adding up your GPA.
- Some schools don't show your rank in your class, such as 168 out of 388, but instead use a quartile system, such as ranking you in the top 25% of your class.
- Some schools show your GPA as "weighted," which means that you get an extra credit point for an honors or AP class.
- Some schools show your "citizenship" record in classes. Did you contribute to the class or were you disruptive?
- Some schools will send a profile of your school with your transcript to colleges showing the community in which the school is located, the student population, how many honors and AP classes are offered, the number of periods in a day that classes are offered, etc.

Part 1: You're Going to be a Freshman . . .

WHAT'S WHAT ON YOUR TRANSCRIPT

A. Your personal information:

Name

Address

Social Security Number (or Student ID number if you don't have a social security number)

Date of Birth

Ethnic Code

NOTE: Parents can request that your social security number, date of birth, and ethnic code be deleted from the transcript when it is sent to various colleges.

B. Abbreviations of the classes you've taken.

C. **Term GPA** is the number of grade points you earn each semester. In the transcript example on the following page, each letter grade is given a number of points, with honors classes getting an extra point:

English 1 Honors (with an extra point for honors)	B	= 4 points
Freehand Drawing 1	A	= 4 points
Spanish 1	B	= 3 points
Algebra 1	B	= 3 points
PE 9	B	= 3 points
Intro to Science 1	C	= 2 points
Government/Law 1	B	= 3 points

Add the points up and you get 22 points. Then divide that total (22) by the number of classes this student took, which is 7. Carry that out to 4 decimal places and you get 3.1429 grade points.

Cumulative GPA is found by taking the number of grade points from all your previous semesters and adding them up and then dividing them by the number of semesters. Let's look again at this student's transcript for the second semester:

Computer Apps	B	= 3 points
English 2 Honors (with an extra point for honors)	C	= 3 points
Freehand Drawing 2	A	= 4 points
Spanish 2	B	= 3 points
Algebra 2	B	= 3 points
Intro to Science 2	A	= 4 points
Government/Law 2	B	= 3 points

Add the points up and you get 23 points. Then divide that total (23) by 7 (the number of classes) and carry that figure out 4 decimals to get 3.2857 points. Add the two semesters' points (3.1429 and 3.2857) together and divide by the number of semesters, which is 2, and you get the cumulative GPA of 3.2143.

D. Letter grade you earned in each class.

E. Number of absences in each class.

F. Number of credits you earned in each class—you get one credit per class and you need 44 to graduate at this high school. Every school district has a different number of classes you need to graduate or, in some states, every district might be the same.

G. In this transcript, the letter G instead of an A, B, C, D, or F indicates that this course is not taken into account when figuring out your GPA. An "H" would indicate that you dropped the class without a penalty, like an "F". This student didn't drop any classes.

H. **Unofficial Transcript** means that it hasn't been signed or stamped with an official stamp. Transcripts are mailed directly to the school or colleges of your choice. Sometimes they can be transported by the student in a sealed envelope.

I. The date you entered the high school.

J. The date you left the high school.

K. Overall weighted—if your school gives extra points for honors or AP classes when figuring out your GPA, it will be noted here.

L. Your final cumulative GPA.

M. The total amount of credits you attempted.

N. Your class standing and the number of students who were in your senior class when you graduated. This student was 168 out of 388 students in the senior class.

O. Total Credits Earned in High School.

P. Notes about the clubs, sports, and committees in which you participated can be added here with verification from the person responsible for that extracurricular activity.

Q. Signature—the transcript must be signed and have an official seal in order to be accepted as an official transcript.

Chapter 1: The Big Jump to High School

Colorado Springs Dist 11
Unofficial Transcript

Doherty High School   719-328-6400
4515 Barnes Rd
Colorado Springs, CO 80917

Entry Date	Counselor	Graduation Date
09/01/2003		05/20/2007
Exit Date	**Exit Reason**	**Diploma Type**
06/06/2007	W19-Graduated	High School Diploma
GPA Type	**GPA**	**Crdt Atmpt**	**Class Rank**
Overall Weighted	3.0476	42.0000	168 of 388

Issued To	Print Date
	09/08/2006
	1 of 1

Total Credits Earned   44.0000

Subject Cd	Course	Mrk1	Abs	Credits
Doherty High School Grd 09 Semester 1 02/00				
EN	English 1, Honors	B	3	1.0000
HU	Frhand Drwng1	A	5	1.0000
HU	Spanish 1	B	4	1.0000
MA	Algebra 1	B	5	1.0000
PE	PE 9	B	7	1.0000
SC	Intro to Science 1	C	6	1.0000
SS	Gov/Law 1	B	5	1.0000
TERM:	GPA 3.1429	CREDITS 7.0000		
CUMULATIVE:	GPA 3.1429	CREDITS 7.0000		
Doherty High School Grd 09 Semester 2 06/00				
CM	Computer Apps	B	1	1.0000
EN	English 2, Honors	C	1	1.0000
HU	Frhand Drwng2	A	2	1.0000
HU	Spanish 2	B	4	1.0000
MA	Algebra 2	B	1	1.0000
SC	Intro to Science 2	A	1	1.0000
SS	Gov/Law 2	B	3	1.0000
TERM:	GPA 3.2857	CREDITS 7.0000		
CUMULATIVE:	GPA 3.2143	CREDITS 14.0000		
Doherty High School Grd 10 Semester 1 01/01				
E3	English 3	B	3	1.0000
HL	Health	C	1	1.0000
HU	Spanish 3	B	1	1.0000
MA	Geometry 1	B	2	1.0000
PA	Todays Foods	B	1	1.0000
SC	Biology 1	B	3	1.0000
SS	World & US History 3	C	2	1.0000
TERM:	GPA 2.7143	CREDITS 7.0000		
CUMULATIVE:	GPA 3.0476	CREDITS 21.0000		
Doherty High School Grd 10 Semester 2 06/01				
E4	English 4	B	1	1.0000
HU	Frhand Drwng3	A	6	1.0000
HU	Spanish 4	B	6	1.0000
MA	Geometry 2	C	3	1.0000
PE	PE 10	B	7	1.0000
SC	Biology 2	B	7	1.0000
SS	World & US History 4	C	6	1.0000
TERM:	GPA 2.8571	CREDITS 7.0000		
CUMULATIVE:	GPA 3.0000	CREDITS 28.0000		
Doherty High School Grd 11 Semester 1 01/02				
A1	Hist: US & World 5	C	9	1.0000
E5	English 5	B	9	1.0000
HU	Psychology	B	3	1.0000
MA	Algebra 3	B	1	1.0000
PA	Automotive Tech 1	A	5	1.0000
TERM:	GPA 3.0000	CREDITS 5.0000		
CUMULATIVE:	GPA 3.0000	CREDITS 33.0000		
Doherty High School Grd 11 Semester 2 05/02				
A2	Hist: US & World 6	B	7	1.0000
E6	English 6	B	1	1.0000
EL	Student Tutor	G	4	1.0000
HU	Psychology, Advanced	A	9	1.0000
MA	Algebra 4	B	4	1.0000
TERM:	GPA 3.2500	CREDITS 5.0000		
CUMULATIVE:	GPA 3.0270	CREDITS 38.0000		
Doherty High School Grd 12 Semester 1 12/02				
CE	Cons Econ	B	3	1.0000
EN	Creative Writing	A	5	1.0000
EN	Senior Speed Reading 1	B	7	1.0000
PE	PE	A	9	1.0000
PE	Physical Ed	G		1.0000
SC	College Prep Chem 1	C	9	1.0000
TERM:	GPA 3.2000	CREDITS 6.0000		
CUMULATIVE:	GPA 3.0476	CREDITS 44.0000		

Mrk 1: Course Grade

Student Notes

_____
School Official's Signature

Part 1: You're Going to be a Freshman . . .

TIPS FOR A SMOOTH START

Write down a list of things you want to accomplish. If you have a rough idea of where you're headed, you'll have an easier time getting there. You've already set goals for yourself. Maybe it was to score more points on a video game than the kid down the street. Maybe it was to ride a bike faster or do more maneuvers on a skateboard. When you get into high school, it's important to set goals for yourself from the start. Obviously, the goals will change over time, but having a list of goals—like I want to make the football team; I want to take some honors classes; I want to run for class president; I want to be the editor of the school yearbook—will help you stay motivated and give you something to work toward.

Make your goals specific. For example:

A vague goal is:

I want to be a better student than I was in middle school.

A specific goal is:

The reason I wasn't a good student in middle school is because I didn't turn in my homework. Starting off in high school, I'm going to turn in all my homework on time.

ADVICE FROM A SENIOR

"When I was a freshman, I was intimidated by the older kids' appearance of greatness and their accomplishments. I thought, 'Wow, I can't get to their level.' But don't give up because you think there's too much competition, especially if it's something you really want to do."

Kristen Seghers, Senior
West Windsor-Plainsboro High School South
Princeton Junction, New Jersey

Get involved in clubs and activities immediately. We've already talked about how clubs and activities help narrow your interests and focus you on what you want to do in the future. But extracurricular activities serve another very important purpose for high school freshmen. You'll find friends who like the same things you do. You'll be with older kids so you'll get to know some juniors and seniors. You'll gain confidence in yourself as you work together with other kids. You'll become comfortable with being in high school a lot quicker than if you hang around on the fringes looking in instead of being in the middle of the action, whether it's on a soccer team, chess club, or—whatever!

Get organized. In high school, being organized does not mean showing up in class on time with your teeth brushed. Being organized is brought to a whole different level in high school. Some kids are naturally this way. In middle school, they knew what homework had to be done, when it was due, and what was required. In high school, the list of things to organize gets longer. You still have to show up on time and whether your teeth are brushed is up to you, but you do have to have all the supplies you need with you.

> **PARENT PERSPECTIVE**
>
> *"Every Friday afternoon before leaving school, Jessica gets her locker organized. It's easy for it to get out of control because kids are stuffing things in there all week. Then they can't find something when they need it and the time between classes is so short."*
>
> Jodi Domsky
> *Parent of Jessica, who just started ninth grade and was very organized in middle school.*

That sparkly pink pen in your hand won't do to take the test the teacher just handed you. Your teacher specifically told you to bring a blue or black ballpoint. Now where is it? I thought I put it in my backpack. Oh no, here's the sandwich I forgot to eat yesterday on top of my history homework. Your room may be a disaster, but your notebooks, binders, and calendar need to be in tip-top shape.

You're organizing for more classes and carrying around a lot more books and papers than you ever did in middle school. You're going to be involved in sports and clubs. Unless you're organized, you're going to spend more time dealing with chaos and confusion and moldy sandwiches than getting your homework done

Chapter 1: The Big Jump to High School

> **ADVICE FROM A TEACHER**
>
> "Typically, middle school students get one big binder with four to five dividers. All their classes' materials are in one binder. It doesn't work that way for high school. They have too much. They can't put homework, notes, handouts and other pieces of paper in one section of the binder. When the binder system fails by mid-October, then they take everything that was in the binder and stuff it in a backpack. Now it's a 15-minute ordeal to find something in the backpack."
>
> Heidi Pimentel
> Spanish teacher
> Pioneer High School
> San Jose, California

and having all the fun there is to have in high school. Each week in high school goes by at blazing speed and things can get out of control very quickly.

This is what organized students know:

- What was assigned in each class
- When the homework is due
- When the next test is scheduled
- What I need to bring to each class
- Where the supplies I need are located

Organization skills will stay with you the rest of your life. Now's a great time to learn how easy your life will be when you're organized.

ADVICE FROM A JUNIOR

I wasn't very organized and should have been. In middle school, you don't have as many classes as in high school. It's harder to plan for seven classes instead of three or four a day.

Matt Wolf, Junior
Doherty High School
Colorado Springs, Colorado

The way to get organized is to set up a system. It can be someone else's system or your own. The important thing is to have some way to keep track of when assignments are due, when tests are coming, and what nights are taken up with practices or meetings. Each week, go through and set up a new schedule for the coming week. It sounds like a lot of work, but when Thursday hits and your head is spinning, you'll be glad you have a schedule to hang on to. You could have three tests on the same day. Wouldn't it be helpful to know that way ahead of time instead of remembering the day of the tests?

Manage your time. Time management is a term that you've probably heard and put into the "I'll deal with that when I get older" category. Guess what, you're older! You have to take your time and manage it, which means figuring out what you have to do and how much time you have to do it.

It's going to be easy to say, "I'll do my homework after dinner," but you have to take into account that basketball practice doesn't end until 8 p.m., and when you get home you'll want something to eat. So, in reality, you're doing homework until 10 or 11 o'clock, and you have to get up at 6 o'clock.

In high school, your workload increases as you move into the upper classes. If you don't learn how to manage your time, you will only have to struggle that much harder. Plus you have all those other activities eating away at the 24 hours in each day.

Ask questions. You've heard the saying, "No question is a stupid question." Well, kids going into ninth grade seem to forget the "NO" part of that sentence and instead rephrase it as "All my questions are stupid." No matter if you went down the wrong hall and can't find your classroom. No matter if you need help in signing up for a club you really want to join. No matter if you didn't understand what the teacher was saying. The guidance counselors and teachers are there to help you get adjusted and pointed in the right direction.

Take advantage of the help the guidance counselors can give you. You'd be amazed at the number of things you can find in the guidance office—advice on good study habits, advice on planning for college, advice about what to do with that class in which you're having a problem. Use it, because it's there for you.

FROM THE GUIDANCE OFFICE

"As students transition to high school, it is important to develop self-advocacy skills. If you need or want something, you will have to seek out the resources to get the help or support that you desire. If you are struggling academically in a particular subject, you need to seek out your teacher for extra help. Your school counselor is an excellent resource to help you develop your self-advocacy skills and to help problem-solve other situations. Once you are in college, your parents will not be there, so start early so you will feel comfortable approaching the resources available."

Leslie Fisher
Lead Counselor
West Windsor-Plainsboro High School South
Princeton Junction, New Jersey

BEWARE OF THE BLACK HOLE OF THE BACKPACK

It looks like an ordinary backpack (or whatever it is you use to carry your books and school papers), but don't be fooled by its innocent appearance. Somewhere between the time you get out of middle school and into high school, it turns into a black hole—casually destroying finished homework, cheerfully ripping through notes you saved for a test, cunningly hiding the special pen you like.

You may have been organized in junior high school, but once you get into high school, the backpack can turn into an endless pit into which you stuff everything; however, whatever it is you need to find in its endless depths cannot be found without a major search and rescue.

The reason for this dilemma that will suddenly appear in your life is that in high school, you've got a lot more papers to organize. Homework is given in most classes. You're getting handouts that have to be saved for a test that will come up in three weeks, along with that list of notes of supplies you're supposed to bring to science class and the day planner you bought.

You must ramp up the way you keep things organized to keep up with high school. One suggestion is to get a three-subject spiral notebook for each class. Section one is for taking notes in class. Section two is for homework. Section three is for tearing out sheets of paper. You now have everything you need for one subject in one notebook. The pages can't come out unless you tear them out and it's chronological, so you can look back at past notes and tell what was discussed when.

With this system, or any other that suits you best, your backpack will turn into an ordinary useful bag, and when your history teacher asks you to pull out the notes from last week's class, you will know exactly where to find them.

TOP 10 MISTAKES

Everyone makes mistakes, but if you can avoid these TOP 10 as you begin your freshman year, you'll be in much better shape. Drum roll, please. We'll start with the worst.

1. **My freshman year doesn't count. My senior year is far away. If I mess up, I can always get back on track in the tenth grade.** While it's true you can make up for bad choices and slip-ups, your freshman year is the foundation upon which the rest of your high school years, and then college, are built. Freshman year isn't practice or a trial period—it's the real thing!

2. **I'm picking this class because my friend is taking it.** Your friend picked the class in beginning biology because she's always liked squiggly green bugs. You don't like looking in microscopes. You won't find out what a mistake you've made until you're way behind on homework and have failed several tests, when you could have been getting As in that writing class you wanted to take but didn't.

3. **I'll just skip this class. One day won't make a difference.** Not so. In high school, attendance counts. Many schools have policies that cause you to lose credits if you miss class a certain number of times. Even the best of students will miss classes because of illness or other unforeseen events. But remember, much of the teaching in high school is cumulative, meaning that each day is built on what happened in the class the day before. If you get out of the loop, it's really hard to get back in.

4. **I don't need to write down that assignment. I'll remember it.** Most likely, you'll only remember the assignment until you leave the classroom, then it's history. By the time you get home, you have a vague recollection of what the teacher said you had to do. Then you have to call someone in the class to ask about the assignment and that person isn't home, so you miss doing the homework.

5. **I spilled soda on my homework and now I'll be late turning it in if I do it over, so I'll just forget about it.** You should talk to your teacher about making up lost or forgotten homework. Even though the teacher will probably take off some points, you guarantee getting no points if you don't turn it in at all! So, while the assignment may be late, at least it will be counted. Don't be afraid to ask your teacher about turning in late assignments—better late than never!

6. **Sorry, I can't join that club, I have to study all the time.** In your freshman year, it's especially important to become part of the school community. Not only will you get to know other kids who like the same things you do, but you'll also explore what you like to do.

7. **Everyone else in this class understood what the teacher just said except me, so I won't ask him to explain it.** You will be surprised to know that if you didn't understand or need more explanation, probably everyone else feels the same way too. Be brave. Ask the question and have everyone else in your class silently thanking you. Plus, more importantly, you'll understand what the teacher was saying.

8. **I don't want to talk to the teacher about the problems I'm having with her class.** Teachers aren't mind-readers. They have no clue that you're struggling until they see your work. If you're having problems, it's okay to say, "I just don't get fractions." Teachers love to teach, and part of teaching is helping students understand things.

9. **There's a situation at school that's making me uncomfortable. I'll just tell my friend about it and not go to the counselor's office.** Big or small, serious or not, whatever problems you're having or whatever situations are bothering you, your high school counselors are there to help you, protect you, guide you, comfort you. Your best friend may be able to sympathize with your problem, but chances are your friend can't solve the issue as effectively as a counselor or teacher can.

10. **I really don't need all that much sleep.** That may have been true during the summer when you could sleep late. Now you're up and out with the sunrise. Trouble is, when you go to bed late, you find yourself nodding off in first period. All that brain power you are using to adjust to high school takes energy. Energy comes from a good night's sleep.

MAKE SURE YOUR PARENTS READ THIS!

Some of you have been through the process of transitioning your son or daughter from middle school to high school. For some of you, it's your first time. Helen Erbe, a guidance counselor at Jackson Memorial High School in Jackson, New Jersey, has been a guidance counselor in middle school, elementary school, and now in high school. She says that having been at all levels, the transitions from elementary to middle and middle to high school are the most traumatic for your kids. The range of emotions swings from fearful to happy and back again. The transition brings out all your child's insecurities. But the cumulative wisdom of other parents and guidance counselors can help you help your children. Here are some tried and tested tips.

- Find out what tryouts for high school clubs, activities, and sports take place in the summer and see if your child may be interested in joining.
- While your child is still in middle school, take her to the high school on casual trips, such as to the library, to the swimming pool, to a play, so she will already be familiar with the building and things to do before ninth grade starts.
- Before high school starts, take your child on a test run to walk the halls and meet teachers who are there early to set up their classrooms. Then let him come back by himself for another test run.
- Encourage involvement in school activities other than just sports. In general, the students who are involved in extracurriculars enjoy school and have greater academic success. Advise your child to start gradually in the freshman year with a few activities and then add more as she moves toward her senior year.
- Help your child set up a system to organize homework assignments, test dates, and other activities.
- Give your child space to try things on her own. Get her to advocate for her interests and needs on her own. School administrators and teachers love parent involvement but it's important to let kids deal with some of the issues alone.
- Set realistic goals for your child. It's good for children to be challenged but if the goals are too ambitious, children give up reaching for any goals.

JUMP-START YOUR FUTURE

Come on, admit it. You know that big question—what will I do when I graduate from high school?—is right around the corner. Some of your classmates know what they want to do, but you're freaking out about all of the decisions you still have to make.

You've got a lot of possibilities from which to choose. Maybe you'll attend a two-year or four-year college or a vocational or career college. Or you'll join the armed services. Or perhaps you'll go right into the workplace with a full-time job. But before you march across that stage to get your diploma, *Peterson's Get a Jump!* will help you to begin thinking about your options and to open up doors you never knew existed.

Chapter 2

A LOOK AT YOURSELF

Deciding what to do with your life is a lot like flying. Just look at the many ways you can fly and the many directions your life can take.

A TEACHER ONCE asked her students to bring something to class that flies. Students brought kites, balloons, and models of airplanes, blimps, hot-air balloons, helicopters, spaceships, gliders, and seaplanes. But when class began, the teacher explained that the lesson was about career planning, not flying.

She was making the point that your plans for life after high school can take many forms. How you will make the journey is an individual matter. That's why it's important to know who you are and what you want before taking off.

You may not choose your life's career by reading *Peterson's Get a Jump!* (GAJ), but you'll learn how to become part of the decision-making process and find resources that can help you plan your future.

READY TO FLY?

Just having a high school diploma is not enough for many occupations. But, surprise, surprise, neither is a college degree. Different kinds of work require different kinds of training. Knowing how to operate a particular type of equipment, for instance, takes special skills and work experience that you might not learn in college. Employers always want to hire the best-qualified people available, but this does not mean that they always choose those applicants who have the most education. The *type* of education and training you have is just as important as *how much*. Right now, you're at the point in your life where you can choose how much and what kind of education and training you want to get.

If you have a definite career goal in mind, like being a doctor, you probably already know what it will take in terms of education. You're looking at about four years of college, then four years of medical school, and, in most states, one year of residency. Cosmetologists, on the other hand, complete a state-approved training program that ranges from eight to eighteen months.

But for most of you, deciding what to do after high school is not so easy. Perhaps you haven't chosen a field of work yet. You might just know for certain that you want a job that will give you status and a big paycheck. Or maybe you know what you want to do, but you're not sure what kind of education you'll need. For instance, you may love fixing cars, and the idea of being an auto mechanic sounds great. But you need to decide whether to learn on the job, attend a vocational school, seek an apprenticeship, or pursue a combination of these options.

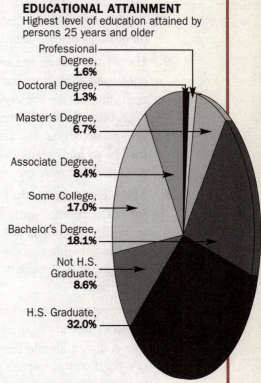

EDUCATIONAL ATTAINMENT
Highest level of education attained by persons 25 years and older

Professional Degree, **1.6%**
Doctoral Degree, **1.3%**
Master's Degree, **6.7%**
Associate Degree, **8.4%**
Some College, **17.0%**
Bachelor's Degree, **18.1%**
Not H.S. Graduate, **8.6%**
H.S. Graduate, **32.0%**

Source: U.S. Census Bureau, Current Population Survey, March 2005

THE TOP 10 REASONS TO CONTINUE YOUR EDUCATION

Continuing your education after high school is one choice that can give you a good start no matter what your final career decision is. There are many good reasons to do so. If you think college is not for you at all, take a look at this list. It just might change your mind.

10. **Fulfill a dream—or begin one.** Some people hope to become teachers or scientists. For many, continuing their education provides the opportunity to make that wish a reality for themselves or their family.

9. **Have fun.** Classes are an important part of continued education, but there are plenty of opportunities for some great times outside the classroom. There are hundreds of sports, clubs, groups, activities, and associations just waiting for you to join. Many people say that their college years were the best years of their lives.

8. **Make connections that can link you to future jobs.** The friends, professors, supervisors, and classmates you meet after high school will provide valuable ties for future jobs, committees, and associations within the community.

7. **Become part of a cultural stew.** As you have probably already figured out, not everyone is like you. Nor should they be. Being in college is a good way to expose yourself to many types of people from various backgrounds and geographic locations, with different viewpoints and opinions. You may discover that you like people and things you never knew existed.

6. **Meet new people.** By furthering your education, you will widen your circle of friends and, chances are, form meaningful lifelong relationships.

5. **Do what you love doing and get paid for it.** Have you ever taken a test during which everything clicked or played a video game and caught on immediately? This is what happens when you combine education and training with the right job. Work becomes more like play, which is far more satisfying and rewarding than just going through the motions.

4. **Exercise your mind.** Just as physical exercise keeps your body in shape, mental exercise keeps your mind free of cobwebs. No matter what your area of interest, education holds the key to the most interesting and challenging information you can imagine. Explore your outer limits and become a lifelong learner.

3. **Earn a higher income.** Although money isn't everything, it is necessary for survival. A good education prepares you to become a solid member of society. (See the chart below, "Increase Your Earning Power.")

2. **Learn critical-thinking and analytical skills.** More than any other skill, education teaches you to think. Furthering your learning will help you to think critically, organize and analyze information, and write clearly.

1. **You won't get left behind.** In the twenty-first century, you need to be prepared to change jobs and continually learn new skills in order to keep up with changes in industry, communications, and technology. Education and training will give you that preparation.

Breaking Down Barriers

INCREASE YOUR EARNING POWER

People with more education tend to earn more money. Look at the average yearly earnings of workers over the age of 25 by education level.

Professional Degree	$98,600
Doctoral Degree	$79,300
Master's Degree	$61,300
Bachelor's Degree	$51,000
Associate Degree	$40,600
Some College	$37,000
High School Diploma	$31,600
Less Than High School Diploma	$25,000

Source: U.S. Census Bureau, 2006

Continuing Your Education

Some of you may say, "Forget the reasons why I *should* continue my education. I *can't* because (fill in the blank)." Let's see if your objections stand up.

I can't.

Nobody in my family has ever gone to college.

You can!

You can be the first! It's a little scary and not always easy, but just think how great you'll feel being the first person in your family to receive a degree, diploma, or certificate.

I can't.

My grades are not good enough.

You can!

Don't let less-than-perfect grades stand in your way. Different institutions have different requirements, including what grades they accept. Schools also evaluate you for admission as a whole person, including your participation in extracurricular activities; your talents, such as academics and athletics; and your employment and volunteer history. There are also classes that you can take to improve your skills in various subject areas. Get a tutor now or form a study group to improve your grades as much as possible. Talk to your guidance counselor about what the appropriate curriculum for you is so you'll have more options when making decisions about continuing your education.

I can't.

I can't afford it.

You can!

Many families cannot afford to pay education costs completely out of pocket. That's why there are so many opportunities for financial aid, scholarships, grants, and work-study programs. Federal, state, school-sponsored, private, and career-specific financial aid resources are available to students who take the time to look. Talk to a guidance counselor, go to the library, and look on the Internet. Read the "Financial Aid Dollars and Sense" chapter of this guide for more information about how to finance your continued education. Be creative and persistent. It can happen for you.

I can't.

I don't know how to apply or where I want to go.

You can!

Fortunately, there are resources to help you decide which institution to select. Talk to friends, family members, neighbors, your guidance counselor, pastor, coach, or librarian. Take a look at the Appendices at the back of this guide for listings of two-year and four-year colleges, as well as vocational and career colleges in your state.

I can't.

I think it may be too difficult for me.

You can!

Think back to something you have done in your life that seemed too difficult in the beginning. Didn't you find that once you began, put your mind to it, and stuck with it that you succeeded? You can do almost anything if you set your mind to it and are willing to work for it.

I can't.

I'm not sure I'll fit in.

You can!

One of the best things about furthering your education is the chance to meet new people and be part of new experiences in new surroundings. Colleges and other continuing education options attract a wide variety of students from many different backgrounds. Chances are you won't have any problem finding someone else with interests that are similar to yours. Because schools differ in size, location, student body, and lifestyle, you'll surely find one that meets your needs. Advance visits and interviews can help you determine which school is right for you.

Part 2: Jump-Start Your Future

FASTEST-GROWING OCCUPATIONS

Want to have a career that's going places? Check out this chart to see which occupations are expected to grow the fastest by the year 2014 and what type of training you'll need to get the job.

Occupation	Expected Openings	Required Education
Home Health Aides	974,000	On-the-job training
Network Systems and Data Communications Analysts	357,000	Bachelor's degree
Medical Assistants	589,000	On-the-job training
Physician Assistants	93,000	Bachelor's degree
Computer Software Engineers, Applications	682,000	Bachelor's degree
Physical Therapist Assistants	85,000	Associate degree
Dental Hygienists	226,000	Associate degree
Computer Software Engineers, Systems Software	486,000	Bachelor's degree
Dental Assistants	382,000	On-the-job training
Personal and Home Care Aides	988,000	On-the-job training
Network and Computer Systems Administrators	385,000	Bachelor's degree
Database Administrators	144,000	Bachelor's degree
Physical Therapists	211,000	Master's degree
Forensic Science Technicians	13,000	Associate degree
Veterinary Technologists and Technicians	81,000	Associate degree
Diagnostic Medical Sonographers	57,000	Associate degree
Physical Therapist Aides	57,000	On-the-job training
Occupational Therapist Assistants	29,000	Associate degree
Medical Scientists, except Epidemiologists	97,000	Doctoral degree
Occupational Therapists	123,000	Master's degree
Preschool Teachers, except Special Education	573,000	Postsecondary vocational award
Cardiovascular Technologists and Technicians	60,000	Associate degree
Postsecondary Teachers	2,153,000	Doctoral degree
Hydrologists	11,000	Master's degree
Computer Systems Analysts	640,000	Bachelor's degree
Hazardous Materials Removal Workers	50,000	On-the-job training
Biomedical Engineers	13,000	Bachelor's degree
Employment, Recruitment, and Placement Specialists	237,000	Bachelor's degree
Environmental Engineer	64,000	Associate degree
Paralegals and Legal Assistants	291,000	Bachelor's degree

Source: Bureau of Labor Statistics, November 2005 Monthly Labor Review

I can't.

I don't even know what I want to do with my life.

You can!

Many students don't know this about themselves until they get to experience some of the possibilities. Take the "Self-Assessment Inventory" on page 26 to help you determine what your interests and talents are. Read "Choosing Your Major" on page 101 for a listing of the most popular college majors and their related careers.

I can't.

There is no way I can pursue my education full-time.

You can!

Part-time students are becoming the norm. In fact, a recent study determined that 43 percent of undergraduate students attend school part-time. Most schools offer evening and weekend classes, and many offer work-study opportunities to help students pay for their education. Also, some employers will pay or reimburse you if you are working and want to further your education. If you are enrolled part-time, it does take longer to graduate. But if full-time enrollment is not an option for you, don't give up the opportunity to continue your education. There are many nontraditional ways to achieve your goals.

CHOOSING A CAREER YOU'LL BE HAPPY WITH

Did you know that of the estimated 15 million people searching for employment in the American job market, approximately 12 million are looking for a new occupation or a different employer? That's an awful lot of people who aren't happy with their jobs. Avoid being one of them by taking some time to consider what it is you really want to do now, while you're still in school. Is there a particular type of job you've always dreamed of doing? Or perhaps you're one of the many high school students who say:

Chapter 2: A Look At Yourself

"I Kind of Know What I Want, But I'm Not Really Sure."

A good way to gather information about potential occupations is by talking with people who have achieved goals that are similar to yours. Talk to teachers, neighbors, and adult friends about their work experiences. The formal name for that activity is an "informational interview." You're interviewing them about the work they do—not to get a job from them but to gather information about their jobs.

If you don't have any contacts in a field that sparks your interest, do some poking around in the workplace. For instance, if you're interested in a career in nursing, you could visit a hospital, doctor's office, or nursing home. Most people love to talk about themselves, so don't be afraid to ask if they'll chat with you about their profession. Offering to volunteer your services can be the best way to know whether you'll be happy doing that type of work.

"I Don't Have a Clue About What I Want to Do."

If you're completely unsure about what kind of work you'd like to do, contact a career counselor who can help you explore your options and possibly administer some interest and aptitude tests. You also might think about contacting a college career planning and placement office, a vocational school placement office, the counseling services of community agencies, or a private counseling service, which may charge you a fee. Many high schools offer job-shadowing programs, where students actually shadow someone in a particular occupation for an entire day or more. Don't forget that as a high school student, your best resource is your high school guidance counselor. Take a look at the list of the "Fastest-Growing Occupations" on page 24 to get a sampling of the careers with the largest projected job growth in the coming years.

ON THE HUNT FOR INFORMATION

Regardless of how unsure you may be about what you want to do after high school, here's a list of things you can do to get the information you need to head in the right direction. Many people start off thinking they want one career and end up doing something completely different. But this is a good place to begin:

- Investigate careers both in and out of school. Participate in mentoring, job shadowing, and career day opportunities whenever possible.
- Get some on-the-job experience in a field that interests you.
- Research two-year and four-year colleges, vocational/career colleges, and apprenticeship programs.
- Participate in school and state career development activities.
- Prepare for and take aptitude and college entrance tests.

Here are a few Web sites where you can receive valuable direction by completing a career interest questionnaire or by reading about various occupations:

Peterson's

www.petersons.com

On Peterson's Web site, you can read helpful articles about the workplace and search for undergraduate academic and career-oriented degree and certificate programs.

Occupational Outlook Handbook

www.bls.gov/oco

The Bureau of Labor Statistics, an agency within the U.S. Department of Labor, produces this Web site, which offers more information than you'll ever need about specific careers.

SELF-ASSESSMENT INVENTORY

In addition to looking to outside sources for information, there's another rich source of data: yourself. Knowing what you want to do begins with knowing yourself—the real you. The better you understand your own wants and needs, the better you will be able to make decisions about your career goals and dreams. This self-assessment inventory can help.

Whom do you admire most, and why?

What is your greatest strength?

What is your greatest talent?

What skills do you already have?

DESCRIBE HOW YOU CURRENTLY USE THESE SKILLS IN YOUR LIFE:

Athletic ability

Mechanical ability

Ability to work with numbers

Leadership skills

Teaching skills

Artistic skills

Analytical skills

CHECK THE AREAS THAT MOST INTEREST YOU:

- ☐ Providing a practical service for people
- ☐ Self-expression in music, art, literature, or nature
- ☐ Organizing and record keeping
- ☐ Meeting people and supervising others
- ☐ Helping others in need, either mentally, spiritually, or physically
- ☐ Solving practical problems
- ☐ Working in forestry, farming, or fishing
- ☐ Working with machines and tools
- ☐ Taking care of animals
- ☐ Physical work outdoors
- ☐ Protecting the public via law enforcement or fire fighting
- ☐ Medical, scientific, or mathematical work
- ☐ Selling, advertising, or promoting

WHAT GIVES YOU SATISFACTION?

Answer the following questions True (T) or False (F).

T F I get satisfaction not from personal accomplishment, but from helping others.

T F I'd like to have a job in which I can use my imagination and be inventive.

T F In my life, money will be placed ahead of job security and personal interests.

T F It is my ambition to have a direct impact on other people's lives.

T F I am not a risk-taker and would prefer a career that offers little risk.

T F I enjoy working with people rather than by myself.

T F I would not be happy doing the same thing all the time.

WHAT MATTERS THE MOST TO YOU?

Rate the items on the list below from 1 to 10, with 10 being extremely important and 1 being not at all important.

___ Good health   ___ Seeing the world
___ Justice   ___ Love
___ Marriage/family ___ Fun
___ Faith   ___ Power
___ Fame   ___ Individualism
___ Beauty   ___ Charity
___ Safety   ___ Honor
___ Friendship   ___ Intelligence
___ Respect   ___ Wealth
___ Accomplishment

Mapping Your Future

www.mapping-your-future.org

On this site, you can find out how to choose a career and how to reach your career goals. You can also pick up useful tips on job hunting, resume writing, and job interviewing techniques. This site also provides a ten-step plan for determining and achieving your career goals.

University of Waterloo Career Development Manual

www.cdm.uwaterloo.ca/

This site provides a thorough online career interest survey and strategies you can use to get the job that's right for you.

LiveCareer

www.livecareer.com

LiveCareer is a San Francisco-based company founded by Sigma Assessment Systems, Inc. and a group of leading career professionals and investors. Since 1967, they have developed innovative practical assessment solutions that have helped more than 300,000 people make important career decisions.

HotJobs.com

www.hotjobs.com

Includes information about thousands of job and career fairs, advice on resumes, and much more.

Chapter 2: A Look At Yourself

WHAT WOULD YOU DO IF YOU WERE IN A BLIZZARD SURVIVAL SITUATION?

Check the one that would be your most likely role.

- ☐ The leader
- ☐ The one who explains the situation to the others
- ☐ The one who keeps morale up
- ☐ The one who invents a way to keep warm and melt snow for water
- ☐ The one who listens to instructions and keeps the supplies organized
- ☐ The one who positions sticks and rocks to signal SOS

LOOKING AHEAD AND LOOKING BACK

What are your goals for the next five years?

Where would you like to be in ten years?

What was your favorite course, and why?

What was your least favorite course, and why?

Who was your favorite teacher, and why?

What are your hobbies?

What are your extracurricular activities?

What jobs have you held?

What volunteer work, if any, have you performed?

Have you ever shadowed a professional for a day? If so, what did you learn?

Do you have a mentor? If so, who? What have you learned from this person?

Do you want to stay close to home, or would you prefer to travel to another city after high school?

WHAT ARE YOUR CAREER GOALS?

The interests, skills, and knowledge supporting my career goals are:

To fulfill my career goals, I will need additional skills and knowledge in:

I will obtain the additional skills and knowledge by taking part in the following educational activities:

I will need a degree, certification, and/or specialized training in:

When I look in the classified ads of the newspaper, the following job descriptions sound attractive to me:

WHAT ARE YOUR IMMEDIATE PLANS AFTER HIGH SCHOOL?

After high school, I plan to:

- ☐ Work full-time
- ☐ Work part-time and attend school
- ☐ Attend college full-time
- ☐ Attend technical college
- ☐ Enter the military

WHAT WILL YOU NEED TO GET WHERE YOU'RE GOING?

The information I have given indicates that I will be selecting courses that are primarily:

- ☐ College path (Four-year or two-year education that offers liberal arts courses combined with courses in your area of interest.)
- ☐ Vocational path (One or more years of education that include hands-on training for a specific job.)
- ☐ Combination of the two

MY PERFECT JOB WOULD BE ...

Let your imagination run wild. You can have any job you want. What's it like? Start by describing to yourself the following:

Work conditions What hours are you willing to work? Do you feel most satisfied in an environment that is indoors/outdoors, varied/regular, noisy/quiet, or casual/traditional?

Duties What duties do you feel comfortable carrying out? Do you want to be a leader, or do you perform best as a team player?

People Do you want to work with other people or more independently? How much people contact do you want/need?

Education How much special training or education is required? How much education are you willing to seek? Can you build upon the education or experience you have to date? Will you need to gain new education or experience?

Benefits What salary and benefits do you expect? Are you willing to travel?

Disadvantages There are disadvantages with almost any job. Can you imagine what the disadvantages may be? Can you confirm or disprove these beliefs by talking to someone or researching the industry or job further? If these disadvantages really exist, can you live with them?

Personal qualities What qualities do you want in the employer you ultimately choose? What are the most important qualities that you want in a supervisor? In your coworkers?

Look over your responses to this assessment. Do you see recurring themes in your answers that start to show you what kind of career you might like? If not, there are many more places to get information to decide where your interests lie. You can go to your guidance counselor for advice. You can take the Campbell ™ Interest and Skills Inventory, the Strong Interest Inventory, the Self-Directed Search, or other assessment tests that your guidance counselor recommends.

Chapter 3

THE FIRST STEPS TO A CAREER

Don't be too surprised when your summer job turns into your career.

THE WORD "CAREER" has a scary sound to it when you're still in high school. Careers are for college graduates or those who have been in the workplace for years. But unless you grew up knowing for sure that you wanted to fly airplanes or be a botanist, what will you do? You'll be happy to know that interests you have now can very possibly lead to a college major or into a career. A job at a clothing store, for instance, could lead to a career designing clothes. Perhaps those hours you spend stealing cars in Grand Theft Auto will lead to a career creating video games! Maybe you babysit and love being around kids, so teaching becomes an obvious choice. Perhaps cars fascinate you, and you find out you want to fix them for a living.

This chapter will show you how you can begin exploring your interests—sort of like getting into a swimming pool starting with your big toe, rather than plunging in. Vocational/career and tech-prep programs, summer jobs, and volunteering are all ways you can test various career paths to decide if you like them.

THE VOCATIONAL/CAREER EDUCATION PATH

If you're looking for a more real-world education, add yourself to the nearly 11 million youths and adults who are getting a taste of the workplace through vocational and career education programs offered in high schools across the nation. These programs are designed to help you develop competency in the skills you'll need in the workplace as well as in school.

What makes this kind of program different is that you learn in the classroom and in the "real world" of the workplace. Not only do you learn the academics in school, but you also get hands-on training by job shadowing, working under a mentor, and actually performing a job outside of school. Your interests and talents are usually taken into consideration, and you can choose from a variety of traditional, high-tech, and service industry training programs. Take a look at the following categories and see what piques your interest.

STUDENT COUNSEL

Q: What do you like about vocational training?

A: I jumped into the tech center my first year when I was a junior because I thought it was a good way to get out of school. But as the year went on, I said, "Hey, this is a good place to be because it's giving me job experience, and I'm learning how to dress and present myself like I was at a real job." I go during the first 3 or last 3 hours out of the school day. When we're in class, we get to do real jobs for people who ask our instructor for help. Then our teacher lets our creative minds go. We just designed a CD cover. One guy here designed a motorcycle and built it, and now he has three people asking him to come and work for them.

Trisha Younk
Tuscola County Tech Center
Reese High School
Reese, Michigan

Chapter 3: The First Steps to a Career

FROM THE GUIDANCE OFFICE

Q: What if going to college is not for me?

A: When adults ask kids what they want to do as a career, kids feel pressured. They think adults want them to identify with one single career. But there are more than 40,000 job titles a person can hold. We tell kids to pick a path first. When you exit high school, there are three paths you can take. One is to the workplace. One leads to the military as a career or as a stepping stone. The third leads to more education—a professional degree, a four-year degree, or a two-year degree. They have to determine which path they'll take.

One of the main selling points about getting career education in high school is that nearly every employer wants you to have some experience before you are hired. In career tech, students are in a workplace environment and can list their time as work experience, and they'll have previous employers who can vouch for them.

Lenore Lemanski
Counselor, Technology Center
Tuscola ISD
Caro, Michigan

Agricultural education. These programs prepare students for careers in agricultural production, animal production and care, agribusiness, agricultural and industrial mechanics, environmental management, farming, horticulture and landscaping, food processing, and natural resource management.

Business education. Students prepare for careers in accounting and finance and computer and data processing as well as administrative/secretarial and management/supervisory positions in professional environments (banking, insurance, law, public service).

Family and consumer sciences. These programs prepare students for careers in child care, food management and production, clothing and interiors, and hospitality and facility care. Core elements include personal development, family life and planning, resource management, and nutrition and wellness.

Trade and industrial and health occupations. Students prepare for careers in auto mechanics, the construction trades, cosmetology, electronics, graphics, public safety, and welding. Health occupation programs offer vocational training for careers in dental and medical assisting, practical nursing, home health care, and medical office assisting.

Marketing education. These programs prepare students for careers in sales, retail, advertising, food and restaurant marketing, and hotel management.

There are many vocational/career education programs available; the kinds listed above represent only a few of the possibilities. To find a program that suits your interests and that is located near you, refer to the college and university listings in the Appendix of this book. Or, you can get more information about vocational education programs by calling 202-245-7700 or e-mailing the U.S. Department of Education, Office of Vocational and Adult Education via its Web site, www.ed.gov/about/offices/list/ovae/index.html.

THE TECH-PREP PATH

An even more advanced preparation for the workplace and/or an associate degree from a college is called tech-prep. It's an educational path that combines college-prep and vocational/technical courses of study.

During the sequence of courses, the focus is on blending academic and vocational/technical competencies. When you graduate from high school, you'll be able to jump right into the workforce or get an associate degree. But if you want to follow this path, you've got to plan for it starting in the ninth grade. Ask your guidance counselor for more information.

USING THE SUMMER TO YOUR ADVANTAGE

When you're sitting in class, a summer with nothing to do might seem appealing. But after you've listened to all of your CDs, aced all of your video games, hung out at the same old mall, and talked to your friends on the phone about being bored, what's left? How about windsurfing on a cool, clear New England lake? Horseback riding along breathtaking mountain trails? Parlez français in Paris? Trekking through spectacular canyon lands or living with a family in Costa Rica, Spain, Switzerland, or Japan? Exploring college majors or possible careers? Helping out on an archeological dig or community-service project? Along the way, you'll meet some wonderful people and maybe even make a couple of lifelong friends.

Interested? Get ready to pack your bags and join the 1 million kids and teens who will be having the summer of a lifetime at thousands of terrific camps, academic programs, sports clinics, arts workshops, internships, volunteer opportunities, and travel adventures throughout North America and abroad.

Oh, you don't have the money, you say? Not to worry. There are programs to meet every budget, from $50 workshops to $5,000 world treks and sessions that vary in length from just a couple of hours to a couple of months.

For a list of summer opportunities, take a look at the Appendix in this book. You can also find out about summer opportunities by visiting www.petersons.com.

FROM THE GUIDANCE OFFICE

Q: What options are open to students who take high school career/technology classes and who feel they can't go to college?

A: Students have the opportunity to develop many skills through classes, student organizations, and career/technology classes during high school. These skills form an essential core that they can use to continue on to college, enter the job market, or participate in additional training after graduation. When students can identify those skills and make the connection by applying and expanding their skills as lifelong learners, then the possibilities are endless.

Linda S. Sanchez
Career and Technology Counselor
South San Antonio I.S.D.
Career Education Center
San Antonio, Texas

FLIP BURGERS AND LEARN ABOUT LIFE

A lot of teenagers who are anxious to earn extra cash spend their summers in retail or food service since those jobs are plentiful. If you're flipping burgers or helping customers find a special outfit, you might think the only thing you're getting out of the job is a paycheck. Think again. You will be amazed to discover that you have gained far more.

Being employed in these fields will teach you how to get along with demanding (and sometimes downright unpleasant) customers, how to work on a team, and how to handle money and order supplies. Not only do summer jobs teach you life skills, but they also offer ways to explore potential careers. What's more, when you apply to college or for a full-time job after high school graduation, the experience will look good on your application.

Sometimes, summer jobs become the very thing you want to do later in life. Before committing to a college major, summer jobs give you the opportunity to try out many directions. Students who think they want to be engineers, lawyers, or doctors might spend the summer shadowing an engineer, being a gofer in a legal firm, or volunteering in a hospital.

However, rather than grab the first job that comes along, find out where your interests are and build on what is natural for you. Activities you take for granted provide clues to what you are good at. What about that bookcase you built? Or those kids you love to baby-sit? Same thing with that big party you arranged. The environments you prefer provide other hints, too. Perhaps you feel best in the middle of a cluttered garage instead of surrounded by people. That suggests certain types of jobs.

Getting a summer job while in high school is the first step in a long line of work experiences to come. And the more experience you have, the better you'll be at getting jobs all your life.

TRY YOUR HAND AT AN INTERNSHIP

Each year, thousands of interns work in a wide variety of places, including corporations, law firms, government agencies, media organizations, interest groups, clinics, labs, museums, and historical sites. How popular are internships? Consider the recent trends. In the early 1980s, only 1 in 36 students completed an internship or other experiential learning program. Compare this to 2006, where one study found that 62 percent of college students had planned for a summer internship. And an increasing number of high school students are signing up for internships now, too.

The Employer's Perspective

Employers consider internships a good option in both healthy and ailing economies. In healthy economies, managers often struggle to fill their positions with eager workers who can adapt to changing technologies. Internships offer a low-cost way to get good workers into "the pipeline" without offering them a full-time position up front. In struggling economies, on the other hand, downsizing often requires employers to lay off workers without thinking about who will cover their responsibilities. Internships offer an inexpensive way to offset position losses resulting from these disruptive layoffs.

The Intern's Perspective

If you are looking to begin a career or supplement your education with practical training, internships are a good bet for several reasons.

1. **Internships offer a relatively quick way to gain work experience and develop job skills.** Try this exercise. Scan the Sunday want ads of your newspaper. Choose a range of interesting advertisements for professional positions that you would consider taking. List the desired or required job skills and work experiences specified in the ads. How many of these skills and experiences do you have? Chances are, if you are still in school, you don't have most of the skills and experience that employers require of their new hires. What do you do?

   The growing reality is that many entry-level positions require skills and experiences that schools and part-time jobs don't provide. Sure, you know your way around a computer. You have some customer service experience. You may even have edited your school's newspaper or organized your junior prom. But you still lack the relevant skills and on-the-job experiences that many hiring managers require. A well-chosen internship can offer a way out of this common dilemma by providing you job training in an actual career field. Internships help you take your existing knowledge and skills and apply them in ways that will help you compete for good jobs.

2. **Internships offer a relatively risk-free way to explore a possible career path.** Believe it or not, the best internship may tell you what you *don't* want to do for the next ten or twenty years. Think about it. If you put all your eggs in one basket, what happens if your dream job turns out to be the exact opposite of what you want or who you are? Internships offer a relatively low-cost opportunity to "try out" a career field to see if it's right for *you*.

3. **Internships offer real opportunities to do career networking and can significantly increase your chances of landing a good full-time position.** Have you heard the saying: "It's not what you know, but who you know"? The reality is that who you know (or who knows you) can make a big difference in your job search. Studies show that fewer than 20 percent of job placements occur through traditional application methods, including newspaper and trade journal advertisements, employment agencies, and career fairs. Instead, 60 to 90 percent of jobs are found through personal contacts and direct application.

Career networking is the exchange of information with others for mutual benefit. Your career network can tell you where the jobs are and help you compete for them. Isn't it better to develop your networking skills now, when the stakes aren't as high, than later when you are competing with everyone else for full-time jobs? The internship hiring process and the weeks you actually spend on the job provide excellent opportunities to talk with various people about careers, your skills, and ways to succeed.

VOLUNTEERING IN YOUR COMMUNITY

You've probably heard the saying that money isn't everything. Well, it's true, especially when it comes to volunteering and community service. There are a number of benefits you'll get that don't add up in dollars and cents but do add up to open doors in your future.

Community service looks good on a college application. Admissions staff members look for applicants who have volunteered and done community service in addition to earning good grades. You could have gotten top grades, but if that's all that's on your application, you won't come across as a well-rounded person.

Community service lets you try out careers. How will you know you'll like a certain type of work if you haven't experienced it? For instance, you might think you want to work in the health-care field. Volunteering in a hospital will let you know if this is really what you want to do.

Community service is an American tradition. You'll be able to meet some of your own community's needs and join with all of the people who have contributed their talents to our country. No matter what your talents, there are unlimited ways for you to serve your community. Take a look at your interests, and then see how they can be applied to help others.

Here are some ideas to get you started:

- **Do you like kids?** Volunteer at your local parks and recreation department, for a Little League team, or as a big brother or sister.
- **Planning a career in health care?** Volunteer at a blood bank, clinic, hospital, retirement home, or hospice. There are also several organizations that raise money for disease research.
- **Interested in the environment?** Volunteer to assist in a recycling program. Create a beautification program for your school or community. Plant trees and flowers or design a community garden.
- **Just say no.** Help others stay off drugs and alcohol by volunteering at a crisis center, hotline, or prevention program. Help educate younger kids about the dangers of drug abuse.
- **Lend a hand.** Collect money, food, or clothing for the homeless. Food banks, homeless shelters, and charitable organizations need your help.
- **Is art your talent?** Share your knowledge and skills with youngsters, the elderly, or local arts organizations that depend on volunteers to help present their plays, recitals, and exhibitions.
- **Help fight crime.** Form a neighborhood watch or organize a group to clean up graffiti.
- **Your church or synagogue may have projects that need youth volunteers.** The United Way, your local politician's office, civic groups, and special interest organizations also provide exceptional opportunities to serve your community. Ask your principal, teachers, or counselors for additional ideas.

For more information on joining in the spirit of youth volunteerism, write to the Federal Citizen Information Center, Pueblo, Colorado 81009, and request the *Catch the Spirit* booklet. Also check out the FCIC's Web site at www.pueblo.gsa.gov.

Part 3

THE ROAD TO MORE EDUCATION

SOME PEOPLE WAKE up at age 3 and announce that they want to be doctors, teachers, or marine biologists—and they do it.

They're the exceptions. Many high school students don't have a clue about what they want to be. They dread the question, "So, what are you going to do after graduation?" Unfortunately, some of those same people are also the ones who end up in careers that don't satisfy them.

You don't have to plan the rest of your life down to the last detail, but you can start to take some general steps toward your future and lay the groundwork. Then, when you do decide what you want to do, you'll be able to seize hold of your dream and go with it.

PLANNING YOUR EDUCATION WHILE IN HIGH SCHOOL

Some people are planners. Then there are the non-planners. Either way, we've got a plan for you!

NON-PLANNERS see the words "plan" and "future" and say, "Yeah, yeah, I know." Meanwhile, they're running out the door for an appointment they were supposed to be at 5 minutes ago.

Unfortunately, when it comes time to really do something about those goals and future hopes, the non-planners often discover that much of what should have been done wasn't done—which is not good when they're planning their future after high school. What about those classes they should have taken? What about those jobs they should have volunteered for? What about that scholarship they could have had if only they'd found out about it sooner?

But there is hope for poor planners. Now that you've thought about yourself and the direction you might want to go after graduating, you can use this chapter to help you plan what you should be doing and when you should be doing it, while still in high school.

Regardless of what type of education you're pursuing after high school, here's a plan to help you get there.

YOUR EDUCATION TIMELINE

Use this timeline to help you make sure you're accomplishing everything you need to accomplish on time.

Ninth Grade

- As soon as you can, meet with your guidance counselor to begin talking about colleges and careers.
- Make sure you are enrolled in the appropriate college-preparatory or tech-prep courses.
- Get off to a good start with your grades. The grades you earn in ninth grade will be included in your final high school GPA and class rank.
- College might seem a long way off now, but grades really do count toward college admission and scholarships.
- Explore your interests and possible careers. Take advantage of Career Day opportunities.
- Get involved in extracurricular activities (both school and non-school-sponsored).
- Talk to your parents about planning for college expenses. Continue or begin a savings plan for college.
- Look at the college information available in your counselor's office and school and public libraries. Use the Internet to check out college Web sites. Visit Peterson's at www.petersons.com to start a list of colleges that might interest you.
- Tour a nearby college, if possible. Visit relatives or friends who live on or near a college campus. Check out the dorms, go to the library or student center, and get a feel for college life.

Part 3: The Road to More Education

- Investigate summer enrichment programs. Visit www.petersons.com for some neat ideas about summer opportunities.

Tenth Grade

Fall

- In October, take the Preliminary SAT/National Merit Scholarship Qualifying Test (PSAT/NMSQT) for practice. When you fill out your test sheet, check the box that releases your name to colleges so you can start receiving brochures from them.

- Ask your guidance counselor about the American College Testing program's PLAN® (Pre-ACT) assessment program, which helps determine your study habits and academic progress and interests. This test will prepare you for the ACT next year.

- Take geometry if you have not already done so. Take biology and a second year of a foreign language.

- Become familiar with general college entrance requirements.

- Participate in your school's or state's career development activities.

- Visit www.petersons.com for advice on test taking and general college entrance requirements.

Winter

- Discuss your PSAT score with your counselor.

- The people who read college applications aren't looking just for grades. Get involved in activities outside the classroom. Work toward leadership positions in the activities that you like best. Become involved in community service and other volunteer activities.

- Read, read, read. Read as many books as possible from a comprehensive reading list, like the one on pages 42 and 43.

- Read the newspaper every day to learn about current affairs.

- Work on your writing skills—you'll need them no matter what you do.

- Find a teacher or another adult who will advise and encourage you to write well.

Spring

- Keep your grades up so you can have the highest GPA and class rank possible.

- Ask your counselor about postsecondary enrollment options and Advanced Placement (AP) courses.

- Continue to explore your interests and careers that you think you might like.

- Begin zeroing in on the type of college you would prefer (two-year or four-year, small or large, rural or urban). To get an idea of what's available, take a look at college profiles on Petersons.com.

- If you are interested in attending a military academy such as West Point or Annapolis, now is the time to start planning and getting information.

- Write to colleges and ask for their academic requirements for admission.

PARENT PERSPECTIVE

Q: When should parents and their children start thinking about preparing for college?

A: The discussion needs to start in middle school. If parents don't expose their children to these concepts at that time, then it can be too late in the game. Children need to take the right courses in high school. Many kids here end up going to junior colleges because they don't meet the minimum requirements when they graduate. Many universities and private colleges don't count some of the classes kids take in high school. You can't wait until the child is 18 and then say, "Maybe we should do something about getting into college."

Kevin Carr
Parent
Oak Park, California

Chapter 4: Planning Your Education While in High School

PARENT PERSPECTIVE

Q: How involved should parents get in the selection of a college for their children?

A: Parents are getting more involved than ever before in supporting their children in the college process. This phenomenon is due to two factors:

(1) This generation of parents has been much more involved with their children in dealing with the outside world than were their parents.

(2) The investment made by today's parents is much more than that made by parents 20 or 30 years ago. As parents focus on the cost of this big-ticket item, there's interest to be more involved, to get the proper return.

Parents certainly should be involved in the college selection and application process. Studies clearly indicate that parental support in this process and throughout the college years can make a big difference in the success of a student. But this process also should be a learning opportunity in decision making for students. In that regard, parents shouldn't direct the student but provide input and the framework to assist their students.

Parents should not feel uncomfortable making suggestions to help their children through the thought and selection process—especially when it comes to identifying schools that their pocketbooks can accommodate. However, the child must be comfortable with the final decision and must have ultimate responsibility for the selection of the school. When students have made the final decision, it can help in their level of commitment because they've invested in it. They have a responsibility to do well and complete their academics at that location.

Richard Flaherty
President, College Parents of America

- Visit a few more college campuses. Read all of the mail you receive from colleges. You may see something you like.
- Attend college fairs.
- Keep putting money away for college. Get a summer job.
- Consider taking SAT Subject Tests in the courses you took this year while the material is still fresh in your mind. These tests are offered in May and June.

Eleventh Grade

Fall

- Meet with your counselor to review the courses you've taken, and see what you still need to take.
- Check your class rank. Even if your grades haven't been that good so far, it's never too late to improve. Colleges like to see an upward trend.
- If you didn't do so in tenth grade, sign up for and take the PSAT/NMSQT. In addition to National Merit Scholarships, this is the qualifying test for the National Scholarship Service and Fund for Negro Students and the National Hispanic Recognition Program.
- Make sure that you have a social security number.
- Take a long, hard look at why you want to continue your education after high school so you will be able to choose the best college or university for your needs.
- Make a list of colleges that meet your most important criteria (size, location, distance from home, majors, academic rigor, housing, and cost). Weigh each of the factors according to their importance to you.
- Continue visiting college fairs. You may be able to narrow your choices or add a college to your list.
- Speak to college representatives who visit your high school.
- If you want to participate in Division I or Division II sports in college, start the certification process. Check with your counselor to make sure you are taking a core curriculum that meets NCAA requirements.
- If you are interested in one of the military academies, talk to your guidance counselor about starting the application process now.

Part 3: The Road to More Education

6 STUDY SKILLS THAT LEAD TO SUCCESS

1. **SET A REGULAR STUDY SCHEDULE.** No one at college is going to hound you to do your homework. Develop the study patterns in high school that will lead to success in college. Anyone who has ever pulled an all-nighter knows how much you remember when you are on the downside of your fifth cup of coffee and no sleep—not much! Nothing beats steady and consistent study habits.

2. **SAVE EVERYTHING.** To make sure your history notes don't end up in your math notebook and your English papers don't get thrown at the bottom of your friend's locker, develop an organized system for storing your papers. Stay on top of your materials, and be sure to save quizzes and tests. It is amazing how questions from a test you took in March can miraculously reappear on your final exam.

3. **LISTEN.** Teachers give away what will be on the test by repeating themselves. If you pay attention to what the teacher is saying, you will probably notice what is being emphasized. If what the teacher says in class repeats itself in your notes and in review sessions, chances are that material will be on the test. So really listen.

4. **TAKE NOTES.** If the teacher has taken the time to prepare a lecture, then what he or she says is important enough for you to write down. Develop a system for reviewing your notes. After each class, rewrite them, review them, or reread them. Try highlighting the important points or making notes in the margins to jar your memory.

5. **USE TEXTBOOKS WISELY.** What can you do with a textbook besides lose it? Use it to back up or clarify information that you don't understand from your class notes. Reading every word may be more effort than it is worth, so look at the book intelligently. What is in boxes or highlighted areas? What content is emphasized? What do the questions ask about in the review sections?

6. **FORM A STUDY GROUP.** Establish a group that will stay on task and ask one another the questions you think the teacher will ask. Compare notes to see if you have all the important facts. And discuss your thoughts. Talking ideas out can help when you have to respond to an essay question.

Winter

- Collect information about college application procedures, entrance requirements, tuition and fees, room and board costs, student activities, course offerings, faculty composition, accreditation, and financial aid. The Internet is a good way to visit colleges and obtain this information. Begin comparing the schools by the factors that you consider to be most important.

- Discuss your PSAT score with your counselor.

- Begin narrowing down your college choices. Find out if the colleges you are interested in require the SAT, ACT, or SAT Subject Tests for admission.

- Register for the SAT and additional SAT Subject Tests, which are offered several times during the winter and spring of your junior year (see the "Tackling the Tests" chapter for a schedule). You can take them again in the fall of your senior year if you are unhappy with your scores.

- Register for the ACT, which is usually taken in April or June. You can take it again late in your junior year or in the fall of your senior year, if necessary.

- Begin preparing for the tests you've decided to take.

- Have a discussion with your parents about the colleges in which you are interested. Examine financial resources, and gather information about financial aid. Check out the "Financial Aid Dollars and Sense" chapter for a step-by-step explanation of the financial aid process.

- Set up a filing system with individual folders for each college's correspondence and printed materials.

Spring

- Meet with your counselor to review senior-year course selection and graduation requirements.

- Discuss ACT/SAT scores with your counselor. Register to take the ACT and/or SAT again if you'd like to try to improve your score.

- Discuss the college essay with your guidance counselor or English teacher.

- Stay involved with your extracurricular activities. Colleges look for consistency and depth in activities.

ADMISSIONS ADVICE

Q: Other than grades and test scores, what are the most important qualities that you look for in students?

A: We consider the types of classes students have taken. A grade of a B in an honors class is competitive to an A in a regular course. We seek not only academically talented students but those who are well-rounded. They need to submit their interests and activities, letters of recommendation, and writing samples in addition to their test scores. We look for someone that's involved in his or her community and high school, someone that holds leadership positions and has a balance of activities outside of academics. This gives us a look at that person as a whole.

Cheyenna Smith
Admission Counselor
University of Houston
Houston, Texas

- Consider whom you will ask to write your recommendations. Think about asking teachers who know you well and who will write positive letters about you. Letters from a coach, activity leader, or an adult who knows you well outside of school (e.g., volunteer work contact) are also valuable.

- Inquire about personal interviews at your favorite colleges. Call or write for early summer appointments. Make necessary travel arrangements.

- See your counselor to apply for on-campus summer programs for high school students. Apply for a summer job or internship. Be prepared to pay for college applications and testing fees in the fall.

- Request applications from schools you're interested in by mail or via the Internet.

Summer

- Visit the campuses of your top-five college choices.

- After each college interview, send a thank-you letter to the interviewer.

- Talk to people you know who have attended the colleges in which you are interested.

- Continue to read books, magazines, and newspapers.

- Practice filling out college applications, and then complete the final application forms or apply online through the Web sites of the colleges in which you're interested.

- Volunteer in your community.

- Compose rough drafts of your college essays. Have a teacher read and discuss them with you. Polish them, and prepare final drafts. Proofread your final essays at least three times.

- Develop a financial aid application plan, including a list of the aid sources, requirements for each application, and a timetable for meeting the filing deadlines.

Twelfth Grade

Fall

- Continue to take a full course load of college-prep courses.

- Keep working on your grades. Make sure you have taken the courses necessary to graduate in the spring.

- Continue to participate in extracurricular and volunteer activities. Demonstrate initiative, creativity, commitment, and leadership in each.

- To male students: you must register for selective service on your eighteenth birthday to be eligible for federal and state financial aid.

- Talk to counselors, teachers, and parents about your final college choices.

- Make a calendar showing application deadlines for admission, financial aid, and scholarships.

- Check resource books, Web sites, and your guidance office for information on scholarships and grants. Ask colleges about scholarships for which you may qualify. Check out www.petersons.com for information on scholarships.

Part 3: The Road to More Education

- Give recommendation forms to the teachers you have chosen, along with stamped, self-addressed envelopes so your teachers can send them directly to the colleges. Be sure to fill out your name, address, and school name on the top of the form. Talk to your recommendation writers about your goals and ambitions.

- Give School Report forms to your high school's guidance office. Fill in your name, address, and any other required information. Verify with your guidance counselor the schools to which transcripts, test scores, and letters are to be sent. Give your counselor any necessary forms at least two weeks before they are due or whenever your counselor's deadline is, whichever is earlier.

- Register for and take the ACT, SAT, or SAT Subject Tests, as necessary.

- Be sure you have requested (either by mail or online) that your test scores be sent to the colleges of your choice.

- Mail or send electronically any college applications for early decision admission by November 1.

- If possible, visit colleges while classes are in session.

- If you plan to apply for an ROTC scholarship, remember that your application is due by December 1.

- Print extra copies or make photocopies of every application you send.

Winter

- Attend whatever college-preparatory nights are held at your school or by local organizations.

- Send midyear grade reports to colleges. Continue to focus on your schoolwork!

- Fill out the Free Application for Federal Student Aid (FAFSA) and, if necessary, the PROFILE®. These forms can be obtained from your guidance counselor or go to www.fafsa.ed.gov/ to download the forms or to file electronically. These forms may not be processed before January 1, so don't send them before then.

- Mail or send electronically any remaining applications and financial aid forms before winter break. Make sure you apply to at least one college that you know you can afford and where you know you will be accepted.

- Follow up to make sure that the colleges have received all application information, including recommendations and test scores.

- Meet with your counselor to verify that all forms are in order and have been sent out to colleges.

Spring

- Watch your mail between March 1 and April 1 for acceptance notifications from colleges.

- Watch your mail for notification of financial aid awards between April 1 and May 1.

- Compare the financial aid packages from the colleges and universities that have accepted you.

- Make your final choice, and notify all schools of your intent by May 1. If possible, do not decide without making at least one campus visit. Send your nonrefundable deposit to your chosen school by May 1 as well. Request that your guidance counselor send a final transcript to the college in June.

- Be sure that you have received a FAFSA acknowledgment.

- If you applied for a Pell Grant (on the FAFSA), you will receive a Student Aid Report (SAR) statement. Review this notice, and forward it to the college you plan to attend. Make a copy for your records.

- Complete follow-up paperwork for the college of your choice (scheduling, orientation session, housing arrangements, and other necessary forms).

Summer

- If applicable, apply for a Stafford Loan through a lender. Allow eight weeks for processing.
- Receive the orientation schedule from your college.
- Get residence hall assignment from your college.
- Obtain course scheduling and cost information from your college.
- Congratulations! You are about to begin the greatest adventure of your life. Good luck.

CLASSES TO TAKE IF YOU'RE GOING TO COLLEGE

Did you know that classes you take as early as the ninth grade will help you get into college? Make sure you take at least the minimum high school curriculum requirements necessary for college admission. Even if you don't plan to enter college immediately, take the most demanding courses you can handle.

Review the list of Suggested Courses on this page. Some courses, categories, and names vary from state to state, but this list may be used as a guideline. Talk with your guidance counselor to select the curriculum that best meets your needs and skills.

Of course, learning also occurs outside of school. While outside activities will not make up for poor academic performance, skills learned from jobs, extracurricular activities, and volunteer opportunities will help you become a well-rounded student and will strengthen your college or job application.

Getting a Head Start on College Courses

You can take college courses while still in high school so that when you're in college, you'll be ahead of everyone else. The formal name is "postsecondary enrollment." (In Texas, the formal names are "dual credit"—academic credit and articulated credit—and "Tech-Prep.") What it means is that some students can take college courses and receive both high school and college credit for the courses taken. It's like a two-for-one deal!

Postsecondary enrollment is designed to provide an opportunity for qualified high school students to experience more advanced academic work. Participation in a postsecondary enrollment program is not intended to replace courses available in high school but rather to enhance the educational opportunities available to students while in high school. There are two options for postsecondary enrollment:

SUGGESTED COURSES

College-Preparatory Curriculum

ENGLISH. Four units, with emphasis on composition (English 9, 10, 11, 12)

MATHEMATICS. Three units (algebra I, algebra II, geometry) are essential; trigonometry, precalculus, calculus, and computer science are recommended for some fields of study

SOCIAL SCIENCE. Three units (American history, world history, government/economics)

SCIENCE. Four units (earth science, biology, chemistry, physics)

FOREIGN LANGUAGE. Three units (at least 2 years in the same language)

FINE ARTS. One to 2 units

OTHER. Keyboarding, computer applications, computer science I, computer science II, physical education, health

College-Preparatory Curriculum Combined with a Career Education or Vocational Program

ENGLISH. Four units

MATHEMATICS. Three units (algebra I, algebra II, geometry)

SOCIAL SCIENCE. Three units (American history, world history, government/economics)

SCIENCE. Two units (earth science, biology)

FOREIGN LANGUAGE. Three units (at least 2 years in the same language)

FINE ARTS. One to 2 units

OTHER. Keyboarding, computer applications, physical education, and health and half-days at the Career Center during junior and senior years

Option A: Qualified high school juniors and seniors take courses for college credit. Students enrolled under Option A must pay for all books, supplies, tuition, and associated fees.

Option B: Qualified high school juniors and seniors take courses for high school and college credit. For students enrolled under this option, the local school district covers the related costs, provided that the student completes the selected courses. Otherwise, the student and parent will be assessed the costs.

Certain preestablished conditions must be met for enrollment, so check with your high school counselor for more information.

SUGGESTED READING LIST FOR GRADES 9 THROUGH 12

Instead of flipping on the TV or putting on those headphones, how about picking up a book instead? Reading not only will take you to wonderful, unexplored worlds through your imagination, but there are practical gains as well. Reading gives you a more well-rounded background. College admissions and future employers pick up on that. And you'll be able to answer the questions, "Did you read that book? What did you think of it?" How many of the books on this list have you read?

Adams, Richard
Watership Down
Aesop
Fables
Agee, James
A Death in the Family
Anderson, Sherwood
Winesburg, Ohio
Anonymous
Go Ask Alice
Asimov, Isaac
Short Stories
Austen, Jane
Emma
Northanger Abbey
Pride and Prejudice
Sense and Sensibility
Baldwin, James
Go Tell It on the Mountain
Balzac, Honoré de
Père Goriot
Beckett, Samuel
Waiting for Godot
Bolt, Robert
A Man for All Seasons
Brontë, Charlotte
Jane Eyre
Brontë, Emily
Wuthering Heights
Brooks, Gwendolyn
In the Mecca
Riot

Browning, Robert
Poems
Buck, Pearl
The Good Earth
Butler, Samuel
The Way of All Flesh
Camus, Albert
The Plague
The Stranger
Cather, Willa
Death Comes for the Archbishop
My Antonia
Cervantes, Miguel
Don Quixote
Chaucer, Geoffrey
The Canterbury Tales
Chekhov, Anton
The Cherry Orchard
Chopin, Kate
The Awakening
Collins, Wilkie
The Moonstone
Conrad, Joseph
Heart of Darkness
Lord Jim
The Secret Sharer
Victory
Crane, Stephen
The Red Badge of Courage
Dante
The Divine Comedy

Defoe, Daniel
Moll Flanders
Dickens, Charles
Bleak House
David Copperfield
Great Expectations
Hard Times
Oliver Twist
A Tale of Two Cities
Dickinson, Emily
Poems
Dinesen, Isak
Out of Africa
Dostoevski, Fyodor
The Brothers Karamazov
Crime and Punishment
Douglass, Frederick
Narrative of the Life of Frederick Douglass
Dreiser, Theodore
An American Tragedy
Sister Carrie
Early, Gerald
Tuxedo Junction
Eliot, George
Adam Bede
Middlemarch
The Mill on the Floss
Silas Marner

Eliot, T. S.
Murder in the Cathedral
Ellison, Ralph
Invisible Man
Emerson, Ralph Waldo
Essays
Faulkner, William
Absalom, Absalom!
As I Lay Dying
Intruder in the Dust
Light in August
The Sound and the Fury
Fielding, Henry
Joseph Andrews
Tom Jones
Fitzgerald, F. Scott
The Great Gatsby
Tender Is the Night
Flaubert, Gustave
Madame Bovary
Forster, E. M.
A Passage to India
A Room with a View
Franklin, Benjamin
The Autobiography of Benjamin Franklin
Galsworthy, John
The Forsyte Saga

Golding, William
Lord of the Flies
Goldsmith, Oliver
She Stoops to Conquer
Graves, Robert
I, Claudius
Greene, Graham
The Heart of the Matter
The Power and the Glory
Hamilton, Edith
Mythology
Hardy, Thomas
Far from the Madding Crowd
Jude the Obscure
The Mayor of Casterbridge
The Return of the Native
Tess of the D'Urbervilles
Hawthorne, Nathaniel
The House of the Seven Gables
The Scarlet Letter
Hemingway, Ernest
A Farewell to Arms
For Whom the Bell Tolls
The Sun Also Rises
Henry, O.
Stories

Hersey, John
A Single Pebble
Hesse, Hermann
Demian
Siddhartha
Steppenwolf
Homer
The Iliad
The Odyssey
Hughes, Langston
Poems
The Big Sea
Hugo, Victor
Les Misérables
Huxley, Aldous
Brave New World
Ibsen, Henrik
A Doll's House
An Enemy of the People
Ghosts
Hedda Gabler
The Master Builder
The Wild Duck
James, Henry
The American
Daisy Miller
Portrait of a Lady
The Turn of the Screw
Joyce, James
Dubliners
A Portrait of the Artist as a Young Man

Kafka, Franz
The Castle
The Metamorphosis
The Trial

Keats, John
Poems

Kerouac, Jack
On the Road

Koestler, Arthur
Darkness at Noon

Lawrence, Jerome, and Robert E. Lee
Inherit the Wind

Lewis, Sinclair
Arrowsmith
Babbitt
Main Street

Llewellyn, Richard
How Green Was My Valley

Machiavelli
The Prince

MacLeish, Archibald
J.B.

Mann, Thomas
Buddenbrooks
The Magic Mountain

Marlowe, Christopher
Dr. Faustus

Maugham, Somerset
Of Human Bondage

McCullers, Carson
The Heart Is a Lonely Hunter

Melville, Herman
Billy Budd
Moby-Dick
Typee

Miller, Arthur
The Crucible
Death of a Salesman

Monsarrat, Nicholas
The Cruel Sea

Naylor, Gloria
Bailey's Cafe
The Women of Brewster Place

O'Neill, Eugene
The Emperor Jones
Long Day's Journey Into Night
Mourning Becomes Electra

Orwell, George
Animal Farm
1984

Pasternak, Boris
Doctor Zhivago

Poe, Edgar Allan
Short Stories

Remarque, Erich Maria
All Quiet on the Western Front

Rolvaag, O. E.
Giants in the Earth

Rostand, Edmond
Cyrano de Bergerac

Salinger, J. D.
The Catcher in the Rye

Sandburg, Carl
Abraham Lincoln: The Prairie Years
Abraham Lincoln: The War Years

Saroyan, William
The Human Comedy

Sayers, Dorothy
The Nine Tailors

Shakespeare, William
Plays and Sonnets

Shaw, George Bernard
Arms and the Man
Major Barbara
Pygmalion
Saint Joan

Sheridan, Richard B.
The School for Scandal

Shute, Nevil
On the Beach

Sinclair, Upton
The Jungle

Sophocles
Antigone
Oedipus Rex

Steinbeck, John
East of Eden
The Grapes of Wrath
Of Mice and Men

Stowe, Harriet Beecher
Uncle Tom's Cabin

Swift, Jonathan
Gulliver's Travels

Thackeray, William M.
Vanity Fair

Thoreau, Henry David
Walden

Tolstoy, Leo
Anna Karenina
War and Peace

Trollope, Anthony
Barchester Towers

Turgenev, Ivan
Fathers and Sons

Twain, Mark
Pudd'nhead Wilson

Updike, John
Rabbit, Run

Vergil
The Aeneid

Voltaire
Candide

Walker, Alice
The Color Purple
Meridian

Warren, Robert Penn
All the King's Men

Waugh, Evelyn
Brideshead Revisited
A Handful of Dust

Wharton, Edith
The Age of Innocence

White, T. H.
The Once and Future King
The Sword in the Stone

Wilde, Oscar
The Importance of Being Earnest
The Picture of Dorian Gray

Wilder, Thornton
Our Town

Williams, Tennessee
The Glass Menagerie
A Streetcar Named Desire

Wolfe, Thomas
Look Homeward, Angel

Woolf, Virginia
Mrs. Dalloway
To the Lighthouse

Wouk, Herman
The Caine Mutiny

Wright, Richard
Black Boy
Native Son

Source: The National Endowment for the Humanities.

Chapter 5

TACKLING THE TESTS

Unless you've been on another planet for the last two or three years, you've probably heard older high school students buzzing about the alphabet soup list of college entrance exams—SAT, ACT, and PSAT.

SOME OF THE STUDENTS who are getting ready to take one of these tests look like they're in various states of hysteria. Others have been studying for months on end, so when they open their mouths, out pops the definition for "meretricious" or the answer to "What is the ratio of 3 pounds to 6 ounces?" Well, the talk that you've heard about the tests is partly true. They are a big deal and can be crucial to your academic plans. On the other hand, you don't have to walk in cold. Remember that word "planning?" It's a whole lot nicer than the word "panic." Preparing for the tests takes a lot of planning and time, but if you're reading this chapter, you're already ahead of the game.

A FEW FACTS ABOUT THE MAJOR TESTS

The major standardized tests students take in high school are the PSAT, SAT, and ACT. Colleges across the country use them to get a sense of a student's readiness to enter their ivy-covered halls. These tests, or "boards" as they are sometimes called, have become notorious because of how important they can be. There is a mystique that surrounds them. People talk about the "magic number" that will get you into the school of your dreams.

Beware! There is a lot of misinformation out there. First and foremost, these are not intelligence tests; they are reasoning tests designed to evaluate the way you think. These tests assess the basic knowledge and skills you have gained through your classes in school, and they also gauge the knowledge you have gained through outside experience. The tests emphasize academic and nonacademic experiences that educational institutions feel are good indicators of your probable success in college.

THE ACT

The ACT is a standardized college entrance examination that measures knowledge and skills in English, mathematics, reading, and science reasoning and the application of these skills to future academic tasks. The ACT consists of four multiple-choice tests.

Test 1: English

- 75 questions, 45 minutes
- Usage and mechanics
- Rhetorical skills

Test 2: Mathematics

- 60 questions, 60 minutes
- Pre-algebra
- Elementary algebra
- Intermediate algebra
- Coordinate geometry
- Plane geometry
- Trigonometry

Chapter 5: Tackling the Tests

STUDENT COUNSEL

Q: What kept you from stressing out about the tests?

A: The best way I found to prepare was to take practice tests to get to know the questions. At first, I'd set the kitchen timer and practice while ignoring the time, just to see what I could do. Practice is the best because they don't really change the type of questions. You read that in every review book, and it's true.

My advice for dealing with the stress on test day? The night before, I watched movies and had popcorn. When you take the test, definitely bring candy. A candy bar in between each section helps.

Theresa-Marie Russo
Edgemont High School
Scarsdale, New York

Test 3: Reading

- 40 questions, 35 minutes
- Prose fiction
- Humanities
- Social studies
- Natural sciences

Test 4: Science Reasoning

- 40 questions, 35 minutes
- Data representation
- Research summary
- Conflicting viewpoints

Each section is scored from 1 to 36 and is scaled for slight variations in difficulty. Students are not penalized for incorrect responses. The composite score is the average of the four scaled scores. There is also a 30-minute Writing Test that is an optional component of the ACT.

To prepare for the ACT, ask your guidance counselor for a free guidebook called *Preparing for the ACT*. Besides providing general test-preparation information and additional test-taking strategies, this guidebook describes the content and format of the four ACT subject area tests, summarizes test administration procedures followed at ACT test centers, and includes a practice test. Peterson's publishes *The Real ACT Prep Guide* that includes three official ACT tests.

THE SAT

The SAT measures developed verbal and mathematical reasoning abilities as they relate to successful performance in college. It is intended to supplement the secondary school record and other information about the student in assessing readiness for college. There is one unscored, experimental section on the exam, which is used for equating and/or pretesting purposes and can cover either the mathematics or verbal subject area.

Critical Reading

- 67 questions, 70 minutes
- Sentence completion
- Passage-based reading

Math

- 54 questions, 70 minutes
- Multiple-choice
- Student-produced response (grid-ins)

Writing

- 49 questions plus essay, 75 minutes
- Identifying sentence errors
- Improving paragraphs
- Improving sentences
- Essay

Students receive one point for each correct response and lose a fraction of a point for each incorrect response (except for student-produced responses). These points are totaled to produce the raw scores, which are then scaled to equalize the scores for slight variations in difficulty for various editions of the test.

Part 3: The Road to More Education

WHICH SHOULD I TAKE? THE ACT VS. THE SAT

It's not a bad idea to take both. This assures that you will have the test scores required for admission to all schools, because some colleges accept the results of one test and not the other. Some institutions use test results for proper placement of students in English and math courses.

You should take the ACT and SAT during the spring of your junior year, if not earlier. This enables you to retake the test in the fall of your senior year if you're not satisfied with your scores. Also, this makes it possible for institutions to receive all test scores before the end of January. Institutions generally consider the better score when determining admission and placement. Because most scholarship applications are processed between December and April of the senior year, your best score results can then be included in the application.

The critical reading, writing, and math scaled scores range from 200–800 per section. The total scaled score range is from 600–2400.

To prepare for the SAT, you should carefully review the pamphlet, *Taking the SAT*, which you should be able to get from your guidance counselor. Also, most libraries and bookstores stock a large selection of material about the SAT and other standardized tests.

RECOMMENDED TEST-TAKING DATES

Sophomore Year
- October — PSAT/NMSQT and PLAN (for practice, planning, and preparation)
- May–June — SAT Subject Tests (if necessary)

Junior Year
- October — PSAT/NMSQT (for the National Merit Scholarship Program and practice)
- January–June — ACT and/or SAT, SAT Subject Tests (if necessary)

Senior Year
- October–December — ACT and/or SAT, SAT Subject Tests (if necessary)

THE PSAT/NMSQT

The Preliminary SAT/National Merit Scholarship Qualifying Test, better known as the PSAT/NMSQT, is a practice test for the SAT. Many students take the PSAT more than once because scores tend to increase with repetition and because it allows students to become more comfortable with taking standardized tests. During the junior year, the PSAT is also used as a qualifying test for the National Merit Scholarship Program and the National Scholarship Service and Fund for Negro Students. It is also used in designating students for the National Hispanic Scholar Recognition Program. The PSAT includes a writing skills section, which consists entirely of multiple-choice questions. There is, however, no essay section on the PSAT.

Critical Reading
- 48 questions, two 25-minute sections
- Sentence completion
- Passage-based reading

Math
- 38 questions, one 30-minute section
- Multiple-choice
- Student-produced response (grid-ins)

Writing Skills
- 39 questions, one 30-minute section
- Identifying sentence errors
- Improving sentences
- Improving paragraphs

Students receive a score in each content area (critical reading, math, and writing skills). Each score ranges from 20 to 80 and is totaled with the others for the combined score. The total score ranges from 60 to 240.

Selection Index (used for National Merit Scholarship purposes)
- Critical Reading + Math + Writing Skills

- Score Range: 60 to 240
- Mean Junior Score: 147

National Merit Scholarship Program

- Semifinalist Status: Selection Index of 201 to 222
- Commended Student: Selection Index of 199

SAT SUBJECT TESTS

Subject Tests are required by some institutions for admission and/or placement in freshman-level courses. Each Subject Test measures one's knowledge of a specific subject and the ability to apply that knowledge. Students should check with each institution for its specific requirements. In general, students are required to take three Subject Tests (one English, one mathematics, and one of their choice).

Subject Tests are given in the following areas: biology, chemistry, Chinese, French, German, Italian, Japanese, Korean, Latin, literature, mathematics, modern Hebrew, physics, Spanish, U.S. history, and world history. These tests are 1 hour long and are primarily multiple-choice tests. Three Subject Tests may be taken on one test date.

Scored like the SAT, students gain a point for each correct answer and lose a fraction of a point for each incorrect answer. The raw scores are then converted to scaled scores that range from 200 to 800.

THE TOEFL INTERNET-BASED TEST (iBT)

The Test of English as a Foreign Language Internet-Based Test (TOEFL iBT) is designed to help assess a student's grasp of English if it is not the student's first language. Performance on the TOEFL test may help interpret scores on the verbal sections of the SAT. The test consists of four integrated sections: speaking, listening, reading, and writing. The TOEFL iBT emphasizes integrated skills. The computer- and paper-based versions of the TOEFL will continue to be administered in certain countries until the Internet-based version is administered by Educational Testing Service (ETS). For further information, visit www.toefl.org.

WHAT OTHER TESTS SHOULD I KNOW ABOUT?

The AP Program

This program allows high school students to try college-level work and build valuable skills and study habits in the process. Subject matter is explored in more depth in AP courses than in other high school classes. A qualifying score on an AP test—which varies from school to school—can earn you college credit or advanced placement. Getting qualifying grades on enough exams can even earn you a full year's credit and sophomore standing at more than 1,500 higher-education institutions. There are currently thirty-seven AP courses in twenty-two different subject areas, including art, biology, and computer science. Speak to your

---

ADMISSIONS ADVICE

Q: What can students who don't have the best grades do to improve their chances of getting into the college of their choice?

A: We encourage students to take the SAT or ACT more than once and see how they do. There are options for students who may not meet the academic requirements because they've had to work or are gifted in other areas, such as art or athletics, or who perhaps have been through something tragic. We ask them to submit letters of recommendations, a personal statement, and any other documentation that might help support their cases. What were the factors that affected their grades? What else can they offer the university?

We often encourage students who still may not meet the requirements to start at a community college and then transfer. We'll look at their college credit vs. their high school credit. They can prove to us that they can handle a college curriculum.

Cheyenna Smith
Admission Counselor
University of Houston

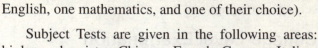

guidance counselor for information about your school's offerings.

College-Level Examination Program (CLEP)

The CLEP enables students to earn college credit for what they already know, whether it was learned in school, through independent study, or through other experiences outside of the classroom. Approximately 2,900 colleges and universities now award credit for qualifying scores on one or more of the 34 CLEP exams. The exams, which are 90 minutes in length and are primarily multiple choice, are administered at participating colleges and universities. For more information, check out the Web site at www.collegeboard.com/clep.

Armed Services Vocational Aptitude Battery (ASVAB)

ASVAB is a career exploration program consisting of a multi-aptitude test battery that helps students explore their interests, abilities, and personal preferences. A career exploration workbook gives students information about the workplace, and a career information resource book helps students match their personal characteristics to the working world. Finally, an occupational outlook handbook describes in detail approximately 250 civilian and military occupations. Students can use ASVAB scores for military enlistment up to two years after they take the test. A student can take the ASVAB as a sophomore, junior, or senior, but students cannot use their sophomore scores to enter the armed forces. Ask your guidance counselor or your local recruiting office for more information. Also, see Chapter 11, "The Military Option."

General Educational Development (GED) Test

If you have not completed your high school education, you may earn an equivalence by taking the GED test, sponsored by your state Department of Education. However, taking the GED test is not a legitimate reason for dropping out of school. In fact, it is more difficult to get into the armed services with only a GED, and some employees have difficulty getting promoted without a high school diploma.

You're eligible to take the GED if you are not enrolled in high school, have not yet graduated from high school, are at least 16 years old, and meet your local requirements regarding age, residency, and length of time since leaving school.

There are five sections to the GED test, covering writing skills, social studies, science, reading comprehension, and mathematics. Part II of the Writing Skills Test requires writing an essay. The GED costs an average of $35 but can vary from state to state, and the application fee may be waived under certain circumstances. You should contact your local GED office to arrange to take the exam. Call 800-62-MYGED to find your local GED office and for more information.

WHAT CAN I DO TO PREPARE FOR THESE TESTS?

Know what to expect. Get familiar with how the tests are structured, how much time is allowed, and the directions for each type of question. Get plenty of rest the night before the test and eat breakfast that morning.

There are a variety of products, from books to software to videos, available to help you prepare for most standardized tests. Find the learning style that suits you best. As for which products to buy, there are two major categories—those created by the test makers and those created by private companies. The best approach is to talk to someone who has been through the process and find out which product or products he or she recommends.

Some students report significant increases in scores after participating in coaching programs. Longer-term programs (40 hours) seem to raise scores more than short-term programs (20 hours), but beyond 40 hours, score gains are minor. Math scores appear to benefit more from coaching than verbal scores.

Preparation Resources

There are a variety of ways to prepare for standardized tests—find a method that fits your schedule and your budget. But you should definitely prepare. Far too many students walk into these tests cold, either because they find standardized tests frightening or annoying or they just haven't found the time to study. The key is that these exams are standardized. That means these tests are largely the same from administration to administration; they always test the same concepts. They have to, or else you couldn't compare the scores of people who took the tests on different dates. The numbers or words may change, but the underlying content doesn't.

So how do you prepare? At the very least, you should review relevant material, such as math formulas and commonly tested vocabulary words, and know the directions for each question type or test section. You should take at least one practice test and review your mistakes so you don't make them again on test day. Beyond that, you know best how much preparation you need. You'll also find lots of material in libraries or bookstores to help you: books and software from the test makers and from other publishers (including Peterson's) or live courses that range from national test-preparation companies to teachers at your high school who offer classes. Peterson's interactive and personalized SAT Online Course at www.petersonstestprep.com is another resource you'll want to check out.

THE TOP 10 WAYS *NOT* TO TAKE THE TEST

10. Cramming the night before the test.
9. Not becoming familiar with the directions before you take the test.
8. Not becoming familiar with the format of the test before you take it.
7. Not knowing how the test is graded.
6. Spending too much time on any one question.
5. Not checking spelling, grammar, and sentence structure in essays.
4. Second-guessing yourself.
3. Forgetting to take a deep breath to keep from—
2. Losing It!
1. Writing a one-paragraph essay.

Chapter 6

THE COLLEGE SEARCH

Now that you have examined your interests, talents, wants, and needs in great detail, it's time to start investigating colleges.

THE BEST RESOURCES

There are thousands of colleges and universities in the United States, so before you start filling out applications, you need to narrow down your search. There are a number of sources that will help you do this.

WELCOME TO *PETERSON'S COLLEGE PLANNER!*

Is the traditional process of searching for colleges getting old—fast? Well, log on to www.petersons.com and access *Peterson's College Planner*, your free personalized monthly e-planner from Peterson's.

In addition to using the interactive search that lets you see detailed profiles of thousands of colleges, you can register for My Peterson's. There you can build a master list of potential schools to research and compare, find the financial aid you need to pay for your education, learn everything you need to know about admission tests, and much more.

Each month, we focus on what is important in college planning—giving you the head's up on what you (yes, you!) need to be doing right now to get ahead. It's easy, and because everything is stored in one place, you don't have to worry about staying organized!

Save time. Keep your sanity. Start planning for college today at www.petersons.com.

Your Guidance Counselor

Your guidance counselor is your greatest asset in the college search process. He or she has access to a vast repository of information, from college bulletins and catalogs to financial aid applications. She knows how well graduates from your high school have performed at colleges across the country, and has probably even visited many of the colleges to get some firsthand knowledge about the schools she has recommended. The more your guidance counselor sees you and learns about you, the easier it is for her to help you. So make sure you stop by her office often, whether it's to talk about your progress or just to say "hi."

Your Teachers

Use your teachers as resources, too. Many of them have had twenty to thirty years of experience in their field. They have taught thousands of students and watched them go off to college and careers. Teachers often stay in contact with graduates and know about their experiences in college and may be familiar with the schools you are interested in attending. Ask your teachers how they feel about the match between you and your choice of schools and if they think you will be able to succeed in that environment.

Your Family

Your family needs to be an integral part of the college selection process, whether they are financing your education or not. They have opinions and valuable advice. Listen to them carefully. Try to absorb all their information and see if it applies to you. Does it fit with who you are and what you want? What works and what doesn't work for you? Is some of what they say dated? How long ago were their experiences, and how relevant are they today? Take in the information, thank them for their concern, compare what they have said with the information you are gathering, and discard what doesn't fit.

PARENT PERSPECTIVE

Q: Now that you've been through the process of getting three of your children into college, what's your best advice for parents and teens?

A: Apply early and meet deadlines. Both of our older sons were sitting there after high school graduation wondering why they were on college waiting lists: "I have good grades. I can't figure it out." At eighteen, they don't see tomorrow, much less way down the line, but do you want to deal with their heartbreak at not getting into the college where they want to be? It's their future. It's hard because they're in their senior year and you want it to be fun for them. However, you see the reality out there that they will be facing for the rest of their lives. They don't want to look at it, but you have to keep bringing them back to it—not in a preachy way. If they start earlier than their senior year, it won't be as much of a shock when they become seniors.

Jeanette and Amedee Richard
San Antonio, Texas

Colleges and Universities

Don't forget to go to college fairs. Usually held in large cities in the evening, they are free and sponsored by your local guidance counselors' association and the National Association of College Admissions Counselors (NACAC). The admissions counselors of hundreds of colleges, vocational/career colleges, and universities attend college fairs each year. Whether your questions are as general as what the overall cost of education is at a particular institution or as specific as how many biology majors had works published last year, the admissions office works to assist you in locating the people who can answer your questions. Bring a shopping bag for all the information you will get.

Admissions officers also visit high schools. Don't forget to attend these meetings during your junior and senior years. In general, college admissions counselors come to a school to get a general sense of the high school and the caliber and personality of the student body. Although it is difficult to make an individual impression at these group sessions, the college counselors do take names on cards for later contact, and you will occasionally see them making notes on the cards when they are struck by an astute questioner. It is helpful to attend these sessions because consistent contact between a student and a college is tracked by colleges and universities. An admissions decision may come down to examining the size of your admissions folder and the number of interactions you have had with the school over time.

College and university brochures and catalogs are a good place to look, too. After reading a few, you will discover that some offer more objective information than others. You will also start to learn what information colleges think is essential to present. That's important. If one college's brochure does not present the same information as most of the other college brochures, you have to ask yourself why. What might this say about the college's academic offerings, athletic or extracurricular programs, or campus life? What does the campus look like? How is the campus environment presented in the brochure? The brochures should present clues to what schools feel are their important majors, what their mission is, and on which departments they are spending their budgets. Take the time to do these informational resources justice. They have a great deal to say to the careful reader.

A college's Web site can give you a glimpse of campus life that does not appear in the college's brochure and catalog. It is true that the virtual tour will show you the shots that the college marketing department wants you to see, highlighting the campus in the best light, but you can use the home page to see other things, too. Read the student newspaper. Visit college-sponsored chat rooms. Go to the department in the major you are investigating. Look at the Course Bulletin to see what courses are required.

ONLINE HELP

To help you find two-year and four-year colleges or universities in your specific region, take a look at the Appendix in the back of this book for a listing of schools in each state. Then check out the following online resources for additional information on college selection, scholarships, student information, and much more.

Peterson's College Search. Petersons.com provides information and tools that will help you prepare, search, and pay for college. You can search for a

Part 3: The Road to More Education

CRITERIA TO CONSIDER

Depending on your personal interests, the following characteristics should play a role in helping you narrow down the field of colleges you are considering.

AFFILIATION
- Public
- Private, independent
- Private, church affiliated
- Proprietary

SIZE
- Very small (fewer than 1,000 students)
- Small (1,000–3,999 students)
- Medium (4,000–8,999 students)
- Large (9,000–19,999 students)
- Very large (more than 20,000 students)

COMMUNITY
- Rural
- Small town
- Suburban
- Urban

LOCATION
- In your hometown
- Less than 3 hours from home
- More than 3 hours from home

HOUSING
- Dorm
- Off-campus apartment
- Home
- Facilities and services for students with disabilities

STUDENT BODY
- All male
- All female
- Coed
- Minority representation
- Primarily one religious denomination
- Primarily full-time students
- Primarily part-time students
- Primarily commuter students
- Primarily residential students

ACADEMIC ENVIRONMENT
- Majors offered
- Student-faculty ratio
- Faculty teaching reputation
- Instruction by professors versus teaching assistants
- Facilities (such as classrooms and labs)
- Libraries
- Independent study available
- International study available
- Internships available

FINANCIAL AID
- Scholarships
- Grants
- Loans
- Work-study program
- Part-time or full-time jobs

SUPPORT SERVICES
- Academic counseling
- Career/placement counseling
- Personal counseling
- Student health facilities

ACTIVITIES/SOCIAL CLUBS
- Clubs, organizations
- Greek life
- Athletics, intramurals

ATHLETICS
- Division I, II, or III
- Sports offered
- Scholarships available

SPECIALIZED PROGRAMS
- Honors programs
- Services for students with disabilities or special needs

---

school by name or location. In addition to college search and selection tools, Petersons.com also offers tips on financial aid, test preparation, and online applications.

The National Association for College Admission Counseling. This home page offers information for professionals, students, and parents. The Internet address is www.nacacnet.org.

U.S. Department of Education. This federal agency's National Center for Education Statistics produces reports on every level of education, from elementary to postgraduate. Dozens are available for downloading. You can hook up with these and other links at www.ed.gov/index.jsp.

CAMPUS VISITS

You've heard the old saying, "A picture is worth a thousand words." Well, a campus visit is worth a thousand brochures. Nothing beats walking around a campus to get a feel for it. Some students report that all they needed to know that they loved or hated a campus was to drive through it. Then there is the true story of the guy who applied to a school because it had a prestigious name. Got accepted. Didn't visit, and when he arrived to move into the dorms, discovered to his horror it was an all-male school. A visit would have taken care of that problem.

The best time to experience the college environment is during the spring of your junior year or the fall of your senior year. Although you may have more time to visit colleges during your summer off, your observations will be more accurate when you can see the campus in full swing. Open houses are a good idea and provide you with opportunities to talk to students, faculty members, and administrators. Write or call in advance to take student-conducted campus tours. If possible, stay overnight in a dorm to see what living at the college is really like.

Bring your transcript so that you are prepared to interview with admission officers. Take this opportunity to ask questions about financial aid and other services that are available to students. You can get a good snapshot of campus life by reading a copy of the student newspaper. The final goal of the campus visit is to study the school's personality and decide if it matches yours. Your parents should be involved with the campus visits so that you can share your impressions. Here are some additional campus visit tips:

- ☑ Read campus literature prior to the visit.
- ☑ Ask for directions, and allow ample travel time.
- ☑ Make a list of questions before the visit.
- ☑ Dress in neat, clean, and casual clothes and shoes.
- ☑ Ask to meet one-on-one with a current student.

Chapter 6: The College Search

- Ask to meet personally with a professor in your area of interest.
- Ask to meet a coach or athlete in your area of interest.
- Offer a firm handshake.
- Use good posture.
- Listen, and take notes.
- Speak clearly, and maintain eye contact with people you meet.
- Don't interrupt.
- Be honest, direct, and polite.
- Be aware of factual information so that you can ask questions of comparison and evaluation.
- Be prepared to answer questions about yourself. Practice a mock interview with someone.
- Don't be shy about explaining your background and why you are interested in the school.
- Ask questions about the background and experiences of the people you meet.
- Convey your interest in getting involved in campus life.
- Be positive and energetic.
- Don't feel as though you have to talk the whole time or carry the conversation yourself.
- Relax, and enjoy yourself.
- Thank those you meet, and send thank-you notes when appropriate.

After you have made your college visits, use the "College Comparison Worksheet" on page 56 to rank the schools in which you're interested. This will help you decide not only which ones to apply to, but also which one to attend once you receive your acceptance letters.

THE COLLEGE INTERVIEW

Not all schools require or offer an interview. However, if you are offered an interview, use this one-on-one time to evaluate the college in detail and to sell yourself to the admission officer. The following list of questions can help you collect the information you may need to know.

WRITING TO A COLLEGE FOR INFORMATION

If neither you nor your guidance counselor has an application for a college that you are interested in, write a brief letter to the college admissions office to request an application.

Date

Your Name
Street Address
City, State, Zip

Office of Admission
Name of College
Street Address
City, State, Zip

To Whom It May Concern:

I am a (freshman, sophomore, junior, senior) at (name of your school) and will graduate in (month) (year).

Please send me the following information about your college: a general information brochure, program descriptions, an admission application, financial aid information, and any other information that might be helpful. I am considering _____ as my major field of study (optional, if you know your preferred field of study).

I am interested in visiting your campus, taking a campus tour, and meeting with an admission counselor and a financial aid officer. I would also like to meet with an adviser or professor in the (your preferred field of study) department, if possible. I will contact you in a week to set up a time that is convenient.

If you would like to contact me directly, I can be reached at (your phone number with area code and e-mail address). Thank you.

Sincerely,

(Signature)
Your Name

- How many students apply each year? How many are accepted?
- What are the average GPA and average ACT or SAT score(s) for those accepted?
- How many students in last year's freshman class returned for their sophomore year?
- What is the school's procedure for credit for Advanced Placement high school courses?

(Continued on page 56)

Part 3: The Road to More Education

THE MATCHING GAME Read each question and respond by circling Y (Yes), N (No), or C (Combination). Complete all the questions and return to the top. Highlight each action that coordinates with your answer, and then read it. Where you chose C, highlight both actions. Is there a pattern? Do the questions seem to lead to a certain type of college or university? Certain size? Certain location? Read the suggestions at the end of "The Matching Game" for more ideas.

Question	Yes/No/Combination	Action
1. Do I have a goal in life?	Y N C	**Y:** State it._____. **N:** Don't worry, many students start college without knowing what they want to do. Look into colleges that specialize in the arts and sciences.
2. Do I know what I want to achieve with a college diploma?	Y N C	**Y:** List specifically what your goals are. _____ **N:** Think about what college can offer you.
3. Do I want to broaden my knowledge?	Y N C	**Y:** Consider a liberal arts college. **N:** You might need to consider other options or educational opportunities.
4. Do I want specific training?	Y N C	**Y:** Investigate technical colleges or professional training programs in universities. **N:** You don't know what you want to study? Don't worry, only 20 pecent of seniors who apply to college are sure.
5. Am I looking for a balanced workload?	Y N C	**Y:** When you are visiting colleges, ask students about how they handle the workload. **N:** Check the workload carefully. If no one is on campus on a sunny day, it may not be the school for you
6. Am I self-directed enough to finish a four-year college program?	Y N C	**Y:** Consider only four-year colleges and universities. **N:** Maybe a two-year junior or community college is a better way to begin your college experience. Also consider a vocational/career college.
7. Do I know what I do well?	Y N C	**Y:** Identify majors related to your abilities. _____ **N:** Spend a little more time asking yourself questions about your interests. Speak to your counselor and do an interest inventory.
8. Do I like to spend time learning any one subject more than others?	Y N C	**Y:** List majors related to that area. _____ **N:** Look at your high school courses. Which ones do you like better than others? _____
9. Do I know what matters to me and what my values are?	Y N C	**Y:** Look for the schools that talk about the values on their campus. Do the values confirm or conflict with your values? **N:** Values are less important to you, so places that really expound their values may seem confining to you.
10. Do I need to be in affluent surroundings?	Y N C	**Y:** Look at the schools that deliver that package. Check the small, private liberal arts colleges. **N:** How strong is your reaction against this setting? If it is strong, check larger, more diverse settings, like an urban school.
11. Am I going to college for the financial gains?	Y N C	**Y:** What majors are going to give you the payback you want? Look at business colleges and professional programs, like premed. **N:** If a big financial payback does not interest you, look at social service majors, like counseling, teaching, and social work.
12. Am I focused?	Y N C	**Y:** Search out the programs that will offer you the best options. **N:** Avoid those schools whose programs are not strong in your focused area.
13. Am I conservative in my views and behavior?	Y N C	**Y:** The political policies of schools are important. Look into them carefully. You might look at the schools in the Midwest or the South. **N:** If you're a liberal, look closely at the political climate. Check the schools in the Northeast and on the West Coast.

Chapter 6: The College Search

14.	Do I need to be around people who are similar to me?	Y N C	**Y:** If you are African American, check the historically black colleges. If socioeconomic level or a certain look is important to you, study the student populations carefully during campus visits. If it is religious orientation you are interested in, look into religiously sponsored colleges and universities. **N:** Look at large, midsize, and small universities in urban settings.
15.	Are the name and prestige of the school important to me?	Y N C	**Y:** Look into the Ivies and the competitive schools to see if you are eligible and what they offer you. Broaden your search to include other colleges and compare their offerings to your specific needs and interests. **N:** Don't exclude the well-known institutions if they fit in every other way.
16.	Do I like sports?	Y N C	**Y:** Large universities with Division I teams will give you all the sports you need—as a competitor or a fan. If you do not want to compete at that level, check schools in other divisions. Look at the liberal arts colleges for athletes. **N:** Look into smaller universities and liberal arts colleges with good teams.
17.	Am I a techie?	Y N C	**Y:** Check for computer engineering courses at technical universities and large universities near research centers and major computer business areas. Ask about hardwiring, e-mail, and computer packages before you enroll. **N:** It still helps to know what computer services are available where you enroll.
18.	Do I need to live in or be near a city?	Y N C	**Y:** How close to a city do you need to be? In the city or an hour away? Do you still want a campus feel? Consider these questions as you visit campuses. **N:** Do you need space, natural beauty, and peaceful surroundings to think? Look into small liberal arts schools in rural and suburban settings. Explore universities in the Midwest and South.
19.	Will I need counseling for support?	Y N C	**Y:** Investigate the quality of student services and the mechanism for accessing them. Smaller schools often pride themselves on their services. Look at liberal arts colleges. Universities connected to medical centers often provide extensive services. **N:** It is still good to know what is offered.
20.	Do I need an environment in which questioning is important?	Y N C	**Y:** Liberal arts colleges, honors colleges, and smaller universities place an emphasis on academic inquiry. **N:** You like to hear others discuss issues, gather as much information and opinions as you can, and think it over by yourself. Try the university setting.

Suggestions

Here are some ideas for you to consider based on the way you answered the questions.

1. If you answered *no* to numbers 2 and 3, why not investigate apprenticeships, vocational/career colleges, armed services options, and certification or two-year college programs?
2. If you answered *yes* to numbers 4, 11, and 17, technical or professional colleges and universities with hands-on training may give you the education you want.
3. If you answered *yes* to numbers 9, 10, and 20, you are leaning toward a liberal arts setting.
4. If you answered *yes* to numbers 5 and 6, examine the competitive and Ivy League colleges.
5. If you answered *no* to numbers 9, 10, 14, and 20 and yes to 16, 17, and 18, larger universities may offer you the best options.

Once you have completed your self-evaluation, made a decision whether college is for you, have some ideas about your personality and likes and dislikes, and can relate them to the different personalities of colleges, it is time to gather information. It needs to be quality information from the right sources. The quality of information you put into your search now will determine whether your list of colleges will represent a good or a bad match.

Part 3: The Road to More Education

- As a freshman, will I be taught by professors or teaching assistants?
- How many students are there per teacher?
- When is it necessary to declare a major?
- Is it possible to have a double major or to declare a major and a minor?
- What are the requirements for the major in which I am interested?
- How does the advising system work?
- Does this college offer study abroad, cooperative programs, or academic honors programs?
- What is the likelihood, due to overcrowding, of getting closed out of the courses I need?
- What technology is available, and what are any associated fees?
- How well equipped are the libraries and laboratories?
- Are internships available?
- How effective is the job placement service of the school?
- What is the average class size in my area of interest?
- Have any professors in my area of interest recently won any honors or awards?
- What teaching methods are used in my area of interest (lecture, group discussion, fieldwork)?
- How many students graduate in four years in my area of interest?
- What are the special requirements for graduation in my area of interest?
- What is the student body like? Age? Sex? Race? Geographic origin?
- What percentage of students live in dormitories? In off-campus housing?
- What percentage of students go home for the weekend?

COLLEGE COMPARISON WORKSHEET

Fill in your top five selection criteria and any others that may be of importance to you. Once you narrow your search of colleges to five, fill in the colleges across the top row. Using a scale of 1 to 5, where 1 is poor and 5 is excellent, rate each college by your criteria. Total each column to see which college rates the highest based upon your criteria.

SELECTION CRITERIA	COLLEGE 1	COLLEGE 2	COLLEGE 3	COLLEGE 4	COLLEGE 5
1.					
2.					
3.					
4.					
5.					
OTHER CRITERIA					
6.					
7.					
8.					
9.					
10.					
TOTAL					

Sample criteria (Use this list as a starting point—there may be other criteria important to you not listed here.): Arts facilities, athletic facilities, audiovisual center, campus setting, class size, classrooms/lecture halls, computer labs, dining hall, dorms, financial aid, fraternity/sorority houses, majors offered, religious facilities, professor profiles, student-faculty ratio, student profile, student union, surrounding community.

Chapter 6: The College Search

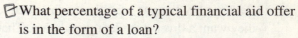

STUDENT COUNSEL

Q: How did you choose the college you're attending?

A: I followed my instincts in not going for a big name school. I went where I thought I would get the most out of the school, not necessarily because of its reputation. I considered seven schools, and once I was accepted, I looked at the location and courses they offered and the financial aid I could get.

Chay Linn Park
Pacific University

- What are some of the regulations that apply to living in a dormitory?
- What are the security precautions taken on campus and in the dorms?
- Is the surrounding community safe?
- Are there problems with drug and alcohol abuse on campus?
- Do faculty members and students mix on an informal basis?
- How important are the arts to student life?
- What facilities are available for cultural events?
- How important are sports to student life?
- What facilities are available for sporting events?
- What percentage of the student body belongs to a sorority/fraternity?
- What is the relationship between those who belong to the Greek system and those who don't?
- Are students involved in the decision-making process at the college? Do they sit on major committees?
- In what other activities can students get involved?
- What percentage of students receive financial aid based on need?
- What percentage of students receive scholarships based on academic ability?
- What percentage of a typical financial aid offer is in the form of a loan?
- If my family demonstrates financial need on the FAFSA (and PROFILE®, if applicable), what percentage of the established need is generally awarded?
- How much did the college increase the cost of room, board, tuition, and fees from last year?
- Do opportunities for financial aid, scholarships, or work-study increase each year?
- When is the admission application deadline?
- When is the financial aid application deadline?
- When will I be notified of the admission decision?
- If there is a deposit required, is it refundable?

Keep in mind that you don't need to ask all these questions—in fact, some of them may have already been answered for you in the catalog, on the Web site, or in the interview. Ask only the questions for which you still need answers.

SHOULD YOU HEAD FOR THE IVY LEAGUE?

Determining whether to apply to one of the eight Ivy League schools is something about which you should think long and hard. Sure, it can't hurt to toss your application into the ring if you can afford the application fee and the time you'll spend writing the essays. But if you want to figure out if you'd be a legitimate candidate for acceptance at one of these top-tier schools, you should understand the type of student that they look for and how you compare, says John Machulsky, a guidance counselor at Lawrence High School in New Jersey. Take a look at these statistics:

- On average only 15 percent or fewer applicants are accepted at Ivy League colleges each year.
- Most Ivy League students have placed in the top 10 percent of their class.

- Because Ivy League schools are so selective, they want a diverse student population. That means they want students that represent not only the fifty states but also a wide selection of other countries.

Lirio Jimenez, a guidance counselor at New Brunswick High School in New Jersey, says that being accepted by an Ivy League school is a process that starts in the ninth grade. You should select demanding courses and maintain good grades in those courses throughout all four years of high school. Get involved in extracurricular activities as well, and, of course, do well on your standardized tests. When it comes time to apply for college, select at least three schools: one ideal, one possible, and one shoe-in. Your ideal can be an Ivy League if you wish.

Peterson's Get a Jump! certainly doesn't want to discourage you from applying to one of these prestigious schools. We're in your corner and want to see you get the best education possible. However, students are sometimes more concerned about getting accepted than with taking a hard look at what a school has to offer them. Often, a university or college that is less competitive than an Ivy may have exactly what you need to succeed in the future. Keep that in mind as you select the colleges that will offer you what you need.

STUDENT COUNSEL

Q: What made you choose to apply to an Ivy League school?

A: My mother recommended that I apply to Princeton. She said, "Why not just try? What do you have to lose? All they can tell you is no." I was afraid of being rejected. I wasn't a straight-A student, and I thought they weren't going to want me—they get thousands of applications. Through the whole college process I had a whole lot of self-doubt. Looking back, I realize that you won't know if you don't try. Take the chance and fill out the application. If you don't get in, it doesn't mean you're less intelligent. It just wasn't the correct fit.

Zoelene Hill
Princeton University

MINORITY STUDENTS

African-American, Hispanic, Asian-American, and Native-American high school students have a lot of doors into higher education opening for them. In fact, most colleges want to respond to the social and economic disadvantages of certain groups of Americans. They want to reflect the globalization of our economy. They want their student populations to look like the rest of America, which means people from many different backgrounds and ethnic groups. This isn't just talk either. You'll find that most colleges have at least one member of the admissions staff who specializes in recruiting minorities.

One of the reasons college admissions staff are recruiting minorities and want to accommodate their needs is because there are more minorities thinking of attending college—and graduating. Let's put some numbers to these statements. A November 2006 report from the American Council on Education (ACE) found that minority enrollment at U.S. colleges and universities over the ten years between 1993 and 2003 increased by 50.7 percent. In 2003, there were 4.7 million minority students, constituting 27.8 percent of all students.

Peterson's Get a Jump! has a lot of information in this section to help you make decisions about college and paying for college. Perhaps the most important information we can give you is that if you want to go to college, you can. There are a lot of organizations ready to assist you. So go for it. See the list of organizations in this section and check with the colleges in which you're interested to connect with the minority affairs office.

Academic Resources for Minority Students

In addition to churches, sororities and fraternities, and college minority affairs offices, minority students can receive information and assistance from the following organizations:

ASPIRA

ASPIRA's mission is to empower the Puerto Rican and Latino community through advocacy and the education and leadership development of its youth.

1444 Eye Street, NW, Suite 800
Washington, D.C. 20005
202-835-3600
www.aspira.org

INROADS

A national career-development organization that places and develops talented minority youth (African-American, Hispanic-American, and Native-American) in business and industry.

10 South Broadway, Suite 700
St. Louis, Missouri 63102
314-241-7488
www.inroads.org

National Action Council for Minorities in Engineering (NACME)

An organization that aims to provide leadership and support for the national effort to increase the representation of successful African-American, American Indian, and Latino women and men in engineering and technology and math- and science-based careers.

440 Hamilton Avenue, Suite 302
White Plains, New York 10601-1813
914-539-4010
www.nacme.org

National Association for the Advancement of Colored People (NAACP)

The purpose of the NAACP is to improve the political, educational, social, and economic status of minority groups; to eliminate racial prejudice; to keep the public aware of the adverse effects of racial discrimination; and to take lawful action to secure its elimination, consistent with the efforts of the national organization.

4805 Mt. Hope Drive
Baltimore, Maryland 21215
877-NAACP-98 (toll-free)
www.naacp.org

SHOULD YOU ATTEND A HISTORICALLY BLACK COLLEGE OR UNIVERSITY?

Choosing which college to attend is usually a difficult decision for anyone to make, but when an African-American student is considering attending a historically black college or university (HBCU), a whole other set of family and cultural issues are raised.

There are many valid reasons that favor one or the other. Some are obvious differences. Parents and their children have to be honest with themselves and take a long, hard look at the needs of the student and how the campus environment can fulfill them. To help you decide, here are some questions to ask:

DO I KNOW WHAT'S REALLY IMPORTANT TO ME?

Look at the reasons why you want a degree and what you want to achieve with it. Is the choice to attend an HBCU yours or your family's? Do you have a particular field of study you want to pursue? Sometimes students can get so caught up in applying to a particular institution, they don't realize it doesn't even offer their major.

HOW WILL THIS CAMPUS FIT MY PLANS FOR THE FUTURE?

There's no substitute for doing your homework about the campuses you're seriously considering. Know the reputation of those campuses in the community and among employers and the general population. Find out about student retention, graduation, and placement rates.

DOES THIS CAMPUS HAVE THE FACILITIES AND LIVING CONDITIONS THAT SUIT MY COMFORT LEVEL?

Finding a campus where you're comfortable is a big factor in choosing a college. What do you want in campus facilities and living conditions? For instance, if you currently attend a small private high school in a suburban setting, perhaps you wouldn't like living on a large urban campus with peers who don't mirror your kind of background.

WHAT LEVEL OF SUPPORT WILL I GET ON CAMPUS?

Students considering institutions where few people are like them should look at the available support systems and organizations that will be available to them. Parents need to feel comfortable with the contact person on campus.

When all the factors that determine the choice of a college are laid out, the bottom line is which institution best meets your needs. For some African-American students, an HBCU is the best choice. For others, it's not. African-American students reflect many backgrounds, and there is no single decision that will be right for everyone.

Part 3: The Road to More Education

STUDENT COUNSEL

Q: How did you make the decision to attend a historically black college or university?

A: Selecting a college was one of the hardest decisions I've ever had to make. As a recipient of the National Achievement Scholarship and a National History Day winner, I was offered scholarships to a number of colleges across the country, including many HCBUs. I tried to figure out which institution would be able to give me the most help in achieving my goals. I finally decided on Florida A&M University (FAMU) in my hometown of Tallahassee.

There are many pluses to attending college in my hometown. By living on campus, I have the freedom to make my own decisions and live as a young adult while being close to the loving support of my parents. Also, FAMU will help me succeed in my objective of obtaining a bachelor's degree in broadcast journalism. As I look back, I am glad that I, unlike some of my high school peers, did not rush to judgment during the process of choosing a college. I am very happy with my decision.

Larry Rivers
Florida A&M University

The National Urban League

The Campaign for African-American Achievement of the National Urban League provides services for African-Americans and economically disadvantaged people. These services include basic academic development, GED test preparation for youths and adults, after-school tutoring for children, parent training classes, scholarships, an annual tour of historically black colleges and universities, and summer employment for youths.

> 120 Wall Street
> New York, New York 10005
> 212-558-5300
> www.nul.org

United Negro College Fund (UNCF)

The UNCF serves to enhance the quality of education by raising operating funds for its 39 member colleges and universities, providing financial assistance to deserving students, and increasing access to technology for students and faculty at historically black colleges and universities.

> 8260 Willow Oaks Corporate Drive
> P.O. Box 10444
> Fairfax, Virginia 22031-8044
> 800-331-2244 (toll-free)
> www.uncf.org

The American Indian Higher Education Consortium (AIHEC)

AIHEC's mission is to support the work of tribal colleges and the national movement for tribal self-determination through four objectives: maintain commonly held standards of quality in American Indian education; support the development of new tribally controlled colleges; promote and assist in the development of legislation to support American Indian higher education; and encourage greater participation by American Indians in the development of higher education policy.

> 121 Oronoco Street
> Alexandria, Virginia 22314
> 703-838-0400
> www.aihec.org

The Gates Millennium Scholars (GMS)

The Gates Millennium Scholars, funded by a grant from the Bill & Melinda Gates Foundation, was established in 1999 to provide outstanding African-American, American-Indian/Alaska Natives, Asian-Pacific Islander Americans, and Hispanic-American students with an opportunity to complete an undergraduate college education in all discipline areas and a graduate education for those students pursuing studies in mathematics, science, engineering, education, or library science. The goal of GMS is to promote academic excellence and to provide an opportunity for thousands of outstanding students with significant financial need to reach their fullest potential.

> P.O. Box 10500
> Fairfax, Virginia 22031-8044
> 877-690-4677 (toll-free)
> www.gmsp.org

Hispanic Association of Colleges and Universities (HACU)

The Hispanic Association of Colleges and Universities is a national association representing the accredited colleges and universities in the United

States where Hispanic students constitute at least 25 percent of the total student enrollment. HACU's goal is to bring together colleges and universities, corporations, government agencies, and individuals to establish partnerships for promoting the developing Hispanic-serving colleges and universities; improving access to and the quality of postsecondary education for Hispanic students; and meeting the needs of business, industry, and government through the development and sharing of resources, information, and expertise.

> 8415 Datapoint Drive, Suite 400
> San Antonio, Texas 78229
> 210-692-3805
> www.hacu.net

Hispanic Scholarship Fund (HSF)

The Hispanic Scholarship Fund is the nation's leading organization supporting Hispanic higher education. HSF was founded in 1975 with a vision to strengthen the country by advancing college education among Hispanic Americans. In support of its mission, HSF provides the Latino community with college scholarships and educational outreach support.

> 55 Second Street, Suite 1500
> San Francisco, California 94105
> 877-473-4636 (toll-free)
> www.hsf.net

STUDENTS WITH DISABILITIES GO TO COLLEGE

The Americans with Disabilities Act (ADA) requires educational institutions at all levels, public and private, to provide equal access to programs, services, and facilities. Schools must be accessible to students, as well as to employees and the public, regardless of any disability. To ensure such accessibility, they must follow specific requirements for new construction, alterations or renovations, academic programs, and institutional policies, practices, and procedures. Students with specific disabilities have the right to request and expect accommodations, including auxiliary aids and services that enable them to participate in and benefit from all programs and activities offered by or related to a school.

TIPS FOR STUDENTS WITH DISABILITIES

- Document your disability with letters from your physician(s), therapist, case manager, school psychologist, and other service providers.
- Get letters of support from teachers, family, friends, and service providers that detail how you have succeeded despite your disability.
- Learn the federal laws that apply to students with disabilities.
- Research support groups for peer information and advocacy.
- Visit several campuses.
- Look into the services available, the pace of campus life, and the college's programs for students with disabilities.
- Ask about orientation programs, including specialized introductions for, or about, students with disabilities.
- Ask about flexible, individualized study plans.
- Ask if the school offers technology such as voice synthesizers, voice recognition, and/or visual learning equipment to its students.
- Ask about adapted intramural/social activities.
- Ask to talk with students who have similar disabilities to hear about their experiences on campus.
- Once you select a college, get a map of the campus and learn the entire layout.
- If you have a physical disability, make sure the buildings you need to be in are accessible to you. Some, even though they comply with the ADA, aren't as accessible as others.
- Be realistic. If you use a wheelchair, for example, a school with an exceptionally hilly campus may not be your best choice, no matter what other accommodations it has.

To comply with ADA requirements, many high schools and universities offer programs and information to answer questions for students with disabilities and to assist them both in selecting appropriate colleges and in attaining full inclusion once they enter college. And most colleges and universities have disabilities services offices to help students negotiate the system. When it comes time to apply to colleges, write to the ones that you're interested in to find out what kinds of programs they have in place. When it comes time to narrow down your choices, make a request for a visit.

What Is Considered a Disability?

A person is considered to have a disability if he or she meets at least one of three conditions. The individual must:

1. have a documented physical or mental impairment that substantially limits one or more major life activities, such as personal self-care, walking, seeing, hearing, speaking, breathing, learning, working, or performing manual tasks;
2. have a record of such an impairment; or
3. be perceived as having such an impairment.

Physical disabilities include impairments of speech, vision, hearing, and mobility. Other disabilities, while less obvious, are similarly limiting; they include diabetes, asthma, multiple sclerosis, heart disease, cancer, mental illness, mental retardation, cerebral palsy, and learning disabilities.

Learning disabilities refer to an array of biological conditions that impede a person's ability to process and disseminate information. A learning disability is commonly recognized as a significant deficiency in one or more of the following areas: oral expression, listening comprehension, written expression, basic reading skills, reading comprehension, mathematical calculation, or problem solving. Individuals with learning disabilities also may have difficulty with sustained attention, time management, or social skills.

If you have a disability, you will take the same steps to choose and apply to a college as other students, but you should also evaluate each college based on your special need(s). Get organized, and meet with campus specialists to discuss your specific requirements. Then, explore whether the programs, policies, procedures, and facilities meet your specific situation.

It is usually best to describe your disability in a letter attached to the application so the proper fit can be made between you and the school. You will probably need to have your psychoeducational evaluation and testing record sent to the school. Some colleges help with schedules and offer transition courses, reduced course loads, extra access to professors, and special study areas to help address your needs.

Remember, admission to college is a realistic goal for any motivated student. If you invest the time and effort, you can make it happen.

STUDENT COUNSEL

The following quotes are from students who attend a college that offers services for learning disabled students.

"I have delayed development. I need help getting things done, and I need extra time for tests. As long as I'm able to go up to teachers and ask questions, I do well on tests."

—Anita

"I have dyslexia. I thought the term 'disabilities services' was for people with visual and hearing impairments. But when I got here, I found it covered a variety of disabilities. It was like Christmas. You got everything you wanted and more."

—Debra

"I am hard of hearing. I was always afraid I wouldn't be able to hear what [teachers] said. It's hard to read lips and listen at the same time. With note takers, I still get what I need even if the teacher moves around. They want you to make it through."

—Jeannette

DIRECTORY FOR STUDENTS WITH DISABILITIES

The following resources can help students, families, and schools with the legal requirements for accommodating disabilities. They can also link you with other groups and individuals that are knowledgeable in students' rights and the process of transition into post-secondary education.

Also, there are special interest, education, support, and advocacy organizations for persons with particular disabilities. Check with your counselor or contact one of the following organizations for information:

ACT Administration

Standard-Time National Testing with Accommodations

ACT Test Administration
P.O. Box 168
Iowa City, Iowa 52243-0168
319-337-1510

Extended-Time National Testing (up to 5 hours testing time or 5 hours, 45 minutes if taking the Writing Test)

ACT Registration
P.O. Box 414
Iowa City, Iowa 52243-0414
319-337-1270

Association on Higher Education and Disability (AHEAD)

107 Commerce Center Drive
Suite 204
Huntersville, NC 28078
704-947-7779
www.ahead.org

Attention Deficit Disorder Association (ADDA)

15000 Commerce Parkway
Suite C
Mount Laurel, NJ 08054
856-439-9099
www.add.org

Children and Adults with Attention-Deficit/Hyperactivity Disorders (CHADD)

8181 Professional Place,
Suite 150
Landover, Maryland 20785
800-233-4050 (toll-free)
www.chadd.org

Council for Learning Disabilities

11184 Antioch Road, Box 405
Overland Park, KS 66210
913-491-1011
www.cldinternational.org

HEATH Resource Center National Clearinghouse on Postsecondary Education for Individuals with Disabilities

The George Washington University
HEATH Resource Center
2121 K Street, NW, Suite 220
Washington, D.C. 20037
800-544-3284 (toll-free)
www.heath.gwu.edu

International Dyslexia Association

The Chester Building, Suite 382
8600 LaSalle Road
Baltimore, Maryland 21286-2044
410-296-0232
www.interdys.org

Learning Disabilities Association of America (LDA)

4156 Library Road
Pittsburgh, Pennsylvania 15234
412-341-1515
www.ldanatl.org

National Center for Learning Disabilities (NCLD)

381 Park Avenue South,
Suite 1401
New York, New York 10016
888-575-7373 (toll-free)
www.ncld.org

National Dissemination Center for Children with Disabilities

P.O. Box 1492
Washington, D.C. 20013
800-695-0285 (toll-free)
www.nichcy.org

Recording for the Blind & Dyslexic

20 Roszel Road
Princeton, New Jersey 08540
866-RFBD-585
www.rfbd.org

SAT Services for Students with Disabilities

The College Board Services for Students with Disabilities
P.O. Box 6226
Princeton, New Jersey 08541-6226
609-771-7137
www.collegeboard.com

Chapter 7

APPLYING TO COLLEGE

The big moment has arrived. It's time to make some decisions about where you want to apply.

Once your list is finalized, the worst part is filling out all the forms accurately and getting them in by the deadlines. Because requirements differ, you should check with all the colleges that you are interested in attending to find out what documentation is needed and when it is due.

WHAT SCHOOLS LOOK FOR IN PROSPECTIVE STUDENTS

As if you were sizing up the other team to plan your game strategy, you'll need to understand what admissions committees want from you as you assemble all the pieces of your application.

Academic record: Admission representatives look at the breadth (how many), diversity (which ones), and difficulty (how challenging) of the courses on your transcript.

Grades: You should show consistency in your ability to work to your potential. If your grades are not initially good, colleges look to see that significant improvement has been made. Some colleges have minimum grade point averages that they are willing to accept.

Class rank: Colleges may consider the academic standing of a student in relation to the other members of his or her class. Are you in the top 25 percent of your class? Top half? Ask your counselor for your class rank.

Standardized test scores: Colleges look at test scores in terms of ranges. If your scores aren't high but you did well academically in high school, you shouldn't be discouraged. There is no set formula for admission. Even at the most competitive schools, some students' test scores are lower than you would think.

Extracurricular activities: Colleges look for depth of involvement (variety and how long you participated), initiative (leadership), and creativity demonstrated in activities, service, or work.

Recommendations: Most colleges require a recommendation from your high school guidance counselor. Some ask for references from teachers or other adults. If your counselor or teachers don't know you well, you should put together a student resume, or brag sheet, that outlines what you have done during your four years of high school. In this chapter, you'll

PARENT PERSPECTIVE

Q: How did you help your daughter get into college?

A: The key is to start early, like in the junior year. We didn't do that. At this point in the fall of our daughter's senior year, deadlines are coming up, and we haven't really looked at any colleges yet or gone on visits. It's kind of like choosing a house to buy without going to the house. The parent's role is to ask a lot of questions to get your child to figure out exactly what it is he or she wants to do. It's a big decision.

We hired a financial aid consultant who is helping us look at different colleges. The biggest worry is the FAFSA form. If you get it wrong, and they send it back to you—you have to start all over again. In the meantime, you're behind and others are getting grants. The whole process is very confusing, and there's no one to walk you through it. We've looked at different colleges on the Internet, and college fairs are a good resource. Plus, our daughter has done a lot on her own.

Doug and Judy Ames
Colorado Springs, Colorado

Chapter 7: Applying to College

PARENT PERSPECTIVE

Q: What can parents do to help their children make decisions about colleges?

A: Parents and teens should visit college campuses early and trust their gut feelings about whether the campus feels right. Above all, don't be blinded by name-brand colleges and the strong peer pressure that seems to steer your teen in the direction of prestigious colleges. Just as in shopping for clothing: Would you rather have a name brand or something that fits you well and makes you feel comfortable?

Ask your teen some questions. Do you really want to live in a pressure-cooker for the next four years? Some students thrive in a highly competitive environment, but many do not—even if they are excellent students. Before making a final decision, a teen should spend three or four days at the two colleges that interest him or her the most.

Senior year in high school is a time when teens go through many changes and experiment with many different roles. This can be bewildering to parents. Be patient. Realize that the time is equally bewildering to your son or daughter. Parents can be supportive and understanding, even though their teen may seem to be pushing them away. Offer guidance about choosing the right college, even though your teen might seem to be rejecting it. Teens hear everything, though they might not show it.

Marilyn Wedge, Ph.D.
Parent, family therapist, and educational consultant
Agoura Hills, California

find a worksheet that will help you put together your resume.

College interview: An interview is required by most colleges with highly selective procedures. For further information, see "The College Interview" in the previous chapter.

ADMISSION PROCEDURES

Your first task in applying is to get application forms. That's easy. You can get them from your high school's guidance department, at college fairs, or by calling or writing to colleges and requesting applications. (See "Writing to a College for Information" in the previous chapter.) The trend, however, is leaning toward online applications, which are completed at the school's Web site. Admission information can be gathered from college representatives, catalogs, Web sites, and directories; alumni or students attending the college; and campus visits. Take a look at "Dos and Don'ts for Filling out Your Applications" on page 70 for some guidelines.

Which Admission Option Is Best for You?

One of the first questions you will be asked on applications for four-year colleges and universities is which admission option you want. What they're talking about is whether you want to apply early action, early decision, deferred admission, etc.

Four-year institutions generally offer the following admissions options:

Early admission: A student of superior ability is admitted into college courses and programs before completing high school.

Early decision: A student declares a first-choice college, requests that the college decide on acceptance early (between November and January), and agrees to enroll if accepted. Students with a strong high school record who are sure they want to attend a certain school should consider early decision admission. (See "More on Early Decision," on the next page.)

Early action: This is similar to early decision, but if a student is accepted, he or she has until the regular admission deadline to decide whether or not to attend.

Early evaluation: A student can apply under early evaluation to find out if the chance of acceptance is good, fair, or poor. Applications are due before the regular admission deadline, and the student is given an opinion between January and March.

Regular admission: This is the most common option offered to students. A deadline is set for when all applications must be received, and all notifications are sent out at the same time.

Rolling admission: The college accepts students who meet the academic requirements on a first-come, first-served basis until it fills its freshman class. No strict application deadline is specified. Applications are reviewed and decisions are made immediately (usually within two to three weeks). This method is commonly used at large state universities, so students should apply early for the best chance of acceptance.

Open admission: Virtually all high school graduates are admitted, regardless of academic qualifications.

Deferred admission: An accepted student is allowed to postpone enrollment for a year. See the section on taking a gap year at the end of this chapter.

If you're going to a two-year college, these options also apply to you. Two-year colleges usually have an "open-door" admission policy, which means that high school graduates may enroll as long as space is available. Sometimes vocational/career colleges are somewhat selective, and competition for admission may be fairly intense for programs that are highly specialized.

More on Early Decision

Early decision is a legally binding agreement between you and the college. If the college accepts you, you pay a deposit within a short period of time and sign an agreement stating that you will not apply to other colleges. To keep students from backing out, some colleges mandate that applicants' high school counselors cannot send transcripts to other institutions.

> **STUDENT COUNSEL**
>
> **Q:** What made you want to apply to college early decision?
>
> **A:** I visited lots of schools in Pennsylvania, but the minute I walked on the campus at Gettysburg, I knew I wanted to come here. I liked the way the campus was set up. It was small, and everything was together. The student-teacher ratio was low, and it had a good political science program. It had everything that I wanted.
>
> But if you want to go early decision, you have to visit the schools to be able to compare and contrast the different campuses. Many of the schools will have the same things, like small class size, but the way you feel about the campus is the largest factor because that's where you will be living. I visited Gettysburg four times, so when I went early decision, I was confident about it. I realized it was a huge step and knew I had to be sure. But after visiting here so many times, I knew I'd be unhappy anywhere else.
>
> *Kelly Keegan*
> *Gettysburg College*

In many ways, early decision is a win-win for both students and colleges. Students can relax and enjoy their senior year of high school without waiting to see if other colleges have accepted them. And colleges know early in the year who is enrolled and can start planning the coming year.

When Is Early Decision the Right Decision?

For good and bad reasons, early decision is a growing trend, so why not just do it? Early decision is an excellent idea that comes with a warning. It's not a good idea unless you have done a thorough college search and know without a shred of doubt that this is the college for you. Don't go for early decision unless you've spent time on the campus, in classes and dorms, and you have a true sense of the academic and social climate of that college.

Early decision can get sticky if you change your mind. Parents of students who have signed agreements and then want to apply elsewhere get angry at high school counselors, saying they've taken away their rights to choose among colleges. They try to force them to send out transcripts even though their children have committed to one college. To guard against this scenario, some colleges ask parents and students to sign a statement signifying their understanding that early decision is a binding plan. Some high schools now have their own form for students and parents to sign acknowledging that they completely realize the nature of an early decision agreement.

The Financial Reason Against Early Decision

Another common argument against early decision is that if an institution has you locked in, there's no incentive to offer applicants the best financial packages. The consensus seems to be that if you're looking to play the financial game, don't apply for early decision.

However, some folks argue that the best financial aid offers are usually made to attractive applicants. In general, if a student receives an early decision offer, they fall into that category and so would get "the sweetest" financial aid anyway. That doesn't mean that there aren't colleges out there using financial incentives to get students to enroll. A strong candidate who applies to six or eight schools and gets admitted to them all will look at how much money the colleges throw his or her way before making a decision.

Before You Decide...

If you're thinking about applying for early decision at a college, ask yourself these questions first. You'll be glad you did.

- Why am I applying early decision?
- Have I thoroughly researched several colleges and do I know what my options are?
- Do I know why I'm going to college and what I want to accomplish there?
- Have I visited several schools, spent time in classes, stayed overnight, and talked to professors?
- Do the courses that the college offers match my goals?
- Am I absolutely convinced that one college clearly stands out above all others?

MORE MUMBO JUMBO

Besides confusing terms like deferred admission, early decision, and early evaluation, just discussed, you'll most likely stumble upon some additional terms that might bamboozle you. Here, we explain a few more:

Academic Calendar

Traditional semesters: Two equal periods of time during a school year.

Early semester: Two equal periods of time during a school year. The first semester is completed before Christmas.

Trimester: Calendar year divided into three equal periods of time. The third trimester replaces summer school.

Quarter: Four equal periods of time during a school year.

4-1-4: Two equal terms of about four months separated by a one-month term.

Accreditation

Accreditation is recognition of a college or university by a regional or national organization, which indicates that the institution has met its objectives and is maintaining prescribed educational standards. Colleges may be accredited by one of six regional associations of schools and colleges and by any one of many national specialized accrediting bodies.

Specialized accreditation of individual programs is granted by national professional organizations. This is intended to ensure that specific programs meet or exceed minimum requirements established by the professional organization. States may require that students in some professions that grant licenses graduate from an accredited program as one qualification for licensure.

Accreditation is somewhat like receiving a pass/fail grade. It doesn't differentiate colleges and universities that excel from those that meet minimum requirements. Accreditation applies to all programs within an institution, but it does not mean that all programs are of equal quality within an institution. Accreditation does not guarantee transfer recognition by other colleges. Transfer decisions are made by individual institutions.

Affiliation

Not-for-profit colleges are classified into one of the following categories: state-assisted, private/independent, or private/church-supported. The institution's affiliation does not guarantee the quality or nature of the institution, and it may or may not have an effect on the religious life of students.

State-assisted colleges and universities and private/independent colleges do not have requirements related to the religious activity of their students. The influence of religion varies among private/church-supported colleges. At some, religious services or study are encouraged or required; at others, religious affiliation is less apparent.

Articulation Agreement

Articulation agreements facilitate the transfer of students and credits among state-assisted institutions of higher education by establishing transfer procedures and equitable treatment of all students in the system.

One type of articulation agreement links two or more colleges so that students can continue to make progress toward their degree, even if they must attend different schools at different times. For example, some states' community colleges have agreements with their state universities that permit graduates of college parallel programs to transfer with junior standing.

A second type of articulation agreement links secondary (high school) and postsecondary institutions to allow students to gain college credit for relevant vocational courses. This type of agreement saves students time and tuition in the pursuit of higher learning.

Because articulation agreements vary from school to school and from program to program, it is recommended that students check with their home institution and the institution they are interested in attending in order to fully understand the options available to them and each institution's specific requirements.

Cross-Registration

Cross-registration is a cooperative arrangement offered by many colleges and universities for the purpose of increasing the number and types of courses offered at any one institution. This arrangement allows students to cross-register for one or more courses at any participating host institution. While specific cross-registration program requirements may vary, typically a student can cross-register without having to pay the host institution additional tuition.

If your college participates in cross-registration, check with your home institution concerning any additional tuition costs and request a cross-registration form. Check with your adviser and registrar at your home institution to make sure that the course you plan to take is approved, and then contact the host institution for cross-registration instructions. Make sure that there is space available in the course you want to take at the host institution, as some host institutions give their own students registration priority.

To participate in cross-registration, you may need to be a full-time student (some programs allow part-time student participation) in good academic and financial standing at your home institution. Check with both colleges well in advance for all of the specific requirements.

THE COMPLETE APPLICATION PACKAGE

Freshman applications can be filed any time after you have completed your junior year of high school. Colleges strongly recommend that students apply by April (at the latest) of their senior year in order to be considered for acceptance, scholarships, financial aid, and housing. College requirements may vary, so always read and comply with specific requirements. In general, admission officers are interested in the following basic materials:

- A completed and signed application and any required application fee.

- An official copy of your high school transcript, including your class ranking and grade point average. The transcript must include all work completed as of the date the application is submitted. Check with your guidance counselor for questions about these items. If you apply on line, you must inform your guidance counselor and request that he or she send your transcript to the schools to which you are applying. Your application will not be processed without a transcript.

- An official record of your ACT or SAT scores.

- Other items that may be required include letters of recommendation, an essay,

(Continued on page 70)

Chapter 7: Applying to College

COLLEGE APPLICATION CHECKLIST Keep track of your applications by inserting a check mark or the completion date in the appropriate column and row.

	College 1	College 2	College 3	College 4
Campus visit				
Campus interview				
Letters of recommendation				
NAME:				
Date requested				
Date followed-up				
NAME:				
Date requested				
Date followed-up				
NAME:				
Date requested				
Date followed-up				
Counselor recommendation form to counselor				
Secondary school report form to counselor				
Test scores requested				
Transcripts sent				
Application completed				
Essay completed				
All signatures collected				
Financial aid forms enclosed				
Application fee enclosed				
Copies made of all forms and documentation enclosed in application packet				
Postage affixed/return address on envelope				
Letters of acceptance/denial/wait list received				
Colleges notified of intent				
Tuition deposit sent				
Housing and other forms submitted to chosen college				
Orientation scheduled				

PETERSON'S GET A JUMP!

Part 3: The Road to More Education

the secondary school report form and midyear school report (sent in by your guidance counselor after you fill out a portion of the form), and any financial aid forms required by the college.

Use the "College Application Checklist" on the previous page to make sure you have what you need before you send everything off.

Filling out the Forms

Filling out college applications can seem like a daunting task, but there are six easy steps to follow for the successful completion of this part of the process.

Step 1: Practice Copies

Make a photocopy of each application of each college to which you plan to apply. Since the presentation of your application may be considered an important aspect in the weighting for admission, you don't want to erase, cross out, or use white-out on your final application. Make all your mistakes on your copies. When you think you have it right, then transfer the information to your final original copy or go online to enter it on the college's electronic application. Remember, at the larger universities, the application packet may be the only part of you they see.

Step 2: Decide on Your Approach

What is it about your application that will grab the admission counselor's attention so that it will be pulled out of the sea of applications on his or her desk for consideration? Be animated and interesting in what you say. Be memorable in your approach to your application, but don't overdo it. You want the admissions counselor to remember you, not your Spanish castle made of popsicle sticks. Most importantly, be honest and don't exaggerate your academics and extracurricular activities. Approach this process with integrity every step of the way. First of all, it is the best way to end up in a college that is the right match for you. Second, if you are less than truthful, the college will eventually learn about it.

DOS AND DON'TS FOR FILLING OUT YOUR APPLICATIONS

One of the most intimidating steps of applying for admission to college is filling out all the forms. This list of dos and don'ts will help you put your best foot forward on your college applications.

DO

- Read applications and directions carefully.
- Make sure that everything that is supposed to be included is enclosed.
- Make copies of applications, and practice filling one out before you complete the original.
- Fill out your own applications. Type the information yourself to avoid crucial mistakes.
- Start with the simple applications and then progress to the more complex ones.
- Type or neatly print your answers, and then proofread the applications and essays several times for accuracy. Also ask someone else to proofread them for you.
- If asked, describe how you can make a contribution to the schools to which you apply.
- Be truthful, and do not exaggerate your accomplishments.
- Keep a copy of all materials you submit to colleges.
- Be thorough and on time.

DON'T

- Use correction fluid. If you type your application, use a correctable typewriter or the liftoff strips to correct mistakes. Better yet, fill out your application online.
- Write in script. If you don't have access to a computer, print neatly.
- Leave blank spaces. Missing information may cause your application to be sent back or delayed while admission officers wait for complete information.
- Be unclear. If the question calls for a specific answer, don't try to dodge it by being vague.
- Put it off!

How will they know? You have to supply support materials to accompany your application, things like transcripts and recommendations. If you tell one story and they tell another, the admissions office will notice the disparity—another red flag!

Step 3: Check the Deadlines

In September of your senior year, organize your applications in chronological order. Place the due dates for your final list of schools next to their names on your stretch, target, and safety list and on your "College Application Checklist." Work on the earliest due date first.

Step 4: Check the Data on You

You need to make sure that the information you will be sending to support your applications is correct. The first thing to double check is your transcript. This is an important piece because you must send a transcript with each application you send to colleges. Take a trip to the guidance office and ask for a "Transcript Request Form." Fill out the request for a formal transcript, indicating that you are requesting a copy for yourself and that you will pick it up. Pay the fee if there is one.

When you get your transcript, look it over carefully. It will be several pages long and will include everything from the titles of all the courses that you have taken since the ninth grade along with the final grade for each course and community service hours you have logged each year. Check the information carefully. It is understandable that with this much data, it is easy to make an input error. Because this information is vital to you and you are the best judge of accuracy, it is up to you to check it. Take any corrections or questions you have back to your guidance counselor to make the corrections. If it is a questionable grade, your counselor will help you find out what grade should have been posted on your transcript. Do whatever needs to be done to make sure your transcript has been corrected no later than October 1 of your senior year.

Step 5: List Your Activities

When you flip through your applications, you will find a section on extracurricular activities. It is time to hit your computer again to prioritize your list of extracurricular activities and determine the best approach for presenting them to your colleges. Some students will prepare a resume and include this in every application they send. Other students will choose to develop an "Extracurricular, Academic, and Work Experience Addendum" and mark those specific sections of their application as "See attached Addendum."

If you are a powerhouse student with a great deal to say in this area, it will take time to prioritize your involvement in activities and word it succinctly yet interestingly. Your "Brag Sheet" will help (see "The Brag Sheet" on page 72). Put those activities that will have the strongest impact, show the most consistent involvement, and demonstrate your leadership abilities at the top of the list. This will take time, so plan accordingly. If you feel you have left out important information because the form limits you, include either an addendum or your resume as a back-up.

Step 6: Organize Your Other Data

What other information can you organize in advance of sitting down to fill out your applications?

The Personal Data Section

Most of this section is standard personal information that you will not have any difficulty responding to, but some items you will need to think about. For example, you may find a question that asks, "What special college or division are you applying to?" Do you have a specific school in mind, like the College of Engineering? If you are not sure about your major, ask yourself what interests you the most and then enter that college. Once you are in college and have a better sense of what you want to do, you can always change your major later.

The application will provide an optional space to declare ethnicity. If you feel you would like to declare an area and that it would work to your advantage for

(Continued on page 73)

Part 3: The Road to More Education

THE BRAG SHEET

At the beginning of this chapter, we described how a student resume can help your guidance counselors and teachers write their letters of recommendation for you. Putting together a list of your accomplishments will also help you organize all of the information you will need to include when you fill out your college applications.

ACADEMICS

GPA (Grade Point Average) _____

THE HONORS COURSES I HAVE TAKEN ARE:

English _____
History _____
Math _____
Science _____
Language _____
Electives _____

THE AP COURSES I HAVE TAKEN ARE:

English _____
History _____
Math _____
Science _____
Language _____
Electives _____

STANDARDIZED TEST SCORES

PSAT _____
1st SAT _____
2nd SAT _____
ACT _____

SAT SUBJECT TESTS

Test 1 _____ Score _____
Test 2 _____ Score _____
Test 3 _____ Score _____

SPECIAL TALENTS

I have received the following academic awards:
_____
_____
_____
_____

I have performed in these theatrical productions: _____
_____

I lettered in the following sports: _____
_____

I have played on the following traveling teams: _____
_____
_____

I am a member of the following musical groups: _____
_____

EXTRACURRICULAR ACTIVITIES

I participate on a regular basis in the following extracurricular activities: _____
_____

I have held the following offices: _____
_____
_____

I have established the following extracurricular organizations:
_____
_____

I have held the following after-school and summer jobs: _____
_____
_____

GOALS

I plan to major in the following area in college: _____
_____

admission, consider completing this section of the application.

You are also going to need your high school's College Entrance Examination Board (CEEB) number. That is the number you needed when you filled out your test packets. It is stamped on the front of your SAT and ACT packets, or, if you go to the guidance department, they'll tell you what it is.

The Standardized Testing Section

Applications ask you for your test dates and scores. Get them together accurately. All your College Board scores should be recorded with the latest test results you have received. Your latest ACT record will only have the current scores unless you asked for all your past test results. If you have lost this information, call these organizations or go to your guidance department. Your counselor should have copies. Be sure the testing organizations are sending your official score reports to the schools to which you're applying. If you are planning to take one of these tests in the future, the colleges will want those dates, too; they will wait for those scores before making a decision. If you change your plans, write the admissions office a note with the new dates or the reason for canceling.

The Senior Course Load Section

Colleges will request that you list your present senior schedule by semester. Set this information up in this order: List any AP or honors-level full-year courses first, as these will have the most impact. Then list other required full-year courses and then required semester courses, followed by electives. Make sure you list first-semester and second-semester courses appropriately. Do not forget to include physical education if you are taking it this year.

Your Recommendation Writers

Most schools will require you to submit two or three letters of recommendation from adults who know you well.

Guidance Counselor Recommendations

Nearly all colleges require a letter of recommendation from the applicant's high school guidance counselor. Some counselors will give students an essay question that they feel will give them the background they need in order to structure a recommendation. Other counselors will canvass a wide array of individuals who know a student in order to gather a broader picture of the student in various settings. No one approach is better than the other. Find out which approach is used at your school. You will probably get this information as a handout at one of those evening guidance programs or in a classroom presentation by your school's guidance department. If you are still not sure you know what is expected of you or if the dog has eaten those papers, ask your guidance counselor what is due and by what date. Make sure that you complete the materials on time and that you set aside enough of your time to do them justice.

Teacher Recommendations

In addition to the recommendation from your counselor, colleges may request additional recommendations from your teachers. Known as formal recommendations, these are sent directly to the colleges by your subject teachers. Most colleges require at least one formal recommendation in addition to the counselor's recommendation. However, many competitive institutions require two, if not three, academic recommendations. Follow a school's directions regarding the exact number. A good rule-of-thumb is to have recommendations from teachers in two subject areas (e.g., English and math).

Approach your recommendation writers personally to request that they write for you. If they agree, provide them with a copy of your Brag Sheet. On the other hand, you may be met with a polite refusal on the order of "I'm sorry, but I'm unable to write for you. I've been approached by so many seniors already that it would be difficult for me to accomplish your recommendation by your due dates." This teacher may really be overburdened with requests for recommendations, especially if this is a senior English teacher, or the teacher may be giving you a signal that someone else may be able to write a stronger piece for you. Either way, accept the refusal politely, and seek another recommendation writer.

How do you decide whom to ask? Here are some questions to help you select your writers:

- ☑ How well does the teacher know you?
- ☑ Has the teacher taught you for more than one course? (A teacher who taught you over a two- to three-year period has seen your talents and skills develop.)
- ☑ Has the teacher sponsored an extracurricular activity in which you made a contribution?
- ☑ Do you get along with the teacher?
- ☑ Does the college/university indicate that a recommendation is required or recommended from a particular subject-area instructor?
- ☑ If you declare an intended major, can you obtain a recommendation from a teacher in that subject area?

Other Recommendation Writers

Consider getting recommendations from your employer, your rabbi or pastor, the director of the summer camp where you worked for the last two summers, and so on—but only if these additional letters are going to reveal information about you that will have a profound impact on the way a college will view your candidacy. Otherwise, you run the risk of overloading your application with too much paper.

Writing the Application Essay

Application essays show how you think and how you write. They also reveal additional information about you that is not in your other application material. Not all colleges require essays, and those that do often have a preferred topic. Make sure you write about the topic that is specified and keep to the length of pages or words. If the essay asks for 300 words, don't submit 50 or 500. Some examples of essay topics include:

Tell us about yourself. Describe your personality and a special accomplishment. Illustrate the unique aspects of who you are, what you do, and what you want out of life. Share an experience that made an impact on you, or write about something you have learned from your parents.

Tell us about an academic or extracurricular interest or idea. Show how a book, experience, quotation, or idea reflects or shapes your outlook and aspirations.

Tell us why you want to come to our college. Explain why your goals and interests match the programs and offerings of that particular school. This question requires some research about the school. Be specific.

Show us an imaginative side of your personality. This question demands originality but is a great opportunity to show off your skills as a writer. Start writing down your thoughts and impressions well before the essay is due. Think about how you have changed over the years so that if and when it comes time to write about yourself, you will have plenty of information. Write about something that means a lot to you, and support your thoughts with reasons and examples. Then explain why you care about your topic.

The essay should not be a summary of your high school career. Describe yourself as others see you, and

---

FROM THE GUIDANCE OFFICE

Q: Why are essays so important to the college application?

A: Students focus more on grades than anything else. They think grades are the be-all and end-all and that an SAT score will get them in. For most selective schools, that's just one piece of the pie. Many of the schools in the upper 20 percent of competitive schools consider the essay more heavily. Essays show whether the student is a thinker, creative, and analytical. They're looking for the type of personality that can shine rather than one that simply can spit out names and dates. When everyone has high SATs in a pool of applicants, the essay is what makes one student stand out over another.

Patsy Lovelady
Counselor
MacArthur High School
San Antonio, Texas

use a natural, conversational style. Use an experience to set the scene in which you will illustrate something about yourself. For example, you might discuss how having a disabled relative helped you to appreciate life's simple pleasures. Or you may use your athletic experiences to tell how you learned the value of teamwork. The essay is your chance to tell something positive or enriching about yourself, so highlight an experience that will make the reader interested in you.

Outline in the essay what you have to offer the college. Explain why you want to attend the institution and how your abilities and goals match the strengths and offerings at the university. Write, rewrite, and edit. Do not try to dash off an essay in one sitting. The essay will improve with time and thought. Proofread and concentrate on spelling, punctuation, and content. Have someone else take a look at your essay. Make copies and save them after mailing the original.

Admission officers look for the person inside the essay. They seek students with a breadth of knowledge and experiences, someone with depth and perspective. Inner strength and commitment are admired, too. Not everyone is a winner all the time. The essay is a tool you can use to develop your competitive edge. Your essay should explain why you should be admitted over other applicants.

As a final word, write the essay from the heart. It should have life and not be contrived or one-dimensional. Avoid telling them what they want to hear; instead, be yourself.

SPECIAL INFORMATION FOR ATHLETES

If you weren't a planner before, but you want to play sports while in college or go to college on an athletic scholarship, you'd better become a planner now. There are many regulations and conditions you need to know ahead of time so that you don't miss out on possible opportunities.

First, think about whether or not you have what it takes to play college sports. It's a tough question to ask, but it's a necessary one. In general, playing college sports requires both basic skills and natural

SAMPLE APPLICATION ESSAY

Here is one student's college application essay. She answered the question, "Indicate a person who has had a significant influence on you, and describe that influence."

Mrs. Morrone did not become my guidance counselor until my sophomore year of high school. During my first meeting with her, I sat across from her in an uncomfortable vinyl chair and refused to meet her eyes as I told her about my long and painful shyness, how I detested oral reports, and how I feared raising my hand in class or being called on to answer a question—all because I didn't want to be the center of attention.

She did not offer me advice right away. Instead, she asked me more about myself—my family, my friends, what kinds of music, books, and movies I liked. We talked easily, like old friends, and it was not long before I began to look forward to our weekly meetings. Her office was one of the few places where I felt like I could be myself and let my personality shine through, where I knew that I was accepted and liked unconditionally.

In November of that year, the drama club announced auditions for the spring play, *The Glass Menagerie*. I had studied it in English class and it was one of my favorites; not surprisingly, I identified strongly with the timid Laura. I talked with Mrs. Morrone about the play and how much I liked theater. At one point I sighed, "I'd love to play Laura."

"Why don't you try out for the show?" Mrs. Morrone suggested.

The very idea of performing, onstage, in a spotlight, in front of dozens of people frightened me. She did not press the matter, but at the end of the session she encouraged me to bring a copy of the play to our next few meetings and read some of the character's lines, "just for fun." I did, and found myself gradually transforming into Laura as I recited her lines with increasing intensity.

After a couple of these amateur performances, she told me that I was genuinely good as Laura, and she would love to see me at least audition for the part. "I would never force you to do it," she said, "but I would hate to see you waste your potential." I insisted that I was too frightened, but she promised that she would come and watch my audition. She told me to pretend she was the only person in the audience.

A week later, I did read for the part of Laura. Mrs. Morrone beamed with pride in the back of the auditorium. I discovered that I truly enjoyed acting; slipping into another character cracked the shell that I had built around myself. I did not get the part, but I had found a passion that enriched my life in immeasurable ways. I owe Mrs. Morrone so much for putting me on the path to becoming a professional actress and for helping me to finally conquer my shyness. Without her quiet support and strength, none of this would have come to pass.

Part 3: The Road to More Education

> **FROM THE GUIDANCE OFFICE**
>
> **Q:** What's a big mistake high school athletes make when thinking about college?
>
> **A:** Some athletes think that their athletic ability alone will get them a scholarship and do not believe that their academics must be acceptable. The Division I or II schools cannot offer scholarships if the student has not met the academic standards required by the school for admission. Our counselors start reminding students in the freshman year and every year after that the courses they take do make a difference in how colleges view their transcripts. Students can't start preparing in their senior year of high school.
>
> *Sue Bradshaw*
> *Guidance Counselor*
> *Sterling High School*
> *Baytown, Texas*

ability, a solid knowledge of the sport, overall body strength, speed, and sound academics. Today's athletes are stronger and faster because of improved methods of training and conditioning. They are coached in skills and techniques, and they begin training in their sport at an early age. Remember, your talents will be compared with those from across the United States and around the world.

Second, know the background. Most college athletic programs are regulated by the National Collegiate Athletic Association (NCAA), an organization that has established rules on eligibility, recruiting, and financial aid. The NCAA has three membership divisions: Division I, Division II, and Division III. Institutions are members of one or another division according to the size and scope of their athletic programs and whether they provide athletic scholarships.

If you are planning to enroll in college as a freshman and you wish to participate in Division I or Division II athletics, you must be certified by the NCAA Initial-Eligibility Clearinghouse (www.ncaaclearinghouse.net). The Clearinghouse was established as a separate organization by the NCAA member institutions to ensure consistent interpretation of NCAA initial-eligibility requirements for all prospective student athletes at all member institutions.

You should start the certification process when you are a junior in high school. Check with your counselor to make sure you are taking a core curriculum that meets NCAA requirements. Also, register to take the ACT or SAT as a junior. Submit your Student Release Form (available in your guidance counseling office) to the Clearinghouse by the beginning of your senior year.

Initial Eligibility of Freshman Athletes for Division I and II

Students who plan to participate in NCAA Division I or II college sports must obtain the Student Release Form from their high school, complete it, and send it to the NCAA Clearinghouse. This form authorizes high schools to release student transcripts, including test scores, proof of grades, and other academic information, to the Clearinghouse. It also authorizes the Clearinghouse to release this information to the colleges that request it. The form and corresponding fee must be received before any documents will be processed. (Fee waivers are available for economically disadvantaged students. Check with your counselor for fee waiver information.)

Students must also make sure that the Clearinghouse receives ACT and/or SAT score reports. Students can have score reports sent directly to the Clearinghouse by entering a specific code (9999) printed in the ACT and SAT registration packets.

Once a year, high schools will send an updated list of approved core courses, which lists each course offering that meets NCAA core course requirements. The Clearinghouse personnel will validate the form. Thereafter, the Clearinghouse will determine each student's initial eligibility. Collegiate institutions will request information from the Clearinghouse on the initial eligibility of prospective student-athletes. The Clearinghouse will make a certification decision and report it directly to the institution.

Three types of eligibility are possible:

1. Certification of eligibility for expense-paid campus visits.

2. Preliminary certification of eligibility to participate in college sports (appears likely to meet all NCAA requirements but not yet graduated).

Chapter 7: Applying to College

ATHLETIC RESUME

Name _____

Address _____

_____

High school address and phone number

_____

_____

_____

Coach's name _____

Height/weight _____

Foot speed (by specific event) _____

Position played _____

Weight classification _____

GPA _____

Class rank _____

ACT or SAT scores (or when you plan to take them)_____

_____

Athletic records held_____

_____

All-state teams _____

Special awards _____

Off-season accomplishments _____

Weightlifting exercises _____

Vertical jumps _____

Push-ups _____

Bench jumps _____

Shuttle run _____

Leadership characteristics _____

Former successful athletes from your high school

_____

Outstanding capabilities_____

Citizenship _____

Alumni parents/relatives _____

Include the following with your resume:

- Team schedule with dates and times
- Videotape with jersey number identified
- Newspaper clippings about you and/or your team

3. Final certification granted when proof of graduation is received.

Additional information about the Clearinghouse can be found in the *Guide for the College-Bound Student-Athlete*, published by the NCAA. To get a copy of this guide, call 800-638-3731 (toll-free). You can also visit the NCAA Web site at www.ncaa.org.

National Association of Intercollegiate Athletics (NAIA) Regulations

The National Association of Intercollegiate Athletics (NAIA) has different eligibility requirements for student-athletes. To be eligible to participate in intercollegiate athletics as an incoming freshman, two of the following three requirements must be met:

1. Have a 2.0 (C) or higher cumulative final grade point average in high school.

2. Have a composite score of 18 or higher on the ACT or an 860 total score or higher on the SAT Critical Reading and Math sections.

3. Have a top-half final class rank in his or her high school graduating class.

Student-athletes must also have on file at the college an official ACT or SAT score report from the appropriate national testing center. Results reported on the student's high school transcript are not acceptable. Students must request that their test scores be forwarded to the college's admission office.

If you have additional questions about NAIA eligibility, contact them at:
NAIA
23500 W. 105th Street
Olathe, Kansas 66051
913-791-0044
www.naia.org

AUDITIONS AND PORTFOLIOS

If you decide to study the arts, such as theater, music, or fine arts, you may be required to audition or show your portfolio to admissions personnel. The following tips will help you showcase your talents and skills when preparing for an audition or portfolio review.

Part 3: The Road to More Education

STUDENT COUNSEL

Q: What's it like going to an art school?

A: This is not your normal college experience. You totally immerse yourself in art and commit all your time to it. It's intense and can be stressful. The teachers are great. Most are working professionals. The student body is impressive. I have people in my class who are 35 and have gone to a regular college.

Coming from high school, it's hard to get into an art school. You're disadvantaged because you haven't worked. I suggest going to the portfolio days in high school where schools will evaluate your portfolio and you can get an idea of where you want to go. Since my sophomore year in high school, I kept in touch with the admissions person I talked to at portfolio day. She followed me along and saw my interest.

Eric Davidson
Art Center
Pasadena, California

Music Auditions

High school students who wish to pursue a degree in music, whether it is vocal or instrumental, typically must audition. If you're a singer, prepare at least two pieces in contrasting styles. One should be in a foreign language, if possible. Choose from operatic, show music, or art song repertories, and make sure you memorize each piece. If you're an instrumentalist or pianist, be prepared to play scales and arpeggios, at least one etude or technical study, and a solo work. Instrumental audition pieces need not be memorized. In either field, you may be required to do sight-reading.

When performing music that is sight-read, you should take time to look over the piece and make certain of the key and time signatures before proceeding with the audition. If you're a singer, you should bring a familiar accompanist to the audition.

"My advice is to ask for help from teachers, try to acquire audition information up front, and know more than is required for the audition," says one student. "It is also a good idea to select your audition time and date early."

"Try to perform your solo in front of as many people as you can as many times as possible," says another student. "You may also want to try to get involved in a high school performance."

Programs differ, so students are encouraged to call the college and ask for audition information. In general, music departments seek students who demonstrate technical competence and performance achievement.

Admission to music programs varies in degree of competitiveness, so you should audition at a minimum of three colleges and a maximum of five to amplify your opportunity. The degree of competitiveness varies also by instrument, especially if a renowned musician teaches a certain instrument. Some colleges offer a second audition if you feel you did not audition to your potential. Ideally, you will be accepted into the music program of your choice, but keep in mind that it's possible to not be accepted. You must then make the decision to either pursue a music program at another college or consider another major at that college.

Dance Auditions

At many four-year colleges, an open class is held the day before auditions. A performance piece that combines improvisation, ballet, modern, and rhythm is taught and then students are expected to perform the piece at auditions. Professors look for coordination, technique, rhythm, degree of movement, and body structure. The dance faculty members also assess your ability to learn and your potential to complete the curriculum. Dance programs vary, so check with the college of your choice for specific information.

Art Portfolios

A portfolio is simply a collection of your best pieces of artwork. The pieces you select to put in your portfolio should demonstrate your interest and aptitude for a serious education in the arts. A well-developed portfolio can help you gain acceptance into a prestigious art college and increase your chances of being awarded a scholarship in national portfolio competitions. The pieces you select should show diversity in technique and variety in subject matter. You may show work in any medium (oils, photography, watercolors, pastels, etc.) and in either black-and-white or color. Your portfolio can include classroom assignments as well as independent projects. You can also include your sketchbook.

Specialized art colleges request that you submit an average of ten pieces of art, but remember that quality is more important than quantity. The admission office staff will review your artwork and transcripts to assess your skill and potential for success. Some schools have you present your portfolio in person; however, some schools allow students to mail artwork if distance is an issue. There is no simple formula for success other than hard work. In addition, there is no such thing as a "perfect portfolio," nor any specific style or direction to achieve one.

Tips for Pulling Your Portfolio Together:

- Try to make your portfolio as clean and organized as possible.
- It is important to protect your work, but make sure the package you select is easy to handle and does not interfere with the viewing of the artwork.
- Drawings that have been rolled up are difficult for the jurors to handle and view. You may shrink-wrap the pieces, but it is not required.
- Avoid loose sheets of paper between pieces. Always spray fixative on any pieces that could smudge.
- If you choose to mount or mat your work (not required), use only neutral gray tones, black, or white.
- Slides should be presented in a standard 8 × 11 plastic slide sleeve.
- Label each piece with your name, address, and high school.

Theater Auditions

Most liberal arts colleges do not require that students audition to be accepted into the theater department unless they offer a Bachelor of Fine Arts (B.F.A.) degree in theater. You should apply to the college of your choice prior to scheduling an audition. You should also consider spending a full day on campus so that you may talk with theater faculty members and students, attend classes, meet with your admission counselor, and tour the facilities.

Although each college and university has different requirements, you should prepare two contrasting monologues taken from plays of your choice if you're auditioning for a B.F.A. acting program. Musical theater requirements generally consist of one up-tempo musical selection and one ballad, as well as one monologue from a play or musical of your choice. The total of all your pieces should not exceed 5 minutes. Music for the accompanist, a resume of your theater experience, and a photo are also required.

Tips to Get You Successfully through an Audition:

- Choose material suitable for your age.
- If you choose your monologue from a book of monologues, you should read the entire play and be familiar with the context of your selection.
- Select a monologue that allows you to speak directly to another person; you should play only one character.
- Memorize your selection.
- Avoid using characterization or style, as they tend to trap you rather than tapping deeper into inner resources.

For more information about visual and performing arts colleges, check out *Peterson's College Guide for Visual Arts Majors* and *Peterson's College Guide for Performing Arts Majors,* available wherever books are sold.

THE GAP-YEAR OPTION

What is a gap year? The term "gap year" originated in the U.K. and usually refers to time taken between high school and college—or while in college—to travel, do service work, and explore areas of interest. It is a long-standing tradition for British students. In the United States, the gap-year option is a more recent phenomenon. 1980 heralded the first independent gap-year counseling service, the Center for Interim Programs, and, at that time, taking a structured break between high school and college was highly unusual. Since then, the gap year has been steadily gaining popularity and acceptance by students, parents, guidance counselors, and colleges alike.

Ten Good Reasons to Take a Gap Year

1. It is harder to take this kind of time when you are older!
2. K–12 years of schooling = potential burnout.
3. Find your passion or determine what is not of interest to you.
4. Choose and create your life for a year.
5. Follow up on interests and enhance prospective studies.
6. Gain practical skills and work experience (resume building before college or seeking a job).
7. Increase your level of self-confidence and maturity from independent travel and real-world experience.
8. Improve your chances for college acceptance.
9. Determine your college focus and avoid changing majors and incurring additional costs.
10. Experience an easier transition from college to the work world.

How Does the Gap Year Work?

The majority of students interested in a gap year apply to colleges in their senior year and then request a year's deferral once accepted. Aside from state universities that may not offer the option of a deferred year, colleges are usually happy to defer a student because they realize that an extra year of maturity and life experience often translates into an overall better student. Other students wait to apply to college until halfway through their gap year when they have a better idea of where they want to go and what they want to study.

What Is a Successful Gap-Year Experience?

The best gap-year experiences usually involve several programs in different areas of interest with at least one based outside of the United States. Good structure and planning are key components for a successful year. The following is just one example:

June–August: work a job at home to help pay for expenses

September–December: cultural study program teaching in schools in Costa Rica for three months with twelve other students and two leaders (Spanish fluency and teaching experience as primary benefits)

December: home for holiday break (and working on college applications)

January–March: internship in politics, photojournalism, radio stations, marketing, computers, or teaching in cities in England or New Zealand (experience in potential career interest as primary benefit)

April–May: short, intensive workshops in filmmaking or learning how to run a recording studio, or outdoor work in conservation or national parks in Australia or the United States

June–August: some free travel and/or working a job again at home

It is important to know that you can tailor a year to match your particular interests, whether those interests are outdoor education, conservation work, kids, social-service work, animals, healing arts/medicine, studio arts, language study, cultural immersion, professional internships, etc.

Chapter 7: Applying to College

A MESSAGE FOR PARENTS

"I suspect that most parents value any process that fosters independence and happy self-confidence. If the process can guide their young adult toward a meaningful and fulfilling career, there is even greater incentive to take part. A well-constructed gap year can offer all of this—and the invaluable benefit of a life enriched by varied experience and the inspiration to continue to create such a life."

Holly Bull
President of the Center for Interim Programs
from "The Possibilities of the Gap Year," The Chronicle of Higher Education, July 7, 2006.

How to Plan the Best Gap Year

There are a variety of resources available now that can assist students and parents in planning a fulfilling gap year. These resources range from books on the topic to independent gap-year counselors to the Internet. Preparation and thorough research definitely add to the success of a gap-year experience.

Useful books

Some of these books include sample student scenarios and programs:

The Gap-Year Advantage, by Karl Haigler and Rae Nelson
Taking Time Off, by Colin Hall and Ron Lieber
Teenage Liberation Handbook, by Grace Llewellyn
Success Without College, by Linda Lee

Gap-year counseling organizations

Working with a gap-year consultant can save a lot of research time and weed out potentially poor program options.

The Center for Interim Programs (www.interimprograms.com)
LEAPNow (www.leapnow.org)
Taking Off (www.takingoff.net)
Time Out Associates (www.timeoutassociates.com)

FINANCIAL AID DOLLARS AND SENSE

Getting financial aid can be intimidating—but don't let that stop you.

Finding the money you need to attend a two- or four-year institution or vocational/career college is a challenge, but you can do it if you devise a strategy well before you actually start applying to college. Financial aid comes from a lot of different sources. But this is where GAJ comes in. You'll find lots of help in this guide in locating those sources and obtaining advice. Financial aid is available to help meet both direct educational costs (tuition, fees, books) and personal living expenses (food, housing, transportation).

Times have changed to favor the student in the financial aid process. Because the pool of potential traditional college students is somewhat limited, colleges and universities are competing to attract the top students to their school. In fact, some colleges and universities not only use financial aid as a method to help students fund their college education but often as a marketing and recruitment tool. This puts students and families at an advantage, one that should be recognized and used for bargaining power.

It used to be that colleges and universities offered need-based and merit-based financial aid to only needy and/or academically exceptional students. Now some schools offer what might be called incentive or tuition discount aid to encourage students to choose them over another college. This aid, which is not necessarily based on need or merit, is aimed at students who meet the standards of the college but who wouldn't necessarily qualify for traditional kinds of aid.

A BIRD'S-EYE VIEW OF FINANCIAL AID

You and your family should be assertive in negotiating financial aid packages. It used to be that there was no room for such negotiation, but in today's environment, it is wise to be a comparison shopper. Families should wait until they've received all of their financial offers and then talk to their first-choice college to see if the college can match the better offers from other colleges.

To be eligible to receive federal/state financial aid, you must maintain satisfactory academic progress toward a degree or certificate. This criterion is established by each college or university. You'll also need a valid social security number, and all male students must register for selective service on their eighteenth birthday.

You apply for financial aid during your senior year. Every school requires the Free Application

PROJECTED COLLEGE EXPENSES

The following chart estimates the cost of one year of college education, including tuition, room, and board. Estimates are based on a 6 percent annual increase.

School Year	Public 4-Year	Private 4-Year
2006–2007	$12,127	$29,026
2007–2008	13,580	32,500
2010–2011	16,000	38,350
2014–2015	19,800	47,500

Source: The College Entrance Examination Board, "Trends in College Pricing, 2004"

FINANCIAL AID GLOSSARY

ASSETS. The amount a family has in savings and investments. This includes savings and checking accounts, a business, a farm or other real estate, and stocks, bonds, and trust funds. Cars are not considered assets, nor are such possessions as stamp collections or jewelry. The net value of the principal home is counted as an asset by some colleges in determining their own awards but is not included in the calculation for eligibility for federal funds.

CITIZENSHIP/ELIGIBILITY FOR AID. To be eligible to receive federally funded college aid, a student must be one of the following:

1. A U.S. citizen;
2. A non-citizen national;
3. A permanent resident with an I-151 or I-551 without conditions;
4. A participant in a suspension of deportation case pending before Congress; or
5. A holder of an I-94 showing one of the following designations: "Refugee," "Asylum Granted," "Indefinite Parole" and/or "Humanitarian Parole," "Cuban/Haitian Entrant, Status Pending," or "Conditional Entrant" (valid if issued before April 1, 1980).

Individuals in the United States on an F1 or F2 visa or on a J1 or J2 exchange visa cannot get federal aid.

COOPERATIVE EDUCATION. A program offered by many colleges in which students alternate periods of enrollment with periods of employment, usually paid, and that can lengthen the usual baccalaureate program to five years.

EXPECTED FAMILY CONTRIBUTION (EFC). A figure determined by a congressionally mandated formula that indicates how much of a family's resources should be considered "available" for college expenses. Factors such as taxable and nontaxable income and the value of family assets are taken into account to determine a family's financial strength. Allowances for maintaining a family and future financial needs are then taken into consideration before determining how much a family should be able to put toward the cost of college.

INDEPENDENT STUDENT. A student who reports only his or her own income and assets (and that of a spouse, if relevant) when applying for federal financial aid. Students are automatically considered independent at 24 years of age. Students who are under 24 will be considered independent if they are:

- married as of the date of filing the FAFSA.
- provide more than half the support of a legal dependent other than a spouse.
- a veteran of the U.S. Armed Forces.
- an orphan or ward of the court.
- classified as independent by a college's financial aid administrator because of other unusual circumstances.
- a graduate or professional student.

MERIT-BASED AID. Any form of financial aid awarded on the basis of personal achievement or individual characteristics without reference to financial need.

SUBSIDIZED LOAN. While enrolled at least half-time, this loan does not accrue interest. For Subsidized Federal Stafford and/or Direct Loans, the government pays the interest to the lender on behalf of the borrower while the student is in college and during approved grace periods.

---

for Federal Student Aid (FAFSA), which cannot be filed until after January 1 of your senior year. Your application will be processed in about 4 weeks if you use the paper application or about one week if you apply on line at www.fafsa.ed.gov. You'll then receive a Student Aid Report (SAR), which will report the information from the FAFSA and show your calculated Expected Family Contribution (EFC—the number used in determining your eligibility for federal student aid). Each school you listed on the application, as well as your state of legal residence, will also receive your FAFSA information. If you are applying to higher-cost colleges or some scholarship programs, you also may have to file the PROFILE® application. This should be completed in September or October of your senior year. More information on the PROFILE is available from your high school guidance office or on the Web at www.collegeboard.org. There is a fee charged with the PROFILE.

Part 3: The Road to More Education

COLLEGE FUNDS AVAILABLE

Use this chart to estimate resources that will be available for college expenses. Check your progress at the end of your sophomore and junior years to see if your plans for seeking financial aid need to be revised.

YOUR RESOURCES	Estimated amount available	Actual amount: 11th grade	Actual amount: 12th grade
Savings and other assets			
Summer earnings			
Part-time work during school year			
Miscellaneous			
PARENTS' RESOURCES			
From their current income			
From college savings			
Miscellaneous (insurance, annuities, stocks, trusts, home equity, property assets)			
TOTAL			

Source: American College Testing Program

You must reapply for federal aid every year. Also, if you decide to transfer to another school, your aid doesn't necessarily go with you. Check with your new school to find out what steps you must take to continue receiving aid. You should plan any transfer at least three months in advance.

Once you've decided to which schools you want to apply, talk to the financial aid officers of those schools. There is no substitute for getting information from the source when it comes to understanding your financial aid options. That personal contact can lead you to substantial amounts of financial aid.

If you qualify for admission, don't let the sticker price of the college or program scare you away, because you may get enough financial assistance to pay for the education you want. Don't rule out a private institution until you have received the financial aid package from the school. Private colleges, in order to attract students from all income levels, offer significant amounts of financial aid. Public-supported institutions tend to offer less financial aid because the lower tuition acts as a form of assistance. In addition, students attending school in their home state often have more aid possibilities than if they attend an out-of-state college. Use the "College Funds Available" chart on this page to determine how much you and your family can contribute to your education and the "College Cost Comparison Worksheet" on the following page to figure out which schools best suit you financially.

TYPES OF FINANCIAL AID

Be sure that you understand the differences between the types of financial aid so you are fully prepared to apply for each. One or more of these financial resources may make it possible to pursue the education you want.

Grants: Grants are usually given to students with financial need. But the term is also used for athletics (Division I only), academics, demographics, and special talents. Grants do not have to be repaid.

Scholarships: Scholarships, also called "merit aid," are awarded for academic excellence or other special talents or abilities. Repayment is not required.

Loans: Student loans, which have very favorable terms and conditions, are sponsored by the federal government, state governments, and through commercial lending institutions. The Financial Aid Office is the best source of information on student loans. These must be repaid, generally after you graduate or leave school.

College Work-Study: College Work-Study is a federally sponsored program that enables colleges to hire students for employment. If eligible, students work a limited number of hours throughout the school year. Many colleges use their own funds to hire students to work in the many departments and offices on campus. If you do not receive a federal work-study grant, you should contact the Student Employment Office or the Financial Aid Office to help locate nonfederal work-study positions that may be available.

Financial Aid Programs: The federal government is the single largest source of financial aid for students, making more than an estimated $94 billion available in loans, grants, and other aid to millions of students. In addition, a number of sources of financial aid are available to students from state governments, private lenders, foundations, and private sources, and the colleges and universities themselves.

FEDERAL GRANTS

The federal government offers a number of educational grants, which are outlined below:

Federal Pell Grant

The Federal Pell Grant is the largest grant program in the nation; about 5.3 million students receive awards annually. This grant is intended to be the base or starting point of assistance for lower-income families. Eligibility for a Federal Pell Grant depends on the EFC, or Expected Family Contribution. (See the "Financial Aid Glossary" for a description of commonly used terms.) The actual Pell Grant award amounts depend on how much funds are appropriated by Congress each year. The maximum for the 2006–07 school year was $4,050. How much you will receive depends not only on your EFC, but also on your cost of attendance and whether you're a full-time or part-time student.

Federal Supplemental Educational Opportunity Grant (FSEOG)

As its name implies, the Federal Supplemental Educational Opportunity Grant (FSEOG) provides additional need-based federal grant money to supplement the Federal Pell Grant. Each participating college is given funds to award to especially needy students. The maximum award is $4,000 per year, but the amount a student receives depends on the college's policy, the availability of FSEOG funds, the total cost of education, and the amount of other aid awarded.

COLLEGE COST COMPARISON WORKSHEET

Chart your course to see which college or university best fits your financial resources. Your totals in expenses and funds available should be the same amount. If not, you have a funding gap, meaning that you have more expenses than funds available.

EXPENSES	College 1	College 2	College 3	College 4
Tuition and fees	$	$	$	$
Books and supplies	$	$	$	$
Room and board	$	$	$	$
Transportation	$	$	$	$
Miscellaneous	$	$	$	$
TOTAL	$	$	$	$
FUNDS AVAILABLE				
Student and parent contributions	$	$	$	$
Grants	$	$	$	$
Scholarships	$	$	$	$
Work-study	$	$	$	$
TOTAL	$	$	$	$
Funding gap	$	$	$	$

Academic Competitiveness Grants (ACG)

The ACG is one of the two new grant programs and is available for the first time for the 2006–07 school year for first-year students who graduated from high school after January 1, 2006, and for second-year students who graduated from high school after January 1, 2005. This grant is in addition to the student's Federal Pell Grant. U.S. citizens who are eligible for a Pell Grant and are enrolled full-time can receive the ACG for $750 in the first year and $1300 in the second year of college. Students must have completed a rigorous secondary school program of study as defined by the federal government and their state. Students must maintain a 3.0 grade point average to be eligible for the program. Application is made by filing the FAFSA. Students will be given a chance to self-identify themselves for consideration and may be selected automatically by their college. The financial aid office will award the grant to eligible students.

National Smart Grants

SMART grants are available during the third and fourth years of undergraduate study to full-time students who are eligible for the Federal Pell Grant and who are majoring in physical, life, or computer sciences, mathematics, technology, or engineering or in a foreign language determined critical to national security. The student must also have maintained a cumulative grade point average (GPA) of at least 3.0 in course work required for the major. U.S. citizens who are eligible for a Pell Grant and are enrolled full-time can receive the $4000 grant. Students must maintain a 3.0 grade point average to be eligible for the program. Application is made by filing the FAFSA. The postsecondary school listed on the student's FAFSA will determine whether the student meets all of the eligibility requirements. The financial aid office will award the grant to eligible students.

FEDERAL SCHOLARSHIPS

The following comprise the scholarships available through the federal government:

ROTC Scholarships

The Armed Forces (Army, Air Force, Navy, Marines) may offer up to a four-year scholarship that pays full college tuition plus a monthly allowance; however, these scholarships are very competitive and based upon GPA, class rank, ACT or SAT scores, and physical qualifications. Apply as soon as possible before December 1 of your senior year. Contact the headquarters of each of the armed forces for more information: Army, 800-USA-ROTC; Air Force, 800-423-USAF; Navy, 800-USA-NAVY; Marines, 800-MARINES (all numbers are toll-free).

Scholarships from Federal Agencies

Federal agencies—such as the CIA, NASA, Department of Agriculture, and Office of Naval Research—offer an annual stipend as well as a scholarship. In return, the student must work for the agency for a certain number of years or else repay all the financial support. See your counselor for more information.

Robert C. Byrd Honors Scholarship

To qualify for this state-administered scholarship, you must demonstrate outstanding academic achievement and excellence in high school as indicated by class rank, high school grades, test scores, and leadership activities. Award amounts of $1,500 are renewable for four years. Contact your high school counselor for application information. Deadlines may vary per state, so also contact your state's Department of Education.

FINANCIAL AID ADVICE

Q: What do you wish students and their parents knew about financial aid?

A: They don't know they should get their financial application filed early enough, so if we run into snags, it can be corrected. They make mistakes, such as not answering the question about the amount of taxes paid the previous year. A lot of parents think that if they didn't send in a check to the IRS, they didn't pay taxes. Something as simple as that causes a lot of problems. If their financial information is recorded incorrectly, it can really mess them up. They should read all the information on the financial aid form, and if they have questions, they should ask someone. Speaking from my experience, if you can't get in touch with the college you're child is thinking of attending, then call a local college. Any time an application doesn't go through the system smoothly, it can cause major problems.

Now that you can apply over the Internet, the applications are much simpler and worded in layman's terms. If applicants miss filling in some information, that will trigger a warning that they omitted something. I realize that not all students have access to the Internet, but they can go to the public library and look into getting onto the Internet there.

Trudy Masters, Financial Aid Officer
Lee College
Baytown, Texas

Chapter 8: Financial Aid Dollars and Sense

FEDERAL LOANS

Following are methods through which you may borrow money from the federal government:

Federal Perkins Loan

This loan provides low-interest (5 percent) aid for students with exceptional financial need. The Federal Perkins Loans are made through the college's Financial Aid Office—that is, the college is the lender. For undergraduate study, you may borrow a maximum of $4,000 per year for up to five years of undergraduate study and may take up to ten years to repay the loan, beginning nine months after you graduate, leave school, or drop below half-time status. No interest accrues while you are in school and, under certain conditions (e.g., if you teach in a low-income area, work in law enforcement, are a full-time nurse or medical technician, or serve as a Peace Corps or VISTA volunteer), some or all of your loans may be either partially paid or cancelled in full. Payments also can be deferred under certain conditions, such as unemployment.

FFEL Stafford Loan

A Federal Family Education (FFEL) Stafford Loan may be borrowed from a participating commercial lender, such as a bank, credit union, or savings and loan association. This is a fixed rate of 6.8 percent loan. If you qualify for a need-based subsidized FFEL Stafford Loan, the interest is paid by the federal government while you are enrolled in school. There is also an unsubsidized FFEL Stafford Student Loan that is not based on need and for which you are eligible, regardless of your family income.

The maximum amount you may borrow as a dependent student is $3,500 for freshmen, $4,500 for sophomores, and $5,500 for juniors and seniors, with a maximum of $23,000 for your undergraduate program. The maximum amount for independent students is $7,500 for freshmen, $8,500 for sophomores, and $10,500 for juniors and seniors, with a maximum of $46,000 for your undergraduate program. (The subsidized amount for independent

FINANCIAL AID RESOURCES

You can use these numbers for direct access to federal and state agencies and processing services.

FEDERAL STUDENT AID INFORMATION CENTER

Provides duplicate student aid reports and aid applications to students. Also answers questions on student aid, mails Department of Education publications, makes corrections to applications, and verifies college federal aid participation. Call 800-4-Fed-Aid (toll-free) or visit their Web site at www.studentaid.ed.gov.

VETERANS BENEFITS ADMINISTRATION

Provides dependent education assistance for children of disabled veterans. College-bound students should call the VBA to determine whether or not they qualify for assistance, what the benefits are, and if a parent's disability qualifies them for benefits. Call 888-442-4551 (toll-free) or visit their Web site at www.gibill.va.gov.

ACT FINANCIAL AID NEED ESTIMATOR (FANE)

Mails financial tabloids to students, provides information on filling out financial aid forms, and estimates financial aid amounts. Also mails financial need estimator forms. Forms are also accessible online. Go to www.ACT.org or call 319-337-1000.

COLLEGE SCHOLARSHIP SERVICE (PROFILE®)

Provides free applications and registration forms for federal student aid. Helps students fill out applications. Call 305-829-9793 or visit http://profileonline.collegeboard.com/index.jsp.

COLLEGE FOR TEXANS

Here is everything a Texan needs to know about preparing for, applying for, and paying for college or technical school. It's all in one up-to-date, easy-to-navigate site as big as the state itself. And remember $4 billion is available every year to help Texans attend college. Go to www.collegefortexans.com for more information.

students is the same as for dependent students, based on financial need.) There may be up-front origination fees charged for these loans that are deducted from the loan proceeds.

To apply for a FFEL Stafford Student Loan, you must first complete a FAFSA to determine eligibility for the subsidized amount of your loan. You should contact your school's Financial Aid Office to determine the most efficient method of selecting a lender, since many schools have established a preferred lender list. If your school does not have a preferred lender list, contact any local financial institution in your area or your state's Department of Higher Education for assistance. The lender will help you through the process, including a one-time signing of a promissory note. The proceeds of the loan, less any fees, will be sent to your college to be credited to your account.

If you qualify for a subsidized Stafford Loan, you don't have to pay interest while in school. For an unsubsidized Stafford Loan, you will be responsible for paying the interest from the time the loan is disbursed. However, most FFEL lenders will permit you to delay making payments and will add the interest to your loan. Once the repayment period starts, you should contact the lender and/or your school's Financial Aid Office to discuss repayment options. For many students, it is wise to consider consolidating all of your student loans into one loan program.

William D. Ford Federal Direct Loans

The Federal Direct Loan program is very similar to the FFEL Stafford Loan program except that the school serves as the lender. There is no need to contact a private financial institution for your student loans. About 30 percent of all U.S. colleges participate in the Direct Loan program. The terms and conditions of the two loan programs are essentially the same. There are many repayment plans available to meet your needs, and these will be explained to you during your "exit interview" during your final term of school.

Parent Loans for Undergraduate Students (PLUS)

The PLUS loans are for parents of dependent students and are designed to help families with cash-flow problems. There is no needs test to qualify, and the loans are made by FFEL lenders or directly by the Department of Education. The loan has a fixed interest rate of 7.9 percent; parents can borrow up to the cost of your education, less other financial aid received. Repayment begins sixty days after the money is advanced. There may be an origination fee of up to 4 percent charged for these loans. Parent borrowers must generally have a good credit record to qualify for PLUS loans.

The PLUS loan will be processed under either the Direct or the FFEL system, depending on the type of loan program for which the college has contracted.

Nursing Student Loan Program

These loans are awarded to nursing students with demonstrated financial need. This loan has a 5 percent interest rate, repayable after completion of studies. Repayment is to be completed within ten years. Contact your college's Financial Aid Office for deadline and other information, including maximum borrowing amounts.

THINKING AHEAD TO PAYING BACK YOUR STUDENT LOAN

More than ever before, loans have become an important part of financial assistance. The majority of students find that they must borrow money to finance their education. If you accept a loan, you are incurring a financial obligation. You will have to repay the loan in full, along with all of the interest and any additional fees (collection, legal, etc.). Since you will be making loan payments to satisfy the loan obligation, carefully consider the burden your loan amount will impose on you after you leave college. Defaulting on a student loan can jeopardize your financial future. Borrow intelligently.

FROM THE GUIDANCE OFFICE

Q: Why might higher-priced institutions still be affordable?

A: Parents and students ask what college is going to cost and how they will pay for it. I tell them to start early and keep looking. Don't discount a school because of cost. Private schools have a higher price tag, but they do have financial aid packages that are bigger than you might expect.

Kids need some help to initiate searches for scholarships. Get them on the Internet. Each year, we have a group of students who start early and get their applications in and recommendations written. Then there's the group of procrastinators who miss out on opportunities of getting into the college of their choice. It can be a big disappointment.

Nadine Boyer
Counselor
East Richland High School
Olney, Illinois

Some Repayment Options

A number of repayment options are available to borrowers of federally guaranteed student loans.

The Standard Repayment Plan requires fixed monthly payments (at least $50) over a fixed period of time (up to ten years). The length of the repayment period depends on the loan amount. This plan usually results in the lowest total interest paid because the repayment period is shorter than under the other plans.

The Extended Repayment Plan allows loan repayment to be extended over a period from generally twelve to thirty years, depending on the total amount borrowed. Borrowers still pay a fixed amount each month (at least $50), but usually monthly payments will be less than under the Standard Repayment Plan. This plan may make repayment more manageable; however, borrowers usually will pay more interest because the repayment period is longer.

The Graduated Repayment Plan allows payments to start out low and increase every two years. This plan may be helpful to borrowers whose incomes are low initially but will increase steadily. A borrower's monthly payments must be at least half but may not be more than one-and-a-half times what he or she would pay under Standard Repayment. As in the Extended Repayment Plan, the repayment period will usually vary from twelve to thirty years, depending on the total amount borrowed. Again, monthly payments may be more manageable at first because they are lower, but borrowers will pay more interest because the repayment period is longer.

The Income Contingent Repayment Plan bases monthly payments on adjusted gross income (AGI) and the total amount borrowed. This is currently only available to students who participate in Direct Loans; however, some FFEL lenders and guaranty agencies provide income-sensitive repayment plans. As income rises or falls each year, monthly payments will be adjusted accordingly. The required monthly payment will not exceed 20 percent of the borrower's discretionary income as calculated under a published formula. Borrowers have up to twenty-five years to repay; after that time, any unpaid amount will be discharged, and borrowers must pay taxes on the amount discharged. In other words, if the federal government forgives the balance of a loan, the amount is considered to be part of the borrower's income for that year.

OTHER FEDERAL PROGRAMS

The following programs offer alternative ways to earn money for college:

Federal Work-Study (FWS)

The Federal Work-Study program provides both on- and off-campus jobs to students who have financial need. Funding for this program is from federal grants to the institutions, plus a partial match from the employer. Students work on an hourly basis and are paid at least the minimum wage. Students are allowed to work up to the amount of the grant authorized by the college. Contact the Financial Aid Office for more information.

AmeriCorps

AmeriCorps engages 50,000 Americans age 17 and older in intensive service to meet community needs in education, the environment, public safety, homeland security, and other areas. Members serve with national nonprofit organizations like Habitat for Humanity, the American Red Cross, and Teach for America, as well as with hundreds of smaller community organizations, both secular and faith-based. Other members serve with AmeriCorps*NCCC (National Civilian Community Corps), a team-based residential program for adults ages 18 to 24, or in low-income communities with AmeriCorps*VISTA. In exchange for a year of service, AmeriCorps members earn a Segal AmeriCorps Education Award of $4,725 to pay for college, graduate school, or to pay back qualified student loans. Members who serve part-time receive a partial Award. Some AmeriCorps members may also receive a modest living allowance during their term of service. You should speak to your college's Financial Aid Office for more details about this program and any other initiatives available to students or visit the Web at www.americorps.org.

FAMILIES' GUIDE TO TAX CUTS FOR EDUCATION

Many new tax benefits for adults who want to return to school and for parents who are sending or planning to send their children to college are now available. These tax cuts effectively make the first two years of college universally available, and they give many more working Americans the financial means to go back to school if they want to choose a new career or upgrade their skills. Millions of families are eligible for the HOPE and Lifetime Learning tax credits each year, as well as the taxable income deduction allowed for tuition and fees.

HOPE Scholarship Tax Credit

The HOPE Scholarship tax credit helps make the first two years of college or career school universally available. Students receive a 100 percent tax credit for the first $1,000 of tuition and required fees and a 50 percent credit on the second $1,000. This credit is available for tuition and required fees minus grants, scholarships, and other tax-free educational assistance.

The credit is gradually reduced for families with Adjusted Gross Incomes between $45,000 and $53,000 if single, or between $87,000 and $107,000 if married. These limits are adjusted for inflation every year. The credit can be claimed in two years for students who are in their first two years of college or career school and who are enrolled on at least a half-time basis in a degree or certificate program for any portion of the year. The taxpayer can claim a credit for his own tuition expense or for the expenses of his or her spouse or dependent children.

The Lifetime Learning Tax Credit

This tax credit is targeted at adults who want to go back to school, change careers, or take a course or two to upgrade their skills and to college juniors, seniors, graduate, and professional degree students. A family will receive a 20 percent tax credit for tuition and required fees paid each year and for the first $10,000, with the maximum credit being $2,000. Just like the HOPE Scholarship tax credit, the Lifetime Learning tax credit is available for tuition and required fees minus grants, scholarships, and other tax-free educational assistance. The maximum credit is determined on a per-taxpayer (family) basis, regardless of the number of postsecondary students in the family, and is phased out at the same income levels as the HOPE Scholarship tax credit. Families will be able to claim the Lifetime Learning tax credit for some members of their family and the HOPE Scholarship tax credit for others who qualify in the same year.

Tuition and Fees Tax Deduction

The Tuition and Fees Tax Deduction can reduce the amount of your taxable income by as much as $4,000 per year. This deduction is subtracted from your income, which means you can claim this deduction even if you do not itemize your deductions on Schedule A of Form 1040. This deduction may benefit you if you do not qualify for the HOPE or Lifetime Learning Tax Credits because your income is too high. This program has been continued for the 2006 tax year. Participating in the HOPE and/or Lifetime Tax credits does not preclude participation in this program, as long as the same student is not used

CHECKLIST FOR SENIORS

Applying for financial aid can become confusing if you don't record what you've done and when. Use this chart to keep track of important information. Remember to keep copies of all applications and related information.

COLLEGE APPLICATIONS	COLLEGE 1	COLLEGE 2	COLLEGE 3	COLLEGE 4
Application deadline				
Date sent				
Official transcript sent				
Letters of recommendation sent				
SAT/ACT scores sent				
Acceptance received				
INDIVIDUAL COLLEGE FINANCIAL AID AND SCHOLARSHIP APPLICATIONS				
Application deadline				
Date sent				
Acceptance received				
FREE APPLICATION FOR FEDERAL STUDENT AID (FAFSA), FINANCIAL AID FORM (FAF), AND/OR PROFILE®				
Form required				
Date sent				
School's priority deadline				
PROFILE® ACKNOWLEDGMENT (if filed)				
Date received				
Correct (Y/N)				
Date changes made, if needed				
Date changes were submitted				
STUDENT AID REPORT				
Date received				
Correct (Y/N)				
Date changes made, if needed				
Date changes were submitted				
Date sent to colleges				
FINANCIAL AWARD LETTERS				
Date received				
Accepted (Y/N)				

Source: The Dayton-Montgomery County Scholarship Program

as the basis for each deduction, credit, or exclusion and the family does not exceed the Lifetime Learning maximum per family. The income cut-off for single tax payers is $65,000 (Modified Adjusted Gross Income) and $130,000 for married filers. Single tax payers under $80,000 and married filers under $160,000 qualify for a reduced amount (income limits are based on 2005 information and may be adjusted for the 2006 tax year). Check with the IRS or your accountant for more information.

APPLYING FOR FINANCIAL AID

Applying for financial aid is a process that can be made easier when you take it step by step.

1. **You must complete the Free Application for Federal Student Aid (FAFSA) to be considered for federal financial aid.** Pick up the FAFSA from your high school guidance counselor or college financial aid office or download it from the Department of Education's Web site at

www.fafsa.ed.gov. The FAFSA can be filed after January 1 of the year you will be attending school. Submit the form as soon as possible but never before the first of the year. If you need to estimate income tax information, it is easily amended later in the year.

2. **Apply for any state grants. Most states use the FAFSA for determining state aid, but be sure to check out the specific requirements with your state Higher Education Assistance agency.** Your high school guidance office can answer most questions about state aid programs.

3. **Some schools (usually higher cost private colleges) require an additional form know as the PROFILE®.** This application is needed for institutional grants and scholarships controlled by the school. Check to see if the schools you are applying to require the PROFILE form. The form should be completed in September or October of your senior year. Additional information is available from your high school guidance office or online through the College Board at www.collegeboard.com. There is a fee associated with this form. Some schools may require an institutional aid application. This is usually found with the admission application. Contact each college you are considering to be sure you have filed the required forms.

4. **Complete individual colleges' required financial aid application forms on time.** These deadlines are usually before March 15, but check to be sure. Financial aid funds are limited, and schools usually do not waver on their deadlines. Check and double check all application dates to be sure you are filing on time.

5. **Make sure your family completes the required forms during your senior year of high school.**

6. **Always apply for grants and scholarships before applying for student loans.** Grants and scholarships are essentially free money. Loans must be repaid with interest.

Use the "Checklist for Seniors" on the previous page to keep track of the financial aid application process.

NATIONAL, STATEWIDE, AND LOCAL SCHOLARSHIPS

Without a doubt, the best source for up-to-date information on private scholarships is the Internet. There are a variety of excellent Web sites to explore, including www.petersons.com, among others. The most important thing to be careful about is scholarship scams, where you are asked either to pay for a scholarship search by an independent organization or pay a "processing fee" to a particular organization to receive their scholarship.

State and Local Scholarships

It is not possible within the scope of this book to list all of the sources of state and local scholarship dollars. The following are excellent resources for seeking financial assistance:

- Your guidance counselor
- A high school teacher or coach
- Your high school and elementary school PTA (yes, many elementary school PTAs award scholarships to alumni)
- Your local library
- College admissions office
- Your parents' alma mater
- Your employer
- Your parents' employer
- Professional and social organizations in your community
- The local Financial Aid Office of a college in your area
- Your state Higher Education Assistance Agency

TYPES OF ATHLETIC SCHOLARSHIPS

Colleges and universities offer two basic types of athletic scholarships: the institutional grant, which is an agreement between the athlete and the college, and the conference grant, which also binds the college to the athlete. The difference is that the athlete who signs an institutional grant can change his or her mind and sign with another team. The athlete who signs a conference contract cannot renegotiate another contract with a school that honors conference grants. Here are the various ways that a scholarship may be offered:

Full four-year. Also known as full ride, these scholarships pay for room, board, tuition, and books. Due to the high cost of awarding scholarships, this type of grant is being discouraged by conferences around the country in favor of the one-year renewable contract or the partial scholarship.

Full one-year renewable contract. This type of scholarship, which has basically replaced the four-year grant, is automatically renewed at the end of each school year for four years if the conditions of the contract are met. The recruiter will probably tell you in good faith that the intent is to offer a four-year scholarship, but he is legally only allowed to offer you a one-year grant. You must ask the recruiter as well as other players what the record has been of renewing scholarships for athletes who comply athletically, academically, and socially. Remember—no athlete can receive more than a full scholarship.

One-year trial grant (full or partial). A verbal agreement between you and the institution that at the end of the year, your renewal will be dependent upon your academic and athletic performance.

Partial scholarship. The partial grant is any part of the total cost of college. You may be offered room and board but not tuition and books, or you may be offered just tuition. The possibility exists for you to negotiate to a full scholarship after you complete your freshman year.

Waiver of out-of-state fees. This award is for out-of-state students to attend the college or university at the same fee as an in-state student.

SCHOLARSHIPS FOR MINORITY STUDENTS

The following is just a sample of the many scholarships available to minority students.

Bureau of Indian Affairs Higher ED Grant Programs
1849 C Street, NW/MS 3512-MIB
Washington, D.C. 20240-001
www.oiep.bia.edu

The Gates Millennium Scholars
P.O. Box 10500
Fairfax, Virginia 22031-5044
www.gmsp.org

Hispanic Scholarship Fund College Scholarship Program
55 Second Street, Suite 1500
San Francisco, California 94105
877-473-4636
www.hsf.net

National Achievement® Scholarship Program
1560 Sherman Avenue, Suite 200
Evanston, Illinois 60201-4897
847-866-5100
www.nationalmerit.org

National Association of Multicultural Engineering Program Advocates (NAMEPA) National Scholarship
1133 West Morse Boulevard, Suite 201
Winter Park, Florida 32789
407-647-8839
www.namepa.org

Jackie Robinson Foundation Scholarship
3 West 35th Street, 11th Floor
New York, New York 10001
212-290-8600
www.jackierobinson.org

APPLYING FOR SCHOLARSHIPS

Here are some tips to help make a success of your scholarship hunt.

1. **Start early.** Your freshman year is not too early to plan for scholarships by choosing extracurricular activities that will highlight your strengths, and getting involved in your church and community—all things that are important to those who make scholarship decisions.

2. **Search for scholarships.** The best source of scholarships can be found on the Internet. There are many great Web sites that are free, including www.petersons.com. For more information, you should also check www.finaid.org and www.ed.gov/studentaid. Scholarship information is also available at your local library.

3. **Apply, apply, apply.** One student applied for nearly sixty scholarships and was fortunate enough to win seven. "Imagine if I'd applied for five and only gotten one," she says.

4. **Plan ahead.** It takes time to get transcripts and letters of recommendation. Letters from people who know you well are more effective than letters from prestigious names who you know.

5. **Be organized.** In the homes of scholarship winners, you can often find a file box where all relevant information is stored. This method allows you to review deadlines and requirements every so often. Computerizing the information, if possible, allows you to change and update information quickly.

6. **Follow directions.** Make sure that you don't disqualify yourself by filling the forms out incorrectly, missing the deadline, or failing to supply important information. Type your applications, if possible, and have someone proofread them.

WHAT YOU NEED TO KNOW ABOUT ATHLETIC SCHOLARSHIPS

Whether you're male or female or interested in baseball, basketball, crew, cross-country, fencing, field hockey, football, golf, gymnastics, lacrosse, sailing, skiing, soccer, softball, swimming and diving, tennis, track and field, volleyball, or wrestling, there may be scholarship dollars available for you. But, here's that word again—planning. You must plan ahead if you want to get your tuition paid for in return for your competitive abilities.

At the beginning of your junior year, ask your guidance counselor to help you make sure that you take the required number and mix of academic courses and to inform you of the SAT and ACT score minimums that must be met to play college sports. Also ask your counselor about academic requirements, because you must be certified by the NCAA Clearinghouse, and this process must be started by the end of your junior year.

But before you do all that, think. Do you want and need an athletic scholarship? Certainly, it is prestigious to receive an athletic scholarship, but some athletes compare having an athletic scholarship to having a job at which you are expected to perform. Meetings, training sessions, practices, games, and (don't forget!) studying take away from social and leisure time. Also, with very few full-ride scholarships available, you will most likely receive a partial scholarship or a one-year renewable contract. If your scholarship is not renewed, you may be left scrambling for financial aid. So ask yourself if you are ready for the demands and roles associated with accepting an athletic scholarship.

If you decide that you want an athletic scholarship, you need to market yourself to beat the stiff competition. Think of yourself as a newly designed sports car, and you're selling your speed, look, and all those other goodies to a waiting public. The point is that you're going to have to sell, or market, your abilities to college recruiters. You're the product, and the college recruiter is the buyer. What makes you stand out from the rest?

College recruiters look for a combination of the following attributes when awarding athletic scholarships: academic excellence, a desire to win, self-motivation, ability to perform as a team player, willingness to help others, cooperation with coaching staff, attitude in practice, attitude in games/matches, toughness, strength, optimal height and weight, and excellence.

In order to successfully sell your skills to a college or university, you'll need to take three main steps: 1) locate the colleges and universities that offer scholarships in your sport, 2) contact the institution in a formal manner, and 3) follow up each lead.

Finding and Getting Athletic Scholarships

Ask your coach or assistant coaches for recommendations; learn about the conference or institution from newspaper or television coverage; ask your guidance counselor; review guidebooks, reference books, and the Internet; ask alumni; or attend a tryout or campus visit. You can also call the NCAA to request a recruiting guide for your sport. The following steps can help you snag that scholarship:

1. **Contact the school formally.** Once you make a list of schools in which you are interested, get the names of the head coaches and write letters to the top twenty schools on your list. Then compile a factual resume of your athletic and academic accomplishments. Put together 10 to 15 minutes of video highlights of your athletic performance (with your jersey number noted), get letters of recommendation from your high school coach and your off-season coach, and include a season schedule.

2. **Ace the interview.** When you meet a recruiter or coach, exhibit self-confidence with a firm handshake, by maintaining eye contact, and by making sure that you are well groomed. According to recruiters, the most effective attitude is quiet confidence, respect, sincerity, and enthusiasm.

3. **Ask good questions.** Don't be afraid to probe the recruiter by getting answers to the following questions: Do I qualify athletically and academically? If I am recruited, what would the parameters of the scholarship be? For what position am I being considered? It's okay to ask the recruiter to declare what level of interest he or she has in you.

4. **Follow up.** Persistence pays off when it comes to seeking an athletic scholarship, and timing can be everything. There are four good times when a follow-up letter from your coach or a personal letter from you is extremely effective: prior to your senior season, during or just after the senior season, just prior to or after announced conference-affiliated signing dates or national association signing dates, and mid-to late summer, in case other scholarship offers have been withdrawn or declined.

To sum up, you know yourself better than anyone, so you must look at your skills—both athletic and academic—objectively. Evaluate the skills you need to improve, and keep the desire to improve alive in your heart. Develop your leadership skills, and keep striving for excellence with your individual achievements. Keep your mind open as to what school you want to attend, and keep plugging away, even when you are tired, sore, and unsure. After all, athletes are trained to be winners!

MYTHS ABOUT SCHOLARSHIPS AND FINANCIAL AID

The scholarship and financial aid game is highly misunderstood by many high school students. And high school guidance counselors often lack the time to fully investigate scholarship opportunities and to inform students about them. The myths and misconceptions persist while the truth about scholarships remains hidden, the glittering prizes and benefits unknown to many teenagers.

Myth 1: Scholarships are rare, elusive awards won only by valedictorians, geniuses, and whiz kids.

The truth is that with proper advice and strategies, private scholarships are very much within the grasp of high school students who possess talent and ability in almost any given field. Thousands of high school students like you compete and win.

Myth 2: My chances of being admitted to a college are reduced if I apply for financial aid.

The truth is that most colleges have a policy of "need-blind" admissions, which means that a student's financial need is not taken into account in the admission decision. However, there are a few colleges that do consider ability to pay before deciding whether or not to admit a student. There are a few more that look at ability to pay of those whom they placed on a waiting list to get in or those students who applied late. Some colleges will mention this in their literature, others may not. In making decisions about the college application and financing process, however, families should apply for financial aid if the student needs the aid to attend college.

Myth 3: All merit scholarships are based on a student's academic record.

The truth is that many of the best opportunities are in such areas as writing, public speaking, leadership, science, community service, music and the arts, foreign languages, and vocational-technical skills. So that means you don't always have to have a 3.99 GPA to win if you excel in a certain area.

Myth 4: You have to be a member of a minority group to get a scholarship.

The truth is that there are indeed some scholarships that are targeted toward women and minority students. There are also scholarships for which you must be a member of a specific national club or student organization (such as 4-H and the National Honor Society), which makes these scholarships just as exclusive. But most scholarship opportunities are not exclusive to any one segment of the population.

Myth 5: If you have need for and receive financial aid, it's useless to win a scholarship from some outside organization because the college will just take away the aid that the organization offered.

It's true that if you receive need-based aid, you can't receive more than the total cost of attendance (including room and board, books, and other expenses, not just tuition). If the financial aid that you've been awarded meets the total cost and you win an outside scholarship, colleges have to reduce something. But usually, they reduce the loan or work-study portion of your financial aid award before touching the grant portion that they've awarded you. This means that you won't have to borrow or earn as much. Also, most colleges don't meet your full financial need when you qualify for need-based financial aid. So, if you do win an outside scholarship, chances are that your other aid will not be taken away or reduced.

SCHOLARSHIP SCAMS

Although most scholarship sponsors and most scholarship search services are legitimate, schemes that pose as either legitimate scholarship search services or scholarship sponsors have cheated thousands of families.

These fraudulent businesses advertise in campus newspapers, distribute flyers, mail letters and postcards, provide toll-free phone numbers, and even have sites on the Web. The most obvious frauds operate as scholarship search services or scholarship clearinghouses. Another quieter segment sets up as a scholarship sponsor, pockets the money from the fees and charges that are paid by thousands of hopeful scholarship seekers, and returns little, if anything, in proportion to the amount it collects. A few of these frauds inflict great harm by gaining access to individuals' credit or checking accounts with the intent to extort funds.

The Federal Trade Commission (FTC), in Washington, D.C., has a campaign called Project $cholar$cam to confront this type of fraudulent activity. There are legitimate services; however, a scholarship search service cannot truthfully guarantee that a student will receive a scholarship, and students almost always will fare as well or better by doing their own homework using a reliable scholarship information source, such as *Peterson's Scholarships, Grants & Prizes* or www.petersons.com, than by wasting money and time with a search service that promises a scholarship.

The FTC warns you to be alert for these six warning signs of a scam:

1. **"This scholarship is guaranteed or your money back."** No service can guarantee that it will get you a grant or scholarship. Refund guarantees often have impossible conditions attached. Review a service's refund policies in writing before you pay a fee.

2. **"The scholarship service will do all the work."** Unfortunately, nobody else can fill out the personal information forms, write the essays, and supply the references that many scholarships may require.

3. **"The scholarship will cost some money."** Be wary of any charges related to scholarship information services or individual scholarship applications, especially in significant amounts. Before you send money to apply for a scholarship, investigate the sponsor.

4. **"You can't get this information anywhere else."** In addition to Peterson's, scholarship directories from other publishers are available in any large bookstore, public library, or high school guidance office.

5. **"You are a finalist"** or **"You have been selected by a national foundation to receive a scholarship."** Most legitimate scholarship programs almost never seek out particular applicants. Most scholarship sponsors will contact you only in response to an inquiry because they generally lack the budget to do anything more than this. Should you think that there is any real possibility that you may have been selected to receive a scholarship, before you send any money, investigate first to be sure that the sponsor or program is legitimate.

6. **"The scholarship service needs your credit card or checking account number in advance."** Never provide your credit card or bank account number on the telephone to the representative of an organization that you do not know. Get information in writing first. An unscrupulous operation does not need your signature on a check. It will scheme to set up situations that will allow it to drain a victim's account with unauthorized withdrawals.

In addition to the FTC's six signs, here are some other points to keep in mind when considering a scholarship program:

- Fraudulent scholarship operations often use official-sounding names, containing words such as *federal, national, administration, division, federation,* and *foundation*. Their names are often a slight variant of the name of a legitimate government or private organization. Do not be fooled by a name that seems reputable or official, an official-looking seal, or a Washington, D.C., address.

- If you win a scholarship, you will receive written official notification by mail, not by telephone. If the sponsor calls to inform you, it will follow up with a letter in the mail. If a request for money is made by phone, the operation is probably fraudulent.

- Be wary if an organization's address is a box number or a residential address. If a bona fide scholarship program uses a post office box number, it usually will include a street address and telephone number on its stationery.

- Beware of telephone numbers with a 900-area code. These may charge you a fee of several dollars a minute for a call that could be a long recording that provides only a list of addresses or names.

- Watch for scholarships that ask you to "act now." A dishonest operation may put pressure on an applicant by saying that awards are on a "first-come, first-served" basis. Some scholarship programs will give preference to the earlier qualified applications. However, if you are told, especially on the telephone, that you must respond quickly but that you will not hear about the results for several months, there may be a problem.

- Be wary of endorsements. Fraudulent operations will claim endorsements by groups with names similar to well-known private or government organizations. The Better Business Bureau (BBB) and government agencies do not endorse businesses.

- Don't pay money for a scholarship to an organization that you've never heard of before or whose legitimacy you can't verify. If you have already paid money to such an

Part 3: The Road to More Education

> **FIND MONEY FOR COLLEGE**
>
> Don't have enough money to pay for college? Afraid your family makes too much and you can't get financial aid? Regardless of your financial situation, BestCollegeDeals® helps you quickly and easily identify each college's unique financial aid packages—student loans, grants, discounts, scholarships—and little-known financial deals you've probably never even heard of.
>
> **How does it work? It's simple!**
>
> 1. Provide financial information about your family in a safe, secure environment that ensures your privacy.
>
> 2. Calculate, with help from BestCollegeDeals®, your Estimated Expected Family Contribution (EFC), the amount of money you may be expected to pay toward your college education.
>
> 3. Choose location, enrollment size, and whether you're interested in a public, private, all-women's, or all-men's college or university.
>
> 4. Get a list of colleges, and information about their financial aid offerings, that match your preferences.
>
> 5. Discover great need- and merit-based (merit awards include scholarships, grants, and prizes that are given for academic achievement) financial deals that you can't find anywhere else!
>
> No matter what your level of income, BestCollegeDeals® gives your family personalized support. BestCollegeDeals® helps you and your family better understand the financial aid process. Go to www.bestcollegedeals.com to learn more!

organization and find reason to doubt its authenticity, call your bank to stop payment on your check, if possible, or call your credit card company and tell it that you think you were the victim of consumer fraud.

To find out how to recognize, report, and stop a scholarship scam, you may write to the Federal Trade Commission's Consumer Response Center at 600 Pennsylvania Avenue NW, Washington, D.C. 20580. On the Web, go to www.ftc.gov, or call 877-FTC-HELP (toll-free). You can also check with the Better Business Bureau (BBB), which is an organization that maintains files of businesses about which it has received complaints. You should call both your local BBB office and the BBB office in the area of the organization in question; each local BBB has different records. Call 703-276-0100 to get the telephone number of your local BBB, or look at www.bbb.org for a directory of local BBBs and downloadable BBB complaint forms.

FINANCIAL AID ON THE WEB

A number of good financial aid resources exist on the Web. It is quick and simple to access general financial aid information, links to relevant Web sites, loan information, employment and career information, advice, scholarship search services, interactive worksheets, forms, and free Expected Family Contribution (EFC) calculators.

Also visit the Web sites of individual colleges to find more school-specific financial aid information.

FAFSA Online

The Free Application for Federal Student Aid (FAFSA) can be filed on the Web at www.fafsa.ed.gov. You can download a worksheet from this Web site, since the questions are formatted differently from the paper application. FAFSA on the Web is a much quicker process and helps eliminate errors. To file electronically, the student and one parent will need an electronic signature Personal Identification Number (PIN). To get a PIN, go to www.pin.ed.gov. The pin number will be sent to you within 24 hours.

Nelnet, Inc.

Nelnet is one of the leading education and education finance companies in the United States and is focused on providing quality student loan products and services to students and schools nationwide. Nelnet offers a broad range of financial services and technology-based products, including student loan origination, consolidation and lending, holding, student loan and guarantee servicing, and software solutions. Visit Nelnet's Web site at www.nelnet.net.

The Education Resource Institute (TERI)

TERI is a private, not-for-profit organization that was founded to help middle-income Americans afford a college education. This site contains a database describing programs that aim to increase college attendance from underrepresented groups. (The target population includes students from low-income families and those who are the first in their family to pursue postsecondary education.) Visit TERI's Web site at www.teri.org.

FinAid

This Web site offers numerous links to valuable financial aid information, including scholarship search engines. You can find the site at www.finaid.org.

Mapping Your Future

This site is sponsored by a group of guaranty agencies that participate in the Federal Family Education Loan Program (FFELP). They are committed to providing information about higher education and career opportunities. Information is available to help parents of middle school students plan for college and for adults returning to higher education to learn new skills. You can find this site at www.mapping-your-future.org.

Student Financial Assistance Information, U.S. Department of Education

This page takes you to some of the major publications on student aid, including the latest edition of *The Student Guide*. Visit www.ed.gov/finaid.html.

Peterson's

Get advice on finding sources to pay for college and search for scholarships at www.petersons.com/finaid.

AES

American Education Services (AES) is a division of PHEAA, which has grown from a small student loan guarantor with a volume of only 4,600 student loans in 1964, to one of the largest, full-service financial aid organizations in the nation. AES helps students succeed by giving them the tools to plan for higher education and find money for school, as well as allowing them to manage student loan accounts online. Visit them at www.aessuccess.org.

Chapter 9

WHAT TO EXPECT IN COLLEGE

If you were going on a long trip, wouldn't you want to know what to expect once you reached your destination? The same should hold true for college.

GET A JUMP! CAN'T FILL IN all the details of what you'll find once you begin college. However, we can give you information about some of the bigger questions you might have, such as how to choose your classes or major and how you can make the most of your life outside the classroom.

CHOOSING YOUR CLASSES

College is designed to give you freedom, but at the same time, it teaches you responsibility. You will probably have more free time than in high school, but you will also have more class material to master. Your parents may entrust you with more money, but it is up to you to make sure there's enough money in your bank account when school fees are due. The same principle applies to your class schedule: You will have more decision-making power than ever, but you also need to know and meet the requirements for graduation.

To guide you through the maze of requirements, all students are given an adviser. This person, typically a faculty member, will help you select classes that meet your interests and graduation requirements. During your first year or two at college, you and your adviser will choose classes that meet general education requirements and select electives, or non-required classes, that pique your interests. Early on, it is a good idea to take a lot of general education classes. They are meant to expose you to new ideas and help you explore possible majors. Once you have selected a major, you will be given an adviser for that particular area of study. This person will help you understand and meet the requirements for that major.

In addition to talking to your adviser, talk to other students who have already taken a class you're interested in and who really enjoyed how a professor taught the class. Then try to get into that professor's class when registering. Remember, a dynamic professor can make a dry subject engaging. A boring professor can make an engaging subject dry.

As you move through college, you will notice that focusing on the professor is more important than focusing on the course title. Class titles can be cleverly crafted. They can sound captivating. However, the advice above still holds true: "Pop Culture and Icons" could turn out to be awful, and "Beowulf and Old English" could be a blast.

When you plan your schedule, watch how many heavy reading classes you take in one semester. You don't want to live in the library or the dorm study lounge. In general, the humanities, such as history, English, philosophy, and theology, involve a lot of reading. Math and science classes involve less reading; they focus more on solving problems.

Finally, don't be afraid to schedule a fun class. Even the most intense program of study will let you take a few electives. So take a deep breath, dig in, and explore!

CHOOSING YOUR MAJOR

You can choose from hundreds of majors—from accounting to zoology—but which is right for you? Should you choose something traditional or select a major from an emerging area? Perhaps you already know what career you want, so you can work backward to decide which major will best help you achieve your goals.

If you know what you want to do early in life, you will have more time to plan your high school curriculum, extracurricular activities, jobs, and community service to coincide with your college major. Your college selection process may also focus upon the schools that provide strong academic programs in a certain major.

Where Do I Begin?

Choosing a major usually starts with an assessment of your career interests. Once you have taken the self-assessment test in Part 1, you should have a clearer understanding of your interests, talents, values, and goals. Then review possible majors, and try several on for size. Picture yourself taking classes, writing papers, making presentations, conducting research, or working in a related field. Talk to people you know who work in your fields of interest and see if you like what you hear. Also, try reading the classified ads in your local newspaper. What jobs sound interesting to you? Which ones pay the salary that you'd like to make? What level of education is required in the ads you find interesting? Select a few jobs that you think you'd like and then consult the following list of majors to see which major(s) coincide. If your area of interest does not appear here, talk to your counselor or teacher about where to find information on that particular subject.

Majors and Related Careers

Agriculture

Many agriculture majors apply their knowledge directly on farms and ranches. Others work in industry (food, farm equipment, and agricultural supply companies), federal agencies (primarily in the Departments of Agriculture and the Interior), and state and local farm and agricultural agencies. Jobs might be in research and lab work, marketing and sales, advertising and public relations, or journalism and radio/TV (for farm communications media). Agriculture majors also pursue further training in biological sciences, animal health, veterinary medicine, agribusiness management, vocational agriculture education, nutrition and dietetics, and rural sociology.

Architecture

Architecture and related design fields focus on the built environment as distinct from the natural environment of the agriculturist or the conservationist. Career possibilities include drafting, design, and project administration in architectural, engineering, landscape design, interior design, industrial design, planning, real estate, and construction firms; government agencies involved in construction, housing, highways, and parks and recreation; and government and nonprofit organizations interested in historic or architectural preservation.

Area/Ethnic Studies

The research, writing, analysis, critical thinking, and cultural awareness skills acquired by area/ethnic studies majors, combined with the expertise gained in a particular area, make this group of majors valuable in a number of professions. Majors find positions in administration, education, public relations, and communications in such organizations as cultural, government, international, and (ethnic) community agencies; international trade (import-export); social service agencies; and the communications industry (journalism, radio, and TV). These studies also provide a good background for further training in law, business management, public administration, education, social work, museum and library work, and international relations.

Arts

Art majors most often use their training to become practicing artists, though the settings in which they work vary. Aside from the most obvious art-related career—that of the self-employed artist or craftsperson—many fields require the skills of a visual artist. These include advertising; public relations; publishing; journalism; museum work; television, movies, and theater; community and social service agencies concerned with education, recreation, and entertainment; and teaching. A background in art is also useful if a student wishes to pursue art therapy, arts or museum administration, or library work.

Biological Sciences

The biological sciences include the study of living organisms from the level of molecules to that of populations. Majors find jobs in industry; government agencies; technical writing, editing, or illustrating; science reporting; secondary school teaching (which usually requires education courses); and research and laboratory analysis and testing. Biological sciences are also a sound foundation for further study in medicine, psychology, health and hospital administration, and biologically oriented engineering.

Business

Business majors comprise all the basic business disciplines. At the undergraduate level, students can major in a general business administration program or specialize in a particular area, such as marketing or accounting. These studies lead not only to positions in business and industry but also to management positions in other sectors. Management-related studies include the general management areas (accounting, finance, marketing, and management) as well as special studies related to a particular type of organization or industry. Management-related majors may be offered in a business school or in a department dealing with the area in which the management skills are to be applied. Careers can be found throughout the business world.

Communication

Jobs in communication range from reporting (news and special features), copywriting, technical writing, copyediting, and programming to advertising, public relations, media sales, and market research. Such positions can be found at newspapers, radio and TV stations, publishing houses (book and magazine), advertising agencies, corporate communications departments, government agencies, universities, and firms that specialize in educational and training materials.

Computer, Information, and Library Sciences

Computer and information science and systems majors stress the theoretical aspects of the computer and emphasize mathematical and scientific disciplines. Data processing, programming, and computer technology programs tend to be more practical; they are more oriented toward business than to scientific applications and to working directly with the computer or with peripheral equipment. Career possibilities for computer and information science majors include data processing, programming, and systems development or maintenance in almost any setting: business and industry, banking and finance, government, colleges and universities, libraries, software firms, service bureaus, computer manufacturers, publishing, and communications.

STUDENT COUNSEL

Q: Why did you choose a seven-year premed program instead of a traditional four-year college program?

A: I'm one of those people who knew what I wanted to do since I was very little, so that made choosing easier. If I was not 100 percent sure that I wanted to go into medicine, I would not be in this seven-year program. For students who are interested but not really sure that they want to go into medicine, they should pick a school they will enjoy, get a good education, and then worry about medical school. That way, if they decide in their junior year that medicine is not for them, they have options.

Elliot Servais
Premed
Boston University

Library science gives preprofessional background in library work and provides valuable knowledge of research sources, indexing, abstracting, computer technology, and media technology, which is useful for further study in any professional field. In most cases, a master's degree in library science is necessary to obtain a job as a librarian. Library science majors find positions in public, school, college, corporate, and government libraries and research centers; book publishing (especially reference books); database and information retrieval services; and communications (especially audiovisual media).

Education

Positions as teachers in public elementary and secondary schools, private day and boarding schools, religious and parochial schools, vocational schools, and proprietary schools are the jobs most often filled by education majors. However, teaching positions also exist in noneducational institutions, such as museums, historical societies, prisons, hospitals, and nursing homes, as well as jobs as educators and trainers in government and industry. Administrative (nonteaching) positions in employee relations and personnel, public relations, marketing and sales, educational publishing, TV and film media, test development firms, and government and community social service agencies also tap the skills and interests of education majors.

Engineering and Science Technology

Engineering and science technology majors prepare students for practical design and production work rather than for jobs that require more theoretical, scientific, and mathematical knowledge. Engineers work in a variety of fields, including aeronautics, bioengineering, geology, nuclear engineering, and quality control and safety. Industry, research labs, and government agencies where technology plays a key role, such as in manufacturing, electronics, construction communications, transportation, and utilities, hire engineering as well as engineering technology and science technology graduates regularly. Work may be in technical activities (research, development, design, production, testing, scientific programming, or systems analysis) or in nontechnical areas where a technical degree is needed, such as marketing, sales, or administration.

Foreign Language and Literature

Knowledge of foreign languages and cultures is increasingly recognized as important in today's international world. Language majors possess a skill that is used in organizations with international dealings as well as in career fields and geographical areas where languages other than English are prominent. Career possibilities include positions with business firms with international subsidiaries; import-export firms; international banking; travel agencies; airlines; tourist services; government and international agencies dealing with international affairs, foreign trade, diplomacy, customs, or immigration; secondary school foreign language teaching and bilingual education (which usually require education courses); freelance translating and interpreting (high level of skill necessary); foreign language publishing; and computer programming (especially for linguistics majors).

Health Sciences

Health professions majors, while having a scientific core, are more focused on applying the results of scientific investigation than on the scientific disciplines themselves. Allied health majors prepare graduates to assist health professionals in providing diagnostics, therapeutics, and rehabilitation. Medical science majors, such as optometry, pharmacy, and the premedical profession sequences, are, for the most part, preprofessional studies that comprise the scientific disciplines necessary for admission to graduate or professional school in the health or medical fields. Health service and technology majors prepare students for positions in the health fields that primarily involve services to patients or working with complex machinery and materials. Medical technologies cover a wide range of fields, such as

> **STUDENT COUNSEL**
>
> **Q:** What advice do you have for high school students who are considering going into engineering?
>
> **A:** In high school, take AP courses in a lot of different areas. That gives you an idea of what those subjects will be like in college. I knew I was good at science and math but didn't know which direction would really interest me. I took an AP English course and didn't do so well. Then I took a chemistry course and knew I could see myself digging deeper. An AP course will give you an idea if that subject is something you want to pursue as a major.
>
> Most engineering majors don't have to decide on what engineering discipline they want until their sophomore year. As a freshman, you can take courses and not really know what type of engineering you want. I took an introduction to engineering course, and it convinced me that this is what I want to do. Your freshman year will give you a flavor for different engineering majors so you don't end up in your junior year and realize you don't like that major. The first semester here is totally an adjustment period.
>
> *Michael Romano*
> *Chemical Engineering*
> *Cornell University*

cytotechnology, biomedical technologies, and operating room technology.

Administrative, professional, or research assistant positions in health agencies, hospitals, occupational health units in industry, community and school health departments, government agencies (public health, environmental protection), and international health organizations are available to majors in health fields, as are jobs in marketing and sales of health-related products and services, health education (with education courses), advertising and public relations, journalism and publishing, and technical writing.

Home Economics and Social Services

Home economics encompasses many different fields—basic studies in foods and textiles as well as consumer economics and leisure studies—that overlap with aspects of agriculture, social science, and education. Jobs can be found in government and community agencies (especially those in education, health, housing, or human services), nursing homes, child-care centers, journalism, radio/TV, educational media, and publishing. Types of work also include marketing, sales, and customer service in consumer-related industries, such as food processing and packaging, appliance manufacturing, utilities, textiles, and secondary school home economics teaching (which usually requires education courses).

Majors in social services find administrative positions in government and community health, welfare, and social service agencies, such as hospitals, clinics, YMCAs and YWCAs, recreation commissions, welfare agencies, and employment services. See the "Law and Legal Studies" section for information on more law-related social services.

Humanities (Miscellaneous)

The majors that constitute the humanities (sometimes called "letters") are the most general and widely applicable and the least vocationally oriented of the liberal arts. They are essentially studies of the ideas and concerns of human kind. These include classics, history of philosophy, history of science, linguistics, and medieval studies. Career possibilities for humanities majors can be found in business firms, government and community agencies, advertising and public relations, marketing and sales, publishing, journalism and radio/TV, secondary school teaching in English and literature (which usually requires education courses), freelance writing and editing, and computer programming (especially for those with a background in logic or linguistics).

Law and Legal Studies

Students of legal studies can use their knowledge of law and government in fields involving the making, breaking, and enforcement of laws; the crimes, trials, and punishment of law breakers; and the running of all branches of government at local, state, and federal levels. Graduates find positions of all types in law firms, legal departments of other organizations, the court or prison system, government agencies (such as law enforcement agencies or offices of state and federal attorneys general), and police departments.

(Continued on page 107)

Chapter 9: What to Expect in College

MAKING THAT MAJOR DECISION: REAL-LIFE ADVICE FROM COLLEGE SENIORS

Somewhere between her junior and senior year in high school, Karen Gliebe got the psychology bug. When choosing a major in college, she knew just what she wanted. Justin Bintrim, on the other hand, did a complete 180. He thought he'd study physics, then veered toward philosophy. It wasn't until he took survey courses in literature that he found where his heart really lay, and now he's graduating with a degree in English.

You might find yourself at either end of this spectrum when choosing a major. Either you'll know just what you want or you'll try on a number of different hats before finally settling on one. To give you a taste of what it could be like for you, meet four college seniors who have been through the trials and errors of choosing their majors. Hopefully you'll pick up some pointers from them or at least find out that you don't have to worry so much about what your major will be.

From Grove City College, a liberal arts school in Pennsylvania, meet Karen Gliebe, who will graduate with a degree in psychology, and English major Justin Bintrim. From Michigan State University, meet computer engineering major Seth Mosier and Kim Trouten, who is finishing up a zoology degree. Here's what they had to say:

HOW THEY CHOSE THEIR MAJORS

Karen: During high school, I volunteered at a retirement center, and my supervisor gave me a lot of exposure to applied psychology. After my freshman year in college, I talked to people who were using a psychology degree. You put in a lot of work for a degree and can wonder if it's worth all the work. It helps to talk to someone who has gone through it so you can see if that's what you want to be doing when you graduate.

Justin: I wasn't sure about what my major would be. One professor told me to take survey courses to see if I was interested in the subject. I took English literature, math, psychology, and philosophy. I liked English the best and did well in it. The next semester, I took two English courses and decided to switch my major. My professors told me not to worry about choosing a major. They said to get my feet wet and we'll talk about your major in two years. I decided that if they're not worried about a major, I wouldn't be either, but I still had it on my mind. I was around older students who were thinking about their careers, so I talked to them about the jobs they had lined up.

Seth: I liked computers in high school. In college, I started out in computer science but got sick of coding. My interest in computers made me pick computer science right off the bat. I didn't know about computer engineering until I got to college.

Kim: I wanted to be a veterinarian but after two years decided that I didn't want to go to school for that long. I was still interested in animals and had two options. One was in animal science, which is working more with farm animals, or going into zoology. I decided to concentrate on zoo and aquarium science. Besides being a vet, the closest interaction with animals would be being a zookeeper.

THE ELECTIVES THEY TOOK AND WHY

Karen: My adviser told me to take different classes, so I took philosophy, art, religion, and extra psychology classes that weren't required.

Justin: I was planning to do a double major, but my professors said to take what interested me. English majors have lots of freedom to take different courses, unlike science majors.

Seth: Because I'm in computer engineering, I don't get to take a lot of electives. I am taking a swimming class right now and took a critical incident analysis class where we looked at major accidents. I wanted something that wasn't computer engineering-related but extremely technical.

Kim: I took a kinesiology class, which was pretty much an aerobics class. I needed to work out and figured I could get credit for it. I also took sign language because I'm interested in it.

WHAT THEY'RE GOING TO DO WITH THEIR DEGREES

Karen: I want to go to graduate school and hopefully get some experience working with kids.

Justin: I'm applying to graduate school in English literature and cultural studies. I want to do research and become a college professor.

Seth: I'm going to work for the defense department. It's not the highest offer I've gotten, but it will be the most fun, which is more important to me than the money.

Kim: My goals have changed again. I don't plan on using my degree. I just got married a year ago, and my husband and I want to go into full-time ministry. I'll work for a while, and then we'll go overseas.

THE CHANGES THEY WOULD MAKE IN THE CLASSES THEY TOOK IF THEY COULD

Karen: There are classes I wouldn't necessarily take again. But even though I didn't learn as much as I wanted to, it was worth it. I learned how to work and how to organize my efforts.

Justin: I should have worried less about choosing a major when I first started college. I didn't have the perspective as to how much time I had to choose.

Seth: I have friends who would change the order in which they took their humanities classes. I was lucky enough to think ahead and spread those classes out over the entire time. Most [engineering] students take them their freshman year to get them all out of the way. Later on, they're locked in the engineering building all day. Because I didn't, it was nice for me to get my mind off engineering.

Kim: Something I can't change are the labs. They require a lot of work, and you only get one credit for 3 hours. Some labs take a lot of work outside of class hours. I had a comparative anatomy lab, which kept me busy over entire weekends. I suggest you don't take a lot of classes that require labs all at once.

THEIR ADVICE FOR YOU

Karen: You don't have to know what you want to do with the rest of your life when you get to college. Most people don't even stay with the major they first choose. Colleges recognize that you will see things you may have not considered at first. Some high school students say they won't go to college unless they know what they want to do.

Justin: If it's possible, take a little of this and a little of that. If you're an engineering student, you'll have it all planned out [for you], but if you're a liberal arts major and are not sure, you probably can take something from each department.

Seth: If possible, take AP exams in high school. You'll be able to make a decision about a major. Freshmen who think they want to do engineering suffer through math and physics classes. Then by their sophomore or junior year, they realize they don't want to be engineers. If they'd taken AP classes, they'd know by their freshman year.

Kim: When I changed my major, I was worried that I might have spent a year in classes that wouldn't count toward my new major. But you shouldn't be scared to change majors because if you stick with something you don't like, you'll have to go back and take other classes anyway.

Though these four seniors arrived at a decision about which major they wanted in different ways, they had similar things to say:

- It's okay to change your mind about what you want out of college.
- To find out which major you might want, start with what you like to do.
- Talk to professionals who have jobs in the fields that interest you.
- Ask your professors about what kinds of jobs you could get with the degree you're considering.
- Talk to seniors who will be graduating with a degree in the major you're considering.
- Take electives in areas that interest you, even though they may have nothing to do with your major.
- College is a time to explore many different options, so take advantage of the opportunity.

Mathematics and Physical Sciences

Mathematics is the science of numbers and the abstract formulation of their operations. Physical sciences involve the study of the laws and structures of physical matter. The quantitative skills acquired through the study of science and mathematics are especially useful for computer-related careers. Career possibilities include positions in industry (manufacturing and processing companies, electronics firms, defense contractors, consulting firms); government agencies (defense, environmental protection, law enforcement); scientific/technical writing, editing, or illustrating; journalism (science reporting); secondary school teaching (usually requiring education courses); research and laboratory analysis and testing; statistical analysis; computer programming; systems analysis; surveying and mapping; weather forecasting; and technical sales.

Natural Resources

A major in the natural resources field prepares students for work in areas as generalized as environmental conservation and as specialized as groundwater contamination. Jobs are available in industry (food, energy, natural resources, and pulp and paper companies), consulting firms, state and federal government agencies (primarily the Departments of Agriculture and the Interior), and public and private conservation agencies. See the "Agriculture" and "Biological Sciences" sections for more information on natural resources-related fields.

Psychology

Psychology majors involve the study of behavior and can range from the biological to the sociological. Students can study individual behavior, usually that of humans, or the behavior of crowds. Students of psychology do not always go into the obvious clinical fields, the fields in which psychologists work with patients. Certain areas of psychology, such as industrial/organizational, experimental, and social, are not clinically oriented. Psychology and counseling careers can be in government (such as mental health agencies), schools, hospitals, clinics, private practice, industry, test development firms, social work, and personnel. The careers listed in the "Social Sciences" section are also pursued by psychology and counseling majors.

Religion

Religion majors are usually seen as preprofessional studies for those who are interested in entering the ministry. Career possibilities for religion also include casework, youth counseling, administration in community and social service organizations, teaching in religious educational institutions, and writing for religious and lay publications. Religious studies also prepare students for the kinds of jobs other humanities majors often pursue.

Social Sciences

Social sciences majors study people in relation to their society. Thus, social science majors can apply their education to a wide range of occupations that deal with social issues and activities. Career opportunities are varied. People with degrees in the social sciences find careers in government, business, community agencies (serving children, youth, and senior citizens), advertising and public relations, marketing and sales, secondary school social studies teaching (with education courses), casework, law enforcement, parks and recreation, museum work (especially for anthropology, archaeology, geography, and history majors), preservation (especially for anthropology, archaeology, geography, and history majors), banking and finance (especially for economics majors), market and survey research, statistical analysis, publishing, fundraising and development, and political campaigning.

Technologies

Technology majors, along with trade fields, are most often offered as two-year programs. Majors in technology fields prepare students directly for jobs; however, positions are in practical design and production work rather than in areas that require more theoretical, scientific, and mathematical knowledge.

Engineering technologies prepare students with the basic training in specific fields (e.g., electronics, mechanics, or chemistry) that are necessary to become technicians on the support staffs of engineers. Other technology majors center more on maintenance and repair. Work may be in technical activities, such as production or testing, or in nontechnical areas where a technical degree is needed, such as marketing, sales, or administration. Industries, research labs, and government agencies in which technology plays a key role—such as in manufacturing, electronics, construction, communications, transportation, and utilities—hire technology graduates regularly.

Still Unsure?

Relax! You don't have to know your major before you enroll in college. More than half of all freshmen are undecided when they start school and prefer to get a feel for what's available at college before making a decision. Most four-year colleges don't require students to formally declare a major until the end of their sophomore year or beginning of their junior year. Part of the experience of college is being exposed to new subjects and new ideas. Chances are your high school never offered anthropology. Or marine biology. Or applied mathematics. So take these classes and follow your interests. While you're fulfilling your general course requirements, you might stumble upon a major that appeals to you, or maybe you'll discover a new interest while you're volunteering or participating in other extracurricular activities. Talking to other students might lead to new options you'll want to explore.

Can I Change My Major If I Change My Mind?

Choosing a major does not set your future in stone, nor does it necessarily disrupt your life if you need to change your major. However, there are advantages to choosing a major sooner rather than later. If you wait too long to choose, you may have to take additional classes to satisfy the requirements, which may cost you additional time and money.

THE OTHER SIDE OF COLLEGE: HAVING FUN!

There is more to college than writing papers, reading books, and sitting through lectures. Your social life plays an integral part in your college experience.

Meeting New People

The easiest time to meet new people is at the beginning of something new. New situations shake people up and make them feel just uncomfortable enough to take the risk of extending their hand in friendship. Fortunately for you, college is filled with new experiences. There are the first weeks of being the newest students. This can be quickly followed by being a new member of a club or activity. And with each passing semester, you will be in new classes with new teachers and new faces. College should be a time of constantly challenging and expanding yourself, so never feel that it is too late to meet new people.

But just how do you take that first step in forming a relationship? It's surprisingly easy. The first few weeks of school will require you to stand in many lines. Some will be to buy books; others will be to get meals. One will be to get a student I.D. card. Another will be to register for classes. While standing in line, turn around and introduce yourself to the person behind you. Focus on what you have in common and try to downplay the differences. Soon you will find the two of you have plenty to talk about. When it is time to leave the line, arrange to have coffee later or to see a movie. This will help you form relationships with the people you meet.

Be open to the opportunities of meeting new people and having new experiences. Join clubs and activities. Investigate rock-climbing. Try ballet. Write for the school paper. But most of all, get involved.

Campus Activities

College life will place a lot of demands on you. Your classes will be challenging. Your professors will expect more from you. You will have to budget and manage your own money. But there is a plus side you probably haven't thought of yet: college students do have free time.

The average student spends about three hours a day in class. Add to this the time you will need to spend studying, eating, and socializing, and you will still have time to spare. One of the best ways to use this time is to participate in campus activities.

Intramural Sports

Intramurals are sports played for competition between members of the same campus community. They provide competition and a sense of belonging without the same level of intensity in practice schedules. Anyone can join an intramural sport. Often there are teams formed by dormitories, sororities, or fraternities that play team sports such as soccer, volleyball, basketball, flag-football, baseball, and softball. There are also individual intramural sports such as swimming, golf, wrestling, and diving. If you want to get involved, just stop by the intramural office. Usually it is located near the student government office.

Student Government

Student government will be set up in a way that is probably similar to your high school. Students form committees and run for office. However, student government in college has more power than in high school. The officers address all of their class's concerns directly to the President of the college or university and the Board of Trustees. Most student governments have a branch responsible for student activities that brings in big name entertainers and controversial speakers. You may want to get involved to see how such contacts are made and appearances negotiated.

Community Service

Another aspect of student life is volunteering, commonly called community service. Many colleges offer a range of opportunities. Some allow you to simply commit an afternoon to a cause, such as passing out food at a food bank. Others require an ongoing commitment. For example, you might decide to help an adult learn to read every Thursday at 4 p.m. for three months. Some colleges will link a service commitment with class credit. This will enhance your learning, giving you some real-world experience. Be sure to stop by your community service office and see what is available.

Clubs

There are a variety of clubs on most college campuses spanning just about every topic you can imagine. Amnesty International regularly meets on most campuses to write letters to help free prisoners in foreign lands. Most college majors band together in a club to discuss their common interests and career potential. There are also clubs that are based on the use of certain computer software or that engage in outdoor activities like sailing or downhill skiing. The list is endless. If you cannot find a club for your interest, consider starting one of your own. Stop by the student government office to see what rules you will need to follow. You will also need to find a location to hold meetings and post signs to advertise your club. When you hold your first meeting, you will probably be surprised at how many people are willing to take a chance and try a new club.

Greek Life

A major misconception of Greek life is that it revolves around wild parties and alcohol. In fact, the vast majority of fraternities and sororities focus on instilling values of scholarship, friendship, leadership, and service in their members. From this point forward, we will refer to both fraternities and sororities as fraternities.

Scholarship

A fraternity experience helps you make the academic transition from high school to college. Although the classes taken in high school are challenging, they'll be even harder in college. Fraternities almost always require members to meet certain academic standards. Many hold mandatory study times, keep old class notes and exams on file for study purposes, and make personal tutors available. Members of a fraternity have a natural vested interest in seeing that other members succeed academically, so older members often assist younger members with their studies.

Friendship

Social life is an important component of Greek life. Social functions offer an excellent opportunity for freshmen to become better acquainted with others in the chapter. Whether it is a Halloween party or a formal dance, there are numerous chances for members to develop poise and confidence. By participating in these functions, students enrich friendships and build memories that will last a lifetime. Remember, social functions aren't only parties; they can include such activities as intramural sports and Homecoming.

Leadership

Because fraternities are self-governing organizations, leadership opportunities abound. Students are given hands-on experience in leading committees, managing budgets, and interacting with faculty members and administrators. Most houses have as many as ten officers, along with an array of committee members. By becoming actively involved in leadership roles, students gain valuable experience that is essential for a successful career. Interestingly, although Greeks represent less than 10 percent of the undergraduate student population, they hold the majority of leadership positions on campus.

Service

According to the North-American Interfraternity Council, fraternities are increasingly becoming involved in philanthropies and hands-on service projects. Helping less fortunate people is a major focus of Greek life. This can vary from work with Easter Seals, blood drives, and food pantry collections to community upkeep, such as picking up trash, painting houses, or cleaning up area parks. Greeks also get involved in projects with organizations such as Habitat for Humanity, the American Heart Association, and Children's Miracle Network. By being involved in philanthropic projects, students not only raise money for worthwhile causes, but they also gain a deeper insight into themselves and their responsibility to the community.

ROOMMATES

When you arrive on campus, you will face a daunting task: to live peacefully with a stranger for the rest of the academic year.

To make this task easier, most schools use some type of room assignment survey. This can make roommate matches more successful. For example, two people who prefer to stay up late and play guitar can be matched, while two people who prefer to rise at dawn and hit the track can be a pair. Such differences are easy to ask about on a survey and easy for students to report. However, surveys cannot ask everything, and chances are pretty good that something about your roommate is going to get on your nerves.

In order to avoid conflict, plan ahead. When you first meet, work out some ground rules. Most schools have roommates write a contract together and sign it during the first week of school. Ground rules help eliminate conflict from the start by allowing each person to know what is expected. You should consider the following areas: privacy, quiet time, chores, and borrowing.

When considering privacy, think about how much time alone you need each day and how you and your roommate will arrange for private time. Class schedules usually give you some alone time. Be aware of this; if your class is cancelled, consider going for a cup of coffee or a browse in the bookstore instead of immediately rushing back to your room. Privacy also relates to giving your roommate space when he or she has had a bad day or just needs time to think. Set up clear hours for quiet time. Your dorm will already have some quiet hours established. You may choose to simply reiterate those or add additional time. Just be clear.

Two other potentially stormy issues are chores and borrowing. If there are cleaning chores that need to be shared, make a schedule and stick to it. No one appreciates a sink full of dirty dishes or a dingy shower. Remember the golden rule: do your chores as you wish your roommate would. When it comes to borrowing, set up clear rules. The safest bet is to not allow it; but if you do, limit when, for how long, and what will be done in case of damage.

Another issue many students confront is whether or not to live with a best friend from high school who is attending the same college. Generally, this is a bad idea for several reasons. First, you may think you know your best friend inside and out, but you may be surprised by her personal living habits. There is nothing like the closeness of a dorm room to reveal the annoying routines of your friend. Plus, personalities can change rapidly in college. Once you are away from home, you may be surprised at how you or your friend transforms from shy and introverted to late night partygoer. This can cause conflict. A final downfall is that the two of you will stick together like glue in the first few weeks and miss out on opportunities to meet other people.

Armed with this information, you should have a smooth year with your new roommate. But just in case you are the exception, most colleges will allow students who absolutely cannot get along to move. Prior to moving, each student must usually go through a dispute resolution process. This typically involves your Resident Adviser, you, and your roommate trying to work through your problems in a structured way.

Living with a roommate can be challenging at times, but the ultimate rewards—meeting someone new, encountering new ideas, and learning how to compromise—will serve you well later in life. Enjoy your roommate and all the experiences you will have, both good and bad, for they are all part of the college experience.

COMMUTING FROM HOME

For some students, home during the college years is the same house in which they grew up. Whether you are in this situation because you can't afford to live on campus or because you'd just rather live at home with your family, some basic guidelines will keep you connected with campus life.

By all means, do not just go straight home after class. Spend some of your free time at school. Usually there is a student union or a coffee shop where students gather and socialize. Make it a point to go there and talk to people between classes. Also, get involved in extracurricular activities, and visit classmates in the dorms.

If you drive to school, find other students who want to carpool. Most schools have a commuters' office or club that will give you a list of people who live near you. Sharing a car ride will give you time to talk and form a relationship with someone else who knows about the challenges of commuting.

Commuters' clubs also sponsor a variety of activities throughout the year—give them a try! Be sure also to consider the variety of activities open to all members of the student body, ranging from student government to community service to intramural sports. You may find this takes a bit more effort on your part, but the payoff in the close friendships you'll form will more than make up for it.

HOMESICKNESS

Homesickness in its most basic form is a longing for the stuff of home: your parents, friends, bedroom, school, and all of the other familiar people and objects that make you comfortable. But on another level, homesickness is a longing to go back in time. Moving away to college forces you to take on new responsibilities and begin to act like an adult. This can be scary.

While this condition is often described as a "sickness," no pill will provide a quick fix. Instead, you need to acknowledge that your feelings are a normal reaction to a significant change in your life. Allow yourself to feel the sadness of moving on in life and be open to conversations about it that may crop up in your dorm or among your new friends. After all, everyone is dealing with this issue. Then, make an effort to create a new home and a new life on campus. Create new habits and routines so that this once-strange place becomes familiar. Join activities and engage in campus life. This will help you to create a feeling of belonging that will ultimately be the key to overcoming homesickness.

WHAT IF YOU DON'T LIKE THE COLLEGE YOU PICK?

In the best of all worlds, you compile a list of colleges, find the most compatible one, and are accepted. You have a great time, learn a lot, graduate, and head off to a budding career. However, you may find the college you chose isn't the best of all worlds. Imagine these scenarios:

1. Halfway through your first semester of college, you come to the distressing conclusion that you can't stand being there for whatever reason. The courses don't match your interests. The campus is out in the boonies, and you don't ever want to see another cow. The selection of extracurricular activities doesn't cut it.

2. You have methodically planned to go to a community college for two years and move to a four-year college to complete your degree. Transferring takes you nearer to your goal.

3. You thought you wanted to major in art, but by the end of the first semester, you find yourself more interested in English lit. Things get confusing, so you drop out of college to sort out your thoughts and now you want to drop back in, hoping to rescue some of those credits.

4. You didn't do that well in high school—socializing got in the way of studying. But you've wised up, have gotten serious about your future, and two years of community college have brightened your prospects of transferring to a four-year institution.

Circumstances shift, people change, and, realistically speaking, it's not all that uncommon to transfer. Many people do. The reasons why students transfer run the gamut, as do the institutional policies that govern them. The most common transfers are students who move from a two-year to a four-year university or the person who opts for a career change midstream.

Whatever reasons you might have for wanting to transfer, you will be doing more than just switching academic gears. Aside from potentially losing credits, time, and money, transferring means again adjusting to a new situation. This affects just about all transfer students, from those who made a mistake in choosing a college to those who planned to go to a two-year college and then transferred to a four-year campus. People choose colleges for arbitrary reasons. That's why admissions departments try to ensure a good match between the student and campus before classes begin. Unfortunately, sometimes students don't realize they've made a mistake until it's too late.

The best way to avoid transferring is to extensively research a college or university before choosing it. Visit the campus and stay overnight, talk to admissions and faculty members, and try to learn as much as you can.

Chapter 10

OTHER OPTIONS AFTER HIGH SCHOOL

Years ago, most young people went directly to work after high school. Today, most young people first go to school for more training, but the majority don't go to traditional four-year colleges.

ACCORDING TO SHANNON McBride, Director of the Golden Crescent Tech Prep Partnership in Victoria, Texas, "Only 40 percent of high school graduates attempt to go to a four-year college, and of those, only 25 percent get their degree. And of that 25 percent, only 37 percent use the degree they got in that area."

So why aren't the remaining 60 percent of students choosing a traditional four-year college? The reasons are as varied as the students. Life events can often interfere with plans to attend college. Responsibilities to a family may materialize that make it impossible to delay earning an income for four years. One may have to work and go to school. And traditional colleges demand certain conventions, behaviors, and attitudes that don't fit every kind of person. Some people need a lot of physical activity to feel satisfied, while others just aren't interested in spending day after day sitting, reading, memorizing, and analyzing. Years of strict time management and postponed rewards are more than they can stand.

If any of these reasons ring true with you, there are still postsecondary options for you, all of which will not only allow you to pursue further education but also will train you for a career. Let's take a look at some of these educational directions you can follow.

DISTANCE LEARNING

As a future college student, can you picture yourself in any of these scenarios?

1. **You need some information, but the only place to find it is at a big state university.** Trouble is, it's hundreds of miles away. No problem. You simply go to your local community college and hook up electronically with the university. Voilà! The resources are brought to you.

2. **That ten-page paper is due in a few days, but you still have some last-minute questions to ask the professor before you turn it in.** Only one problem: you won't be able to see the professor until after the paper is due. Being a night owl, you also want to work on it when your roommate is asleep. Not to worry. Since you have the professor's e-mail address, just like all the other students in the class, you simply e-mail your question to her. She replies. You get your answer, finish the paper, and even turn it in electronically.

3. **After graduating from high school, you can't go to college right away, but your employer has a neat hook up with a college that offers courses via the Internet.** During your lunch hours, you and several of your work buddies log in to a class and get college credit.

Not too long ago, if you'd offered these scenarios to high school graduates as real possibilities, they would have thought you were a sci-fi freak. Distance education was not common at all—or if it was, it usually meant getting courses via snail mail or on videotape. Well, today you are in the right place at the right time. Distance education is a reality for countless high school graduates.

What distance education now means is that you can access educational programs and not have to physically be in a classroom on a campus. Through such technologies as cable or satellite television, videotapes and audiotapes, fax, computer modem, computer conferencing and videoconferencing, and other means of electronic delivery, the classroom comes to you—sometimes even if you're sitting in your room in your bunny slippers and it's 2 in the morning.

Distance learning expands the reach of the classroom by using various technologies to deliver university resources to off-campus sites, transmit college courses into the workplace, and enable you to view class lectures in the comfort of your home.

Where and How Can I Take Distance Learning Courses?

The technology for new, cheaper telecommunications technology is getting better all the time, and there is a growing demand for education by people who can't afford either the time or money to be a full-time, on-campus student. To fill that demand, educational networks also are growing and changing how and when you can access college courses.

Most states have established new distance learning systems to advance the delivery of instruction to schools, postsecondary institutions, and state government agencies. Colleges and universities are collaborating with commercial telecommunication entities, including online information services, such as America Online and cable and telephone companies, to provide education to far-flung student constituencies. Professions such as law, medicine, and accounting, as well as knowledge-based industries, are utilizing telecommunications networks for the transmission of customized higher education programs to working professionals, technicians, and managers.

Ways in Which Distance Learning May Be Offered:

- **Credit courses.** In general, if these credit courses are completed successfully, they can be applied toward a degree.

- **Noncredit courses and courses offered for professional certification.** These programs can help you acquire specialized knowledge in a concentrated, time-efficient manner and stay on top of the latest developments in your field. They provide a flexible way for you to prepare for a new career or study for professional licensure and certification. Many of these university programs are created in cooperation with professional and trade associations so that courses are based on real-life workforce needs, and the practical skills learned are immediately applicable in the field.

The Way Distance Learning Works

Enrolling in a distance learning course may simply involve filling out a registration form, making sure that you have access to the equipment needed, and paying the tuition and fees by check, money order, or credit card. In these cases, your applications may be accepted without entrance examinations or proof of prior educational experience.

Other courses may involve educational prerequisites and access to equipment not found in all geographic locations. Some institutions offer detailed information about individual courses, such as a course outline, upon request. If you have access to the Internet and simply wish to review course descriptions, you may be able to peruse an institution's course catalogs electronically by accessing the institution's home page on the Web.

Time Requirements

Some courses allow you to enroll at your convenience and work at your own pace. Others closely adhere to a traditional classroom schedule. Specific policies and time limitations pertaining to withdrawals, refunds, transfers, and renewal periods can be found in the institutional catalog.

Admission to a Degree Program

If you plan to enter a degree program, you should consult the academic advising department of the institution of your choice to learn about entrance requirements and application procedures. You may find it necessary to develop a portfolio of your past experiences and accomplishments that may have resulted in college-level learning.

How Do I Communicate with My Instructor?

Student-faculty exchanges occur using electronic communication (through fax and e-mail). Many institutions offer their distance learning students access to toll-free numbers so students can talk to their professors or teaching assistants without incurring any long-distance charges.

Responses to your instructor's comments on your lessons, requests for clarification of comments, and all other exchanges between you and your instructor will take time. Interaction with your instructor—whether by computer, phone, or letter—is important, and you must be willing to take the initiative.

What Else Does Distance Learning Offer?

Distance learning comes in a variety of colors and flavors. Along with traditional college degrees, you can earn professional certification or continuing education units (CEUs) in a particular field.

College Degrees

There are opportunities for you to earn degrees at a distance at the associate, baccalaureate, and graduate levels. Two-year community college students are now able to earn baccalaureate degrees—without relocating—by transferring to distance learning programs offered by four-year universities. Corporations are forming partnerships with universities to bring college courses to worksites and encourage employees to continue their education. Distance learning is especially popular among people who want to earn their degree part-time while continuing to work full-time. Although on-campus residencies are sometimes required for certain distance learning degree programs, they generally can be completed while employees are on short-term leave or vacation.

Professional Certification

Certificate programs often focus on employment specializations, such as hazardous waste management or electronic publishing, and can be helpful to those seeking to advance or change careers. Also, many states mandate continuing education for professionals such as teachers, nursing home administrators, or accountants. Distance learning offers a convenient way for many individuals to meet professional certification requirements. Health care, engineering, and education are just a few of the many professions that take advantage of distance learning to help their professionals maintain certification.

Many colleges offer a sequence of distance learning courses in a specific field of a profession. For instance, within the engineering profession, certificate programs in computer-integrated manufacturing, systems engineering, test and evaluation, waste management education, and research consortium are offered via distance learning.

Business offerings include distance learning certification in information technology, total quality management, and health services management.

Within the field of education, you'll find distance learning certificate programs in areas such as early reading instruction and special education for the learning handicapped.

Continuing Education Units (CEUs)

If you choose to take a course on a noncredit basis, you may be able to earn continuing education units (CEUs). The CEU system is a nationally recognized system to provide a standardized measure for accumulating, transferring, and recognizing participation in continuing education programs. One CEU is defined as 10 contact hours of participation in an organized continuing education experience under responsible sponsorship, capable direction, and qualified instruction.

COMMUNITY COLLEGES

Two-year colleges or community colleges, are often called "the people's colleges." With their open-door policies (admission is open to individuals with a high school diploma or its equivalent), community colleges provide access to higher education for millions of Americans who might otherwise be excluded from higher education. Community college students are diverse, of all ages, races, and economic backgrounds. While many community college students enroll full-time, an equally large number attend on a part-time basis so they can fulfill employment and family commitments as they advance their education.

Today, there are more than 1,600 community colleges in the United States. They enroll more than 11 million students, who represent more than 40 percent of all undergraduates in the United States. As you can see, millions of first-time freshmen begin their higher education in a community college.

Community colleges are also referred to as either technical or junior colleges, and they may either be under public or independent control. What unites all two-year colleges is that they are regionally accredited, postsecondary institutions, whose highest credential awarded is the associate degree. With few exceptions, community colleges offer a comprehensive curriculum, which includes transfer, technical, and continuing education programs.

Important Factors in a Community College Education

The student who attends a community college can count on receiving quality instruction in a supportive learning community. This setting frees the student to pursue his or her own goals, nurture special talents, explore new fields of learning, and develop the capacity for lifelong learning.

From the student's perspective, four characteristics capture the essence of community colleges:

- They are community-based institutions that work in close partnership with high schools, community groups, and employers in extending high-quality programs at convenient times and places.

- Community colleges are cost effective. Annual tuition and fees at public community colleges average approximately half those at public four-year colleges and less than 15 percent of private four-year institutions. In addition, since most community colleges are generally close to their students' homes, these students can also save a significant amount of money on the room, board, and transportation expenses traditionally associated with a college education.

- They provide a caring environment, with faculty members who are expert instructors, known for excellent teaching and for meeting students at the point of their individual needs, regardless of age, sex, race, current job status, or previous academic preparation. Community colleges join a strong curriculum with a broad range of counseling and career services that are intended to assist students in making the most of their educational opportunities.

- Many offer comprehensive programs, including transfer curricula in such liberal arts programs as chemistry, psychology, and business management, that lead directly to a baccalaureate degree and career programs that prepare students for employment or assist those already employed in upgrading their skills. For those students who need to strengthen their academic skills, community colleges also offer a wide range of developmental programs in mathematics, languages, and learning skills, designed to prepare the student for success in college studies.

Getting to Know Your Two-Year College

The best way to learn about your college is to visit in person. During a campus visit, be prepared to ask a lot of questions. Talk to students, faculty members, administrators, and counselors about the college and its programs, particularly those in which you have a special interest. Ask about available certificates and associate degrees. Don't be shy. Do what you can to dig below the surface. Ask college officials about the

Chapter 10: Other Options After High School

transfer rate to four-year colleges. If a college emphasizes student services, find out what particular assistance is offered, such as educational or career guidance. Colleges are eager to provide you with the information you need to make informed decisions.

The Money Factor

For many students, the decision to attend a community college is often based on financial factors. If you aren't sure what you want to do or what talents you have, community colleges allow you the freedom to explore different career interests at a low cost. For those students who can't afford the cost of university tuition, community colleges let them take care of their basic classes before transferring to a four-year institution. Many two-year colleges can now offer you instruction in your own home through cable television or public broadcast stations or through home study courses that can save both time and money. Look into all your options, and be sure to add up all the costs of attending various colleges before deciding which is best for you.

Working and Going to School

Many two-year college students maintain full-time or part-time employment while they earn their degrees. Over the past decades, a steadily growing number of students have chosen to attend community colleges while they fulfill family and employment responsibilities. To enable these students to balance the demands of home, work, and school, most community colleges offer classes at night and on weekends.

For the full-time student, the usual length of time it takes to obtain an associate degree is two years. However, your length of study will depend on the course load you take: the fewer credits you earn each term, the longer it will take you to earn a degree. To assist you in moving more quickly toward your degree, many community colleges now award credit through examination or for equivalent knowledge gained through relevant life experiences. Be certain to find out the credit options that are available to you at the college in which you are interested. You may discover that it will take less time to earn a degree than you first thought.

Preparation for Transfer

Studies have repeatedly shown that students who first attend a community college and then transfer to a four-year college or university do at least as well academically as the students who entered the four-year institutions as freshmen. Most community colleges have agreements with nearby four-year institutions to make transfer of credits easier. If you are thinking of transferring, be sure to meet with a counselor or faculty adviser before choosing your courses. You will want to map out a course of study with transfer in mind. Make sure you also find out the credit-transfer requirements of the four-year institution you might want to attend.

New Career Opportunities

Community colleges realize that many entering students are not sure about the field in which they

A SCHOLARSHIP FOR CAREER COLLEGE STUDENTS

The *Imagine America* Scholarship can help those who dream of a career but might not be able to achieve it through traditional college education.

What is the Imagine America Scholarship?

Introduced in 1998 by the Career College Foundation, the *Imagine America* Scholarship aims to reduce the growing "skills gap" in America. Any graduating high school senior can be considered for selection for one of the three scholarships awarded to his or her high school. The *Imagine America* Scholarship gives thousands of graduating high school seniors scholarships of $1,000 to be used at hundreds of participating career colleges and schools across the country.

You are eligible for the Imagine America Scholarship if:

- You attend any private postsecondary institution that is accredited by an agency recognized by the U.S. Department of Education.
- You are graduating from high school this year.

To find out more about the *Imagine America* Scholarship Program, talk to your high school counselor or visit www.imagine-america.org for more information.

want to focus their studies or the career they would like to pursue. Community colleges have the resources to help students identify areas of career interest and to set challenging occupational goals.

Once a career goal is set, you can be confident that a community college will provide job-relevant, high-quality occupation and technical education. About half of the students who take courses for credit at community colleges do so to prepare for employment or to acquire or upgrade skills for their current job. Especially helpful in charting a career path is the assistance of a counselor or a faculty adviser, who can discuss job opportunities in your chosen field and help you map out your course of study.

In addition, since community colleges have close ties to their communities, they are in constant contact with leaders in business, industry, organized labor, and public life. Community colleges work with these individuals and their organizations to prepare students for direct entry into the world of work. For example, some community colleges have established partnerships with local businesses and industries to provide specialized training programs. Some also provide the academic portion of apprenticeship training, while others offer extensive job-shadowing and cooperative education opportunities. Be sure to examine all of the career-preparation opportunities offered by the community colleges in which you are interested.

VOCATIONAL/CAREER COLLEGES

Career education is important for every employee as technology continues to change. From the largest employers, such as the U.S. military, defense contractors, IBM, aviation, and health care, down to the company with one and two employees, issues of keeping up with technology and producing goods and services cheaper, faster, and at less cost requires—indeed demands—a skilled, world-class workforce. In good or bad economic times, you will always have a distinct advantage if you have a demonstrable skill and can be immediately productive while continuing to learn and improve. If you know how to use technology, work collaboratively, and find creative solutions, you will always be in demand.

Career colleges offer scores of opportunities to learn the technical skills required by many of today's and tomorrow's top jobs. This is especially true in the areas of computer and information technology, health care, and hospitality (culinary arts, travel and tourism, and hotel and motel management). Career colleges range in size from those with a handful of students to universities with thousands enrolled. They are located in every state in the nation and share one common objective—to prepare students for a successful career in the world of work through a focused, intensive curriculum.

America's career colleges are privately owned and operated for-profit companies. Instead of using tax support to operate, career colleges pay taxes. Because career colleges are businesses, they must be responsive to the workforce needs of their communities or they will cease to exist.

Generally, career colleges prepare you for a specific career. Some will require you to take

MOST POPULAR MAJORS FOR COMMUNITY COLLEGE GRADS

The American Association of Community Colleges conducted a survey in the year 2004 to see what the most popular majors for community college students were. The top 15 majors and their average starting salaries follow:

MAJOR	AVERAGE STARTING SALARY
1. Registered Nursing	$38,419
2. Law Enforcement	$31,865
3. Licensed Practical Nursing	$27,507
4. Radiology	$35,612
5. Computer Technologies	$35,469
6. Automotive	$32,498
7. Nursing Assistant	$16,754
8. Dental Hygiene	$35,956
9. Health Information Technology	$26,578
10. Construction	$34,414
11. Education	$30,810
12. Business	$31,366
13. Networking	$35,938
14. Electronics	$32,734
15. Medical Assistant	$22,953

academic courses such as English or history. Others will relate every class you take to a specific job, such as computer-aided drafting or interior design. Some focus specifically on business or technical fields. Bob Sullivan, a career counselor at East Brunswick High School in East Brunswick, New Jersey, points out that the negative side to this kind of education is that if you haven't carefully researched what you want to do, you could waste a lot of time and money. "There's no room for exploration or finding yourself as opposed to a community college where you can go to find yourself and feel your way around," he explains.

So how do you find the right career college for you? A good place to start is knowing generally what you want to do. You don't have to know the fine details of your goals, but you should have a broad idea, such as a career in allied health or business or computing.

After you've crossed that hurdle, the rest is easy. Since professional training is the main purpose of career colleges, its graduates are the best measure of a school's success. Who hires the graduates? How do their jobs relate to the education they received? Career colleges should be able to provide that data to prospective students. "Career colleges have a different customer than other institutions," notes Stephen Friedheim, President of ESS College of Business in Dallas, Texas. In addition to focusing on the needs of their students, career colleges also want to ensure they meet the needs of the employers who are hiring their graduates. "The assumption is that if you can please the employer, you will please the student," Friedheim explains.

Checking the credentials of a career college is one of the most important steps you should take in your career college search. Though not every career college has to be accredited, it is a sign that the college has gone through a process that ensures quality. It also means that students can qualify for federal grant and loan programs. Furthermore, you should see if the college has met the standards from professional training organizations. In fields such as court reporting and health-related professions, those criteria are paramount.

FINANCIAL AID OPTIONS FOR CAREER AND COMMUNITY COLLEGES

The financial aid process is basically the same for students attending a community college, a career college, or a technical institute as it is for students attending a four-year college. However, there are some details that can make the difference between getting the maximum amount of financial aid and only scraping by.

As with four-year students, the federal government is still your best source of financial aid. Most community colleges and career and technical schools participate in federal financial aid programs. To get detailed information about federal financial aid programs and how to apply for them, read through Chapter 8: "Financial Aid Dollars and Sense." In the meantime, here are some quick tips on where to look for education money.

Investigate federal financial aid programs. You should definitely check out a Federal Pell Grant, which is a need-based grant available to those who can't pay the entire tuition themselves. The Federal Supplemental Educational Opportunity Grant (FSEOG) is for those students with exceptional financial need. You also can take advantage of the Federal Work-Study programs that provide jobs for students with financial aid eligibility in return for part of their tuition. Many two-year institutions offer work-study, but the number of jobs tends to be limited. Also, federal loans make up a substantial part of financial aid for two-year students. Student loans, which have lower interest rates, may be sponsored by the institution or federally sponsored, or they may be available through commercial financial institutions. They are basically the same as those for the traditional four-year college student, such as the Federal Perkins Loan and the Direct Stafford Loan and the Federal Family Education Stafford Loan. In fact, some private career colleges and technical institutes only offer federal loans. You also can find more specific information about federal loans in Chapter 8.

Don't overlook scholarships. What many two-year students don't realize is that they could be eligible for scholarships. Regrettably, many make the assumption

Part 3: The Road to More Education

> **SNAPSHOT OF TWO CAREER COLLEGE STUDENTS**
> **Katrina Dew**
> **Network Systems Administration**
> **Silicon Valley College**
> **Fremont, California**
>
> **ABOUT KATRINA**
>
> Right after high school, Katrina headed for junior college, but she felt like she was spinning her wheels. She wanted something that was goal-oriented. Community college offered too many options. She needed to be focused in one direction.
>
> At first, Katrina thought she would become a physical therapist. Then she realized how much schooling she would need to begin working. Turning to the computer field, she saw some definite benefits. For one, she had messed around with them in high school. She could get a degree and get out in two years. She saw that computer careers are big and getting bigger. Plus, there weren't a lot of women in that field, which signaled more potential for her. But before she switched schools, she visited the career college, talked to students, and sat in on lectures. She really liked the way the teachers related to their students. Along with her technical classes, she's taken algebra, psychology, English composition, and management communication.
>
> **WHAT I LIKE ABOUT BEING A CAREER STUDENT**
>
> "Career colleges are for fast-track-oriented students who want to get out in the work field and still feel that they have an appropriate education."
>
> **Nicholas Cecere**
> **Automotive Techniques Management**
> **Education America/Vale Technical Institute**
> **Blairsville, Pennsylvania**
>
> **ABOUT NICHOLAS**
>
> Nicholas has completely repainted his 1988 Mercury Topaz, redone all the brakes, put in a brand-new exhaust system, and lots of smaller stuff here and there. But he says that's nothing compared to the completely totaled cars some of his classmates haul into the school. Talk about hands-on: they're able to completely restore them while going through the program.
>
> Nicholas didn't always have gasoline running through his veins. In fact, he just recently discovered how much he likes automotives. After graduating from high school, he went to a community college, and after one semester, he left to work at a personal care home. Standing over a sink of dirty dishes made him realize he wanted more than just a job. He started thinking about what he wanted to do and visited a few schools and the body shop where his brother worked. Where others saw twisted car frames, Nicholas saw opportunity and enrolled in the program.
>
> **WHAT I LIKE ABOUT BEING A CAREER STUDENT**
>
> "I compare career college to a magnifying glass that takes the sun and focuses it. You learn just what you need to learn."

that scholarships are only for very smart students attending prestigious universities. You'd be surprised to learn how many community and career colleges offer scholarships. It's critical to talk to the financial aid officer of each school you plan to attend to find out what scholarships might be available.

Two-year students should find out how their state of residence can help them pay for tuition. Every state in the union has some level of state financial aid that goes to community college students. The amounts are dependent on which state you live in, and most aid is in the form of grants.

APPRENTICESHIPS

Some students like working with their hands and have the skill, patience, and temperament to become expert mechanics, carpenters, or electronic repair technicians. If you think you'd enjoy a profession like this and feel that college training isn't for you, then you might want to think about a job that requires apprenticeship training.

To stay competitive, America needs highly skilled workers. But if you're looking for a soft job, forget it. An apprenticeship is no snap. It demands hard work and has tough competition, so you've got to have the will to see it through. An apprenticeship is a program formally agreed upon between a worker and an employer where the employee learns a skilled trade through classroom work and on-the-job training. Apprenticeship programs vary in length, pay, and intensity among the various trades. A person completing an apprenticeship program generally becomes a journeyperson (skilled craftsperson) in that trade.

The advantages of apprenticeships are numerous. First and foremost, an apprenticeship leads to a lasting lifetime skill. As a highly trained worker, you can take your skill anywhere you decide to go. The more creative, exciting, and challenging jobs are put in the hands of the fully skilled worker, the all-around person who knows his or her trade inside out.

Chapter 10: Other Options After High School

WHAT TO LOOK FOR IN A CAREER COLLEGE

A tour of the college is a must! While visiting the campus, do the following:

- **Get a full explanation of the curriculum, including finding out how you will be trained.**
- **Take a physical tour of the classrooms and laboratories and look for cleanliness, modern equipment/computers, and size of classes. Observe the activity in classes: Are students engaged in class, and are lectures dynamic?**
- **Ask about employment opportunities after graduation. What are the placement rates (most current) and list of employers? Inquire about specific placement assistance: resume preparation, job leads, etc. Look for "success stories" on bulletin boards, placement boards, and newsletters.**
- **Find out about tuition and other costs associated with the program. Ask about the financial aid assistance provided to students.**
- **Find out if an externship is part of the training program. How are externships assigned? Does the student have any input as to externship assignment?**
- **Ask if national certification and registration in your chosen field is available upon graduation.**
- **Inquire about the college's accreditation and certification.**
- **Also find out the associations and organizations to which the college belongs. Ask what awards or honors the college has had bestowed.**
- **Ask if the college utilizes an advisory board to develop employer relationships.**
- **Ask about the rules and regulations. What GPA must be maintained? What is the attendance policy? What are grounds for termination? What is the refund policy if the student drops or is terminated? Is there a dress code? What are the holidays of the college?**

Source: Arizona College of Allied Health, Phoenix, Arizona

Skilled workers advance much faster than those who are semiskilled or whose skills are not broad enough to equip them to assume additional responsibilities in a career. Those who complete an apprenticeship have also acquired the skills and judgment that are necessary to go into business for themselves if they choose.

What to Do If You're Interested in an Apprenticeship

If you want to begin an apprenticeship, you have to be at least 16 years old, and you must fill out an application for employment. These applications may be available year-round or only at certain times during the year, depending on the trade in which you're interested.

Federal regulations prohibit anyone under the age of 16 from being considered for an apprenticeship. Some programs require a high school degree or certain course work. Other requirements may include passing certain aptitude tests, proof of physical ability to perform the duties of the trade, and possession of a valid driver's license.

Once you have met the basic program entrance requirements, you'll be interviewed and awarded points on your interest in the trade, your attitude toward work in general, and personal traits, such as appearance, sincerity, character, and habits. Openings are awarded to those who have achieved the most points.

Because an apprentice must be trained in an area where work actually exists and where a certain pay scale is guaranteed upon completion of the program, the wait for application acceptance may be pretty long in areas of low employment. This standard works to your advantage, however. Just think: You wouldn't want to spend one to six years of your life learning a job where no work exists or where the wage is the same as, or just a little above, that of an unskilled or semiskilled laborer.

If you're considering an apprenticeship, the best sources of assistance and information are vocational or career counselors, local state employment security agencies, field offices of state apprenticeship agencies, and regional offices of the Bureau of Apprenticeship and Training (BAT). Apprenticeships are usually registered with the BAT or a state apprenticeship council. Some apprenticeships are not registered at all, although that doesn't necessarily mean that the program isn't valid. To find out if a certain apprenticeship is legitimate, contact your state's apprenticeship agency or a regional office of the BAT. Addresses and phone numbers for these regional offices are listed on the following page. You can also visit the Bureau's Web site at www.doleta.gov/oa/bat.cfm.

BUREAU OF APPRENTICESHIP AND TRAINING OFFICES

NATIONAL OFFICE
Office of Apprenticeship Training
Bureau of Apprenticeship and Training
Frances Perkins Building
200 Constitution Avenue, NW
Washington, DC 20210
Phone: 877-US-2JOBS (toll-free)

REGION I: BOSTON

Mr. John M. Griffin Jr.
Regional Director
USDOL/ETA/OATELS
JFK Federal Building
Room E-370
Boston, MA 02203
Telephone: 617-788-0177
Fax: 617-788-0304
E-mail: Griffin.John@dol.gov

Connecticut
Maine
Massachusetts
New Hampshire
New Jersey
New York
Puerto Rico
Rhode Island
Vermont
Virgin Islands

REGION II: PHILADELPHIA

Mr. Joseph T. Hersh
Regional Director
USDOL/ETA/OATELS
Suite 820-East
170 S. Independence Mall West
Philadelphia, PA 19106-3315
Telephone: 215-861-4830
Fax: 215-861-4833
E-mail: Hersh.Joseph@dol.gov

Delaware
District of Columbia
Maryland
Pennsylvania
Virginia
West Virginia

REGION III: ATLANTA

Mr. Garfield G. Garner, Jr.
Regional Director
USDOL/ETA/OATELS
61 Forsyth Street SW, Rm. 6T71
Atlanta, GA 30303
Telephone: 404-562-2335
Fax: 404-562-2329
E-mail: Garner.Garfield@dol.gov

Alabama
Florida
Georgia
Kentucky
Mississippi
North Carolina
South Carolina
Tennessee

REGION IV: DALLAS

Mr. Steve Opitz
Regional Director
USDOL/ETA/OATELS
Federal Building
525 S. Griffin Street, Rm. 317
Dallas, TX 75202
Telephone: 214-767-4993
Fax: 214-767-4995
E-mail: Opitz.Steve@dol.gov

Arkansas
Colorado
Louisiana
Montana
North Dakota
South Dakota
Texas
Utah
Wyoming

REGION V: CHICAGO

Mr. Terrence Benewich
Regional Director
USDOL/ETA/OATELS
230 South Dearborn Street, Rm. 656
Chicago, IL 60604
Telephone: 312-596-5500
Fax: 312-596-5501
E-mail: Benewich.Terrence@dol.gov

Illinois
Indiana
Iowa
Kansas
Michigan
Minnesota
Missouri
Nebraska
Ohio
Wisconsin

REGION VI: SAN FRANCISCO

Mr. Michael W. Longeuay
Deputy Regional Director
USDOL/ETA/OATELS
71 Stevenson Street, Suite 815
San Francisco, CA 94105
Phone: 415-975-4007
Fax: 415-975-4010
E-mail: Longeuay.Michael@dol.gov

Alaska
Arizona
California
Hawaii
Idaho
Nevada
Oregon
Washington

Chapter 11

THE MILITARY OPTION

Bet you didn't know that the United States military is the largest employer in the country. There's got to be a good reason that so many people get their paychecks from Uncle Sam.

SHOULD I OR SHOULDN'T I WORK FOR THE LARGEST EMPLOYER IN THE UNITED STATES?

Every year, thousands of young people pursue a military career and enjoy the benefits it offers. Yet thousands more consider joining the military and decide against it. Their reasons vary, but many choose not to enlist because they lack knowledge of what a career in the military can offer. Others simply mistrust recruiters based on horror stories they've heard. Sadly, many make the decision against joining the military without ever setting foot in the recruiting office.

But if you are an informed "shopper," you will be able to make an informed choice about whether the military is right for you.

People rarely buy anything based on their needs: Instead, they buy based on their emotions. We see it on a daily basis in advertising, from automobiles to soft drinks. We rarely see an automobile commercial that gives statistics about how the car is engineered, how long it will last, the gas mileage, and other technical specifications. Instead, we see people driving around and having a good time.

The reason for this is that advertising agencies know that you will probably buy something based on how you feel rather than what you think. Because of this tendency to buy with emotion rather than reason, it is important to separate the feelings from the facts. That way, you can base your decision about whether to join the military primarily on the facts.

There are two big questions that you must answer before you can come to any conclusions. First, is the military right for me, and second, if the first answer is yes, which branch is right for me?

Suppose that you have to decide whether to buy a new car or repair your current car. The first choice you make will determine your next course of action. You will have to weigh the facts to determine if you will purchase a new car or not. Once you've decided to buy a car rather than repair your old one, you must then decide exactly what make and model will best suit your needs.

NO HYPE, JUST THE FACTS

So you didn't wake up one morning and know for sure that you're going to join the Navy. One minute you think you'd like the Army, but then you talk to your cousin who convinces you to follow him into the Air Force. But then the neighbor down the street is a Marine, and he's gung ho for you to join up with them. What to do?

Well, a helpful Web site is the answer. Go to www.spear.navy.mil/profile for some really straightforward and non-partisan information about each branch of the military. You'll be able to compare the benefits that each service offers plus pick up other helpful tips and information. The Web site is designed specifically for high school students considering the military.

"Normally the first question we get from people interested in the Air Force is 'What does the Air Force have to offer me?' But I back off and ask them about their qualifications. Sometimes it's easier to go to an Ivy League school than to join the Air Force because of our stringent requirements."

**Master Sergeant Timothy Little
United States Air Force**

Part 3: The Road to More Education

You should make a list of the reasons why you want to join the military before you ever set foot in the recruiter's office. Whether your list is long—containing such items as money for college, job security, opportunity to travel, technical training, and good pay—or contains only one item, such as having full-time employment, the number of items on your list is not what's important. What is important is that you are able to satisfy those reasons, or primary motivators.

Whatever your list contains, the first course of action is to collect your reasons to join the military and put them in order of importance to you. This process, known as rank-ordering, will help you determine if you should proceed with the enlistment process.

"Take two people with the same qualifications who are looking for jobs. The person with the Army background will be that much more competitive. That's due to the fact that he or she is disciplined and knows how to act without being told what to do."
Staff Sergeant Max Burda
United States Army

Rank-ordering your list is a simple process of deciding which motivators are most important to you and then listing them in order of importance. List your most important motivator as number one, your next most important as number two, and so on.

If we apply the car-buying scenario here, your primary motivators may be finding a car that costs under $20,000, gets at least 30 miles to the gallon, has leather interior, is available in blue, and has a sunroof. If you put those motivators in rank order, your list might look something like this:

1. Costs under $20,000
2. Gets at least 30 mpg
3. Has a sunroof
4. Has leather interior
5. Available in blue

You'll notice that the number one, or most important, motivator in this case is cost, while the last, or least important, motivator is color. The more important the motivator, the less likely you'll be willing to settle for something different or to live without it altogether.

After you've rank-ordered your motivators, go down your list and determine whether those motivators can be met by enlisting in the military. If you find that all your motivators can be met by enlisting, that's great; but even if only some of your motivators can be met, you may still want to consider enlisting. Seldom does a product meet all our needs and wants.

CHOOSING WHICH BRANCH TO JOIN

"If you like to travel, we offer more than anyone else. The longest you're underway is generally two to three weeks, with three to four days off in every port and one day on the ship. Prior to pulling in, you can even set up tours."
Chief Petty Officer Keith Horst
United States Navy

If you are seriously considering joining the military, you probably have checked out at least two of the branches. Check them all out, even if it means just requesting literature and reviewing it. A word of caution though: Brochures do not tell the complete story, and it is very difficult to base your decision either for or against a military branch on the contents of a brochure alone. Would you buy a car based solely on the information contained in a brochure? Probably not!

"I tell people that you get paid the same in all the services, and the benefits are the same. What's different about each branch is the environment."
Sergeant Ian Bonnell, Infantry Sergeant
United States Marines

The process of choosing the right branch of the military for you is basically the same process that you used to determine if joining the military was right for you. You should start with your list of primary motivators and use the "yes/no" method to determine whether each branch can meet all or some of those motivators. Once you've determined which branch or branches can best meet your motivators, it's time to compare those branches. Remember to look for the negative aspects as well as the motivators of each of the branches as you compare.

After making your comparisons, you may still find yourself with more than one choice. What do you do then? You could flip a coin, but that's not the wisest idea! Instead, look at some of these factors:

Length of enlistment. Some branches may require a longer term for offering the same benefits that you could receive from another branch.

Advanced pay grade. You may be entitled to an advanced rank in some branches based on certain enlistment options.

"In the Army, you can get training in everything from culinary arts to truck driving and all the way to aviation mechanics, military intelligence, and computer networking."
Staff Sergeant Max Burda
United States Army

Length and type of training. How long will your training take? Usually the longer the training, the more in-depth and useful it is. You'll also want to consider how useful the training will be once you've left the military.

Enlistment bonuses. Be careful when using an enlistment bonus as the only factor in deciding which branch to choose. If it comes down to a tie between two branches and only one offers a bonus, it's not a bad reason to choose that branch.

Additional pay and allowances. There may be additional pay you'd be entitled to that can only be offered by a particular branch. For instance, if you join the Navy, you may be entitled to Sea Pay and Submarine Pay, something obviously not available if you join the Air Force.

Ability to pursue higher education. While all the military branches offer educational benefits, you must consider when you will be able to take advantage of these benefits. If your job requires 12-hour shifts and has you out in the field a lot, when will you be able to attend classes?

"Everyone in the Navy learns how to fight a fire. You get qualified in First Aid and CPR. That's mandatory for every sailor. The only jobs we don't have in the Navy are veterinarians, forest rangers, and rodeo stars."
Chief Petty Officer Keith Horst
United States Navy

Once you have considered these factors, and perhaps some of your own, you should be able to decide which branch is right for you. If you still haven't been able to select one branch over another, though, consider the following:

- Ask your recruiter if you can speak to someone who has recently joined.

- If there is a base nearby, you may be able to get a tour to look at its facilities.

- If you are well versed in Internet chat rooms, you may want to look for ones that cater to military members—then ask a lot of questions.

- Talk to friends and family members who are currently serving in the military. Be careful, however, not to talk to people who have been out of the military for a while, as they probably aren't familiar with today's military. Also, avoid people who left the military under less-than-desirable conditions (for example, someone who was discharged from Basic Training for no compatibility).

If you choose to continue with processing for enlistment, your next step will probably be to take the Armed Services Vocational Aptitude Battery (ASVAB).

I'M JOINING THE AIR FORCE

It didn't take Brian Filipek long to decide he wanted to join the Air Force. But that's if you don't count the times he talked to people who had served in the Air Force or the research he did on the Internet to gather information—and that was before he even set foot inside the recruiter's office. By the time an Air Force recruiter responded to a card Brian had sent in, he was pretty sure he liked what he'd seen so far. "The recruiter didn't have to do any work to convince me," says Brian. After that, it was a matter of going through the pre-qualifying process, like whether he met the height and weight qualifications, and the security forms he had to fill out.

After he enlisted, Brian didn't stop gathering information. Long before he was sent to Basic Training, he found out about Warrior Week, which is held on one of the last weeks in Basic Training. He was already looking forward to it. "I'm an outdoors kind of person," he says. "I want to do the obstacle course and ropes course."

Though the idea of testing his endurance and strength appeals to him, being away from family will be hard. "Granted, your food is cooked for you, but you're still on your own," he says. However, he knows that it's worth it to achieve his goal of education and free job training. Brian acknowledges that the military is not for everyone, but as far as he's concerned, he's sure he's made the right choice.

Brian Filipek, Enlistee
U.S. Air Force

THE ASVAB

The ASVAB, a multiple-aptitude battery of tests designed for use with students in their junior or senior year in high school or in a postsecondary school, as well as those seeking military enlistment, was developed to yield results useful to both students and the military. The military uses the results to determine the qualifications of candidates for enlistment and to help place them in military occupational programs. Schools use ASVAB test results to assist their students in developing future educational and career plans.

Frequently Asked Questions About the ASVAB

What is the Armed Services Vocational Aptitude Battery (ASVAB)?

The ASVAB, sponsored by the Department of Defense, is a multi-aptitude test battery consisting of nine short individual tests covering Word Knowledge, Paragraph Comprehension, Arithmetic Reasoning, Mathematics Knowledge, General Science, Auto and Shop Information, Mechanical Comprehension, Electronics Information, and Assembling Objects. Your ASVAB results provide scores for each individual test, as well as three academic composite scores—Verbal, Math, and Academic Ability—and two career exploration composite scores.

Why should I take the ASVAB?

As a high school student nearing graduation, you are faced with important career choices. Should you go on to college, technical, or vocational school? Would it be better to enter the job market? Should you consider a military career? Your ASVAB scores are measures of aptitude. Your composite scores measure your aptitude for higher academic learning and give you ideas for career exploration.

When and where is the ASVAB given?

ASVAB is administered annually or semiannually at more than 14,000 high schools and postsecondary schools in the United States.

Is there a charge or fee to take the ASVAB?

ASVAB is administered at no cost to the school or to the student.

How long does it take to complete the ASVAB?

ASVAB testing takes approximately 3 hours. If you miss class, it will be with your school's approval.

If I wish to take the ASVAB but my school doesn't offer it (or I missed it), what should I do?

See your school counselor. In some cases, arrangements may be made for you to take it at another high school. Your counselor should call 800-323-0513 (toll-free) for additional information.

How do I find out what my scores mean and how to use them?

Your scores will be provided to you on a report called the ASVAB Student Results Sheet. Along with your scores, you should receive a copy of *Exploring Careers: The ASVAB Workbook*, which contains information that will help you understand your

ASVAB results and shows you how to use them for career exploration. Test results are returned to participating schools within thirty days.

What is a passing score on the ASVAB?

No one "passes" or "fails" the ASVAB. The ASVAB enables you to compare your scores to those of other students at your grade level.

If I take the ASVAB, am I obligated to join the military?

No. Taking the ASVAB does not obligate you to the military in any way. You are free to use your test results in whatever manner you wish. You may use the ASVAB results for up to two years for military enlistment if you are a junior, senior, or postsecondary school student. The military services encourage all young people to finish high school before joining the armed forces.

If I am planning to go to college, should I take the ASVAB?

Yes. ASVAB results provide you with information that can help you determine your capacity for advanced academic education. You can also use your ASVAB results, along with other personal information, to identify areas for career exploration.

Should I take the ASVAB if I plan to become a commissioned officer?

Yes. Taking the ASVAB is a valuable experience for any student who aspires to become a military officer. The aptitude information you receive could assist you in career planning.

Should I take the ASVAB if I am considering entering the Reserve or National Guard?

Yes. These military organizations also use the ASVAB for enlistment purposes.

What should I do if a service recruiter contacts me?

You may be contacted by a service recruiter before you graduate. If you want to learn about the many opportunities available through military service, arrange for a follow-up meeting. However, you are under no obligation to the military as a result of taking the ASVAB.

Is the ASVAB administered other than in the school testing program?

Yes. ASVAB is also used in the regular military enlistment program. It is administered at approximately sixty-five Military Entrance Processing Stations located throughout the United States. Each year, hundreds of thousands of young men and women who are interested in enlisting in the uniformed services (Army, Navy, Air Force, Marines, and Coast Guard) but who did not take the ASVAB while in school are examined and processed at these military stations.

Is any special preparation necessary before taking the ASVAB?

Yes. A certain amount of preparation is required for taking any examination. Whether it is an athletic competition or a written test, preparation is a *must* in order to achieve the best results. Your test scores

I SURVIVED BASIC TRAINING

Although Michael Hipszky was eager to join the Navy, it didn't take long for doubts about his decision to hit him. While he was riding the bus to the Navy's Basic Training facility, he asked himself THE QUESTION—"Why am I putting myself through this mess?" Recalls Michael, "It crosses everyone's mind. As far as I know, in my division, everyone had the same thought. 'I want to go home.' Those first few days are intense."

He figures it's because you lose control the minute you walk through the door on the first day of Basic Training. Someone's telling you (in a very loud voice) how to stand at attention, how to stand in line, how to do just about everything. "So many things go through your head," says Michael. He soon found that if he followed three rules, life got a whole lot easier:

1. **KEEP YOUR MOUTH SHUT.** "Your mouth is your biggest problem," he warns, "talking when you aren't supposed to and saying dumb things."

2. **PAY ATTENTION TO DETAIL.** "They'll say things like, 'Grab the door knob, turn it half to the right, and go through.' A lot of people will just pull it open and get yelled at. They teach you how to fold your clothes and clean the head (toilet). Everything is paying attention to detail," Michael advises.

3. **DON'T THINK FOR YOURSELF.** "Wait to be told what to do," Michael says, recalling the time his group was handed a form and told to wait until ordered to fill it out. Many saw that the form was asking for information like name, date, and division and began filling it out, only to get in trouble because they didn't wait.

Having been through Basic Training, Michael now knows that every little thing—from folding T-shirts the exact way he'd been told to do (arms folded in), to sweeping the floor, to marching—is all part of the training process. "You don't realize it until you're done," he says.

Despite all the yelling and push-ups, Michael values the training he got in the classes. He learned how to put out different kinds of fires, how to manage his money, how to identify aircraft—even etiquette. And that's just for starters.

His lowest point was about halfway through Basic, which, he found out, usually happens for everyone at the same time. "The first half of Basic, everything is so surreal. Then you get halfway through, and finishing up Basic seems so far away. You're always busy, whether you're stenciling your clothes or marching. You march a lot," he says. But then he reached his highest point, which was pass-in review at the end of the training and winning awards. He knew he'd done well. Looking into his future with the Navy, Michael says, "I want to see the world and have the experiences that the Navy can give you." Having finished Basic Training, he's well on his way.

Airman Michael Hipszky
United States Navy

reflect not only your ability but also the time and effort in preparing for the test. The uniformed services use ASVAB to help determine a person's qualification for enlistment and to help indicate the vocational areas for which the person is best suited. Achieving your maximum score will increase your vocational opportunities. So take practice tests to prepare.

BASIC TRAINING: WHAT HAVE I GOTTEN MYSELF INTO?

The main objective of Basic Training is to transform civilians into well-disciplined military personnel in a matter of weeks. Performing such a monumental task takes a lot of hard work, both mentally and physically. For most people, Basic Training ends with a parade on graduation day. For others, though, it ends somewhere short of graduation. It is those "horror stories" that make Basic Training the one biggest fear, or anxiety-inducer, for those considering military enlistment.

Unlike the boot camp you may have heard about from your Uncle Louie or seen on television, today's Basic Training doesn't include the verbal and physical abuse of yesterday. All of the military branches are ensuring that new enlistees are treated fairly and with dignity. Not that enlistees aren't yelled at (because they are); however, the vulgarity and demeaning verbal attacks are a thing of the past. There are, from time to time, incidents involving instructors who contradict the military's policies. These violations, however, receive a lot of attention, are thoroughly investigated, and usually end up with disciplinary action taken against those involved in the abuse.

"A lot of kids are worried about Marine boot camp. They've seen movies or heard stories. Boot camp is not set up to make you fail. It's challenging, but that's the purpose of it. You're learning that no matter what life throws at you, you will be able to improvise, adapt, and overcome."

Sergeant Ian Bonnell, Infantry Sergeant
United States Marines

If you are still uncertain of which branch you'd like to join, do not allow the type of Basic Training you'll receive to be your only deciding factor. If, for example, the Marine Corps meets all your needs and is clearly your first choice, do not select the Air Force because its Basic Training seems easier. Conversely, if the Air Force is clearly your first choice, do not select the Marine Corps because it has the "toughest" Basic Training, and you want to prove you are up to the challenge. Basic Training is a means of your transformation from civilian life to military life. It happens in a relatively short period of time compared to the entire length of your enlistment.

Some Words on Getting through Basic Training

No matter what you may have heard or read elsewhere, there are no secrets to getting through Basic Training; only common sense and preparation will get you through. Here are some do's and don'ts that should help you survive Basic Training for any of the services. Although following these guidelines will not ensure your success at Basic Training, your chances for success will be greatly improved by following them.

Before Arriving at Basic Training

DO:
- Start an exercise program.
- Maintain a sensible diet.
- Stay out of trouble. (For example, pay any traffic fines promptly before leaving for Basic Training.)
- Ensure that all of your financial obligations are in order.
- Bring the required items that you are told to bring.
- Give up smoking.

DON'T:
- Skip preparing yourself physically because you think that Basic Training will whip you into shape.
- Abuse drugs and/or alcohol.
- Have a big send-off party and get drunk the night before you leave for Basic Training.
- Leave home with open tickets, summonses, or warrants.
- Get yourself into heavy debt (such as buying a new car).
- Bring any prohibited items.
- Have your hair cut in a radical manner. (This includes having your head shaved. Men will receive a "very close" haircut shortly after arriving at Basic Training.)
- Have any part of your body pierced, tattooed, or otherwise altered.

PAYING FOR COLLEGE THROUGH THE ARMED SERVICES

You can take any of the following three paths into the armed services—all of which provide opportunities for financial assistance for college.

Enlisted Personnel

All five branches of the armed services offer college-credit courses on base. Enlisted personnel can also take college courses at civilian colleges while on active duty.

"In the Air Force, you're not only getting an education, but also experience. You could go to school for a degree in avionics technology, but in the Air Force, you get the teaching and the experience—real-world, hands-on experience—that makes your education marketable."
Master Sergeant Timothy Little
United States Air Force

ROTC

More than 40,000 college students participate in Reserve Officers' Training Corps (ROTC). Two-, three-, and four-year ROTC scholarships are available to outstanding students. You can try ROTC at no obligation for two years or, if you have a four-year scholarship, for one year. Normally, all ROTC classes, uniforms, and books are free. ROTC graduates are required to serve in the military for a set period of time, either full-time on active duty or part-time in the Reserve or National Guard. Qualifying graduates can delay their service to go to graduate or professional school first.

Part 3: The Road to More Education

WHAT'S MY JOB?—OH, I JUST DRIVE AN ARMORED CARRIER AROUND

Justin Platt thought maybe he would join the Army, but first he had a few doubts to overcome. A big one was his reluctance to be away from friends and family. Another one was the overseas duty—something he definitely didn't want. But his desire to get his foot in the door of medical training won out. When he found out that he could get an education in the Army to become a nurse, his fears flew out the window, and Justin joined the Army. He's glad he did.

Stationed at Fort Carson in Colorado, Justin's been through Basic Training and is on his first stint of active duty working in—you guessed it—the medical field. "I work in an aid station, which is like a mini hospital," he says. He's the one who does the screening for anyone in his battalion who comes into sick call. Okay, it's from 5 a.m. to 7 p.m., but Justin doesn't mind.

Justin's job on active duty doesn't just consist of handing out Band-Aids and cough drops. He's also learning how to drive an armored carrier—not your usual medical training. But in the field, Army medics have to be able to pick up the wounded, which means knowing how to drive what he describes as a souped-up SUV—only instead of tires, it has tracks.

Justin plans to get enough rank to go from green to gold—enlisted to officer. "I'll have to take additional college courses to get a four-year degree," he says. It'll take him about seven years, including his Army duty. Not bad for someone who once had doubts about joining the military.

Private First Class Justin Platt
Fort Carson, Colorado

U.S. Service Academies

Openings at the U.S. service academies are few, so it pays to get information early. Every student is on a full scholarship, but free does not mean easy—these intense programs train graduates to meet the demands of leadership and success.

West Point. The U.S. Military Academy (Army) offers a broad-based academic program with forty-two majors in various fields of study. Extensive training and leadership experience go hand in hand with academics. *www.usma.edu*

Annapolis. The U.S. Naval Academy is a unique blend of tradition and state-of-the-art technology. Its core curriculum includes nineteen major fields of study, and classroom work is supported by practical experience in leadership and professional operations. *www.usna.edu*

Air Force Academy. The U.S. Air Force Academy prepares and motivates cadets for careers as Air Force officers. The academy offers a B.S. degree in thirty-two majors. Graduates receive a reserve commission as a second lieutenant in the Air Force. *www.usafa.edu*

Coast Guard Academy. This broad-based education, which leads to a B.S. degree in eight technical or professional majors, includes a thorough grounding in the professional skills necessary for the Coast Guard's work. *www.cga.edu*

Financing Higher Education through the U.S. Armed Forces

The U.S. military provides a number of options to help students and their parents get financial aid for postsecondary education.

The Active Duty Montgomery GI Bill

The Active Duty Montgomery GI Bill, called "ADMGIB" for short, provides up to 36 months of education benefits to eligible veterans for college, business, technical or vocational courses, correspondence courses, apprenticeship/job training, and flight training. You may be an eligible veteran if you get an Honorable Discharge; you have a High School Diploma or GED, or, in some cases, 12 hours of college credit; AND you meet the necessary requirements related to military service. You MUST have elected to participate in the ADMGIB, which involves giving up $100 of your pay per month for the first twelve months of military service. The monthly benefit paid to you is based on the type of training you take, length of your service, your category, and if the Department of Defense put extra money in your *College* Fund (called "kicker"). You usually have ten years to use your MGIB benefits, but the time limit can be less, in some cases, and longer under certain circumstances.

The Selected Reserve Montgomery GI Bill

The Selected Reserve Montgomery GI Bill (SRMGIB) may be available to you if you are a member of the Selected Reserve. The Selected Reserve includes the Army Reserve, Navy Reserve, Air Force Reserve, Marine Corps Reserve and Coast Guard Reserve, and the Army National Guard and the Air National Guard. You may use this education assistance program for degree programs, certificate or correspondence courses, cooperative training, independent study programs, apprenticeship/on-the-job training, and vocational flight training programs. Remedial, refresher, and deficiency training are available under certain circumstances. Eligibility for this program is determined by the Selected Reserve components. VA makes the payments for this program. Your benefit entitlement ends fourteen years from the date of your eligibility for the program, or on the day you leave the Selected Reserve.

Call toll-free 888-GI-BILL-1 for more information, or visit the Web site at www.gibill.va.gov/.

Tuition Assistance

All branches of the military pay up to 75 percent of tuition for full-time, active-duty enlistees who take courses at community colleges or by correspondence during their tours of duty. Details vary by service.

The Community College of the Air Force

Enlisted Air Force personnel can convert their technical training and military experience into academic credit, earning an associate degree, an occupational instructor's certificate, or a trade school certificate. Participants receive an official transcript from this fully accredited program. You can visit the Community College of the Air Force on line at www.au.af.mil/au/ccaf.

Educational Loan-Repayment Program

The Armed Services can help repay government-insured and other approved loans. Each of the services is free to offer such programs, but individual policies differ.

Other Forms of Tuition Assistance

Each branch of the military offers its own education incentives. To find out more, check with a local recruiting office.

YOU AND THE WORKPLACE

SOME OF YOU WILL GO TO COLLEGE first and then look for jobs. Some of you might work for a few years and then go to college. And many of you will go immediately into the workforce and bypass college altogether. Whenever you become an employee, you'll want to know what you can do to succeed on the job and move to both higher levels of responsibility and more pay.

Chapter 12

JUMP INTO WORK

Almost everyone ends up in the workforce at some point. No matter when you plan to receive that first full-time paycheck, there are some things you'll need to do to prepare yourself for the world of work.

AT EACH GRADE LEVEL, there are specific steps you should take regardless of whether or not you plan to attend college immediately following high school. In fact, college and career timelines should coincide, according to guidance counselors and career specialists, and students should take college-preparatory courses, even if they aren't planning on attending college.

THE COLLEGE/CAREER TIMELINE

The following timeline will help you meet college requirements and prepare you for work. In an effort to make sure that you are adequately preparing for both school and work, incorporate these five steps into your career/college timeline:

1. **Take an aptitude test.** You can do this as early as the sixth grade, but even if you don't do this until high school, it's not too late. By doing so, you will begin to get a feel for what areas you might be good at and enjoy. Your guidance counselor should have a test in his or her office for you to take, or you can try the ASVAB (see page 127). Thousands of high school students take this test every year to discover possible career paths—and taking the ASVAB doesn't require you to join the military!

2. **Beginning in middle school, you should start considering what your options are after high school.** However, if you're only starting to think about this in high school, that's okay, too. Keep a notebook of information gathered from field trips, job-shadowing experiences, mentoring programs, and career fairs to help you make sense of the possibilities open to you. This process should continue through high school. Many schools offer job shadowing and internship programs for students to explore different vocational avenues. Take advantage of these opportunities if you can. Too often, students don't explore the workplace until after they've taken the courses necessary to enter a particular profession, only to discover it wasn't the career they dreamed of after all.

3. **No later than the tenth grade, visit a vocational center to look at the training programs offered.** Some public school systems send students to vocational and career program centers for career exploration.

TAKING A BREAK BETWEEN HIGH SCHOOL AND COLLEGE

Because of the soaring costs of college tuition today, college is no longer a place to "find yourself." It is a costly investment in your future. The career you choose to pursue may or may not require additional education; your research will determine whether or not it's required or preferred. If you decide not to attend college immediately after high school, however, don't consider it to be a closed door. Taking some time off between high school and college is considered perfectly acceptable by employers. Many students simply need a break after thirteen years of schooling. Most experts agree that it's better to be ready and prepared for college; many adults get more out of their classes after they've had a few years to mature.

Source: Street Smart Career Guide: A Step-by-Step Program for Your Career Development.

4. **During your junior and senior years, be sure to create a portfolio of practice resumes, writing samples, and a list of work skills.** This portfolio should also include your high school transcript and letters of recommendation. It will serve as a valuable reference tool when it comes time to apply for jobs.

5. **By tenth or eleventh grade, you should begin focusing on a specific career path.** More employers today are looking for employees who have both the education and work experience that relates to the career field for which they're interviewing. If you are looking for part-time employment, you should consider jobs that pertain to your field of study. Until you start interacting with people in the field, you won't have a realistic feel of what's involved in that profession. If you're planning on heading into the workplace right after high school, take a look at the following pages for a list of careers that don't require a four-year degree.

WRITING YOUR RESUME

Resumes are a critical part of getting a job. A resume is an introduction of your skills to a potential employer. For that reason, your resume must stand out in a crowd because some employers receive dozens of resumes each week. A resume that is too long, cluttered, or disorganized may find its way to the "circular file," also known as the trash can. You can avoid this hazard by creating a resume that is short, presentable, and easy to read.

Remember that a resume is a summary of who you are and an outline of your experiences, skills, and goals. While writing it, you may discover some talents that you weren't aware you had, and that will help boost your confidence for the job search.

Begin by collecting facts about yourself, including where you went to high school, your past and present jobs, activities, interests, and leadership roles. Next to the individual activities, write down what responsibilities you had. For example, something as simple as babysitting requires the ability to settle disagreements and supervise others.

Next, decide on how you would like to format your resume. Most hiring managers expect to see one of two types of resumes: chronological or functional. The chronological resume is the most traditional, supplying the reader with a sequential listing (from present to past) of your accomplishments. Because the emphasis here is on past employment experience, high school and college students with little or no employment history might want to avoid this resume type. A functional resume, on the other hand, highlights a person's abilities rather than his or her work history. Entry-level candidates who want to focus on skills rather than credentials should consider using a functional resume.

(Continued on page 139)

FIND OUT WHAT A *ResumeEdge*™ RESUME CAN DO FOR YOU!

With more than one thousand years of combined resume writing experience, the *ResumeEdge* team of Certified Professional Resume Writers specializes in 40 different industries to provide entry-level job seekers with the best resume and cover letter writing services available anywhere. While you may lack professional experience as a recent graduate, your resume can compensate for this by emphasizing the skills and attributes required by your target position. *ResumeEdge* writers have inside knowledge of what employers look for and market your strengths, potential, and accomplishments more effectively. Tens of thousands of entry-level applicants have shortened their job search time and improved their resume response rate. Visit www.resumeedge.com and find out what a *ResumeEdge* resume can do for you!

Chapter 12: Jump into Work

CAREERS WITHOUT A FOUR-YEAR DEGREE

Some students spend a few years in the workplace before going to college. Others begin their career with a high school diploma, a vocational certificate, or up to two years of education or training after high school.

With that in mind, sometimes it's easier to know what you don't want rather than what you do want. Take a look at the list below, and check off the careers that interest you. Perhaps you've thought of something you'd like to do that isn't on this list. Well, don't dump your hopes. There are many different levels of training and education that can lead you to the career of your dreams. Since this list is not all-inclusive, you should check with your high school counselor or go on line to research the training you'll need for the job or career you want—without a four-year degree. Then talk to your guidance counselor, teacher, librarian, or career counselor for more information about the careers on the list below or those you've researched on your own.

AGRICULTURE AND NATURAL RESOURCES
High school/vocational diploma
- Fisher
- Groundskeeper
- Logger
- Pest Controller

Up to two years beyond high school
- Fish and Game Warden
- Tree Surgeon

APPLIED ARTS (VISUAL)
High school/vocational diploma
- Floral Arranger
- Merchandise Displayer
- Painter (artist)

Up to two years beyond high school
- Cartoonist
- Commercial Artist
- Fashion Designer
- Interior Decorator
- Photographer

APPLIED ARTS (WRITTEN AND SPOKEN)
High school/vocational diploma
- Proofreader

Up to two years beyond high school
- Advertising copywriter
- Legal Assistant

BUSINESS MACHINE/COMPUTER OPERATION
High school/vocational diploma
- Data Entry
- Statistical Clerk
- Telephone Operator
- Typist

Up to two years beyond high school
- Computer Operator
- Motion Picture Projectionist

CONSTRUCTION AND MAINTENANCE
High school/vocational diploma
- Bricklayer
- Construction Laborer
- Elevator Mechanic
- Floor Covering Installer
- Heavy Equipment Operator
- Janitor
- Maintenance Mechanic

Up to two years beyond high school
- Building Inspector
- Carpenter
- Electrician
- Insulation Worker
- Lather
- Painter (construction)
- Pipefitter
- Plumber
- Roofer
- Sheet Metal Worker
- Structural Steel Worker
- Tile Setter

CRAFTS AND RELATED SERVICES
High school/vocational diploma
- Baker/Cook/Chef
- Butcher
- Furniture Upholsterer
- Housekeeper (hotel)
- Tailor/Dressmaker

Up to two years beyond high school
- Dry Cleaner
- Jeweler
- Locksmith
- Musical Instrument Repairer

CREATIVE/PERFORMING ARTS
High school/vocational diploma
- Singer
- Stunt Performer

Up to two years beyond high school
- Actor/Actress
- Dancer/Choreographer
- Musician
- Writer/Author

EDUCATION AND RELATED SERVICES
High school/vocational diploma
- Nursery School Attendant
- Teacher's Aide

ENGINEERING AND RELATED TECHNOLOGIES
High school/vocational diploma
- Biomedical Equipment Technician
- Laser Technician

Up to two years beyond high school
- Aerospace Engineer Technician
- Broadcast Technician
- Chemical Laboratory Technician
- Civil Engineering Technician
- Computer Programmer
- Computer Service Technician
- Electronic Technician
- Energy Conservation Technician
- Industrial Engineering Technician
- Laboratory Tester
- Mechanical Engineering Technician
- Metallurgical Technician
- Pollution Control Technician
- Quality Control Technician
- Robot Technician
- Surveyor (land)
- Technical Illustrator
- Tool Designer
- Weather Observer

FINANCIAL TRANSACTIONS
High school/vocational diploma
- Accounting Clerk
- Bank Teller
- Cashier
- Payroll Clerk
- Travel Agent

Up to two years beyond high school
- Bookkeeper
- Loan Officer

HEALTH CARE (GENERAL)
High school/vocational diploma
- Dental Assistant
- Medical Assistant
- Nursing/Psychiatric Aide

Up to two years beyond high school
- Dietetic Technician
- Nurse (practical)
- Nurse (registered)
- Optometric Assistant
- Physical Therapist's Assistant
- Physician's Assistant
- Recreation Therapist

HEALTH-CARE SPECIALTIES AND TECHNOLOGIES
High school/vocational diploma
- Dialysis Technician

Up to two years beyond high school
- Dental Hygienist
- Dental Laboratory Technician
- EEG Technologist
- EKG Technician
- Emergency Medical Technician
- Medical Laboratory Technician
- Medical Technologist
- Nuclear Medicine Technologist
- Operating Room Technician
- Optician
- Radiation Therapy Technologist
- Radiologic Technologist
- Respiratory Therapist
- Sonographer

PETERSON'S GET A JUMP!

Part 4: You and the Workplace

HOME/BUSINESS EQUIPMENT REPAIR
High school/vocational diploma
- Air-Conditioning/Refrigeration/Heating Mechanic
- Appliance Servicer
- Coin Machine Mechanic

Up to two years beyond high school
- Communications Equipment Mechanic
- Line Installer/Splicer
- Office Machine Servicer
- Radio/TV Repairer
- Telephone Installer

INDUSTRIAL EQUIPMENT OPERATIONS AND REPAIR
High school/vocational diploma
- Assembler
- Blaster
- Boilermaker
- Coal Equipment Operator
- Compressor House Operator
- Crater
- Dock Worker
- Forging Press Operator
- Furnace Operator
- Heat Treater
- Machine Tool Operator
- Material Handler
- Miner
- Sailor
- Sewing Machine Operator

Up to two years beyond high school
- Bookbinder
- Compositor/Typesetter
- Electronic Equipment Repairer
- Electroplater
- Firefighter
- Instrument Mechanic
- Lithographer
- Machine Repairer
- Machinist
- Millwright
- Molder
- Nuclear Reactor Operator
- Patternmaker
- Photoengraver
- Power House Mechanic
- Power Plant Operator
- Printing Press Operator
- Stationery Engineer
- Tool and Die Maker
- Water Plant Operator
- Welder
- Wire Drawer

MANAGEMENT AND PLANNING
High school/vocational diploma
- Administrative Assistant
- Food Service Supervisor
- Postmaster
- Service Station Manager

Up to two years beyond high school
- Benefits Manager
- Building Manager
- Caterer
- Contractor
- Credit Manager
- Customer Service Coordinator
- Employment Interviewer
- Executive Housekeeper
- Funeral Director
- Hotel/Motel Manager
- Importer/Exporter
- Insurance Manager
- Manager (small business)
- Office Manager
- Personnel Manager
- Restaurant/Bar Manager
- Store Manager
- Supermarket Manager

MARKETING AND SALES
High school/vocational diploma
- Auctioneer
- Bill Collector
- Driver (route)
- Fashion Model
- Product Demonstrator
- Salesperson (general)
- Sample Distributor

Up to two years beyond high school
- Claims Adjuster
- Insurance Worker
- Manufacturer's Representative
- Real Estate Agent
- Sales Manager
- Travel Agent
- Travel Guide

PERSONAL AND CUSTOMER SERVICE
High school/vocational diploma
- Barber
- Bartender
- Beautician
- Child-Care Worker
- Counter Attendant
- Dining Room Attendant
- Electrologist
- Flight Attendant
- Host/Hostess
- Houseparent
- Manicurist
- Parking Lot Attendant
- Porter
- Private Household Worker
- Waiter/Waitress

RECORDS AND COMMUNICATIONS
High school/vocational diploma
- Billing Clerk
- Clerk (general)
- File Clerk
- Foreign Trade Clerk
- Hotel Clerk
- Meter Reader
- Postal Clerk
- Receptionist
- Stenographer

Up to two years beyond high school
- Court Reporter
- Legal Secretary
- Library Assistant
- Library Technician
- Medical Records Technician
- Medical Secretary
- Personnel Assistant
- Secretary
- Travel Clerk

SOCIAL AND GOVERNMENT
High school/vocational diploma
- Corrections Officer
- Police Officer
- Security Guard
- Store Detective

Up to two years beyond high school
- Detective (police)
- Hazardous Waste Technician
- Recreation Leader
- Personal/Customer Services

STORAGE AND DISPATCHING
High school/vocational diploma
- Dispatcher
- Mail Carrier
- Railroad Conductor
- Shipping/Receiving Clerk
- Stock Clerk
- Tool Crib Attendant
- Warehouse Worker

Up to two years beyond high school
- Warehouse Supervisor

VEHICLE OPERATION AND REPAIR
High school/vocational diploma
- Automotive Painter
- Bus Driver
- Chauffeur
- Diesel Mechanic
- Farm Equipment Mechanic
- Forklift Operator
- Heavy Equipment Mechanic
- Locomotive Engineer
- Railroad Braker
- Refuse Collector
- Service Station Attendant
- Taxicab Driver
- Truck Driver

Up to two years beyond high school
- Aircraft Mechanic
- Airplane Pilot
- Auto Body Repairer
- Automotive Mechanic
- Garage Supervisor
- Motorcycle Mechanic

Parts of a Resume

At the very least, your resume should include the following components:

Heading: Centered at the top of the page should be your name, address, phone number, and e-mail address.

Objective: In one sentence, tell the employer the type of work for which you are looking.

Education: Beginning with your most recent school or program, include the date (or expected date) of completion, the degree or certificate earned, and the address of the institution. Don't overlook any workshops or seminars, self-study, or on-the-job training in which you have been involved. If any courses particularly lend themselves to the type of work for which you are applying, include them. Mention grade point averages and class rank when they are especially impressive.

Skills and abilities: Until you've actually listed these on paper, you can easily overlook many of them. They may be as varied as the ability to work with computers or being captain of the girl's basketball team.

Work experience: If you don't have any, skip this section. If you do, begin with your most recent employer and include the date you left the job, your job title, the company name, and the company address. If you are still employed there, simply enter your start date and "to present" for the date. Include notable accomplishments for each job. High school and college students with little work experience shouldn't be shy about including summer, part-time, and volunteer jobs, such as lifeguarding, babysitting, delivering pizzas, or volunteering at local parks.

Personal: Here's your opportunity to include your special talents and interests as well as notable accomplishments or experiences.

References: Most experts agree that it's best to simply state that references are available upon request. However, if you do decide to list names, addresses, and phone numbers, limit yourself to no more than three. Make sure you inform any people whom you have listed that they may be contacted.

SAMPLE FUNCTIONAL RESUME

Michele A. Thomas
3467 Main Street
Atlanta, Georgia 30308
404-555-3423
E-mail: mthomas_987654321@yahoo.com

OBJECTIVE

Seeking a sales position in the wireless phone industry

EDUCATION

High School Diploma, June 2005

John F. Kennedy High School, Atlanta, Georgia

SKILLS

Computer literate, IBM: MS Works, MS Word, WordPerfect, Netscape; Macintosh: MS Word, Excel

ACTIVITIES/LEADERSHIP

Student Government secretary, 2004–2005

Key Club vice president, 2003–2004

Future Business Leaders of America

AWARDS

Varsity Swim Club (Captain; MVP Junior, Senior; Sportsmanship Award)
Outstanding Community Service Award, 2004

EXPERIENCE

Sales Clerk, The Limited, Atlanta, Georgia; part-time, September 2004 to present

Cashier, Winn-Dixie Supermarkets, Atlanta, Georgia, Summers 2002 and 2003

INTERESTS

Swimming, reading, computers

REFERENCES

Available upon request

SAMPLE COVER LETTER

Take a look at how this student's cover letter applied the facts outlined in her resume to the job to which she's applying. You can use this letter to help you get started on your own cover letters. Text that appears in all caps below indicates the kind of information you need to include in that section. Before you send your letter, proofread it for mistakes and ask a parent or friend you trust to look it over as well.

(DATE)
June 29, 2007

(YOUR ADDRESS)
3467 Main Street
Atlanta, Georgia 30308
Phone: 404-555-3423
E-mail: mthomas_987654321@yahoo.com

(PERSON—BY NAME—TO WHOM YOU'RE SENDING THE LETTER)
Mr. Charles E. Pence
Manager, Human Resources
NexAir Wireless
20201 East Sixth Street
Atlanta, Georgia 30372

Dear Mr. Pence:

(HOW YOU HEARD OF THE POSITION)
Your job announcement in the *Atlanta Gazette* for an entry-level sales position asked for someone who has both computer and sales skills. **(SOMETHING EXTRA THAT WILL INTEREST THE READER)** My training and past job experience fit both of those categories. I also bring an enthusiasm and desire to begin my career in a communications firm such as NexAir.

(WHAT PRACTICAL SKILLS YOU CAN BRING TO THE POSITION)
A few weeks ago, I graduated from John F. Kennedy High School here in Atlanta. While in school, I concentrated on gaining computer skills on both IBM and Macintosh machines and participated in organizations such as the Key Club, in which I was vice president, and the Future Business Leaders of America.

(RELATE PAST EXPERIENCE TO DESIRED JOB)
As you will see from my resume, I worked as a cashier at Winn-Dixie Supermarket for two summers and am currently employed as a sales clerk at The Limited. From these two positions, I have gained valuable customer service skills and an attention to detail, qualities which I am sure are of utmost importance to you as you make your hiring decision.

I would very much like to interview for the position and am available at your convenience. I look forward to hearing from you soon.

Sincerely,

Michele A. Thomas

Resume-Writing Tips

These tips will help as you begin constructing your resume:

- Keep the resume short and simple. Although senior executives may use as many as two or three pages, recent graduates should limit themselves to one page.

- Capitalize headings.

- Keep sentences short; avoid writing in paragraphs.

- Use language that is simple, not flowery or complex.

- Be specific, and offer examples when appropriate.

- Emphasize achievements.

- Be honest.

- Don't include information about salary or wages unless specifically requested.

- Use high-quality, white, beige, or gray, 8 ½" × 11" paper.

- Make good use of white space by leaving adequate side and top margins on the paper.

- Make what you write presentable and use good business style.

- Because your resume should be a reflection of your personality, write it yourself.

- Avoid gimmicks such as colored paper, photos, or clip art.

- Make good use of bullets or asterisks, underlining, and bold print.

- Proofread your work, and have someone you trust proofread it also.

- Be neat and accurate.

- Never send a resume without a cover letter.

The Cover Letter

Every resume should be accompanied by a cover letter. This is often the most crucial part of your job search because the letter will be the first thing that a potential employer reads. When you include a cover letter, you're showing the employer that you care enough to take the time to address him or her personally and that you are genuinely interested in the job.

Always call the company and verify the name and title of the person to whom you are addressing the letter. Although you will want to keep your letter brief, introduce yourself and begin with a statement that will catch the reader's attention. Indicate the position you are applying for and mention if someone referred you or if you are simply responding to a newspaper ad. Draw attention to yourself by including something that will arouse the employer's curiosity about your experience and accomplishments. A cover letter should request something, most commonly an interview. Sign and date your letter. Then follow up with a phone call a few days after you're sure the letter has been received. Persistence pays!

JOB HUNTING 101

High school is a time for taking classes and learning, developing relationships with others, becoming involved in extracurricular activities that teach valuable life skills, and generally preparing for college or a job. Regardless of where you're headed after high school, you need to learn how to create a favorable impression. That can mean setting some clear, attainable goals for yourself, putting them down on paper in the form of a resume and cover letter, and convincing interviewers that you are, indeed, the person for whom they are looking. In short, learn how to sell yourself. A brief course in Job Hunting 101 will help you do just that.

Marketing Yourself

You can use several approaches to market yourself successfully. Networking, the continual process of contacting friends and relatives, is a great way to get information about job openings. Seventy-five percent of the job openings in this country are not advertised but are filled by friends, relatives, and acquaintances of current employees. From the employer's perspective, there is less risk associated with hiring someone recommended by an employee than hiring someone unknown. Networking is powerful. Everyone has a primary network of people they know and talk to frequently. Those acquaintances know and talk to networks of their own, thereby creating a secondary network for you and multiplying the number of individuals who know what you're looking for in a job.

Broadcasting is another marketing method in which you gather a list of companies that interest you and then mail them letters asking for job interviews. Although the rate of return on your mailings is small, two thirds of all job hunters use this approach, and half of those who use it find a job. You will increase your response rate by addressing your letter to a particular person—the one who has the power to hire you—and by following up with a phone call a few days after the letter has been received. To obtain the manager's name, simply call the company and ask the receptionist for the person's name, job title, and correct spelling. Good resources for finding potential employers include referrals, community agencies, job fairs, newspaper ads, trade directories, trade journals, state indexes, the local chamber of commerce, the Yellow Pages, and the Web. The following tips can help as you begin hunting for the perfect job:

- Job-hunting is time-intensive. Do your homework and take it seriously by using every opportunity available to you.

- Prepare yourself for the fact that there will be far more rejections than acceptances.

- Consider taking a temporary job while you continue the job hunt. It will help pay the bills and give you new skills to boost your resume at the same time.

- Research the activities of potential employers and show that you have studied them when you're being interviewed.

- Keep careful records of all contacts and follow-up activities.

- Don't ignore any job leads—act on every tip you get.

- Stay positive.

With all these thoughts in mind, you should be ready to begin the process of making people believe in you, and that's a major part of being successful in your job hunt.

THE JOB INTERVIEW

You can prevent some of the preinterview jitters by adequately preparing. Remember that you have nothing to lose and that you, too, are doing the choosing. Just as you are waiting and hoping to be offered a job, you have the option of choosing whether or not to accept an offer. It's all right to feel somewhat anxious, but keep everything in perspective. This is an adventure, and you are in control. Most important, remember to be yourself. With all of this in mind, consider some of the following points of the interview process:

- Speak up during the interview, and furnish the interviewer with the information he or she needs in order to make an informed decision. It is especially impressive if you can remember the names of people to whom you've been introduced. People like to be called by name, and it shows that you took the initiative to remember them.

- Always arrive a few minutes early for the interview, and look your best. The way you act and dress tells the interviewer plenty about your attitude and personality. Sloppy dress, chewing gum, and cigarettes have no place at an interview and will probably cut your interview short. Instead, dress professionally and appropriately for the job. Avoid heavy makeup, short skirts, jeans, and untidy or flashy clothing of any kind.

The best way to prepare for the interview is to practice. Have a friend or relative play the role of the interviewer, and go over some of the most commonly asked questions. Learn as much as you can about the company you're interviewing with—it pays to do your homework. When you show a potential employer that you've taken the time and initiative to learn about his or her company, you're showing that you will be a motivated and hardworking employee. Employers fear laziness and minimal effort, looking instead for workers who don't always have to be told what to do and when to do it.

Here is a list of interview questions you can expect to have to answer:

- **Tell me a little bit about yourself.** This is your chance to pitch your qualifications for the job in 2 minutes. Provide a few details about your education, previous jobs you've held, and extracurricular activities that relate to the position for which you're interviewing.

- **Are you at your best when working alone or in a group?** The safest answer is "Both." Most companies today cluster their employees into work groups, so you will need strong interpersonal skills. However, on occasion, you may be required to work on projects alone.

- **What did you like the most about your last job? What did you dislike the most about it?** You should always accentuate the positives in an interview, so focus primarily on what you liked. Also be honest about what you disliked, but then explain how facing the negatives helped you grow as an employee.

- **What are your career goals?** Be sure you've done some research on the company and industry before your interview. When this question comes up, talk realistically about how far you believe your skills and talents will take you and what actions you plan to take to ensure this happens, such as pursuing more education.

Take the time to prepare some answers to these commonly asked questions. For instance, if you haven't set at least one career goal for yourself, do it now. Be ready to describe it to the interviewer. Likewise, you should be able to talk about your last job, including what you liked the most and the least. Adapt your answers so they apply to the job for which you are presently interviewing. Other questions that might be asked include:

- What qualifications do you have?

- Why do you want to work for us?

- Do you enjoy school? Why or why not?

FINDING JOBS ON THE WEB

As mentioned, you can find jobs through your network of friends, family, and acquaintances; through classified ads in the newspaper; and through career Web pages. Here is a listing of popular Web sites that not only offer job search technology but also information on resume writing, interviewing, and other important career advice.

www.monster.com   www.careerbuilder.com

www.hotjobs.com   www.vault.com

- Do you plan to continue your education?
- What do you plan to be doing five years from now?
- What motivates you to do a good job?

If you are seeking a job as a manager, you might respond by saying you liked the varied responsibilities of your past job. Recall that you enjoyed the unexpected challenges and flexible schedule. And when describing what you liked least, make sure you respond with some function or area of responsibility that has nothing to do with the responsibilities of the job you hope to get.

More than likely, you'll be asked to tell the interviewer something about yourself. This is your chance to "toot your horn," but don't ramble. You might ask the interviewer specifically what he or she would like to hear about: your educational background or recent experiences and responsibilities in your present or last job. After he or she chooses, stick to the basics; the next move belongs to the interviewer.

When asked about personal strengths and weaknesses, given that the question is two parts, begin with a weakness so you can end on a strong note with your strengths. Again, try to connect your description of a strength or weakness with the requirements for the job. Naturally, it wouldn't be wise to reveal a serious weakness about yourself, but you can mention how you have changed your shortcomings. You might say, "I like to get my work done fast, but I consciously try to slow down a little to make sure I'm careful and accurate." When it comes to strengths, don't exaggerate, but don't sell yourself short either.

Asking Questions

You can ask questions, too. In fact, the interviewer expects you to ask questions to determine if the job is right for you, just as he or she will be trying to find out if you'll be successful working for his or her company. When you ask questions, it shows that you're interested and want to learn more. When the type of question you ask indicates that you've done your homework regarding the job and the company, your interviewer will be impressed. Avoid asking questions about salary or fringe benefits, anything adversarial, or questions that show you have a negative opinion of the company. It's all right to list your questions on a piece of paper; it's the quality of the question that's important, not whether you can remember it. Here are a few sample questions that you should consider asking if the topics don't come up in your interview:

- What kind of responsibilities come with this job?
- How is the department organized?
- What will be the first project for the new hire to tackle?
- What is a typical career advancement path for a person in this position?
- Who will the supervisor be for this position, and can I meet him or her?
- What is the office environment like? Is it casual or corporate?
- When do you expect to reach a hiring decision?

Following Up

After the interview, follow up with a thank-you note to the interviewer. Not only is it a thoughtful gesture, it triggers the interviewer's memory about you and shows that you have a genuine interest in the job. Your thank-you note should be written in a business letter format and should highlight the key points in your interview.

During the interview process, remember that you will not appeal to everyone who interviews you. If your first experience doesn't work out, don't get discouraged. Keep trying.

SAMPLE THANK-YOU LETTER

After you've interviewed for a job, it's important to reiterate your interest in the position by sending a thank-you letter to those who interviewed you. Take a look at Michele's letter to the manager she interviewed with at NexAir. You can use this letter as a model when the time comes for you to write some thank-you letters.

July 17, 2007

Michele A. Thomas
3467 Main Street
Atlanta, Georgia 30308
Phone: 404-555-3423
E-mail: mthomas_987654321@yahoo.com

Mr. Charles E. Pence
Manager, Human Resources
NexAir Wireless
20201 East Sixth Street
Atlanta, Georgia 30372

Dear Mr. Pence:

It was a pleasure meeting with you Monday to discuss the sales opportunity at NexAir's downtown location. After learning more about the position, it is clear to me that with my background and enthusiasm, I would be an asset to your organization.

As we discussed, my experiences as a cashier at Winn-Dixie Supermarket and as a sales clerk at The Limited have provided me with the basic skills necessary to perform the responsibilities required of a sales representative at NexAir. I believe that with my ability to learn quickly and communicate effectively, I can help NexAir increase sales of its wireless products.

Thank you for the opportunity to interview with your organization. If there is any additional information I can provide about myself, please do not hesitate to call me. I look forward to hearing your decision soon.

Sincerely,

Michele A. Thomas

WHAT EMPLOYERS EXPECT FROM EMPLOYEES

As part of the National City Bank personnel team in Columbus, Ohio, Rose Graham works with Cooperative Business Education (CBE) coordinators in the area who are trying to place high school students in the workplace. When asked what skills she looks for in potential employees, she quickly replies that basic communication skills are at the top of her list. She stresses, "The ability to construct a sentence and put together words cannot be overemphasized." She cites knowledge of the personal computer, with good keyboarding skills, as essential.

In an article published in the *Nashville Business Journal*, Donna Cobble of Staffing Solutions outlined these basic skills for everyday life in the workplace:

Communication. Being a good communicator not only means having the ability to express oneself properly in the English language, but it also means being a good listener. If you feel inferior in any of these areas, it's a good idea to sign up for a public speaking class, read books on the subject, and borrow techniques from professional speakers.

Organization. Organization is the key to success in any occupation or facet of life. The ability to plan, prioritize, and complete a task in a timely fashion is a valuable skill. Check out Chapter 13 for tips on improving your time-management skills.

Problem solving. Companies are looking for creative problem solvers, people who aren't afraid to act on a situation and follow through with their decision. Experience and practice play a major role in your ability to determine the best solution. You can learn these techniques by talking with others about how they solve problems as well as observing others in the problem-solving process.

Sensitivity. In addition to being kind and courteous to their fellow workers, employees need to be sensitive to a coworker's perspective. That might mean putting yourself in the other person's shoes to gain a better understanding of that person's feelings. Employers look for individuals who are able to work on a team instead of those concerned only with their own personal gain.

Judgment. Although closely related to problem solving, good judgment shows up on many different levels in the workplace. It is the ability of a person to assess a situation, weigh the options, consider the risks, and make the necessary decision. Good judgment is built on experience and self-confidence.

Concentration. Concentration is the ability to focus on one thing at a time. Learning to tune out distractions and relate solely to the task at hand is a valuable asset for anyone.

Cooperation. Remember that you're being paid to do a job, so cooperate.

Honesty. Dishonesty shows up in many different ways, ranging from stealing time or property to divulging company secrets. Stay honest.

Initiative. Don't wait to be told exactly what to do. Show some initiative and look around to see what needs to be done next.

Willingness to learn. Be willing to learn how things are done at the company instead of doing things the way you want to do them.

Dependability. Arrive at work on time every day and meet your deadlines.

Enthusiasm. Although not every task you're assigned will be stimulating, show enthusiasm for your work at all times.

Acceptance of criticism. Constructive criticism is necessary for any employee to learn how things should be done. Employees who view criticism as a way to improve themselves will benefit from it.

Loyalty. There is no place for negativity in the workplace. You simply won't be happy working for an employer to whom you're not loyal.

Never fail to show pride in your work, the place where you work, and your appearance. By making these traits a part of your personality and daily performance, you will demonstrate that you are a cut above other employees with equal or better qualifications.

JUMPING ON THE SALARY FAST-TRACK

So the job offer comes, and it's time to talk about money. Unless you are an undiscovered genius, you most likely will start near the bottom of the salary scale if you're heading straight to the workplace after graduating from high school. There's not much room to negotiate a salary since you probably won't be able to say, "Well, I've done this, this, and this. I know what my experience is worth." You will find that most people hiring first-time employees will have a "take-it-or-leave-it" attitude about salary offers. However, according to Amryl Ward, a human resources consultant who has been hiring employees for more than twenty-five years in various human resource positions, there are some things that entry-level employees can do to make themselves more easily hired and, once hired, to get themselves on the fast-track toward more pay:

- **As you interview for the job, be prepared to tell a potential employer why you're worth hiring.** "Bring your skills to the table," says Ward. For instance, you might not think that the job you had during the summer at that big office supply store did anything more than earn you spending money. On the contrary, you learned valuable skills, such as how to be part of a team and how to deal with customers. What about that after-school office job you had? You learned how to answer the phones and how to work with certain software. Think carefully about the jobs you had in high school and what you learned from them. Those are called transferable skills.

- **Once you're hired, be willing to do more than just what the job requires.** Sure, you may be frying fries at the start. But if you come in early and stay late, if you pitch in to help another employee with his or her job, or if you voluntarily clean up the counters and sweep the floor, that says to management, "This employee is a winner. Let's keep him or her in mind the next time a promotion comes up." Soon, you might be managing a crew, then the store.

ON THE JOB

Once you snag that perfect job, there's no time to rest easy. You need to keep your manager happy and instill trust in your coworkers. And at the same time you're doing this, you'll want to watch out for yourself, keep yourself happy, and stay ahead of the learning curve. Here are some ways for you to do just that.

Minding Your Office Etiquette

Okay, so maybe you didn't know which was the salad fork at your cousin Sally's wedding reception. Most likely, though, you can name a few basic rules of etiquette, like not chewing with your mouth open at the dinner table. Now, what about when it comes to the manners you're supposed to have in the workplace? That usually draws a blank if you've never worked in an office setting. How would you know what's the right way to answer the phone or talk to your boss or customers?

Shannon McBride, of the Golden Crescent Tech-Prep Partnership in Victoria, Texas, has seen many students come through his program and land good jobs. He's also seen many of them succeed because they knew how to present themselves in a professional situation. Unfortunately, he can also relate stories of high school graduates who had no clue how to act in the workplace. They didn't realize that when they're working in an office with a group of people, they have to go out of their way to get along and follow the unwritten rules of that workplace. McBride says that means you'll have to size up how others are dressing and match what the office is geared to. For instance, if you work in a business office, most likely you'd wear slacks and a button-down shirt or a nice skirt and top. If you worked in a golf pro shop, you'd wear a golf shirt and shorts. "As much as you want to be an individual," says McBride, "you have to fit in when you're in a business setting. If you want an adult job, you have to act like an adult."

A lot of young people don't grasp how important office etiquette is and blow it off as just some silly rules imposed by adults. But McBride cautions that not following the norms of office etiquette can make or break a job. You can have all the technical talent and know all the latest software applications, but if you're not up on how people dress, talk, and conduct business, your job probably won't last very long. When it comes to getting a job, McBride warns, "First impressions are so important. Bad office etiquette can hurt that first impression." The best advice that we can give is that if you're not sure what the policy is about answering phones, using e-mail or the Internet on the job, or dress codes, ask your boss. He or she won't steer you wrong and will be pleased that you were concerned enough to ask.

Finding a Friendly Face at Work

There you are on the first day of a new job. Everyone looks like they know what they're doing while you stand there feeling really dumb. Even for the most seasoned employee, those first few weeks on the job are tough. Of course, everyone else looks like they know what they're doing because they've been doing it for quite some time. Wouldn't it be nice, though, if you had someone to help you adjust? Someone who would give you those little inside tips everyone else learns with experience. Someone to caution you about things that could go wrong or give you a heads-up when you're doing something that could lead to a reprimand. If you look around the office, you'll find such a person, says Robert Fait, Career Counselor and Instructional Specialist, who is associated with Career and Technology Education in the Katy Independent School district in Katy, Texas.

You might not realize that such a person is a mentor, but in the strict definition of the word, that's what he or she is. Or, as Fait puts it, "Mentors are role models who are willing to assist others with personal education and career goal setting and planning. This caring person shares a listening ear, a comforting shoulder, and an understanding heart." In other words, a mentor is someone who will make you feel comfortable in a new working environment, show you the procedures, and, in the end, help you become more productive.

Unless the company you're working for has a formal mentoring program, mentors don't come with huge signs around their necks that read, "Look here. I'm a mentor. Ask me anything." You have to look for them. Fait advises new employees to look closely at their coworkers and take notice of who demonstrates positive behavior, has strong work habits, and seems trustworthy. Those are the people to approach. "Such workers are usually willing to share their knowledge and insights with others," says Fait.

Who knows? Given some time, you could become a mentor yourself after you've been on the job for a while. Maybe you'll be able to help some new employee who looks kind of bewildered and in need of a friendly hand because you'll remember what it was like to be that new person.

Chapter 13

SURVIVAL SKILLS

Whether you're headed to college or work, you're going to come face-to-face with some intimidating stuff after graduation.

Your level of stress will most likely increase due to the demands of your classes or job and your exposure to alcohol or drugs. Various forms of conflict will arise, and you're going to have to keep up with your own health and nutrition. Seem daunting? It's really not if you keep a level head about you and stick to your core values. This chapter will help you work through the muddier side of life after high school.

SKILLS TO MAKE YOU STRESS-HARDY

Jump out of bed and into the shower. What to wear? Throw that on. Yuck—what's that stain? "Mom, where are my clean socks?" Tick, tock. No time to grab a bite if you want to make the homeroom bell. Skid around the corner and race for the classroom just as the final bell rings. Whoops, forgot your bio book. Sports, clubs, job, homework, friends on the Internet, and finally (sigh) sleep.

Sound like your life? If you're like most high school students, that description probably hits pretty close to home. So now we'll take your already hectic schedule and throw in the fact that you'll soon be graduating and have to figure out what to do with your life. Can you say "stress"?

Some people say that stress actually motivates them to perform better, but we won't talk about those perfect people. For most of you, stress means that you may snap at the dog, slam a few doors, get mad at your dad, and feel down. Maybe you'll even have physical symptoms—upset stomach, rapid heartbeat, sweaty palms, dizziness. The list goes on. Not a good place to be when you're dealing with a huge list of things to do, plus graduation staring you in the face.

How to handle stress has been written about countless times, but out of all the advice that's out there, a few simple pointers can really help you prevent the sweaty palms and nauseated feeling in the pit of your stomach.

- **French fries out, good food in.** Eat at least one hot, balanced meal a day. Healthy, as in veggies, fruits, meats, cheese, grains. Read further along in this chapter for more information about nutrition and health.

- **Sleep.** 7, 8, 10 hours a day. Easier said than done, but well worth it. Sleep will not only get you through high school but also your college and career lives, and it will help you stop feeling like such a frazzled bunch of nerve endings.

- **Hug your dog, cat, rabbit, friend, or mom.** Loneliness breeds stress because then all you've got is yourself and those stressed-out thoughts zooming around in your head.

- **Hang out with friends.** That takes time, but being with people you like and doing fun things eases stress—as long as you don't overdo it.

- **Exercise.** This does not include running down the hall to make the bell. We're talking 20 minutes of heart-pounding perspiration at least three times a week. It's amazing what a little sweat can do to relax you. Believe it or not, good posture helps too.

- **Don't smoke, drink, or use excessive amounts of caffeine.** Whoever told you that partying is the way to relieve stress got it all wrong. Nicotine and alcohol actually take away the things your body needs to fight stress.
- **Simplify your expenses.** Money can be a big stress factor. Think of ways to spend less so that the money you have doesn't have to be stretched so far. Be creative. Share resources. Sell items you no longer use. Maybe put off buying something you've been wanting.
- **Let your feelings out of your head.** It takes time and energy to keep them bottled up inside. Have regular conversations with your parents and siblings so that minor annoyances can be solved when they're still minor.
- **Organize your time.** As in prioritizing and dealing with one small part of your life instead of trying to solve everything in one shot. Read on for more information about time management.
- **Lighten up.** When you've graduated and are into whatever it is you'll end up doing, you'll look back and realize that this was a teensy little part of your life. So look on the bright side. The decisions you'll be making about your future are heavy, but they won't be cut in stone. You can change them if they don't work out.

Stress Busters

Most people get stressed when things are out of control—too many things to do, too many decisions to make, or too much information to digest. If you add not having enough time, enough money, or enough energy to get it all done, you have the perfect recipe for stress.

In the space below, identify what's causing you stress:
_____
_____
_____
_____
_____

Then, choose from these three stress-busting options:

1. **Alter the situation.** Some things you can't control, some things you can. Change the ones you can. If you have too much on your plate and can't possibly do it all, push a few things aside. There's got to be something on the list you can get rid of. (And no, homework is not a choice.) Maybe you need to be able to say no to extra demands. Concentrate on what is important. Make a list of your priorities from the most important to the least, and work your way down.

2. **Avoid the situation—for now.** Step back and ask, "Is this really a problem? Do I really need to solve it now?" This doesn't mean you should procrastinate on things that need to get done. Think of this stress buster as buying some time, taking a break, catching your breath, getting advice, and airing out the situation so that you can deal with it when you're better prepared to handle it.

3. **Accept the situation.** How you perceive your circumstances has a lot to do with how you make decisions about them. Put whatever is stressing you in the perspective of the big picture. How will this really affect me next year or even ten years from now? Look at your circumstances through the lens of your personal values. Think about what feels right to you, not someone else.

Quick Fixes for Stressful Moments

So, you've done all the things we talked about and you're still feeling like you're being pulled in a million directions. If your stressometer has hit the top, use these quick fixes to help you calm down.

- Make the world slow down for a bit. Take a walk. Take a shower. Listen to some soothing music.
- Breathe deeply. Get in tune with the rhythm of your own breathing. Lie or sit down for 15 minutes and just concentrate on relaxing.
- Relax those little knots of tension. Start at your head and work down to your toes.
- Close your eyes and clear your mind. Oops, there comes that nagging thought. Out, out, out! Get rid of the clutter. Imagine yourself in your favorite place: the beach, under a tree, whatever works.
- Close the door to your bedroom, and let out a blood-curdling scream. Walt Whitman knew what he was talking about when he said, "I sound my barbaric yawp over the roofs of the world." Just let your family know what you're doing so they don't come running to your room in fear. You'll be amazed at how much better you feel.
- When all else fails, watch a funny movie. Read the comics. Get in a giggly frame of mind. Those big challenges will quickly be brought down to size.

WINNING THE TIME MANAGEMENT GAME

What is the value of time? Eight dollars an hour? The price of a scholarship because the application is a day late? Time can be a very expensive resource or something you can use to your advantage. Even if you recognize the value of time, managing it is a challenge.

When you live with enough time, life is relaxed and balanced. In order to find that balance, you have to prioritize and plan. Decide what you want and what is important to you. Organize logically and schedule realistically. Overcome obstacles. Change bad habits. Simplify and streamline. Save time when you can. Sound impossible? It's not easy, but you can do it. The secret is held in a Chinese proverb: The wisdom of life is the elimination of nonessentials.

It's All About Control

The good thing about time is that much of it is yours to do with as you wish. You may feel out of control and as if you must run to keep up with the conflicting demands and expectations of your life. But we all have the same number of hours in each day. The key is in how we spend them. The following tips are designed to help you spend your time wisely and to keep you in control of your life.

Prepare a list of your goals and the tasks necessary to accomplish them. This could be by day, week, month, semester, or even year. You may also want to break the list into sections, such as friends and family, school, work, sports, health and fitness, home, personal development, and college preparation.

Prioritize based on time-sensitive deadlines. Use a grading system to code how important each task is. A is "Do It Now," B is "Do It Soon," C is "Do It Later." Understand the difference between "important" and "urgent."

Be realistic about how much you can really do. Analyze how you spend your time now. What can you cut? How much time do you truly need for each task?

Think ahead. How many times have you underestimated how long it will take to do something? Plan for roadblocks, and give yourself some breathing space.

Accept responsibility. Once you decide to do something, commit yourself to it. That doesn't mean that a task that was on the "A" list can't be moved to the "C" list. But be consistent and specific about what you want to accomplish.

Divide and conquer. You may need to form a committee, delegate tasks to your parents, or ask for help from a friend. That is why it is called time management.

Take advantage of your personal prime time. Don't schedule yourself to get up and do homework at 6 a.m.

if you are a night owl. It won't work. Instead, plan complex tasks when you are most efficient.

Avoid procrastination. There are a million ways to procrastinate. And not one of them is good if you really want to get something done. Have you ever noticed that you always find time to do the things you enjoy?

Do the most unpleasant task first. Get it over with. Then it will be all downhill from there.

Don't over-prepare. That is just another way to procrastinate.

Learn to say no to the demands on your time that you cannot afford.

Be enthusiastic, and share your goals with others.

If you work on too many goals at once, you will overwhelm yourself from the start. Remember, what is important is the quality of the time you spend on a task, not the quantity. It doesn't make any difference if you study for 10 hours if you don't recall a thing you've reviewed. The overall goal is to be productive, efficient, and effective, not just busy. You'll also need to pace yourself. All work and no play makes for an unbalanced person.

Use all the benefits of modern technology to help you manage time. You can save lots of time by using a fax, e-mail, or voice mail. If you don't already use a day planner or calendar, you would be wise to invest in one. Write in all the important deadlines, and refer to it often. Block out commitments you know you have so you won't over-schedule yourself. When you do over-schedule yourself or underestimate the time it takes to accomplish a task, learn from your mistakes. But don't get too down on yourself. Give yourself a pep talk every now and then to keep yourself positive and motivated.

MOVING OUT ON YOUR OWN?

As you consider moving away from home either to a college dorm or your own place, some pretty wonderful expectations of what it no doubt will be like will come floating into your head. No more parental rules. On your own. Making your own decisions. Hamburgers forever. Coming and going when you want to. Wait, what's this? Looks like you're out of clothes to wear. No more cereal bowls—they're all in the sink, and they're dirty. Out of milk and the refrigerator's empty. Yikes! What happened to all those warm, fuzzy thoughts about freedom?

Sure, it's nice to be able to come and go as you please, but before you get too far into that pleasant—and unrealistic—mind mode, here are some thoughts you might want to consider as you make plans to become independent. Ozzie Hashley, a guidance counselor at Clinton Community Schools in Clinton, Michigan, works with juniors and seniors in high school. Here is what he says to inform students about six realities of independent life.

1. **If you rent your own place, have you thought about the extra charges in addition to the rent?** Says Hashley, "Many students think only of paying the rent. They don't realize that they'll be responsible for utilities in many cases. Or the money it will take to wash and dry their clothes."

2. **Subsisting on hamburgers and fries sounds yummy, but as you watch a fast food diet eat its way into your paycheck, you'll most likely think about cooking up something yourself.** What will you cook? Who will buy the food? More importantly, who will do the dishes? Dividing up the responsibilities of preparing food is a big aspect of being on your own, especially when sharing a living space.

3. **Medical insurance may not be on your mind as you prepare to graduate—you're probably on your parents' insurance plans right now.** However, once you are established as independent at age 18 and you're living on your own, insurance becomes a big consideration. If you need health care and don't have medical insurance, the bills will be big. So when you get a job, make sure that you have medical coverage. If you're going off to college after high school, you'll most likely be covered under your parents' insurance until age 23.

4. **There's no one to tell you when to come home when you're on your own.** There's also no one to tell you that you're really disorganized when it comes to managing your time. Time management might not sound like a big deal now, but when you have to juggle all the facets of being independent—your job, taking care of your living space and car, your social life—then being able to manage time becomes an important part of life.

5. **Managing your money moves into a whole other realm when you are on your own.** You have to make sure you have enough to pay the rent, your car loan, and insurance, not to mention that movie you wanted to see, the CD you wanted to buy, or those jeans you saw at the mall last week. If you want to eat at the end of the month, budgeting will become an important part of your new independent vocabulary. Ask your parents or an adult you trust to help you set up your budget. Also learn how to balance your checkbook. It's a lot easier to manage your money when you keep track of how much you have in your bank account and how much you spend!

DRUGS AND ALCOHOL: ARE YOU AT RISK?

At risk? Wait a minute. How could you be at risk when the legal drinking age in all fifty states is 21? Chances are, if you're reading this, you're not 21 yet. It's also illegal to smoke or buy any tobacco product before age 18, and possession of any drug for recreational use is illegal, period. So if you drink alcohol before age 21; smoke or buy cigarettes, cigars, or chewing tobacco before age 18; or take any illegal drugs, you could:

- be arrested for driving under the influence (DUI);
- be convicted;
- be required to pay steep fines;
- have your driving privileges suspended;
- get kicked out of school (that's any kind of school, college included);
- get fired;
- go to jail; and/or
- have a criminal record.

A criminal record . . . so what?

Consider this true story. A 29-year-old man who recently received his graduate degree in business was offered a job with a major Fortune-100 corporation. We're talking big bucks, stock options, reserved parking space—the whole nine yards. When the company did a background check and found that he was arrested for a DUI during his freshman year of college, they rescinded their offer. The past can, and will, come back to haunt you. Let's not even think about what would happen down the line if you decide to run for public office.

Think about why you might want to try drinking or doing drugs. For fun? To forget your troubles? To be cool? Are your reasons good enough? Remember the consequences before you make a decision.

How Can I Say No Without Looking Like a Geek?

"It takes a lot more guts to stay sober, awake, and aware than to just get high, get numb, and learn nothing about life," says one former user. "Laugh at people who suggest you drink or take drugs, and then avoid them like the plague."

Friends worth having will respect your decision to say no. And girls—if a guy pressures you to drink or get high, ditch him pronto. You can vice-versa that for guys, too. According to the National Institute on Drug Abuse (NIDA), alcohol and club drugs like GHB or Rohypnol (roofies) make you an easy target for date rape.

The Nitty Gritty

Along with the temporary pleasure they may give you, all drugs (including club drugs, alcohol, and nicotine) have a downside. Alcohol, for example, is a depressant. Even one drink slows down the part of your brain that controls your reasoning. So your judgment gets dull just when you're wondering, "Should I drive my friends home? Should I talk to this guy? Should I have another drink?"

Your body needs about an hour to burn up the alcohol in one drink (one shot of hard liquor, straight or mixed in a cocktail; one glass of wine; or one 12-ounce beer). Nothing, including coffee, will sober you up any faster.

Alcohol helps smart people make bad decisions. In fact, many drugs make you believe that you're thinking even more clearly than usual. Well, guess what? You aren't. Depending on what drug you take, how much, and what you do while you're on it, you're also risking confusion, nausea, headache, sleep problems, depression, paranoia, rape (especially "date rape"), unwanted pregnancy, sexually transmitted diseases (STDs) ranging from herpes to HIV/AIDS, having a baby with a birth defect, memory impairment, persistent psychosis, lung damage, cancer, injuring or killing someone else, and death.

Take a moment now, when your brain is razor sharp, to decide if those consequences are worth the escape you get for 20 minutes one night. You may be saying, "Oh, come on. Only addicts have problems like that." Getting drunk or high doesn't necessarily mean that you're an alcoholic or an addict—but it always means a loss of control.

"So much of addiction is about denial," says one member of Alcoholics Anonymous. "I just didn't think I looked or acted or thought or smelled or lied or cheated or failed like an alcoholic or addict. It was when the drugs and alcohol use started to cause problems in multiple areas of my life that I began to think the problem might reside with me. Friends leaving—in disgust—was what opened my eyes."

> **DID YOU KNOW…**
>
> … that nicotine is as addictive as cocaine and heroin, according to the American Cancer Society?
>
> … that drinking a lot of alcohol fast can kill you on the spot, according to Keystone College?
>
> … that MDMA (Ecstasy, X, Adam, Clarity, Lover's Speed), according to NIDA, may permanently damage your memory?

> **DO I HAVE A PROBLEM?**
> Take the quiz below to see if you're in real trouble with drugs or alcohol.
>
> 1. Do you look forward to drinking or using drugs?
> 2. Do most of your friends drink or do drugs?
> 3. Do you keep a secret supply of alcohol or drugs?
> 4. Can you drink a lot without appearing drunk?
> 5. Do you "power-hit" to get high faster, by binge-drinking, funneling, or slamming?
> 6. Do you ever drink or do drugs alone, including in a group where no one else is doing so?
> 7. Do you ever drink or use drugs when you hadn't planned to?
> 8. Do you ever have blackouts where you can't remember things that happened when you were drunk or high?
>
> If you answered yes to any of these questions, you probably need help. If you have a friend who fits the picture, find a respectful way to bring up your concerns. Don't be surprised if he or she tells you to back off—but don't give up, either. If someone in your family has an alcohol or drug problem, be aware that you may be prone to the same tendency.
>
> Source: Keystone College, La Plume, Pennsylvania

Where Can I Get Help?

If you think you have a problem, or if you think a friend has a problem, try Alcoholics Anonymous or Narcotics Anonymous. If you're not sure, ask yourself the questions in "Do I Have a Problem?" on the top of this page.

Talk to any adult you trust: maybe your doctor, a clergy member, a counselor, or your parents. Health clinics and hospitals offer information and treatment. The American Cancer Society can help you quit smoking. These are only a few places to turn—check out the Yellow Pages and the Web for more.

Alcoholics Anonymous
212-870-3400
www.aa.org

American Cancer Society
800-ACS-2345
www.cancer.org

Narcotics Anonymous
818-773-9999
www.na.org

So, that's the straight stuff. You're at a tough but wonderful age, when your life is finally your own and your decisions really matter. Think about what you value most—and then make your choices.

CONFLICT: HOW TO AVOID IT OR DEFUSE IT

You're walking along and you see a group of kids up ahead . . . and suddenly you're afraid. Or you're about to talk to someone you have a disagreement with, and already you're tense. Or your boyfriend's jealousy is spooking you. What should you do?

All of these situations involve potential conflicts that could get out of hand. Even if you never get into a violent situation, you'll face conflicts with others, as we all do. Learning to spot the warning signs of violence and how to handle conflicts well will bring you lifelong benefits.

What's Your Style?

What do you do when you're faced with a potential conflict? Do you try to get away, no matter what? Do you find yourself bowing to pressure from others? Do you feel like you have to stand and fight, even if you don't want to? Do you wish you had some new ways to handle conflict?

Different situations call for different strategies. First, let's talk about situations where violence is a real possibility. Most of us get a bad feeling before things get violent, but too often, we ignore the feeling. Trust your gut feeling! And whether you're on the street or in school, Fred Barfoot of the Crime Prevention Association of Philadelphia suggests that you keep in mind these tips for avoiding violence:

- Walk like you're in charge and you know where you're going.

- Stick to lighted areas.

- Travel with a trusted friend when possible. On campus, get an escort from security at night. Loners are targets.

- If a person or group up ahead makes you nervous, cross the street immediately—and calmly—as if you'd intended to anyway.

- Call out to an imaginary friend, "Hey, Joe! Wait up!" and then run toward your "friend," away from whoever is scaring you.

- Go right up to the nearest house and ring the bell. Pretend you're expected: "Hey Joe, it's me!" You can explain later.

- If someone threatens you physically, scream.

- If someone assaults you, scream, kick where it hurts, scratch—anything.

- Don't ever get in a car with someone you don't know well or trust, even if you've seen that person around a lot.

- Strike up a conversation with an innocent bystander if you feel threatened by someone else, just to make yourself less vulnerable for a few minutes.

- Wear a whistle around your neck or carry a personal alarm or pepper spray.

- If someone mugs you, hand over your purse, wallet, jewelry—whatever he or she asks for. None of it is worth your life.

- Don't go along with something your gut says is wrong, no matter who says it's okay.

Remember that it's not a sign of weakness to back down if someone's egging you on to fight. Bill Tomasco, principal of Furness High School in Philadelphia, says that pressure from other kids to fight creates much of the violence in schools. If you're being pushed to fight, show true strength: Know that your opponent has a good side too, speak only to that good side, and don't give in to the pressure of the crowd.

Are You Safe at Home?

Locking doors and windows makes sense—but sometimes the danger lies within. A lot of violence occurs in abusive relationships, says Amy Gottlieb, a marriage family therapist intern at the California Family Counseling Center in Encino. To find out if you're at risk, ask yourself whether your partner, roommate, or family member:

- Uses jealousy to justify controlling you
- Puts you down, humiliates you, or pulls guilt trips on you
- Threatens to reveal your secrets or tells lies about you
- Makes all the decisions
- Frightens you, especially if it's on purpose
- Threatens you in any way
- Makes light of abusive behavior or says you provoked it

If any of these things are going on in your relationship, talk about it to an adult you trust, and ask for help.

Talking It Out

If your instincts tell you to get away from a situation, do it. But you can resolve many actual or potential conflicts face to face and gracefully so that everyone walks away feeling good. Read on for some tips on handling conflict from Kare Anderson, a communications expert in Sausalito, California.

Most of us make the mistake of reacting quickly, thinking only of our own needs, and not listening, says Anderson. Try doing the opposite. First and foremost, think about what you really want from the situation, and keep your goal in mind the whole time. But bring up the other person's concerns first. Then, discuss how the situation affects you both. Offer a solution that will benefit you both—and only then talk about how your solution addresses your own needs.

When the other person is talking, really listen—don't just come up with retorts in your head. Always show that you've heard the person before you give your response, especially if you're talking with someone of a different sex, size, or race. Those differences can distract us so much that we actually hear less. If you're female, you may need to s-l-o-w yourself down. Say less than you think you need to. Guys, don't shut down altogether—keep the communication going.

Even if the other person acts like a jerk, be gracious and respectful. Ask questions instead of criticizing. Let someone save face instead of looking like a fool. If you insult or embarrass someone, you may never have that person's full attention again. In short, treat the other person as you'd like to be treated.

What should you do if you're really angry? One teen said, "Thinking about things calms me down." Another said, "Once in a while, we have to cool off for a day and then come back to the discussion." Anger almost always covers up fear. What are you afraid of? Is the reward you want out of this negotiation bigger than your fear? Focus on that reward. Don't forget to breathe—long, slow breaths.

Think about these strategies often, so you'll be more likely to use them when a situation gets hot, instead of just reacting blindly. Use them to plan for negotiations ahead of time, too. Learning to resolve problems with people takes most of us a lifetime—get a jump on it now!

THE LOWDOWN ON SEXUAL HARASSMENT

Has someone ever looked at you, talked to you, or touched you in a way that gave you the creeps, made you self-conscious about your body, or created a sexual mood when it wasn't appropriate? And did you begin to dread seeing this person because he or she just wouldn't quit?

If so, you've encountered sexual harassment. Sexual harassment is inappropriate behavior that:

- is happening to you because of your sex,
- is unwanted (you don't like it),
- is objectively offensive (to a hypothetical "reasonable" man or woman),

- is either severe, persistent, or pervasive, and
- interferes with your work or school experience.

Paul Edison, a domestic and sexual violence prevention educator in Portland, Oregon, says that mostly—just as with crimes like rape—men harass women. But teenage girls are a bit more likely than older women to sexually harass someone, more girl-on-girl harassment goes on with teens, and guys get harassed, too. In some of the most brutal cases coming to light, gay men (or men perceived to be gay) are the targets.

People who sexually harass others fall into three camps, says Edison. Some just seem to be misguided and insensitive. Others get turned on by harassing someone. And a third group does it to intimidate—for example, to drive someone away from a job or just to make him or her feel bad about himself or herself.

So What Do I Do If Someone's Harassing Me?

Experts in self-defense say the best technique is to name the behavior that's bugging you and request that it stop. You might say, "Your hand is on my knee. Please remove it." If the person doesn't quit, you might try writing a letter spelling out what's bothering you and requesting that the person stop—this way, you've confronted the situation directly and you also have a record of your complaint.

But here's the good news, says Edison: You are not expected to handle harassment on your own, especially if the person harassing you is in a position of authority over you, such as a teacher, sergeant, or boss. The authorities at your school or your job should handle it—but they can't do that unless you tell them what's going on.

If you file a complaint, be prepared to describe what happened, when, and where. And make sure you report your concerns to someone who has clear authority to handle sexual harassment complaints, such as the principal or the personnel director.

Often, the person harassing you will stop as soon as he or she gets the clear message that the behavior isn't okay with you, especially if your complaint goes to someone higher up as well. Edison notes that most harassment cases don't end up involving lawyers and lawsuits. You may choose, in serious cases, to register your complaint with the Office of Civil Rights (if you're being harassed at school) or the Equal Employment Opportunity Commission (if you're being harassed at work). You can also file your complaint on different levels at the same time: for example, with your school and the police.

You have the legal right to a school and workplace free from discrimination based on your race, color, religion, sex, national origin, and—depending on where you live, as state and local laws vary—your sexual orientation. You have the right to protection from retaliation if you file a complaint of harassment. So don't be afraid to report a situation if it truly offends you and interferes with your life.

What If I'm Just Being Hypersensitive?

If someone's words or actions make you uncomfortable, that's all the reason you need to ask that person to stop the behavior, no matter how innocent the behavior may be. Trust your feelings—especially if you find you're trying to convince yourself that nothing is wrong.

What Will Happen to the Person Who Has Been Harassing Me?

If your complaint is successfully handled, says Edison, the main thing that will happen is that the person will stop harassing you. People aren't "charged" with sexual harassment unless their behavior includes criminal conduct. But your harasser may face disciplinary action, loss of privileges, suspension, expulsion, lawsuits, or criminal action, depending on the severity of his or her behavior.

How Can I Avoid Harassing Someone?

Sometimes the line between harmless flirting, joking, or complimenting and harassment is pretty thin. How can you stay on the right side of that line?

First, pay attention to your own motives. Be honest with yourself. Do you enjoy watching someone get uncomfortable when you say or do certain things? Do you feel angry with the person for some reason? Do you enjoy exercising your authority over this person in some way? Do you find yourself obsessing about the person? If any of these are true, whatever you're saying or doing probably isn't harmless.

Even if your motives seem harmless to you, be extraordinarily careful about whom and how you touch. You may be comfortable touching people casually—perhaps you'll touch someone's hand or shoulder in conversation—but remember that other people's boundaries may differ from yours.

Pay attention to the person's reactions to you. Are you getting clear green signals when you do or say things around this person, or does the person seem to shrink away from you? Does the person shut down or seem upset when you do or say certain things? If someone's told you clearly that she or he doesn't like it when you do or say certain things, apologize and stop at once. And remember, no means no.

So, if you're faced with something that feels like sexual harassment, remember to trust your feelings, convey them clearly, and get help promptly if you need it.

STAYING HEALTHY IN SPITE OF YOURSELF

When someone—like your mom—asks if you're eating right, do you ever want to say, "Hey, have you looked at my life lately? Do you see a lot of time there for eating right?" Well, how about exercise—are you getting enough? "Yeah, right. I bench-press my backpack when I'm not doing wind sprints to my next class," may be how you reply.

If you're feeling like you can't escape your stress and fatigue, you might be surprised by how much better you'll feel if you keep active and don't just eat junk. Your workload will seem easier. You'll sleep better. You'll look fantastic. And you can stay healthy—even if time and money are in short supply.

But Really, Who Has Time to Exercise?

As one teen says, "Schoolwork gets in the way, and then I want to relax when I have a moment that isn't filled with schoolwork." You can make time for anything, if you choose to. But if you aren't athletic by nature or school or work keeps you going nonstop, exercise is the first thing to go out the window.

However, you don't have to become a gym rat or run miles to get enough exercise. Longer workouts are great if you do them consistently, but you're better off getting little bits of regular exercise than just doing a huge workout every so often or never doing anything. And by "little bits," we mean 15- to 20-minute chunks. Add that to a fast walk to the bus, a frenzied private dance session in your room, or running up the stairs instead of taking the elevator, and you're exercising!

Regardless of how you choose to pump that muscle in the middle of your chest, the important thing is that you're doing something. You'll not only feel better about yourself, but you'll have increased energy to do other things, like study, go to work, or go out with friends.

What Does "Eating Right" Mean Anyway?

Eating right means eating a balance of good foods in moderate amounts. Your diet needn't be complicated or expensive. Dr. Michele Wilson, a specialist in adolescent medicine at the Children's Hospital of Philadelphia, notes that a teen's diet should be heavy in grains—especially whole grains—and light in sugars and fats. It should include a lot of fruits and vegetables and provide you with plenty of protein, calcium, vitamin A, B vitamins, iron, and zinc. Sound complicated?

Well, what's complicated about a bean burrito with cheese? How about pasta with vegetables, meat, or both in the sauce? A banana or some cantaloupe? Stir-fried vegetables with tofu? Carrot sticks with peanut butter? Yogurt? Cereal with milk and fruit? All of these are cheap, quick to make, and great for you.

One teen swears by microwaveable veggie burgers and adds, "Staying away from deep-fried anything is a good plan." Try to avoid things like chips and sweets, says Dr. Wilson, adding that if you're a vegetarian—and especially if you don't eat dairy products or fish—you should make sure you're getting enough protein and iron. And no matter what your diet, drink water—eight glasses a day.

As Long as I'm in Control of What I Eat, I'm Okay, Right?

That depends. Of course, having no control over what you eat is a problem. But "in control" can be good or bad. How severely do you control what and how you eat? Are you obsessed with getting thinner? Do people who love you tell you that you're too thin, and do you take that as a compliment? Do you ever binge secretly or make yourself throw up after a meal? If any of these are true, you may be suffering from anorexia or bulimia.

According to the National Association of Anorexia Nervosa and Associated Disorders (ANAD), eating disorders affect about 7 million women and 1 million men in this country and can lead to serious health problems—even death. "The thing that convinced me to get help was fear—I had to be hospitalized, as I was literally dying from my anorexia," says one woman. Most Americans who are anorexic or bulimic developed their eating disorders in their teens.

We asked some women being treated for eating disorders what they used to see when they looked in the mirror. "Total ugliness," said one. "The smallest dimple in my flesh looked immense," said another. And a third said, "I got rid of the mirrors because they would set me off to where I wouldn't eat for days." Their advice to teens struggling with an eating disorder? "Treat yourself as you wish your parents had treated you," "Ask people you feel close to not to discuss your weight with you," and "Find ways outside of yourself to feel in control." Above all—get help! That means going to someone you trust, whether it be a parent, relative, sibling, friend, doctor, or teacher. Or call ANAD's national hotline at 847-831-3438 for a listing of support groups and referrals in your area.

So If I Eat Right and Exercise, I'm Healthy?

Well, probably. But Dr. Wilson suggests that you keep a few other things in mind too. If you smoke, drink, or do drugs, you're asking for trouble. Aside from their many scarier side effects, all these habits can steal nutrients that you need. If all this sounds like the recipe for a dull and totally uncool life, remember that feeling and looking great are never boring and that vomiting (or dying) after downing the most tequilas in the fastest time looks really uncool. If you're making short-term decisions that will hurt you in the long run, take some time to figure out why. Good health is priceless—just ask any grandparent.

APPENDICES

NOW THAT YOU HAVE DECIDED what types of opportunities you wish to pursue after graduation, you need a jumping-off point for getting more information. The **Appendices** that follow will provide you with a sampling of additional data to help you with your decision-making process.

NOTE: Because of Peterson's comprehensive editorial review and because all material comes directly from institution or organization officials, we believe that the information presented in these **Appendices** is accurate. Nonetheless, errors and omissions are possible in a data collection and processing endeavor of this scope. You should check with the specific institution or organization at the time of application to verify pertinent data that may have changed since the publication of this book.

MIDDLE ATLANTIC STATES

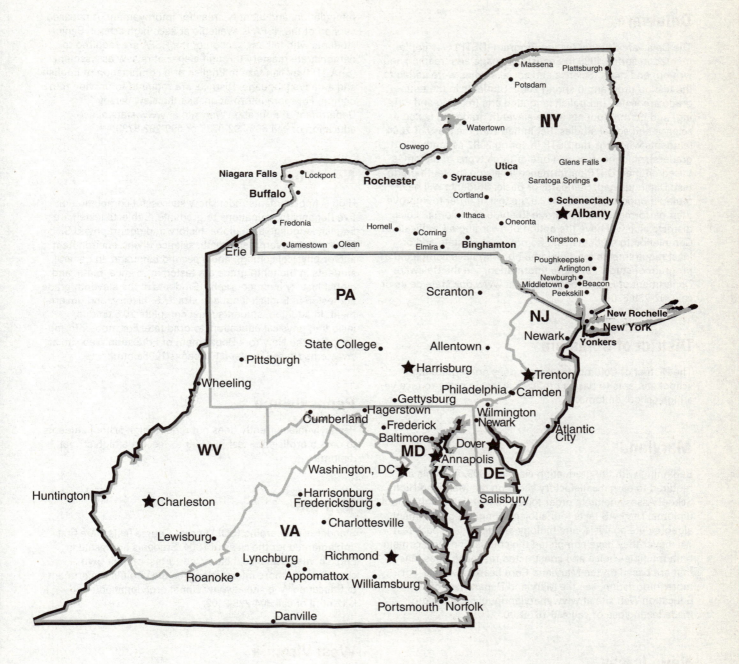

HIGH SCHOOL DIPLOMA TEST REQUIREMENTS

Delaware

The Delaware Student Testing Program (DSTP) was implemented in spring 1998 in English language arts (reading and writing) and math. Science and social studies were added to the testing program in spring 2000. Students in the tenth grade are tested in English language arts (reading and writing) and math. Students in the eleventh grade are tested in science and social studies. Beginning with the class of 2004 (students who took the DSTP in spring 2002 as tenth graders), students received one of three types of diplomas based on their DSTP performance levels on the tenth grade test: Distinguished, Standard, or Basic. Students will have multiple opportunities to retake the test in order to improve their performance and upgrade the type of diploma. Local districts also will have the option of awarding a Certificate of Completion to students who do not meet all state and/or local requirements for a diploma but who have completed a program of study. For more information, see the Delaware Department of Education Web site at www.doe.state.de.us or call 302-739-6700.

District of Columbia

The District of Columbia currently does not require high school students to pass a proficiency test in order to receive a high school diploma.

Maryland

Beginning with the graduating class of 2009, students are required to earn a satisfactory score on the Maryland High School Assessments in order to earn a Maryland high school diploma. The HAS tests four subjects: English, government, algebra/data analysis, and biology. Students take each test whenever they have completed the course. The tests contain both multiple-choice and constructed-response questions that are based on the Maryland Core Learning Goals. For more information, see the Maryland Department of Education Web site at www.marylandpublicschools.org/msde/testing/hsa or call 410-767-0100.

New Jersey

The High School Proficiency Assessment (HSPA) was implemented in March 2002 for the class of 2003. Students are tested in language arts literacy and math. In March 2005, science was added. HSPA data are used to satisfy a part of the graduation requirements, determine a student's needs for remediation, and identify areas for improvement. A released version of the HSPA is available at each high school. Senior students who fail any section of the HSPA are required to demonstrate mastery through a special review assessment (SRA 11) they can take in English or a combination of English and a native language. Districts are required to provide remediation. For more information, see the New Jersey Department of Education Web site at www.state.nj.us/education or call 609-292-8736 or 609-292-8739.

New York

High school students must show successful completion on five Regents Examinations to graduate. Subjects tested are English language arts, global history and geography, U.S. history and government, math, science (living environment and/or physical setting), and a second language. In general, students in the tenth grade are tested in science, math, and global history and geography. Students in the eleventh grade are tested in English language arts, U.S. history, and government. In addition, students must complete 20.5 credits, including physical education, to graduate. For more information, visit the New York Department of Education Web site at www.emsc.nysed.gov/part100/pages/1005a.html.

Pennsylvania

Pennsylvania currently does not require high school students to pass a proficiency test in order to receive a high school diploma.

Virginia

Standards of Learning (SOL) End-of-Course Tests were first implemented for the class of 2004. Students are tested in English, math, science, history, and 1 test of their own choosing. For more information, see the Virginia Department of Education Web site at www.vipnet.org/vipnet/edu-ent/k-12.html or call 804-225-2102.

West Virginia

West Virginia currently does not require high school students to pass a proficiency test in order to receive a high school diploma.

FOUR-YEAR COLLEGES AND UNIVERSITIES

Delaware

Delaware State University
1200 North DuPont Highway
Dover, DE 19901-2277
800-845-2544
www.desu.edu/

Goldey-Beacom College
4701 Limestone Road
Wilmington, DE 19808-1999
800-833-4877
goldey.gbc.edu/

University of Delaware
Newark, DE 19716
302-831-8123
www.udel.edu/

Wesley College
120 North State Street
Dover, DE 19901-3875
800-937-5398
www.wesley.edu/

Wilmington College
320 North DuPont Highway
New Castle, DE 19720-6491
877-967-5464
www.wilmcoll.edu/

District of Columbia

American University
4400 Massachusetts Avenue, NW
Washington, DC 20016-8001
202-885-6000
www.american.edu/

The Catholic University of America
Cardinal Station
Washington, DC 20064
800-673-2772
www.cua.edu/

Corcoran College of Art and Design
500 17th Street NW
Washington, DC 20006-4804
888-CORCORAN
www.corcoran.edu/

Gallaudet University
800 Florida Avenue, NE
Washington, DC 20002-3625
800-995-0550
www.gallaudet.edu/

Georgetown University
37th and O Streets, NW
Washington, DC 20057
202-687-3600
www.georgetown.edu/

The George Washington University
2121 Eye Street, NW
Washington, DC 20052
800-447-3765
www.gwu.edu/

Howard University
2400 Sixth Street, NW
Washington, DC 20059-0002
800-HOWARD-U
www.howard.edu/

Potomac College
4000 Chesapeake Street, NW
Washington, DC 20016
888-686-0876
www.potomac.edu/

Southeastern University
501 I Street, SW
Washington, DC 20024-2788
202-478-8200
www.seu.edu/

Strayer University
1025 15th Street, NW
Washington, DC 20005-2603
888-4-STRAYER
www.strayer.edu/

Trinity (Washington) University
125 Michigan Avenue, NE
Washington, DC 20017-1094
800-IWANTTC
www.trinitydc.edu/

University of the District of Columbia
4200 Connecticut Avenue, NW
Washington, DC 20008-1175
202-274-6110
www.udc.edu/

Maryland

Baltimore Hebrew University
5800 Park Heights Avenue
Baltimore, MD 21215-3996
888-248-7420
www.bhu.edu/

Bowie State University
14000 Jericho Park Road
Bowie, MD 20715-9465
301-860-3415
www.bowiestate.edu/

Capitol College
11301 Springfield Road
Laurel, MD 20708-9759
800-950-1992
www.capitol-college.edu/

College of Notre Dame of Maryland
4701 North Charles Street
Baltimore, MD 21210-2476
800-435-0300
www.ndm.edu/

Columbia Union College
7600 Flower Avenue
Takoma Park, MD 20912-7796
800-835-4212
www.cuc.edu/

Coppin State University
2500 West North Avenue
Baltimore, MD 21216-3698
800-635-3674
www.coppin.edu/

DeVry University
4550 Montgomery Avenue
Suite 100 North
Bethesda, MD 20814-3304
866-338-7934
www.devry.edu/

Frostburg State University
101 Braddock Road
Frostburg, MD 21532-1099
301-687-4201
www.frostburg.edu/

George Meany Center for Labor Studies-The National Labor College
10000 New Hampshire Avenue
Silver Spring, MD 20903
800-GMC-4CDP
www.georgemeany.org/

Goucher College
1021 Dulaney Valley Road
Baltimore, MD 21204-2794
800-468-2437
www.goucher.edu/

Griggs University
PO Box 4437, 12501 Old Columbia Pk
Silver Spring, MD 20914-4437
301-680-6593
www.griggs.edu/

Hood College
401 Rosemont Avenue
Frederick, MD 21701-8575
800-922-1599
www.hood.edu/

The Johns Hopkins University
3400 North Charles Street
Baltimore, MD 21218-2699
410-516-8341
www.jhu.edu/

Loyola College in Maryland
4501 North Charles Street
Baltimore, MD 21210-2699
410-617-5012
www.loyola.edu/

Maple Springs Baptist Bible College and Seminary
4130 Belt Road
Capitol Heights, MD 20743
301-736-3631
www.msbbcs.edu/

Maryland Institute College of Art
1300 Mount Royal Avenue
Baltimore, MD 21217
410-225-2222
www.mica.edu/

McDaniel College
2 College Hill
Westminster, MD 21157-4390
800-638-5005
www.mcdaniel.edu/

Morgan State University
1700 East Cold Spring Lane
Baltimore, MD 21251
800-332-6674
www.morgan.edu/

Mount St. Mary's University
16300 Old Emmitsburg Road
Emmitsburg, MD 21727-7799
800-448-4347
www.msmary.edu/

Ner Israel Rabbinical College
400 Mount Wilson Lane
Baltimore, MD 21208
410-484-7200

Peabody Conservatory of Music of The Johns Hopkins University
1 East Mount Vernon Place
Baltimore, MD 21202-2397
800-368-2521
www.peabody.jhu.edu/

St. John's College
PO Box 2800
Annapolis, MD 21404
800-727-9238
www.stjohnscollege.edu/

St. Mary's College of Maryland
18952 East Fisher Road
St. Mary's City, MD 20686-3001
800-492-7181
www.smcm.edu/

Salisbury University
1101 Camden Avenue
Salisbury, MD 21801-6837
888-543-0148
www.ssu.edu/

Sojourner-Douglass College
500 North Caroline Street
Baltimore, MD 21205-1814
410-276-0306
sdc.edu/

Towson University
8000 York Road
Towson, MD 21252-0001
888-4TOWSON
www.towson.edu/

United States Naval Academy
121 Blake Road
Annapolis, MD 21402-5000
410-293-4361
www.usna.edu/

University of Baltimore
1420 North Charles Street
Baltimore, MD 21201-5779
877-APPLYUB
www.ubalt.edu/

University of Maryland Eastern Shore
Princess Anne, MD 21853-1299
410-651-2200
www.umes.edu/

University of Maryland University College
3501 University Boulevard East
Adelphi, MD 20783
301-985-7000
www.umuc.edu/

University of Maryland, Baltimore County
1000 Hilltop Circle
Baltimore, MD 21250
800-862-2402
www.umbc.edu/

University of Maryland, College Park
College Park, MD 20742
800-422-5867
www.maryland.edu/

University of Phoenix–Maryland Campus
8830 Stanford Boulevard, Suite 100
Columbia, MD 21045-5424
800-228-7240
www.phoenix.edu/

Villa Julie College
Green Spring Valley Road
Stevenson, MD 21153
877-468-3852
www.vjc.edu/

Washington Bible College
6511 Princess Garden Parkway
Lanham, MD 20706-3599
877-793-7227
www.bible.edu/

Washington College
300 Washington Avenue
Chestertown, MD 21620-1197
800-422-1782
www.washcoll.edu/

Yeshiva College of the Nation's Capital
1216 Arcola Avenue
Silver Spring, MD 20902
301-593-2534

New Jersey

Beth Medrash Govoha
617 Sixth Street
Lakewood, NJ 08701-2797
732-367-1060

Bloomfield College
467 Franklin Street
Bloomfield, NJ 07003-9981
800-848-4555
www.bloomfield.edu/

Caldwell College
9 Ryerson Avenue
Caldwell, NJ 07006-6195
888-864-9516
www.caldwell.edu/

Centenary College
400 Jefferson Street
Hackettstown, NJ 07840-2100
800-236-8679
www.centenarycollege.edu/

The College of New Jersey
PO Box 7718
Ewing, NJ 08628
800-624-0967
www.tcnj.edu/

College of Saint Elizabeth
2 Convent Road
Morristown, NJ 07960-6989
800-210-7900
www.cse.edu/

DeVry University
630 US Highway 1
North Brunswick, NJ 08902-3362
866-338-7934
www.devry.edu/

Drew University
36 Madison Avenue
Madison, NJ 07940-1493
973-408-3739
www.drew.edu/

Fairleigh Dickinson University, College at Florham
285 Madison Avenue
Madison, NJ 07940-1099
800-338-8803
www.fdu.edu/

Fairleigh Dickinson University, Metropolitan Campus
1000 River Road
Teaneck, NJ 07666-1914
800-338-8803
www.fdu.edu/

Felician College
262 South Main Street
Lodi, NJ 07644-2117
201-559-6131
www.felician.edu/

Georgian Court University
900 Lakewood Avenue
Lakewood, NJ 08701-2697
800-458-8422
www.georgian.edu/

Kean University
1000 Morris Avenue
Union, NJ 07083
908-737-7100
www.kean.edu/

Monmouth University
400 Cedar Avenue
West Long Branch, NJ 07764-1898
800-543-9671
www.monmouth.edu/

Montclair State University
1 Normal Avenue
Montclair, NJ 07043-1624
800-331-9205
www.montclair.edu/

Four-Year Colleges and Universities

New Jersey City University
2039 Kennedy Boulevard
Jersey City, NJ 07305-1597
888-441-NJCU
www.njcu.edu/

New Jersey Institute of Technology
University Heights
Newark, NJ 07102
800-925-NJIT
www.njit.edu/

Princeton University
Princeton, NJ 08544-1019
609-258-3062
www.princeton.edu/

Rabbi Jacob Joseph School
One Plainfield Ave
Edison, NJ 08817
908-985-6533

Rabbinical College of America
226 Sussex Avenue, PO Box 1996
Morristown, NJ 07962-1996
973-267-9404

Ramapo College of New Jersey
505 Ramapo Valley Road
Mahwah, NJ 07430-1680
201-684-7307
www.ramapo.edu/

The Richard Stockton College of New Jersey
PO Box 195, Jimmie Leeds Road
Pomona, NJ 08240-0195
609-652-4261
www.stockton.edu/

Rider University
2083 Lawrenceville Road
Lawrenceville, NJ 08648-3001
800-257-9026
www.rider.edu/

Rowan University
201 Mullica Hill Road
Glassboro, NJ 08028-1701
856-256-4200
www.rowan.edu/

Rutgers, The State University of New Jersey, Camden
311 North Fifth Street
Camden, NJ 08102-1401
856-225-6498
camden-www.rutgers.edu/

Rutgers, The State University of New Jersey, New Brunswick/Piscataway
New Brunswick, NJ 08901-1281
732-353-1440
www.rutgers.edu/

Rutgers, The State University of New Jersey, Newark
Newark, NJ 07102
973-353-5205
www.newark.rutgers.edu/

Saint Peter's College
2641 Kennedy Boulevard
Jersey City, NJ 07306-5997
888-SPC-9933
www.spc.edu/

Seton Hall University
400 South Orange Avenue
South Orange, NJ 07079-2697
800-THE HALL
www.shu.edu/

Stevens Institute of Technology
Castle Point on Hudson
Hoboken, NJ 07030
800-458-5323
www.stevens.edu/

Talmudical Academy of New Jersey
Route 524
Adelphia, NJ 07710
732-431-1600

Thomas Edison State College
101 West State Street
Trenton, NJ 08608-1176
888-442-8372
www.tesc.edu/

Westminster Choir College of Rider University
101 Walnut Lane
Princeton, NJ 08540-3899
800-96-CHOIR
westminster.rider.edu/

William Paterson University of New Jersey
300 Pompton Road
Wayne, NJ 07470-8420
973-720-2906
ww2.wpunj.edu/

New York

Adelphi University
One South Avenue, PO Box 701
Garden City, NY 11530-0701
800-ADELPHI
www.adelphi.edu/

Albany College of Pharmacy of Union University
106 New Scotland Avenue
Albany, NY 12208-3425
888-203-8010
www.acp.edu/

Alfred University
One Saxon Drive
Alfred, NY 14802-1205
800-541-9229
www.alfred.edu/

Bard College
PO Box 5000
Annandale-on-Hudson, NY 12504
845-758-7472
www.bard.edu/

Barnard College
3009 Broadway
New York, NY 10027-6598
212-854-2014
www.barnard.edu/

Beis Medrash Heichal Dovid
257 Beach 17th Street
Far Rockaway, NY 11691
718-868-2300

Bernard M. Baruch College of the City University of New York
1 Bernard Baruch Way
New York, NY 10010-5585
646-312-1000
www.baruch.cuny.edu/

Beth HaMedrash Shaarei Yosher Institute
4102-10 Sixteenth Avenue
Brooklyn, NY 11204
718-854-2290

Beth Hatalmud Rabbinical College
2127 Eighty-second Street
Brooklyn, NY 11214
718-259-2525

Boricua College
3755 Broadway
New York, NY 10032-1560
212-694-1000
www.boricuacollege.edu/

Briarcliffe College
1055 Stewart Avenue
Bethpage, NY 11714
516-918-3705
www.briarcliffe.edu/

Brooklyn College of the City University of New York
2900 Bedford Avenue
Brooklyn, NY 11210-2889
718-951-5001
www.brooklyn.cuny.edu/

Buffalo State College, State University of New York
1300 Elmwood Avenue
Buffalo, NY 14222-1095
716-878-5519
www.buffalostate.edu/

Canisius College
2001 Main Street
Buffalo, NY 14208-1098
800-843-1517
www.canisius.edu/

Cazenovia College
22 Sullivan Street
Cazenovia, NY 13035-1084
800-654-3210
www.cazenovia.edu/

Central Yeshiva Tomchei Tmimim-Lubavitch
841-853 Ocean Parkway
Brooklyn, NY 11230
718-434-0784

City College of the City University of New York
138th Street and Convent Avenue
New York, NY 10031-9198
212-650-6977
www.ccny.cuny.edu/

Part 5: Appendices

City University of New York System
535 East 80th Street
New York, NY 10021-0767
212-794-5555
www.cuny.edu/

Clarkson University
Potsdam, NY 13699
800-527-6577
www.clarkson.edu/

Colgate University
13 Oak Drive
Hamilton, NY 13346-1386
315-228-7401
www.colgate.edu/

College of Mount Saint Vincent
6301 Riverdale Avenue
Riverdale, NY 10471-1093
800-665-CMSV
www.mountsaintvincent.edu/

The College of New Rochelle
29 Castle Place
New Rochelle, NY 10805-2308
800-933-5923
cnr.edu/

The College of Saint Rose
432 Western Avenue
Albany, NY 12203-1419
800-637-8556
www.strose.edu/

College of Staten Island of the City University of New York
2800 Victory Boulevard
Staten Island, NY 10314-6600
718-982-2000
www.csi.cuny.edu/

Columbia College
116th Street and Broadway
New York, NY 10027
212-854-2522
www.college.columbia.edu/

Columbia University, School of General Studies
2970 Broadway
New York, NY 10027-6939
800-895-1169
www.gs.columbia.edu/

Columbia University, The Fu Foundation School of Engineering and Applied Science
500 West 120th Street
New York, NY 10027
212-854-2522
www.engineering.columbia.edu/

Concordia College
171 White Plains Road
Bronxville, NY 10708-1998
800-YES-COLLEGE
www.concordia-ny.edu/

Cooper Union for the Advancement of Science and Art
30 Cooper Square
New York, NY 10003-7120
212-353-4120
www.cooper.edu/

Cornell University
Ithaca, NY 14853-0001
607-255-5241

The Culinary Institute of America
1946 Campus Drive
Hyde Park, NY 12538-1499
800-CULINARY
www.ciachef.edu/

Daemen College
4380 Main Street
Amherst, NY 14226-3592
800-462-7652
www.daemen.edu/

Darkei Noam Rabbinical College
2822 Avenue J
Brooklyn, NY 11210
718-338-6464

Davis College
400 Riverside Drive
Johnson City, NY 13790
800-331-4137
www.davisny.edu/

DeVry Institute of Technology
30-20 Thomson Avenue
Long Island City, NY 11101
866-338-7934
www.devry.edu/

Dominican College
470 Western Highway
Orangeburg, NY 10962-1210
866-432-4636
www.dc.edu/

Dowling College
Idle Hour Boulevard
Oakdale, NY 11769-1999
800-DOWLING
www.dowling.edu/

D'Youville College
320 Porter Avenue
Buffalo, NY 14201-1084
800-777-3921
www.dyc.edu/

Elmira College
One Park Place
Elmira, NY 14901
800-935-6472
www.elmira.edu/

Eugene Lang College, The New School for Liberal Arts
65 West 11th Street
New York, NY 10011-8601
877-528-3321
www.lang.edu/

Excelsior College
7 Columbia Circle
Albany, NY 12203-5159
888-647-2388
www.excelsior.edu/

Farmingdale State University of New York
Route 110, 2350 Broadhollow Road
Farmingdale, NY 11735
877-4-FARMINGDALE
www.farmingdale.edu/

Fashion Institute of Technology
Seventh Avenue at 27th Street
New York, NY 10001-5992
800-GOTOFIT
www.fitnyc.edu/

Five Towns College
305 North Service Road
Dix Hills, NY 11746-6055
631-424-7000
www.fivetowns.edu/

Fordham University
441 East Fordham Road
New York, NY 10458
800-FORDHAM
www.fordham.edu/

Globe Institute of Technology
291 Broadway, Second Floor
New York, NY 10007
877-394-5623
www.globe.edu/

Hamilton College
198 College Hill Road
Clinton, NY 13323-1296
800-843-2655
www.hamilton.edu/

Hartwick College
One Hartwick Drive
Oneonta, NY 13820-4020
888-HARTWICK
www.hartwick.edu/

Hilbert College
5200 South Park Avenue
Hamburg, NY 14075-1597
716-649-7900
www.hilbert.edu/

Hobart and William Smith Colleges
Geneva, NY 14456-3397
800-245-0100
www.hws.edu/

Hofstra University
100 Hofstra University
Hempstead, NY 11549
800-HOFSTRA
www.hofstra.edu/

Holy Trinity Orthodox Seminary
PO Box 36
Jordanville, NY 13361
315-858-0945
www.hts.edu/

Houghton College
One Willard Avenue
Houghton, NY 14744
800-777-2556
www.houghton.edu/

Hunter College of the City University of New York
695 Park Avenue
New York, NY 10021-5085
212-772-4490
www.hunter.cuny.edu/

Four-Year Colleges and Universities

Iona College
715 North Avenue
New Rochelle, NY 10801-1890
914-633-2502
www.iona.edu/

Ithaca College
100 Job Hall
Ithaca, NY 14850-7020
800-429-4274
www.ithaca.edu/

The Jewish Theological Seminary
3080 Broadway
New York, NY 10027-4649
212-678-8000
www.jtsa.edu/

John Jay College of Criminal Justice of the City University of New
899 Tenth Avenue
New York, NY 10019-1093
877-JOHNJAY
www.jjay.cuny.edu/

The Juilliard School
60 Lincoln Center Plaza
New York, NY 10023-6588
212-799-5000
www.juilliard.edu/

Kehilath Yakov Rabbinical Seminary
206 Wilson Street
Brooklyn, NY 11211-7207
718-963-1212

Keuka College
Keuka Park, NY 14478-0098
800-33-KEUKA
www.keuka.edu/

The King's College
350 Fifth Avenue, 15th Floor Empire State Building
New York, NY 10118
888-969-7200
www.tkc.edu/

Kol Yaakov Torah Center
29 West Maple Avenue
Monsey, NY 10952-2954
914-425-3871
horizons.edu/

Laboratory Institute of Merchandising
12 East 53rd Street
New York, NY 10022-5268
800-677-1323
www.limcollege.edu/

Le Moyne College
1419 Salt Springs Road
Syracuse, NY 13214
800-333-4733
www.lemoyne.edu/

Lehman College of the City University of New York
250 Bedford Park Boulevard West
Bronx, NY 10468-1589
877-Lehman1
www.lehman.cuny.edu/

Long Island University, Brentwood Campus
100 Second Avenue
Brentwood, NY 11717
631-273-5112
www.liu.edu/

Long Island University, Brooklyn Campus
One University Plaza
Brooklyn, NY 11201-8423
800-LIU-PLAN
www.liu.edu/

Long Island University, C.W. Post Campus
720 Northern Boulevard
Brookville, NY 11548-1300
800-LIU-PLAN
www.liu.edu/

Long Island University, Friends World Program
239 Montauk Highway
Southampton, NY 11968
800-287-8093
www.southampton.liu.edu/fw/

Machzikei Hadath Rabbinical College
5407 Sixteenth Avenue
Brooklyn, NY 11204-1805
718-854-8777

Manhattan College
Manhattan College Parkway
Riverdale, NY 10471
718-862-7200
www.manhattan.edu/

Manhattan School of Music
120 Claremont Avenue
New York, NY 10027-4698
917-493-4501
www.msmnyc.edu/

Manhattanville College
2900 Purchase Street
Purchase, NY 10577-2132
800-328-4553
www.manhattanville.edu/

Mannes College The New School for Music
150 West 85th Street
New York, NY 10024-4402
800-292-3040
www.newschool.mannes.edu/

Marist College
3399 North Road
Poughkeepsie, NY 12601-1387
800-436-5483
www.marist.edu/

Marymount Manhattan College
221 East 71st Street
New York, NY 10021-4597
800-MARYMOUNT
www.mmm.edu/

Medaille College
18 Agassiz Circle
Buffalo, NY 14214-2695
716-884-3281
www.medaille.edu/

Medgar Evers College of the City University of New York
1650 Bedford Street
Brooklyn, NY 11225-2298
718-270-4960
www.mec.cuny.edu/

Mercy College
555 Broadway
Dobbs Ferry, NY 10522-1189
800-MERCY-NY
www.mercy.edu/

Mesivta of Eastern Parkway Rabbinical Seminary
510 Dahill Road
Brooklyn, NY 11218-5559
718-438-1002

Mesivta Tifereth Jerusalem of America
145 East Broadway
New York, NY 10002-6301
212-964-2830

Mesivta Torah Vodaath Rabbinical Seminary
425 East Ninth Street
Brooklyn, NY 11218-5299
718-941-8000

Metropolitan College of New York
75 Varick Street
New York, NY 10013-1919
212-343-1234
www.metropolitan.edu/

Mirrer Yeshiva
1795 Ocean Parkway
Brooklyn, NY 11223-2010
718-645-0536

Molloy College
1000 Hempstead Avenue
Rockville Centre, NY 11571-5002
888-4MOLLOY
www.molloy.edu/

Monroe College
Monroe College Way
Bronx, NY 10468-5407
800-55MONROE
www.monroecollege.edu/

Monroe College
434 Main Street
New Rochelle, NY 10801-6410
800-55MONROE
www.monroecollege.edu/

Mount Saint Mary College
330 Powell Avenue
Newburgh, NY 12550-3494
888-937-6762
www.msmc.edu/

Nazareth College of Rochester
4245 East Avenue
Rochester, NY 14618-3790
585-389-2860
www.naz.edu/

Part 5: Appendices

The New School for General Studies
66 West 12th Street
New York, NY 10011-8603
800-862-5039
www.nsu.newschool.edu/

The New School for Jazz and Contemporary Music
55 West 13th Street, 5th Floor
New York, NY 10011
212-229-5896
www.jazz.newschool.edu

New York Institute of Technology
PO Box 8000
Old Westbury, NY 11568-8000
800-345-NYIT
www.nyit.edu/

New York School of Interior Design
170 East 70th Street
New York, NY 10021-5110
800-336-9743
www.nysid.edu/

New York University
70 Washington Square South
New York, NY 10012-1019
212-998-4500
www.nyu.edu/

Niagara University
Niagara University, NY 14109
800-462-2111
www.niagara.edu/

Nyack College
One South Boulevard
Nyack, NY 10960-3698
800-33-NYACK
www.nyack.edu

Ohr Hameir Theological Seminary
Furnace Woods Road
Peekskill, NY 10566
914-736-1500

Ohr Somayach/Joseph Tanenbaum Educational Center
PO Box 334, 244 Route 306
Monsey, NY 10952-0334
914-425-1370
www.ohrsomayach.edu/

Pace University
One Pace Plaza
New York, NY 10038
800-874-7223
www.pace.edu/

Parsons The New School for Design
66 Fifth Avenue
New York, NY 10011-8878
877-528-3321
www.parsons.newschool.edu/

Paul Smith's College of Arts and Sciences
PO Box 265
Paul Smiths, NY 12970-0265
800-421-2605
www.paulsmiths.edu/

Polytechnic University, Brooklyn Campus
Six Metrotech Center
Brooklyn, NY 11201-2990
800-POLYTECH
www.poly.edu/

Pratt Institute
200 Willoughby Avenue
Brooklyn, NY 11205-3899
800-331-0834
www.pratt.edu/

Purchase College, State University of New York
735 Anderson Hill Road
Purchase, NY 10577-1400
914-251-6300
www.purchase.edu/

Queens College of the City University of New York
65-30 Kissena Boulevard
Flushing, NY 11367-1597
718-997-5600
www.qc.edu/

Rabbinical Academy Mesivta Rabbi Chaim Berlin
1605 Coney Island Avenue
Brooklyn, NY 11230-4715
718-377-0777

Rabbinical College Beth Shraga
28 Saddle River Road
Monsey, NY 10952-3035
914-356-1980

Rabbinical College Bobover Yeshiva B'nei Zion
1577 Forty-eighth Street
Brooklyn, NY 11219
718-438-2018

Rabbinical College Ch'san Sofer
1876 Fiftieth Street
Brooklyn, NY 11204
718-236-1171

Rabbinical College of Long Island
201 Magnolia Boulevard
Long Beach, NY 11561-3305
516-431-7414

Rabbinical College of Ohr Shimon Yisroel
215-217 Hewes Street
Brooklyn, NY 11211
718-855-4092

Rabbinical Seminary Adas Yereim
185 Wilson Street
Brooklyn, NY 11211-7206
718-388-1751

Rabbinical Seminary M'kor Chaim
1571 Fifty-fifth Street
Brooklyn, NY 11219
718-851-0183

Rabbinical Seminary of America
76-01 147th Street
Flushing, NY 11367
718-268-4700

Rensselaer Polytechnic Institute
110 8th Street
Troy, NY 12180-3590
800-448-6562
www.rpi.edu/

Roberts Wesleyan College
2301 Westside Drive
Rochester, NY 14624-1997
800-777-4RWC
www.roberts.edu/

Rochester Institute of Technology
One Lomb Memorial Drive
Rochester, NY 14623-5603
585-475-6631
www.rit.edu/

Russell Sage College
45 Ferry Street
Troy, NY 12180-4115
888-VERY SAGE
www.sage.edu/rsc/index.php

St. Bonaventure University
Route 417
St. Bonaventure, NY 14778-2284
800-462-5050
www.sbu.edu/

St. Francis College
180 Remsen Street
Brooklyn Heights, NY 11201-4398
718-489-5472
www.stfranciscollege.edu/

St. John Fisher College
3690 East Avenue
Rochester, NY 14618-3597
800-444-4640
www.sjfc.edu/

St. John's University
8000 Utopia Parkway
Queens, NY 11439
888-9ST JOHNS
www.stjohns.edu/

St. Joseph's College, New York
245 Clinton Avenue
Brooklyn, NY 11205-3688
718-636-6868
www.sjcny.edu/

St. Joseph's College, Suffolk Campus
155 West Roe Boulevard
Patchogue, NY 11772-2399
631-447-3219
www.sjcny.edu/

St. Lawrence University
Canton, NY 13617-1455
800-285-1856
www.stlawu.edu/

St. Thomas Aquinas College
125 Route 340
Sparkill, NY 10976
800-999-STAC
www.stac.edu/

Sage College of Albany
140 New Scotland Avenue
Albany, NY 12208-3425
888-VERY-SAGE
www.sage.edu/sca/index.php

Four-Year Colleges and Universities

Sarah Lawrence College
1 Mead Way
Bronxville, NY 10708-5999
800-888-2858
www.sarahlawrence.edu/

School of Visual Arts
209 East 23rd Street
New York, NY 10010-3994
800-436-4204
www.schoolofvisualarts.edu/

Sh'or Yoshuv Rabbinical College
1 Cedarlawn Avenue
Lawrence, NY 11559-1714
718-327-2048
www.shoryoshuv.org/

Siena College
515 Loudon Road
Loudonville, NY 12211-1462
888-AT-SIENA
www.siena.edu/

Skidmore College
815 North Broadway
Saratoga Springs, NY 12866-1632
800-867-6007
www.skidmore.edu/

State University of New York at Binghamton
PO Box 6000
Binghamton, NY 13902-6000
607-777-2171
www.binghamton.edu/

State University of New York at New Paltz
75 South Manheim Boulevard
New Paltz, NY 12561
845-257-3200
www.newpaltz.edu/

State University of New York at Oswego
7060 Route 104
Oswego, NY 13126
315-312-2250
www.oswego.edu/

State University of New York at Plattsburgh
101 Broad Steet
Plattsburgh, NY 12901-2681
518-564-2040
www.plattsburgh.edu/

State University of New York College at Brockport
350 New Campus Drive
Brockport, NY 14420-2997
585-395-2751
www.brockport.edu/

State University of New York College at Cortland
PO Box 2000
Cortland, NY 13045
607-753-4711
www.cortland.edu/

State University of New York College at Geneseo
1 College Circle
Geneseo, NY 14454-1401
866-245-5211
www.geneseo.edu/

State University of New York College at Old Westbury
PO Box 210
Old Westbury, NY 11568-0210
516-876-3073
www.oldwestbury.edu/

State University of New York College at Oneonta
Ravine Parkway
Oneonta, NY 13820-4015
800-SUNY-123
www.oneonta.edu/

State University of New York College at Potsdam
44 Pierrepont Avenue
Potsdam, NY 13676
877-POTSDAM
www.potsdam.edu/

State University of New York College of Agriculture and Technology at Cobleskill
Cobleskill, NY 12043
800-295-8988
www.cobleskill.edu/

State University of New York College of Environmental Science and Forestry
1 Forestry Drive
Syracuse, NY 13210-2779
800-777-7373
www.esf.edu/

State University of New York Downstate Medical Center
450 Clarkson Avenue
Brooklyn, NY 11203-2098
718-270-2446
www.downstate.edu/

State University of New York Empire State College
1 Union Avenue
Saratoga Springs, NY 12866-4391
800-847-3000
www.esc.edu/

State University of New York Institute of Technology
PO Box 3050
Utica, NY 13504-3050
800-SUNYTEC
www.sunyit.edu/

State University of New York Maritime College
6 Pennyfield Avenue
Throggs Neck, NY 10465-4198
800-642-1874
www.sunymaritime.edu/

State University of New York Upstate Medical University
750 East Adams Street
Syracuse, NY 13210-2334
800-736-2171
www.upstate.edu/

State University of New York, Fredonia
Fredonia, NY 14063-1136
800-252-1212
www.fredonia.edu/

Stony Brook University, State University of New York
Nicolls Road
Stony Brook, NY 11794
800-872-7869
www.sunysb.edu/

Swedish Institute, College of Health Sciences
226 West 26th Street
New York, NY 10001-6700
212-924-5900
www.swedishinstitute.org/

Syracuse University
Syracuse, NY 13244
315-443-3611
www.syracuse.edu/

Talmudical Institute of Upstate New York
769 Park Avenue
Rochester, NY 14607-3046
716-473-2810
www.tiuny.org/

Talmudical Seminary Oholei Torah
667 Eastern Parkway
Brooklyn, NY 11213-3310
718-774-5050

Torah Temimah Talmudical Seminary
507 Ocean Parkway
Brooklyn, NY 11218-5913
718-853-8500

Touro College
27-33 West 23rd Street
New York, NY 10010
212-627-9542
www.touro.edu/

U.T.A. Mesivta of Kiryas Joel
33 Forest Road, Suite 101
Monroe, NY 10950
845-873-9901

Union College
807 Union Street
Schenectady, NY 12308-2311
518-388-6112
www.union.edu/

United States Merchant Marine Academy
300 Steamboat Road
Kings Point, NY 11024-1699
866-546-4778
www.usmma.edu/

United States Military Academy
600 Thayer Road
West Point, NY 10996
845-938-4041
www.usma.edu/

United Talmudical Seminary
82 Lee Avenue
Brooklyn, NY 11211-7900
718-963-9260

University at Albany, State University of New York
1400 Washington Avenue
Albany, NY 12222-0001
518-442-5435
www.albany.edu/

University at Buffalo, the State University of New York
Capen Hall
Buffalo, NY 14260
888-UB-ADMIT
www.buffalo.edu/

University of Rochester
Wilson Boulevard
Rochester, NY 14627-0250
888-822-2256
www.rochester.edu/

Utica College
1600 Burrstone Road
Utica, NY 13502-4892
800-782-8884
www.utica.edu/

Vassar College
124 Raymond Avenue
Poughkeepsie, NY 12604
800-827-7270
www.vassar.edu/

Vaughn College of Aeronautics and Technology
8601 23rd Avenue
Flushing, NY 11369-1037
718-429-6600
www.vaughn.edu/

Wagner College
1 Campus Road
Staten Island, NY 10301-4495
800-221-1010
www.wagner.edu/

Webb Institute
Crescent Beach Road
Glen Cove, NY 11542-1398
516-671-2213
www.webb-institute.edu/

Wells College
170 Main Street
Aurora, NY 13026
800-952-9355
www.wells.edu/

Yeshiva and Kolel Bais Medrash Elyon
73 Main Street
Monsey, NY 10952
845-356-7064

Yeshiva And Kollel Harbotzas Torah
1049 East 15th Street
Brooklyn, NY 11230
718-692-0208

Yeshiva Derech Chaim
1573 39th Street
Brooklyn, NY 11218
718-438-3070

Yeshiva D'Monsey Rabbinical College
2 Roman Boulevard
Monsey, NY 10952
914-352-5852

Yeshiva Gedolah Imrei Yosef D'Spinka
1466 56th Street
Brooklyn, NY 11219
718-851-8721

Yeshiva Karlin Stolin Rabbinical Institute
1818 Fifty-fourth Street
Brooklyn, NY 11204
718-232-7800

Yeshiva of Nitra Rabbinical College
Pines Bridge Road
Mount Kisco, NY 10549
718-384-5460

Yeshiva of the Telshe Alumni
4904 Independence Avenue
Riverdale, NY 10471
718-601-3523

Yeshiva Shaar Hatorah Talmudic Research Institute
117-06 84th Avenue
Kew Gardens, NY 11418-1469
718-846-1940

Yeshiva Shaarei Torah of Rockland
91 West Carlton Road
Suffern, NY 10901
845-352-3431

Yeshiva University
500 West 185th Street
New York, NY 10033-3201
212-960-5400
www.yu.edu/

Yeshivas Novominsk
1569 47th Street
Brooklyn, NY 11219
718-438-2727

Yeshivat Mikdash Melech
1326 Ocean Parkway
Brooklyn, NY 11230-5601
718-339-1090

Yeshivath Viznitz
Phyllis Terrace, PO Box 446
Monsey, NY 10952
914-356-1010

Yeshivath Zichron Moshe
Laurel Park Road
South Fallsburg, NY 12779
914-434-5240

York College of the City University of New York
94-20 Guy R Brewer Boulevard
Jamaica, NY 11451-0001
718-262-2188
www.york.cuny.edu/

Pennsylvania

Albright College
13th and Bern Streets, PO Box 15234
Reading, PA 19612-5234
800-252-1856
www.albright.edu/

Allegheny College
520 North Main Street
Meadville, PA 16335
800-521-5293
www.allegheny.edu/

Alvernia College
400 Saint Bernardine Street
Reading, PA 19607-1799
610-796-3005
www.alvernia.edu/

Arcadia University
450 South Easton Road
Glenside, PA 19038-3295
877-ARCADIA
www.arcadia.edu/

The Art Institute of Pittsburgh
420 Boulevard of the Allies
Pittsburgh, PA 15219
800-275-2470
www.aip.artinstitutes.edu/

Baptist Bible College of Pennsylvania
538 Venard Road
Clarks Summit, PA 18411-1297
800-451-7664
www.bbc.edu/

Bloomsburg University of Pennsylvania
400 East Second Street
Bloomsburg, PA 17815-1301
570-389-4316
www.bloomu.edu/

Bryn Athyn College of the New Church
PO Box 717
Bryn Athyn, PA 19009-0717
267-502-2511
www.brynathyn.edu/

Bryn Mawr College
101 North Merion Avenue
Bryn Mawr, PA 19010-2899
800-BMC-1885
www.brynmawr.edu/

Bucknell University
Lewisburg, PA 17837
570-577-1101
www.bucknell.edu/

Cabrini College
610 King of Prussia Road
Radnor, PA 19087-3698
800-848-1003
www.cabrini.edu/

California University of Pennsylvania
250 University Avenue
California, PA 15419-1394
724-938-4404
www.cup.edu/

Carlow University
3333 Fifth Avenue
Pittsburgh, PA 15213-3165
800-333-CARLOW
www.carlow.edu/

Carnegie Mellon University
5000 Forbes Avenue
Pittsburgh, PA 15213-3891
412-268-2082
www.cmu.edu/

Four-Year Colleges and Universities

Cedar Crest College
100 College Drive
Allentown, PA 18104-6196
800-360-1222
www.cedarcrest.edu/

Central Pennsylvania College
College Hill & Valley Roads
Summerdale, PA 17093-0309
800-759-2727
www.centralpenn.edu/

Chatham College
Woodland Road
Pittsburgh, PA 15232-2826
800-837-1290
www.chatham.edu/

Chestnut Hill College
9601 Germantown Avenue
Philadelphia, PA 19118-2693
800-248-0052
www.chc.edu/

Cheyney University of Pennsylvania
1837 University Circle, PO Box 200
Cheyney, PA 19319-0200
800-CHEYNEY
www.cheyney.edu/

Clarion University of Pennsylvania
890 Wood Street
Clarion, PA 16214
800-672-7171
www.clarion.edu/

College Misericordia
301 Lake Street
Dallas, PA 18612-1098
866-2626363
www.misericordia.edu/

The Curtis Institute of Music
1726 Locust Street
Philadelphia, PA 19103-6107
215-893-5252
www.curtis.edu/

Delaware Valley College
700 East Butler Avenue
Doylestown, PA 18901-2697
215-489-2211
www.devalcol.edu/

DeSales University
2755 Station Avenue
Center Valley, PA 18034-9568
800-228-5114
www.desales.edu

DeVry University
FreeMarkets Center, 210 Sixth Avenue, Suite 200
Pittsburgh, PA 15222-9123
866-77DEVRY
www.devry.edu/

DeVry University
1140 Virginia Drive
Fort Washington, PA 19034
866-338-7934
www.devry.edu/

DeVry University
701 Lee Road, Suite 103
Chesterbrook, PA 19087-5612
610-889-9980
www.devry.edu/

Dickinson College
PO Box 1773
Carlisle, PA 17013-2896
800-644-1773
www.dickinson.edu/

Drexel University
3141 Chestnut Street
Philadelphia, PA 19104-2875
800-2-DREXEL
www.drexel.edu/

Duquesne University
600 Forbes Avenue
Pittsburgh, PA 15282-0001
800-456-0590
www.duq.edu/

East Stroudsburg University of Pennsylvania
200 Prospect Street
East Stroudsburg, PA 18301-2999
877-230-5547
www3.esu.edu/

Eastern University
1300 Eagle Road
St. Davids, PA 19087-3696
800-452-0996
www.eastern.edu/

Edinboro University of Pennsylvania
Edinboro, PA 16444
800-626-2203
www.edinboro.edu/

Elizabethtown College
1 Alpha Drive
Elizabethtown, PA 17022-2298
717-361-1400
www.etown.edu/

Franklin and Marshall College
PO Box 3003
Lancaster, PA 17604-3003
717-291-3953
www.fandm.edu/

Gannon University
University Square
Erie, PA 16541-0001
800-GANNONU
www.gannon.edu/

Geneva College
3200 College Avenue
Beaver Falls, PA 15010-3599
800-847-8255
www.geneva.edu/

Gettysburg College
300 North Washington Street
Gettysburg, PA 17325-1483
800-431-0803
www.gettysburg.edu/

Gratz College
7605 Old York Road
Melrose Park, PA 19027
800-475-4635
www.gratzcollege.edu/

Grove City College
100 Campus Drive
Grove City, PA 16127-2104
724-458-2100
www.gcc.edu/

Gwynedd-Mercy College
Sumneytown Pike, PO Box 901
Gwynedd Valley, PA 19437-0901
215-646-7300
www.gmc.edu/

Harrisburg University of Science and Technology
215 Market Street
Harrisburg, PA 17101
866-HBG-UNIV
www.harrisburgu.net/

Haverford College
370 Lancaster Avenue
Haverford, PA 19041-1392
610-896-1350
www.haverford.edu/

Holy Family University
Grant and Frankford Avenues
Philadelphia, PA 19114-2094
800-637-1191
www.holyfamily.edu/

Hussian School of Art
1118 Market Street
Philadelphia, PA 19107-3679
215-981-0900
www.hussianart.edu/

Immaculata University
1145 King Road
Immaculata, PA 19345
877-428-6328
www.immaculata.edu/

Indiana University of Pennsylvania
Indiana, PA 15705-1087
800-442-6830
www.iup.edu/

Juniata College
1700 Moore Street
Huntingdon, PA 16652-2119
877-JUNIATA
www.juniata.edu/

King's College
133 North River Street
Wilkes-Barre, PA 18711-0801
888-KINGSPA
www.kings.edu/

Kutztown University of Pennsylvania
15200 Kutztown Road
Kutztown, PA 19530-0730
877-628-1915
www.kutztown.edu/

La Roche College
9000 Babcock Boulevard
Pittsburgh, PA 15237-5898
800-838-4LRC
www.laroche.edu/

Part 5: Appendices

La Salle University
1900 West Olney Avenue
Philadelphia, PA 19141-1199
800-328-1910
www.lasalle.edu/

Lafayette College
Easton, PA 18042-1798
610-330-5100
www.lafayette.edu/

Lancaster Bible College
901 Eden Road, PO Box 83403
Lancaster, PA 17608-3403
866-LBC4YOU
www.lbc.edu/

Lebanon Valley College
101 North College Avenue
Annville, PA 17003-1400
866-LVC-4ADM
www.lvc.edu/

Lehigh University
27 Memorial Drive West
Bethlehem, PA 18015-3094
610-758-3100
www.lehigh.edu/

Lincoln University
PO Box 179
Lincoln University, PA 19352
800-790-0191
www.lincoln.edu/

Lock Haven University of Pennsylvania
401 N. Fairview Street
Lock Haven, PA 17745-2390
800-233-8978
www.lhup.edu/

Lycoming College
700 College Place
Williamsport, PA 17701-5192
800-345-3920
www.lycoming.edu/

Mansfield University of Pennsylvania
Academy Street
Mansfield, PA 16933
800-577-6826
www.mansfield.edu/

Marywood University
2300 Adams Avenue
Scranton, PA 18509-1598
800-346-5014
www.marywood.edu/

Mercyhurst College
501 East 38th Street
Erie, PA 16546
800-825-1926
www.mercyhurst.edu/

Messiah College
One College Avenue
Grantham, PA 17027
800-233-4220
www.messiah.edu/

Millersville University of Pennsylvania
PO Box 1002
Millersville, PA 17551-0302
800-MU-ADMIT
www.millersville.edu/

Moore College of Art & Design
20th and the Parkway
Philadelphia, PA 19103
800-523-2025
www.moore.edu/

Moravian College
1200 Main Street
Bethlehem, PA 18018-6650
800-441-3191
www.moravian.edu/

Mount Aloysius College
7373 Admiral Peary Highway
Cresson, PA 16630-1999
888-823-2220
www.mtaloy.edu/

Muhlenberg College
2400 Chew Street
Allentown, PA 18104-5586
484-664-3245
www.muhlenberg.edu/

Neumann College
One Neumann Drive
Aston, PA 19014-1298
800-963-8626
www.neumann.edu/

Peirce College
1420 Pine Street
Philadelphia, PA 19102-4699
888-467-3472
www.peirce.edu/

Pennsylvania College of Art & Design
204 North Prince Street, PO Box 59
Lancaster, PA 17608-0059
717-396-7833
www.pcad.edu/

Pennsylvania College of Technology
One College Avenue
Williamsport, PA 17701-5778
570-327-4761
www.pct.edu/

The Pennsylvania State University–Abington College
1600 Woodland Road
Abington, PA 19001
814-865-4700
www.abington.psu.edu/

The Pennsylvania State University–Altoona College
3000 Ivyside Park
Altoona, PA 16601-3760
800-848-9843
www.aa.psu.edu/

The Pennsylvania State University at Erie–The Behrend College
5091 Station Road
Erie, PA 16563-0001
866-374-3378
www.pserie.psu.edu/

The Pennsylvania State University Berks Campus of the Berks–Lehigh Valley College
Tulpehocken Road, PO Box 7009
Reading, PA 19610-6009
814-865-4700
www.bk.psu.edu/

The Pennsylvania State University–Harrisburg Campus
777 West Harrisburg Pike
Middletown, PA 17057-4898
800-222-2056
www.hbg.psu.edu/

The Pennsylvania State University–University Park Campus
201 Old Main
University Park, PA 16802-1503
814-865-4700
www.psu.edu/

Philadelphia Biblical University
200 Manor Avenue
Langhorne, PA 19047-2990
800-366-0049
www.pbu.edu/

Philadelphia University
School House Lane and Henry Avenue
Philadelphia, PA 19144-5497
215-951-2800
www.philau.edu/

Point Park University
201 Wood Street
Pittsburgh, PA 15222-1984
800-321-0129
www.pointpark.edu/

Robert Morris University
6001 University Boulevard
Moon Township, PA 15108-1189
800-762-0097
www.rmu.edu/

Rosemont College
1400 Montgomery Avenue
Rosemont, PA 19010-1699
800-331-0708
www.rosemont.edu/

St. Charles Borromeo Seminary, Overbrook
100 East Wynnewood Road
Wynnewood, PA 19096
610-785-6271
www.scs.edu/

Saint Francis University
PO Box 600, 117 Evergreen Drive
Loretto, PA 15940-0600
800-342-5732
www.francis.edu/

Saint Joseph's University
5600 City Avenue
Philadelphia, PA 19131-1395
610-660-1300
www.sju.edu/

Four-Year Colleges and Universities

Saint Vincent College
300 Fraser Purchase Road
Latrobe, PA 15650-2690
800-782-5549
www.stvincent.edu/

Seton Hill University
Seton Hill Drive
Greensburg, PA 15601
800-826-6234
www.setonhill.edu/

Shippensburg University of Pennsylvania
1871 Old Main Drive
Shippensburg, PA 17257-2299
717-477-1231
www.ship.edu/

Slippery Rock University of Pennsylvania
1 Morrow Way
Slippery Rock, PA 16057-1383
800-SRU-9111
www.sru.edu/

Susquehanna University
514 University Avenue
Selinsgrove, PA 17870
800-326-9672
www.susqu.edu/

Swarthmore College
500 College Avenue
Swarthmore, PA 19081-1397
800-667-3110
www.swarthmore.edu/

Talmudical Yeshiva of Philadelphia
6063 Drexel Road
Philadelphia, PA 19131-1296
215-473-1212

Temple University
1801 North Broad Street
Philadelphia, PA 19122-6096
888-340-2222
www.temple.edu/

Thiel College
75 College Avenue
Greenville, PA 16125-2181
800-248-4435
www.thiel.edu/

Thomas Jefferson University
Eleventh and Walnut Streets
Philadelphia, PA 19107
877-533-3247
www.jefferson.edu/

University of Pennsylvania
3451 Walnut Street
Philadelphia, PA 19104
215-898-7507
www.upenn.edu/

University of Phoenix–Philadelphia Campus
170 South Warner Road, Suite 200
Wayne, PA 19087-2121
800-228-7240
www.phoenix.edu/

University of Phoenix–Pittsburgh Campus
Penn Center West Six, Suite 100
Pittsburgh, PA 15276
800-228-7240
www.phoenix.edu/

University of Pittsburgh
4200 Fifth Avenue
Pittsburgh, PA 15260
412-624-7488
www.pitt.edu/

University of Pittsburgh at Bradford
300 Campus Drive
Bradford, PA 16701-2812
800-872-1787
www.upb.pitt.edu/

University of Pittsburgh at Greensburg
1150 Mount Pleasant Road
Greensburg, PA 15601-5860
724-836-9880
www.upg.pitt.edu/

University of Pittsburgh at Johnstown
450 Schoolhouse Road
Johnstown, PA 15904-2990
800-765-4875
www.upj.pitt.edu/

The University of Scranton
800 Linden Street
Scranton, PA 18510
888-SCRANTON
www.scranton.edu/

The University of the Arts
320 South Broad Street
Philadelphia, PA 19102-4944
800-616-ARTS
www.uarts.edu/

University of the Sciences in Philadelphia
600 South 43rd Street
Philadelphia, PA 19104-4495
215-596-8810
www.usip.edu/

Ursinus College
Box 1000, Main Street
Collegeville, PA 19426-1000
610-409-3200
www.ursinus.edu/

Valley Forge Christian College
1401 Charlestown Road
Phoenixville, PA 19460
800-432-8322
www.vfcc.edu/

Villanova University
800 Lancaster Avenue
Villanova, PA 19085-1699
610-519-4000
www.villanova.edu/

Washington & Jefferson College
60 South Lincoln Street
Washington, PA 15301
888-WANDJAY
www.washjeff.edu/

Waynesburg College
51 West College Street
Waynesburg, PA 15370-1222
800-225-7393
www.waynesburg.edu/

West Chester University of Pennsylvania
University Avenue and High Street
West Chester, PA 19383
610-436-3414
www.wcupa.edu/

Westminster College
319 South Market Street
New Wilmington, PA 16172-0001
724-946-7100
www.westminster.edu/

Widener University
One University Place
Chester, PA 19013-5792
888-WIDENER
www.widener.edu/

Wilkes University
84 West South Street
Wilkes-Barre, PA 18766-0002
800-945-5378
www.wilkes.edu/

Wilson College
1015 Philadelphia Avenue
Chambersburg, PA 17201-1285
800-421-8402
www.wilson.edu/

Yeshiva Beth Moshe
930 Hickory Street, PO Box 1141
Scranton, PA 18505-2124
717-346-1747

York College of Pennsylvania
York, PA 17405-7199
800-455-8018
www.ycp.edu/

VIRGINIA

Argosy University/Washington D.C.
1550 Wilson Boulevard, Suite 600
Arlington, VA 22209
866-703-2777
www.argosyu.edu/

The Art Institute of Washington
1820 North Fort Meyer Drive, Ground Floor
Arlington, VA 22209
877-303-3771
www.artinstitutes.edu/arlington/

Averett University
420 West Main Street
Danville, VA 24541-3692
800-AVERETT
www.averett.edu/

Bluefield College
3000 College Drive
Bluefield, VA 24605-1799
800-872-0175
www.bluefield.edu/

Part 5: Appendices

Bridgewater College
402 East College Street
Bridgewater, VA 22812-1599
800-759-8328
www.bridgewater.edu/

Christendom College
134 Christendom Drive
Front Royal, VA 22630-5103
800-877-5456
www.christendom.edu/

Christopher Newport University
1 University Place
Newport News, VA 23606-2998
800-333-4268
www.cnu.edu/

The College of William and Mary
PO Box 8795
Williamsburg, VA 23187-8795
757-221-4223
www.wm.edu/

DeVry University
1751 Pinnacle Drive, Suite 250
McLean, VA 22102-3832
703-556-9669
www.devry.edu/

DeVry University
2450 Crystal Drive
Arlington, VA 22202
866-563-3900
www.devry.edu/

Eastern Mennonite University
1200 Park Road
Harrisonburg, VA 22802-2462
800-368-2665
www.emu.edu/

Emory & Henry College
PO Box 947
Emory, VA 24327-0947
800-848-5493
www.ehc.edu/

Ferrum College
PO Box 1000
Ferrum, VA 24088-9001
800-868-9797
www.ferrum.edu/

George Mason University
4400 University Drive
Fairfax, VA 22030
703-993-2398
www.gmu.edu/

Hampden-Sydney College
PO Box 667
Hampden-Sydney, VA 23943
800-755-0733
www.hsc.edu/

Hampton University
Hampton, VA 23668
800-624-3328
www.hamptonu.edu/

Hollins University
PO Box 9603
Roanoke, VA 24020-1603
800-456-9595
www.hollins.edu/

James Madison University
800 South Main Street
Harrisonburg, VA 22807
540-568-5681
www.jmu.edu/

Jefferson College of Health Sciences
PO Box 13186
Roanoke, VA 24031-3186
888-985-8483
www.jchs.edu/

Liberty University
1971 University Boulevard
Lynchburg, VA 24502
800-543-5317
www.liberty.edu/

Longwood University
201 High Street
Farmville, VA 23909
800-281-4677
www.longwood.edu/

Lynchburg College
1501 Lakeside Drive
Lynchburg, VA 24501-3199
800-426-8101
www.lynchburg.edu/

Mary Baldwin College
201 East Frederick Street
Staunton, VA 24401-3610
800-468-2262
www.mbc.edu/

Marymount University
2807 North Glebe Road
Arlington, VA 22207-4299
800-548-7638
www.marymount.edu/

Norfolk State University
700 Park Avenue
Norfolk, VA 23504
757-823-8396
www.nsu.edu/

Old Dominion University
5115 Hampton Boulevard
Norfolk, VA 23529
800-348-7926
www.odu.edu/

Patrick Henry College
One Patrick Henry Circle
Purcellville, VA 20132
540-338-1776
www.phc.edu/

Radford University
PO Box 6890, RU Station
Radford, VA 24142
800-890-4265
www.radford.edu/

Randolph-Macon College
PO Box 5005
Ashland, VA 23005-5505
800-888-1762
www.rmc.edu/

Randolph-Macon Woman's College
2500 Rivermont Avenue
Lynchburg, VA 24503-1526
800-745-7692
www.rmwc.edu/

Regent University
1000 Regent University Drive
Virginia Beach, VA 23464-9800
800-373-5504
www.regent.edu/

Roanoke College
221 College Lane
Salem, VA 24153-3794
800-388-2276
www.roanoke.edu/

Saint Paul's College
115 College Drive
Lawrenceville, VA 23868-1202
800-678-7071
www.saintpauls.edu/

Shenandoah University
1460 University Drive
Winchester, VA 22601-5195
800-432-2266
www.su.edu/

Southern Virginia University
One College Hill Drive
Buena Vista, VA 24416
800-229-8420
www.southernvirginia.edu/

Stratford University
7777 Leesburg Pike, Suite 100 South
Falls Church, VA 22043
800-444-0804
www.stratford.edu/

Sweet Briar College
Sweet Briar, VA 24595
800-381-6142
www.sbc.edu/

University of Management and Technology
1901 North Fort Myers Drive
Arlington, VA 22209
703-516-0035
www.umtweb.edu/

University of Mary Washington
1301 College Avenue
Fredericksburg, VA 22401-5358
800-468-5614
www.umw.edu/

University of Northern Virginia
10021 Balls Ford Road
Manassas, VA 20109
703-392-0771
www.unva.edu/

University of Phoenix–Northern Virginia Campus
11730 Plaza American Drive, Suite 2000
Reston, VA 20190
800-228-7240
www.phoenix.edu/

University of Phoenix–Richmond Campus
6802 Paragon Place, Suite 420
Richmond, VA 23230
800-228-7240
www.phoenix.edu/

Four-Year Colleges and Universities

University of Richmond
28 Westhampton Way
University of Richmond, VA 23173
800-700-1662
www.richmond.edu/

University of Virginia
Charlottesville, VA 22903
434-982-3200
www.virginia.edu/

The University of Virginia's College at Wise
1 College Avenue
Wise, VA 24293
888-282-9324
www.uvawise.edu/

Virginia Commonwealth University
901 West Franklin Street
Richmond, VA 23284-9005
800-841-3638
www.vcu.edu/

Virginia Intermont College
1013 Moore Street
Bristol, VA 24201-4298
800-451-1842
www.vic.edu/

Virginia Military Institute
Lexington, VA 24450
800-767-4207
www.vmi.edu/

Virginia Polytechnic Institute and State University
Blacksburg, VA 24061
540-231-6267
www.vt.edu/

Virginia State University
1 Hayden Street
Petersburg, VA 23806-0001
800-871-7611
www.vsu.edu/

Virginia Union University
1500 North Lombardy Street
Richmond, VA 23220-1170
800-368-3227
www.vuu.edu/

Virginia University of Lynchburg
2058 Garfield Avenue
Lynchburg, VA 24501-6417
804-528-5276
www.vulonline.org/

Virginia Wesleyan College
1584 Wesleyan Drive
Norfolk, VA 23502-5599
800-737-8684
www.vwc.edu/

Washington and Lee University
Lexington, VA 24450-0303
540-458-8710
www.wlu.edu/

Westwood College–Arlington Ballston Campus
1901 North Ft. Myer Drive
Arlington, VA 22209
877-268-5218
www.westwood.edu

World College
5193 Shore Drive, Suite 105
Virginia Beach, VA 23455-2500
800-696-7532
www.worldcollege.edu/

West Virginia

Alderson-Broaddus College
1 College Hill Drive
Philippi, WV 26416
800-263-1549
www.ab.edu/

American Public University System
111 West Congress Street
Charles Town, WV 25414
877-468-6268
www.apus.edu/

Appalachian Bible College
PO Box ABC
Bradley, WV 25818
800-678-9ABC
www.abc.edu/

Bethany College
Main Street
Bethany, WV 26032
800-922-7611
www.bethanywv.edu/

Bluefield State College
219 Rock Street
Bluefield, WV 24701-2198
800-654-7798
www.bluefieldstate.edu/

Concord University
Vermillion Street, PO Box 1000
Athens, WV 24712-1000
888-384-5249
www.concord.edu/

Davis & Elkins College
100 Campus Drive
Elkins, WV 26241-3996
800-624-3157
www.davisandelkins.edu/

Fairmont State University
1201 Locust Avenue
Fairmont, WV 26554
800-641-5678
www.fairmontstate.edu/

Glenville State College
200 High Street
Glenville, WV 26351-1200
304-462-4128
www.glenville.edu/

Marshall University
One John Marshall Drive
Huntington, WV 25755
304-696-3160
www.marshall.edu/

Mountain State University
Box 9003
Beckley, WV 25802-9003
800-766-6067
www.mountainstate.edu/

Ohio Valley University
One Campus View Drive
Vienna, WV 26105-8000
877-446-8668
www.ovu.edu/

Salem International University
223 West Main Street, PO Box 500
Salem, WV 26426-0500
800-283-4562
www.salemiu.edu/

Shepherd University
PO Box 3210
Shepherdstown, WV 25443-3210
800-344-5231
www.shepherd.edu/

University of Charleston
2300 MacCorkle Avenue, SE
Charleston, WV 25304-1099
800-995-GOUC
www.ucwv.edu/

West Liberty State College
PO Box 295
West Liberty, WV 26074
800-732-6204
www.wlsc.edu/

West Virginia State University
Post Office Box 1000
Institute, WV 25112-1000
800-987-2112
www.wvstateu.edu/

West Virginia University
University Avenue
Morgantown, WV 26506
800-344-9881
www.wvu.edu/

West Virginia University Institute of Technology
405 Fayette Pike
Montgomery, WV 25136
888-554-8324
www.wvutech.edu/

West Virginia Wesleyan College
59 College Avenue
Buckhannon, WV 26201
800-722-9933
www.wvwc.edu/

Wheeling Jesuit University
316 Washington Avenue
Wheeling, WV 26003-6295
800-624-6992
www.wju.edu/

TWO-YEAR COLLEGES

Delaware

Delaware College of Art and Design
600 North Market Street
Wilmington, DE 19801
302-622-8000
www.dcad.edu/

Delaware Technical & Community College, Jack F. Owens Campus
PO Box 610
Georgetown, DE 19947
302-856-5400
www.dtcc.edu/

Delaware Technical & Community College, Stanton/Wilmington Campus
400 Stanton-Christiana Road
Newark, DE 19713
302-571-5366
www.dtcc.edu/

Delaware Technical & Community College, Terry Campus
100 Campus Drive
Dover, DE 19904-1383
302-857-1020
www.dtcc.edu/terry/

Maryland

Allegany College of Maryland
12401 Willowbrook Road, SE
Cumberland, MD 21502-2596
301-784-5000
www.allegany.edu/

Anne Arundel Community College
101 College Parkway
Arnold, MD 21012-1895
410-777-2240
www.aacc.edu/

Baltimore City Community College
2901 Liberty Heights Avenue
Baltimore, MD 21215-7893
410-462-8300
www.bccc.state.md.us/

Baltimore International College
Commerce Exchange, 17 Commerce Street
Baltimore, MD 21202-3230
800-624-9926
www.bic.edu/

Carroll Community College
1601 Washington Road
Westminster, MD 21157
410-386-8430
www.carrollcc.edu/

Cecil Community College
One Seahawk Drive
North East, MD 21901-1999
410-287-1002
www.cecilcc.edu/

Chesapeake College
PO Box 8
Wye Mills, MD 21679-0008
410-822-5400
www.chesapeake.edu/

College of Southern Maryland
8730 Mitchell Road, PO Box 910
La Plata, MD 20646-0910
800-933-9177
www.csmd.edu/

The Community College of Baltimore County
800 South Rolling Road
Baltimore, MD 21228-5381
410-455-4392
www.ccbcmd.edu/

Frederick Community College
7932 Opossumtown Pike
Frederick, MD 21702-2097
301-846-2466
www.frederick.edu/

Garrett College
687 Mosser Road
McHenry, MD 21541
301-387-3044
www.garrettcollege.edu/

Hagerstown Business College
18618 Crestwood Drive
Hagerstown, MD 21742-2797
800-422-2670
www.hagerstownbusinesscol.org/

Hagerstown Community College
11400 Robinwood Drive
Hagerstown, MD 21742-6590
301-790-2800
www.hagerstowncc.edu/

Harford Community College
401 Thomas Run Road
Bel Air, MD 21015-1698
410-836-4311
www.harford.edu/

Howard Community College
10901 Little Patuxent Parkway
Columbia, MD 21044-3197
410-772-4856
www.howardcc.edu/

ITT Technical Institute
11301 Red Run Boulevard
Owings Mills, MD 21117
443-394-7115
www.itt-tech.edu/

Montgomery College
900 Hungerford Drive
Rockville, MD 20850
301-279-5034
www.montgomerycollege.org/

Prince George's Community College
301 Largo Road
Largo, MD 20774-2199
301-336-6000
www.pgcc.edu/

TESST College of Technology
803 Glen Eagles Court
Towson, MD 21286-2201
800-48-TESST
www.tesst.com/

TESST College of Technology
1520 South Caton Avenue
Baltimore, MD 21227-1063
410-644-6400
www.tesst.com/

TESST College of Technology
4600 Powder Mill Road
Beltsville, MD 20705
301-937-8448
www.tesst.com/

Wor-Wic Community College
32000 Campus Drive
Salisbury, MD 21804
410-334-2895
www.worwic.edu/

New Jersey

Assumption College for Sisters
350 Bernardsville Road
Mendham, NJ 07945-0800
973-543-6528
www.acscollegeforsisters.org/

Atlantic Cape Community College
5100 Black Horse Pike
Mays Landing, NJ 08330-2699
800-645-CHIEF
www.atlantic.edu/

Bergen Community College
400 Paramus Road
Paramus, NJ 07652-1595
201-447-7193
www.bergen.edu/

Berkeley College
44 Rifle Camp Road
West Paterson, NJ 07424-3353
800-446-5400
www.berkeleycollege.edu/

Brookdale Community College
765 Newman Springs Road
Lincroft, NJ 07738-1597
732-842-1900
www.brookdalecc.edu/

Burlington County College
Route 530
Pemberton, NJ 08068-1599
609-894-9311
www.bcc.edu/

Camden County College
PO Box 200
Blackwood, NJ 08012-0200
888-228-2466
www.camdencc.edu/

County College of Morris
214 Center Grove Road
Randolph, NJ 07869-2086
888-226-8001
www.ccm.edu/

Cumberland County College
PO Box 1500, College Drive
Vineland, NJ 08362-1500
856-691-8600
www.cccnj.edu/

Essex County College
303 University Avenue
Newark, NJ 07102-1798
973-877-3119
www.essex.edu/

Gibbs College
630 West Mount Pleasant Avenue, Route 10
Livingston, NJ 07039
888-316-0444
www.gibbsnj.edu/

Gloucester County College
1400 Tanyard Road
Sewell, NJ 08080
856-468-5000
www.gccnj.edu/

Hudson County Community College
25 Journal Square
Jersey City, NJ 07306
201-656-2020
www.hccc.edu/

Mercer County Community College
1200 Old Trenton Road, PO Box B
Trenton, NJ 08690-1004
800-392-MCCC
www.mccc.edu/

Middlesex County College
2600 Woodbridge Avenue, PO Box 3050
Edison, NJ 08818-3050
732-548-6000
www.middlesexcc.edu/

Ocean County College
College Drive, PO Box 2001
Toms River, NJ 08754-2001
732-255-0304
www.ocean.edu/

Passaic County Community College
One College Boulevard
Paterson, NJ 07505-1179
973-684-6304
www.pccc.cc.nj.us/

Raritan Valley Community College
PO Box 3300
Somerville, NJ 08876-1265
908-526-1200
www.raritanval.edu/

Salem Community College
460 Hollywood Avenue
Carneys Point, NJ 08069-2799
856-351-2707
www.salemcc.org/

Somerset Christian College
10 Liberty Square, PO Box 9035
Zarephath, NJ 08890-9035
800-234-9305
www.somerset.edu/

Sussex County Community College
1 College Hill
Newton, NJ 07860
973-300-2219
www.sussex.edu/

Union County College
1033 Springfield Avenue
Cranford, NJ 07016-1599
908-709-7127
www.ucc.edu/

Warren County Community College
475 Route 57 West
Washington, NJ 07882-4343
908-835-2300
www.warren.edu/

New York

Adirondack Community College
640 Bay Road
Queensbury, NY 12804
518-743-2200
www.sunyacc.edu/

American Academy McAllister Institute of Funeral Service
450 West 56th Street
New York, NY 10019-3602
212-757-1190
www.a-a-m-i.org/

American Academy of Dramatic Arts
120 Madison Avenue
New York, NY 10016-7004
800-463-8990
www.aada.org/

The Art Institute of New York City
75 Varick Street, 16th Floor
New York, NY 10013
800-654-2433
www.ainyc.aii.edu/

ASA Institute, The College of Advanced Technology
151 Lawrence Street, 2nd Floor
Brooklyn, NY 11201
718-522-9073
www.asa-institute.com/

Berkeley College-New York City Campus
3 East 43rd Street
New York, NY 10017-4604
800-446-5400
www.berkeleycollege.edu/

Berkeley College-Westchester Campus
99 Church Street
White Plains, NY 10601
800-446-5400
www.berkeleycollege.edu/

Borough of Manhattan Community College of the City University of New York
199 Chambers Street
New York, NY 10007-1097
212-220-1265
www.bmcc.cuny.edu/

Bramson ORT College
69-30 Austin Street
Forest Hills, NY 11375-4239
718-261-5800
www.bramsonort.edu/

Bronx Community College of the City University of New York
University Avenue & West 181st Street
Bronx, NY 10453
718-289-5888
www.bcc.cuny.edu/

Broome Community College
PO Box 1017
Binghamton, NY 13902-1017
607-778-5001
www.sunybroome.edu/

Bryant and Stratton College
1259 Central Avenue
Albany, NY 12205-5230
518-437-1802
www.bryantstratton.edu/

Bryant and Stratton College
1225 Jefferson Road
Rochester, NY 14623-3136
585-292-5627
www.bryantstratton.edu/

Bryant and Stratton College
150 Bellwood Drive
Rochester, NY 14606
585-720-0660
www.bryantstratton.edu/

Bryant and Stratton College
953 James Street
Syracuse, NY 13203-2502
315-472-6603
www.bryantstratton.edu/

Bryant and Stratton College, Amherst Campus
Audubon Business Center, 40 Hazelwood Drive
Amherst, NY 14228
716-677-9500
www.bryantstratton.edu/

Bryant and Stratton College, Buffalo Campus
465 Main Street, Suite 400
Buffalo, NY 14203
716-884-9120
www.bryantstratton.edu/

Two-Year Colleges

Bryant and Stratton College, Lackawanna Campus
1214 Abbott Road
Lackawanna, NY 14218-1989
716-677-9500
www.bryantstratton.edu/

Bryant and Stratton College, North Campus
8687 Carling Road
Liverpool, NY 13090-1315
315-652-6500
www.bryantstratton.edu/

Business Informatics Center, Inc.
134 South Central Avenue
Valley Stream, NY 11580-5431
516-561-0050

Cayuga County Community College
197 Franklin Street
Auburn, NY 13021-3099
315-255-1743
www.cayuga-cc.edu/

Clinton Community College
136 Clinton Point Drive
Plattsburgh, NY 12901-9573
800-552-1160
clintoncc.suny.edu/

Cochran School of Nursing
967 North Broadway
Yonkers, NY 10701
914-964-4316
www.riversidehealth.org/

The College of Westchester
325 Central Avenue, PO Box 710
White Plains, NY 10602
800-333-4924
www.cw.edu/

Columbia-Greene Community College
4400 Route 23
Hudson, NY 12534-0327
518-828-4181
www.sunycgcc.edu/

Corning Community College
One Academic Drive
Corning, NY 14830-3297
607-962-9221
www.corning-cc.edu/

Crouse Hospital School of Nursing
736 Irving Avenue
Syracuse, NY 13210
315-470-7481
www.crouse.org/nursing/

Dorothea Hopfer School of Nursing at The Mount Vernon Hospital
53 Valentine Street
Mount Vernon, NY 10550
914-664-8000
www.ssmc.org/

Dutchess Community College
53 Pendell Road
Poughkeepsie, NY 12601-1595
845-431-8000
www.sunydutchess.edu/

Ellis Hospital School of Nursing
1101 Nott Street
Schenectady, NY 12308
518-243-4471
www.ehson.org/

Elmira Business Institute
303 North Main Street
Elmira, NY 14901
800-843-1812
www.ebi-college.com/

Erie Community College
121 Ellicott Street
Buffalo, NY 14203-2698
716-851-1588
www.ecc.edu/

Erie Community College, North Campus
6205 Main Street
Williamsville, NY 14221-7095
716-851-1588
www.ecc.edu

Erie Community College, South Campus
4041 Southwestern Boulevard
Orchard Park, NY 14127-2199
716-851-1588
www.ecc.edu/

Eugenio María de Hostos Community College of the City University of New York
500 Grand Concourse
Bronx, NY 10451
718-518-4444
www.hostos.cuny.edu/

Finger Lakes Community College
4355 Lakeshore Drive
Canandaigua, NY 14424-8395
585-394-3500
www.flcc.edu/

Fiorello H. LaGuardia Community College of the City University of New York
31-10 Thomson Avenue
Long Island City, NY 11101-3071
718-482-5114
www.lagcc.cuny.edu/

Fulton-Montgomery Community College
2805 State Highway 67
Johnstown, NY 12095-3790
518-762-4651
www.fmcc.suny.edu/

Gamla College
1213 Elm Avenue
Brooklyn, NY 11230
718-339-4747

Genesee Community College
1 College Road
Batavia, NY 14020-9704
800-CALL GCC
www.genesee.edu/

Helene Fuld College of Nursing of North General Hospital
1879 Madison Avenue
New York, NY 10035-2709
212-423-2768
www.helenefuld.edu/

Herkimer County Community College
Reservoir Road
Herkimer, NY 13350
315-866-0300
www.herkimer.edu

Hudson Valley Community College
80 Vandenburgh Avenue
Troy, NY 12180-6096
518-629-4603
www.hvcc.edu/

Institute of Design and Construction
141 Willoughby Street
Brooklyn, NY 11201-5317
718-855-3661
www.idcbrooklyn.org/

Interboro Institute
450 West 56th Street
New York, NY 10019-3602
212-399-0091
www.interboro.com/

Island Drafting and Technical Institute
128 Broadway
Amityville, NY 11787
631-691-8733
www.idti.edu/

ITT Technical Institute
13 Airline Drive
Albany, NY 12205
518-452-9300
www.itt-tech.edu/

ITT Technical Institute
235 Greenfield Parkway
Liverpool, NY 13088
315-461-8000
www.itt-tech.edu/

ITT Technical Institute
2295 Millersport Highway, PO Box 327
Getzville, NY 14068
716-689-2200
www.itt-tech.edu/

Jamestown Business College
7 Fairmount Avenue, Box 429
Jamestown, NY 14702-0429
716-664-5100
www.jbcny.org/

Jamestown Community College
525 Falconer Street
Jamestown, NY 14701-1999
716-665-5220
www.sunyjcc.edu/

Part 5: Appendices

Jefferson Community College
1220 Coffeen Street
Watertown, NY 13601
315-786-2277
www.sunyjefferson.edu/

Katharine Gibbs School
320 South Service Road
Melville, NY 11747-3785
631-370-3300
www.gibbsmelville.com/

Katharine Gibbs School
200 Park Avenue
New York, NY 10166-0005
212-867-9300
www.katharinegibbs.com/

Kingsborough Community College of the City University of New
2001 Oriental Blvd, Manhattan Beach
Brooklyn, NY 11235
718-368-4600
www.kbcc.cuny.edu/

Long Island Business Institute
6500 Jericho Turnpike
Commack, NY 11725
631-499-7100
www.libi.edu/commack/index.html

Long Island College Hospital School of Nursing
340 Court Street
Brooklyn, NY 11231
718-780-1071
www.futurenurselich.org/

Maria College
700 New Scotland Avenue
Albany, NY 12208-1798
518-438-3111
www.mariacollege.edu/

Memorial Hospital School of Nursing
600 Northern Boulevard
Albany, NY 12204
518-471-3260
www.nehealth.com/html/NEH_Schools.asp?L1=6&L2=31

Mildred Elley
800 New Louden Road
Latham, NY 12110
800-622-6327
www.mildred-elley.edu/

Mohawk Valley Community College
1101 Sherman Drive
Utica, NY 13501-5394
315-792-5640
www.mvcc.edu/

Monroe Community College
1000 East Henrietta Road
Rochester, NY 14623-5780
585-292-2000
www.monroecc.edu/

Nassau Community College
1 Education Drive
Garden City, NY 11530-6793
516-572-7345
www.ncc.edu/

New York Career Institute
11 Park Place- 4th Floor
New York, NY 10007
212-962-0002
www.nyci.com/

New York City College of Technology of the City University of New York
300 Jay Street
Brooklyn, NY 11201-2983
718-260-5500
www.citytech.cuny.edu/

New York College of Health Professions
6801 Jericho Turnpike
Syosset, NY 11791-4413
800-922-7337
www.nycollege.edu/

Niagara County Community College
3111 Saunders Settlement Road
Sanborn, NY 14132-9460
716-614-6200
www.niagaracc.suny.edu/

North Country Community College
23 Santanoni Avenue, PO Box 89
Saranac Lake, NY 12983-0089
888-TRY-NCCC
www.nccc.edu/

Olean Business Institute
301 North Union Street
Olean, NY 14760-2691
716-372-7978
www.obi.edu/

Onondaga Community College
4941 Onondaga Road
Syracuse, NY 13215-2099
315-488-2201
www.sunyocc.edu/

Orange County Community College
115 South Street
Middletown, NY 10940-6437
845-341-4030
www.orange.cc.ny.us/

Phillips Beth Israel School of Nursing
310 East 22nd Street, 9th Floor
New York, NY 10010-5702
212-614-6176
www.futurenursebi.org

Plaza College
7409 37th Avenue
Jackson Heights, NY 11372-6300
718-779-1430
www.plazacollege.edu/

Queensborough Community College of the City University of New
222-05 56th Avenue
Bayside, NY 11364
718-631-6307
www.qcc.cuny.edu/

Rochester Business Institute
1630 Portland Avenue
Rochester, NY 14621
585-266-0430
www.rochester-institute.com/

Rockland Community College
145 College Road
Suffern, NY 10901-3699
800-722-7666
www.sunyrockland.edu/

St. Elizabeth College of Nursing
2215 Genesee Street
Utica, NY 13501
315-798-8253
www.stemc.org/

Saint Joseph's Hospital Health Center School of Nursing
206 Prospect Avenue
Syracuse, NY 13203
315-448-5040
www.sjhsyr.org/nursing/

Saint Vincent Catholic Medical Centers School of Nursing
175-05 Horace Harding Expressway
Fresh Meadows, NY 11365
718-357-0500
www.svcmcny.org/

Samaritan Hospital School of Nursing
2215 Burdett Avenue
Troy, NY 12180
518-271-3285
www.nehealth.com/

Schenectady County Community College
78 Washington Avenue
Schenectady, NY 12305-2294
518-381-1370
www.sunysccc.edu/

Simmons Institute of Funeral Service
1828 South Avenue
Syracuse, NY 13207
800-727-3536
www.simmonsinstitute.com/

State University of New York College of Agriculture and Technology at Morrisville
PO Box 901
Morrisville, NY 13408-0901
315-684-6000
www.morrisville.edu/

State University of New York College of Environmental Science & Forestry, Ranger School
PO Box 48, 257 Ranger School Road
Wanakena, NY 13695
800-777-7373
www.esf.edu/

State University of New York College of Technology at Alfred
Alfred, NY 14802
800-4-ALFRED
www.alfredstate.edu/

State University of New York College of Technology at Canton
Cornell Drive
Canton, NY 13617
800-388-7123
www.canton.edu/

State University of New York College of Technology at Delhi
Main Street
Delhi, NY 13753
800-96-DELHI
www.delhi.edu/

Suffolk County Community College
533 College Road
Selden, NY 11784-2899
631-451-4110
www.sunysuffolk.edu/

Sullivan County Community College
112 College Road
Loch Sheldrake, NY 12759
845-434-5750
www.sullivan.suny.edu/

Taylor Business Institute
23 West 17th Street, 7th floor
New York, NY 10011
212-229-1963
www.tbiglobal.com/

TCI–The College of Technology
320 West 31st Street
New York, NY 10001-2705
212-594-4000
www.tciedu.com/

Tompkins Cortland Community College
170 North Street, PO Box 139
Dryden, NY 13053-0139
607-844-8222
www.sunytccc.edu/

Trocaire College
360 Choate Avenue
Buffalo, NY 14220-2094
716-827-2459
www.trocaire.edu/

Ulster County Community College
Cottekill Road
Stone Ridge, NY 12484
800-724-0833
www.sunyulster.edu/

Utica School of Commerce
201 Bleecker Street
Utica, NY 13501-2280
800-321-4USC
www.uscny.edu/

Villa Maria College of Buffalo
240 Pine Ridge Road
Buffalo, NY 14225-3999
716-896-0700
www.villa.edu/

Westchester Community College
75 Grasslands Road
Valhalla, NY 10595-1698
914-606-6735
www.sunywcc.edu/

Wood Tobe–Coburn School
8 East 40th Street
New York, NY 10016
212-686-9040
www.woodtobecoburn.com/

Pennsylvania

Academy of Medical Arts and Business
2301 Academy Drive
Harrisburg, PA 17112-1012
717-545-4747
www.acadcampus.com/

Allied Medical and Technical Careers
166 Slocum Street
Forty Fort, PA 18704-2936
717-288-8400
www.alliedteched.com/

Antonelli Institute
300 Montgomery Avenue
Erdenheim, PA 19038
800-722-7871
www.antonelli.edu/

The Art Institute of Philadelphia
1622 Chestnut Street
Philadelphia, PA 19103-5198
800-275-2474
www.aiph.artinstitutes.edu/

Berean Institute
1901 West Girard Avenue
Philadelphia, PA 19130-1599
215-763-4833
www.bereaninstitute.org/

Berks Technical Institute
2205 Ridgewood Road
Wyomissing, PA 19610-1168
800-821-4662
www.berkstech.com/

Bidwell Training Center
1815 Metropolitan Street
Pittsburgh, PA 15233-2234
412-323-4000
www.bidwell-training.org/

Bradford School
125 West Station Square Drive, Suite 129
Pittsburgh, PA 15219
800-391-6810
www.bradfordpittsburgh.edu/

Bradley Academy for the Visual Arts
1409 Williams Road
York, PA 17402-9012
800-864-7725
www.bradleyacademy.net/

Bucks County Community College
275 Swamp Road
Newtown, PA 18940-1525
215-968-8119
www.bucks.edu/

Business Institute of Pennsylvania
628 Arch Street, Suite B105
Meadville, PA 16335
814-724-0700
www.biop.edu/

Business Institute of Pennsylvania
335 Boyd Drive
Sharon, PA 16146
800-289-2069
www.biop.edu/

Butler County Community College
College Drive, PO Box 1203
Butler, PA 16003-1203
888-826-2829
www.bc3.edu/

Cambria-Rowe Business College
422 South 13th Street
Indiana, PA 15701
724-483-0222
www.crbc.net/

Cambria-Rowe Business College
221 Central Avenue
Johnstown, PA 15902-2494
814-536-5168
www.crbc.net/

Career Training Academy
105 Mall Boulevard, Suite 300 West, Expo Mart
Monroeville, PA 15146
412-372-3900
www.careerta.com/

Career Training Academy
1500 Northway Mall, Suite 200
Pittsburgh, PA 15237
412-367-4000
www.careerta.com/

Career Training Academy
950 Fifth Avenue
New Kensington, PA 15068-6301
412-367-4000
www.careerta.com/

Center for Advanced Manufacturing & Technology
5451 Merwin Lane
Erie, PA 16510
888-834-4226
www.gocamtech.com/

CHI Institute
520 Street Road
Southampton, PA 18966-3747
800-336-7696
www.chitraining.com/

CHI Institute, RETS Campus
Lawrence Park Shopping Center, Rt. 320 & Lawrence Road
Broomall, PA 19008
610-353-7630
www.chitraining.com/

Commonwealth Technical Institute
727 Goucher Street
Johnstown, PA 15905-3092
814-255-8200
www.hgac.org/

Community College of Allegheny County
800 Allegheny Avenue
Pittsburgh, PA 15233-1894
412-237-4581
www.ccac.edu/

Community College of
    Beaver County
One Campus Drive
Monaca, PA 15061-2588
800-335-0222
www.ccbc.edu/

Community College of
    Philadelphia
1700 Spring Garden Street
Philadelphia, PA 19130-3991
215-751-8230
www.ccp.edu/

Consolidated School of
    Business
1605 Clugston Road
York, PA 17404
800-520-0691
www.csb.edu/

Consolidated School of
    Business
2124 Ambassador Circle
Lancaster, PA 17603
717-764-9550
www.csb.edu/

Dean Institute of Technology
1501 West Liberty Avenue
Pittsburgh, PA 15226-1103
412-531-4433
home.earthlink.net/
    ~deantech/

Delaware County Community
    College
901 South Media Line Road
Media, PA 19063-1094
800-543-0146
www.dccc.edu/

Douglas Education Center
130 Seventh Street
Monessen, PA 15062
724-684-3684
www.douglas-school.com/

DuBois Business College
1 Beaver Drive
DuBois, PA 15801-2401
814-371-6920
www.dbcollege.com/

Duff's Business Institute
100 Forbes Avenue, Suite
    1200
Pittsburgh, PA 15222
888-279-3314
www.duffs-institute.com/

Erie Business Center, South
170 Cascade Galleria
New Castle, PA 16101-3950
724-658-9066
www.eriebc.com/

Erie Business Center, Main
246 West Ninth Street
Erie, PA 16501-1392
800-352-3743
www.eriebc.edu/

Erie Institute of Technology
5539 Peach Street
Erie, PA 16509
866-868-3743
www.erieit.org/

Harcum College
750 Montgomery Avenue
Bryn Mawr, PA 19010-3476
800-345-2600
www.harcum.edu/

Harrisburg Area Community
    College
1 HACC Drive
Harrisburg, PA 17110-2999
717-780-2406
www.hacc.edu/

ICM School of Business &
    Medical Careers
10 Wood Street at Fort Pitt
    Boulevard
Pittsburgh, PA 15222-1977
800-441-5222
www.icmschool.com/

Information Computer
    Systems Institute
2201 Hangar Place
Allentown, PA 18103-9504
610-841-3333
www.icsinstitute.com/

International Academy of
    Design & Technology
555 Grant Street
Pittsburgh, PA 15219
800-447-8324
www.iadtpitt.com/

JNA Institute of Culinary Arts
1212 South Broad Street
Philadelphia, PA 19146
215-468-8880
www.culinaryarts.com/

Johnson College
3427 North Main Avenue
Scranton, PA 18508-1495
800-2-WE-WORK
www.johnson.edu/

Kaplan Career
    Institute–Harrisburg
5650 Derry Street
Harrisburg, PA 17111-3518
800-431-1995
www.getinfokaplancareer
    institute.com/Kaplan
    InstitutePortal/Kaplan
    InstituteCampuses/
    Pennsylvania/Harrisburg

Katharine Gibbs School
2501 Monroe Boulevard
Norristown, PA 19403
866-PAGIBBS
www.pagibbs.com/

Keystone College
One College Green
La Plume, PA 18440
877-4COLLEGE
www.keystone.edu/

Lackawanna College
501 Vine Street
Scranton, PA 18509
570-961-7841
www.lackawanna.edu/

Lancaster General College of
    Nursing & Health
    Sciences
410 North Lime Street
Lancaster, PA 17602
717-290-4912
www.lancastergeneral.org/
    content/LG_Collegeof
    Nursing.asp

Lansdale School of Business
201 Church Road
North Wales, PA 19454-4148
215-699-5700
www.lsbonline.com/

Laurel Business Institute
11-15 Penn Street
Uniontown, PA 15401
724-439-4900
www.laurel.edu/

Lehigh Carbon Community
    College
4525 Education Park Drive
Schnecksville, PA 18078-
    2598
610-799-1575
www.lccc.edu/

Lehigh Valley College
2809 East Saucon Valley Road
Center Valley, PA 18034
800-227-9109
www.lehighvalley.edu/

Lincoln Technical Institute
5151 Tilghman Street
Allentown, PA 18104-3298
610-398-5301
www.lincolntech.com/

Lincoln Technical Institute
9191 Torresdale Avenue
Philadelphia, PA 19136-1595
800-238-8381
www.lincolntech.com/

Luzerne County Community
    College
1333 South Prospect Street
Nanticoke, PA 18634-9804
570-740-0200
www.luzerne.edu/

Manor College
700 Fox Chase Road
Jenkintown, PA 19046
215-884-2216
www.manor.edu/

McCann School of Business
    & Technology
2650 Woodglen Road
Pottsville, PA 17901
570-622-7622
www.mccannschool.com/

Median School of Allied
    Health Careers
125 7th Street
Pittsburgh, PA 15222-3400
800-570-0693
www.medianschool.edu/

Metropolitan Career Center
100 South Broad Street
Philadelphia, PA 19110
215-568-9215
www.metropolitancareer
    center.org/

Two-Year Colleges

Montgomery County Community College
340 DeKalb Pike
Blue Bell, PA 19422-0796
215-641-6551
www.mc3.edu

New Castle School of Trades
New Castle Youngstown Road, Route 422 RD1
Pulaski, PA 16143-9721
800-837-8299
www.ncstrades.com/

Newport Business Institute
941 West Third Street
Williamsport, PA 17701-5855
800-962-6971
www.newportbusiness.com/

Newport Business Institute
945 Greensburg Road
Lower Burrell, PA 15068-3929
800-752-7695
www.nbi.edu

North Central Industrial Technical Education Center
651 Montmorenci Avenue
Ridgway, PA 15853
800-242-5872

Northampton County Area Community College
3835 Green Pond Road
Bethlehem, PA 18020-7599
610-861-5506
www.northampton.edu/

Oakbridge Academy of Arts
1250 Greensburg Road
Lower Burrell, PA 15068
800-734-5601
www.akvalley.com/oakbridge/

Orleans Technical Institute–Center City Campus
1845 Walnut Street, Suite 700
Philadelphia, PA 19103-4707
215-854-1853
www.jevs.org/schools_svs.asp

Pace Institute
606 Court Street
Reading, PA 19601
610-375-1212
www.paceinstitute.com/

Penn Commercial Business and Technical School
242 Oak Spring Road
Washington, PA 15301
724-222-5330
www.penncommercial.net/

Penn Foster Career School
925 Oak Street
Scranton, PA 18515
800-233-4191
www.pennfoster.edu/

Pennco Tech
3815 Otter Street
Bristol, PA 19007-3696
215-824-3200
www.penncotech.com/

Pennsylvania Culinary Institute
717 Liberty Avenue
Pittsburgh, PA 15222-3500
800-432-2433
www.paculinary.com/

Pennsylvania Highland Community College
PO Box 68
Johnstown, PA 15907-0068
814-532-5300
www.pennhighlands.edu/

Pennsylvania Institute of Technology
800 Manchester Avenue
Media, PA 19063-4098
800-422-0025
www.pit.edu/

The Pennsylvania State University, Beaver Campus of the Commonwealth College
100 University Drive
Monaca, PA 15061
877-564-6778
www.br.psu.edu/

The Pennsylvania State University, Delaware County Campus of the Commonwealth College
25 Yearsley Mill Road
Media, PA 19063-5596
610-892-1350
www.de.psu.edu/

The Pennsylvania State University, DuBois Campus of the Commonwealth College
College Place
DuBois, PA 15801-3199
800-346-7627
www.ds.psu.edu/

The Pennsylvania State University, Fayette Campus of the Commonwealth College
1 University Drive, PO Box 519
Uniontown, PA 15401-0519
877-568-4130
www.fe.psu.edu/

The Pennsylvania State University, Hazleton Campus of the Commonwealth College
Hazleton, PA 18202-1291
800-279-8495
www.hn.psu.edu/

The Pennsylvania State University, Lehigh Valley Campus of the Berks-Lehigh Valley College
8380 Mohr Lane
Fogelsville, PA 18051-9999
610-285-5000
www.lv.psu.edu/

The Pennsylvania State University, McKeesport Campus of the Commonwealth College
4000 University Drive
McKeesport, PA 15132-7698
412-675-9000
www.mk.psu.edu/

The Pennsylvania State University, Mont Alto Campus of the Commonwealth College
Campus Drive
Mont Alto, PA 17237-9703
800-392-6173
www.ma.psu.edu/

The Pennsylvania State University, New Kensington Campus of the Commonwealth College
3550 7th Street Road, RT 780
New Kensington, PA 15068-1798
888-968-7297
www.nk.psu.edu/

The Pennsylvania State University, Schuylkill Campus of the Capital College
200 University Drive
Schuylkill Haven, PA 17972-2208
570-385-6000
www.sl.psu.edu/

The Pennsylvania State University, Shenango Campus of the Commonwealth College
147 Shenango Avenue
Sharon, PA 16146-1537
724-983-2814
www.shenango.psu.edu/

The Pennsylvania State University, Wilkes-Barre Campus of the Commonwealth College
PO PSU
Lehman, PA 18627-0217
800-966-6613
www.wb.psu.edu/

The Pennsylvania State University, Worthington Scranton Campus of the Commonwealth College
120 Ridge View Drive
Dunmore, PA 18512-1699
570-963-2500
www.sn.psu.edu/

The Pennsylvania State University, York Campus of the Commonwealth College
1031 Edgecomb Avenue
York, PA 17403-3398
800-778-6227
www.yk.psu.edu/

Pittsburgh Institute of Aeronautics
PO Box 10897
Pittsburgh, PA 15236-0897
800-444-1440
www.pia.edu/

Part 5: Appendices

Pittsburgh Institute of Mortuary Science, Incorporated
5808 Baum Boulevard
Pittsburgh, PA 15206-3706
800-933-5808
www.pims.edu/

Pittsburgh Technical Institute
1111 McKee Road
Oakdale, PA 15071
800-784-9675
www.pti.edu/

The PJA School
7900 West Chester Pike
Upper Darby, PA 19082-1926
800-RING-PJA
www.pjaschool.com/

Reading Area Community College
PO Box 1706
Reading, PA 19603-1706
610-372-4721
www.racc.edu/

Rosedale Technical Institute
215 Beecham Drive, Suite 2
Pittsburgh, PA 15205-9791
800-521-6262
www.rosedaletech.org/

The Restaurant School at Walnut Hill College
4207 Walnut Street
Philadelphia, PA 19104-3518
877-925-6884
www.walnuthillcollege.edu/

Schuylkill Institute of Business and Technology
171 Red Horse Road
Pottsville, PA 17901
570-622-4835
www.sibt.edu/

South Hills School of Business & Technology
480 Waupelani Drive
State College, PA 16801-4516
888-282-7427
www.southhills.edu/

South Hills School of Business & Technology
508 58th Street
Atloona, PA 16602
814-944-6134
www.southhills.edu/

Thaddeus Stevens College of Technology
750 East King Street
Lancaster, PA 17602-3198
717-299-7730
www.stevenscollege.edu/

Triangle Tech, Inc.–DuBois School
PO Box 551
DuBois, PA 15801-0551
800-874-8324
www.triangle-tech.edu/

Triangle Tech, Inc.–Erie School
2000 Liberty Street
Erie, PA 16502-2594
800-TRI-TECH
www.triangle-tech.com/

Triangle Tech, Inc.–Greensburg School
222 East Pittsburgh Street, Suite A
Greensburg, PA 15601-3304
800-874-8324
www.triangle-tech.com/

Triangle Tech, Inc.–Pittsburgh School
1940 Perrysville Avenue
Pittsburgh, PA 15214-3897
800-874-8324
www.triangle-tech.edu/

Triangle Tech, Inc.–Sunbury School
RR #1, Box 51
Sunbury, PA 17801
570-988-0700
www.triangle-tech.com/

Tri-State Business Institute
5757 West 26th Street
Erie, PA 16506
814-838-7673
www.tsbi.org/

University of Pittsburgh at Titusville
PO Box 287
Titusville, PA 16354
888-878-0462
www.upt.pitt.edu/

Valley Forge Military College
1001 Eagle Road
Wayne, PA 19087-3695
800-234-8362
www.vfmac.edu/

Western School of Health and Business Careers
421 Seventh Avenue
Pittsburgh, PA 15219-1907
800-333-6607
www.westernschool.com/

Western School of Health and Business Careers
1 Monroeville Center, Suite 250, Route 22, 3824 Northern Pike
Monroeville, PA 15146-2142
412-373-6400
www.westernschool.com/

Westmoreland County Community College
400 Armbrust Road
Youngwood, PA 15697-1898
724-925-4064
www.wccc-pa.edu/

The Williamson Free School of Mechanical Trades
106 South New Middletown Road
Media, PA 19063
610-566-1776
www.williamson.edu/

Winner Institute of Arts & Sciences
One Winner Place
Transfer, PA 16154
888-414-2433
www.winner-institute.edu/

WyoTech
500 Innovation Drive
Blairsville, PA 15717
800-822-8253
www.wyotech.com/

Yorktowne Business Institute
West Seventh Avenue
York, PA 17404
800-840-1004
www.ybi.edu/

YTI Career Institute–York
1405 Williams Road
York, PA 17402-9017
800-227-9675
www.yti.edu/

Virginia

ACT College
1100 Wilson Boulevard
Arlington, VA 22209
www.healthtraining.com

Advanced Technology Institute
5700 Southern Boulevard
Virginia Beach, VA 23462
www.aticareers.com

Aviation Institute of Maintenance–Manassas
9821 Godwin Drive
Manassas, VA 20110
877-604-2121
www.aviationmaintenance.edu/aviation-washington-dc.asp

Aviation Institute of Maintenance–Virginia Beach
1429 Miller Store Road
Virginia Beach, VA 23455
888-349-5387
www.aviationmaintenance.edu/aviation-norfolk.asp

Beta Tech
1610 Forest Avenue - Ste214
Richmond, VA 23229
804-673-7110

Blue Ridge Community College
PO Box 80
Weyers Cave, VA 24486-0080
540-453-2332
www.brcc.edu/

Bryant and Stratton College, Richmond
8141 Hull Street Road
Richmond, VA 23235-6411
804-745-2444
www.bryantstratton.edu/

Bryant and Stratton College, Virginia Beach
301 Centre Pointe Drive
Virginia Beach, VA 23462-4417
757-499-7900
www.bryantstratton.edu/

Two-Year Colleges

Central Virginia Community College
3506 Wards Road
Lynchburg, VA 24502-2498
434-832-7600
www.cvcc.vccs.edu/

Dabney S. Lancaster Community College
100 Dabney Drive, PO Box 1000
Clifton Forge, VA 24422
540-863-2815
www.dl.vccs.edu/

Danville Community College
1008 South Main Street
Danville, VA 24541-4088
800-560-4291
www.dcc.vccs.edu/

Eastern Shore Community College
29300 Lankford Highway
Melfa, VA 23410-3000
877-871-8455
www.es.cc.va.us/

ECPI College of Technology
1001 Omni Boulevard, #100
Newport News, VA 23606
757-838-9191
www.ecpi.edu/

ECPI College of Technology
5555 Greenwich Road
Virginia Beach, VA 23462
800-986-1200
www.ecpi.edu/

ECPI Technical College
4305 Cox Road
Glen Allen, VA 23060
800-986-1200
www.ecpitech.edu/

ECPI Technical College
5234 Airport Road
Roanoke, VA 24012
800-986-1200
www.ecpi.net/

ECPI Technical College
800 Moorefield Park Drive
Richmond, VA 23236
800-986-1200
www.ecpitech.edu/

Everest College
801 North Quincy Street, Suite 501
Arlington, VA 22203
703-248-8887
www.parks-college.com/

Germanna Community College
2130 Germanna Highway
Locust Grove, VA 22508-2102
540-891-3016
www.gcc.vccs.edu/

ITT Technical Institute
300 Gateway Centre Parkway
Richmond, VA 23235
804-330-4992
www.itt-tech.edu/

ITT Technical Institute
7300 Boston Boulevard
Springfield, VA 22153
866-817-8324
www.itt-tech.edu/

ITT Technical Institute
863 Glenrock Road, Suite 100
Norfolk, VA 23502-3701
757-466-1260
www.itt-tech.edu/

ITT Technical Institute
14420 Abermarle Point Place, Suite 100
Chantilly, VA 20151
888-895-8324
www.itt-tech.edu/

J. Sargeant Reynolds Community College
PO Box 85622
Richmond, VA 23285-5622
804-523-5029
www.reynolds.edu

John Tyler Community College
13101 Jefferson Davis Highway
Chester, VA 23831-5316
804-796-4150
www.jtcc.edu/

Lord Fairfax Community College
173 Skirmisher Lane
Middletown, VA 22645
800-906-5322
www.lfcc.edu/

Medical Careers Institute
5501 Greenwich Road
Virginia Beach, VA 23462
757-497-8400
www.medical.edu

Medical Careers Institute
800 Moorefield Park Drive, Suite 302
Richmond, VA 23236-3659
804-521-0400
www.medicalcareersinstitute.com/

Medical Careers Institute
1001 Omni Boulevard, Suite 200
Newport News, VA 23606
757-873-2423
www.medicalcareersinstitute.com/

Mountain Empire Community College
PO Drawer 700
Big Stone Gap, VA 24219-0700
276-523-2400
www.me.vccs.edu/

National College
51 B Burgess Road
Harrisonburg, VA 22801-9709
800-664-1886
www.national-college.edu/

National College
100 Logan Street, PO Box 629
Bluefield, VA 24605-1405
800-664-1886
www.national-college.edu/

National College
1819 Emmet Street
Charlottesville, VA 22901
800-664-1886
www.national-college.edu/

National College
734 Main Street
Danville, VA 24541-1819
800-664-1886
www.national-college.edu/

National College
1813 East Main Street
Salem, VA 24153
800-664-1886
www.national-college.edu/

National College
10 Church Street, PO Box 232
Martinsville, VA 24114
800-664-1866
www.national-college.edu/

National College
104 Candlewood Court
Lynchburg, VA 24502-2653
800-664-1886
www.national-college.edu/

New River Community College
PO Box 1127
Dublin, VA 24084-1127
540-674-3600
www.nr.cc.va.us/

Northern Virginia Community College
4001 Wakefield Chapel Road
Annandale, VA 22003-3796
703-323-3000
www.nv.cc.va.us/

Patrick Henry Community College
PO Box 5311
Martinsville, VA 24115-5311
276-638-8777
www.ph.vccs.edu/

Paul D. Camp Community College
PO Box 737, 100 North College Drive
Franklin, VA 23851-0737
757-569-6700
www.pc.vccs.edu/

Piedmont Virginia Community College
501 College Drive
Charlottesville, VA 22902-7589
434-9616540
www.pvcc.edu/

Rappahannock Community College
12745 College Drive
Glenns, VA 23149-2616
804-758-6742
www.rcc.vccs.edu/

Richard Bland College of The College of William and Mary
11301 Johnson Road
Petersburg, VA 23805-7100
804-862-6225
www.rbc.edu/

Southside Virginia
   Community College
109 Campus Drive
Alberta, VA 23821-9719
434-949-1012
www.sv.vccs.edu/

Southwest Virginia
   Community College
PO Box SVCC
Richlands, VA 24641-1101
276-964-7300
www.sw.edu/

TESST College of Technology
6315 Bren Mar Drive
Alexandria, VA 22312-6342
800-48-TESST
www.tesst.com/

Thomas Nelson Community
   College
PO Box 9407
Hampton, VA 23670-0407
757-825-2800
www.tncc.edu/

Tidewater Community
   College
121 College Place
Norfolk, VA 23510
757-822-1068
www.tcc.edu/

Tidewater Tech
2697 Dean Drive, Suite 100
Virginia Beach, VA 23452
757-340-2121
www.tidetech.com/

Virginia Highlands
   Community College
PO Box 828
Abingdon, VA 24212-0828
877-207-6115
www.vhcc.edu/

Virginia Western Community
   College
PO Box 14007
Roanoke, VA 24038
540-857-7231
www.virginiawestern.edu/

Westwood College–
   Annandale Campus
7611 Little River Turnpike,
   3rd Floor
Annadale, VA 22003
800-281-2978
www.westwood.edu/
   locations/virginia-
   colleges/annandale-
   college.asp

Wytheville Community
   College
1000 East Main Street
Wytheville, VA 24382-3308
276-223-4700
www.wcc.vccs.edu/

West Virginia

Blue Ridge Community and
   Technical College
400 West Stephen Street
Martinsburg, WV 25401
304-260-4380
www.blueridgectc.edu/

Community & Technical
   College at West Virginia
   University
Institute of Technology
Montgomery, WV 25136
888-554-8324
ctc.wvutech.edu/

Eastern West Virginia
   Community and Technical
   College
HC 65 Box 402
Moorefield, WV 26836
877-982-2322
www.eastern.wvnet.edu/

Huntington Junior College
900 Fifth Avenue
Huntington, WV 25701-2004
304-697-7550
www.huntingtonjunior
   college.com/

International Academy of
   Design & Technology
2000 Green River Drive
Fairmont, WV 26554-9790
888-406-8324
iadtwv.com/

Marshall Community and
   Technical College
One John Marshall Drive
Huntington, WV 25755
304-696-3160
www.marshall.edu/ctc/

Mountain State College
1508 Spring Street
Parkersburg, WV 26101-3993
800-841-0201
www.mountainstate.org/

National Institute of
   Technology
5514 Big Tyler Road
Cross Lanes, WV 25313-1390
888-741-4271
www.nitschools.com/

New River Community and
   Technical College
167 Dye Drive
Beckley, WV 25801
304-255-5821
www.nrctc.org/

Pierpont Community and
   Technical College of
   Fairmont State University
1201 Locust Avenue
Fairmont, WV 26554
800-641-5678
www.fairmontstate.edu/

Potomac State College of
   West Virginia University
Fort Avenue
Keyser, WV 26726-2698
800-262-7332
www.potomacstatecollege.
   edu/

Southern West Virginia
   Community and Technical
   College
Dempsey Branch Road,
   PO Box 2900
Mount Gay, WV 25637-2900
304-792-7160
www.southern.wvnet.edu/

Valley College
287 Aikens Center
Martinsburg, WV 25401
304-263-0878
www.valleycollege.com/

West Virginia Business
   College
1052 Main Street
Wheeling, WV 26003
304-232-0361
www.stratuswave.com/
   ~wvbc/

West Virginia Business
   College
116 Pennsylvania Avenue
Nutter Fort, WV 26301
304-624-7695
www.stratuswave.com/
   ~wvbc/

West Virginia Junior College
176 Thompson Drive
Bridgeport, WV 26330
304-363-8824
www.wvjc.com/

West Virginia Junior College
1000 Virginia Street East
Charleston, WV 25301-2817
304-345-2820
www.wvjc.com/

West Virginia Junior College
148 Willey Street
Morgantown, WV 26505-5521
304-296-8282
www.wvjc.com/

West Virginia Northern
   Community College
1704 Market Street
Wheeling, WV 26003-3699
304-233-5900
www.northern.wvnet.edu/

West Virginia State
   Community and Technical
   College
Thomas W. Cole, Jr.,
   Complex, PO Box 1000
Institute, WV 25112
800-987-2112
www.wvsctc.edu/

West Virginia University at
   Parkersburg
300 Campus Drive
Parkersburg, WV 26104-8647
304-424-8223
www.wvup.edu/

VOCATIONAL/CAREER COLLEGES

Delaware

Dawn Training Centre, Inc.
105 Tall Oaks Ct., Tall Oaks Business Center
Wilmington, DE 19805-1511
302-633-9075

Delaware College of Art and Design
600 North Market St.
Wilmington, DE 19801
302-622-8000
www.dcad.edu/

Delaware Technical & Community College, Jack F. Owens Campus
PO Box 610
Georgetown, DE 19947
302-856-5400
www.dtcc.edu/

Delaware Technical & Community College, Stanton/Wilmington Campus
400 Stanton-Christiana Rd.
Newark, DE 19713
302-454-3900
www.dtcc.edu/

Delaware Technical & Community College, Terry Campus
100 Campus Dr.
Dover, DE 19904-1383
302-857-1000
www.dtcc.edu/terry/

Star Technical Institute
631 West Newport Pike, Graystone Plaza
Wilmington, DE 19804
302-999-7827

District of Columbia

Potomac College
4000 Chesapeake St., NW
Washington, DC 20016
202-686-0818
www.potomac.edu/

Sanz School, Inc.
1511 K St., NW, Ste. 210
Washington, DC 20005
202-628-5800

Strayer University
1133 15th St. NW, Ste. 200
Washington. DC 20005
202-419-0400
www.strayer.edu

Strayer University at Takoma Park
6830 Laurel St. NW
Washington, DC 20012
www.strayer.edu

Maryland

Abbie Business Institute
5310 Spectrum Dr.
Frederick, MD 21703
301-694-0211

All-State Career School
2200 Broening Hwy., Ste. 160
Baltimore, MD 21224
410-631-1818

Allegany College of Maryland
12401 Willowbrook Rd., SE
Cumberland, MD 21502-2596
301-784-5000
www.allegany.edu/

Anne Arundel Community College
101 College Pkwy.
Arnold, MD 21012-1895
410-647-7100
www.aacc.edu/

Baltimore City Community College
2901 Liberty Heights Ave.
Baltimore, MD 21215-7893
410-462-8300
www.bccc.state.md.us/

Baltimore International College
Commerce Exchange, 17 Commerce St.
Baltimore, MD 21202-3230
410-752-4710
www.bic.edu/

Baltimore School of Massage
6401 Dogwood Rd.
Baltimore, MD 21207
410-944-8855
www.bsom.com/

Carroll Community College
1601 Washington Rd.
Westminster, MD 21157
410-386-8000
www.carrollcc.edu/

Cecil Community College
One Seahawk Dr.
North East, MD 21901-1999
410-287-6060
www.cecilcc.edu/

Chesapeake College
PO Box 8
Wye Mills, MD 21679-0008
410-822-5400
www.chesapeake.edu/

College of Southern Maryland
8730 Mitchell Rd., PO Box 910
La Plata, MD 20646-0910
301-934-2251
www.csmd.edu/

Diesel Institute of America
Route 40, Box 69
Grantsville, MD 21536
301-895-5138

Empire Beauty School–Baltimore
5633 Reisterstown Rd.
Baltimore, MD 21215
800-223-3271, ext. 2414
www.empire.edu

Frederick Community College
7932 Opossumtown Pike
Frederick, MD 21702-2097
301-846-2400
www.frederick.edu/

Garrett College
687 Mosser Rd.
McHenry, MD 21541
301-387-3000
www.garrettcollege.edu/

Hagerstown Business College
18618 Crestwood Dr.
Hagerstown, MD 21742-2797
301-739-2670
www.hagerstownbusinesscol.org/

Hagerstown Community College
11400 Robinwood Dr.
Hagerstown, MD 21742-6590
301-790-2800
www.hagerstowncc.edu/

Hair Academy, Inc.–New Carrollton
8435 Old Annapolis Rd.
New Carrollton, MD 20784
301-459-2509

Harford Community College
401 Thomas Run Rd.
Bel Air, MD 21015-1698
410-836-4000
www.harford.edu/

Howard Community College
10901 Little Patuxent Pkwy.
Columbia, MD 21044-3197
410-772-4800
www.howardcc.edu/

Lincoln Technical Institute
9325 Snowden River Pkwy.
Columbia, MD 21046
410-290-7100

Medix Schools
700 York Rd.
Towson, MD 21204
410-337-5155

Prince George's Community College
301 Largo Rd.
Largo, MD 20774-2199
301-336-6000
www.pgcc.edu/

Sanford-Brown Institute
8401 Corporate Dr., Ste. 500
Landover, MD 20785
301-918-8221
www.uds-landover.com/

TESST College of Technology
1520 South Caton Ave.
Baltimore, MD 21227-1063
410-644-6400
www.tesst.com/

TESST College of Technology
4600 Powder Mill Rd.
Beltsville, MD 20705
301-937-8448
www.tesst.com/

TESST College of Technology
803 Glen Eagles Ct.
Towson, MD 21286-2201
410-296-5350
www.tesst.com/

Wor-Wic Community College
32000 Campus Dr.
Salisbury, MD 21804
410-334-2800
www.worwic.edu/

New Jersey

Academy of Massage Therapy
401 S. Van Brunt St., # 204
Englewood, NJ 07631
201-568-3220
www.academyofmassage.com

Berdan Institute
265 State Route 46
Totowa, NJ 07512
973-256-3444
www.berdaninstitute.com/

Bergen Community College
400 Paramus Rd.
Paramus, NJ 07652-1595
201-447-7100
www.bergen.edu/

Berkeley College
44 Rifle Camp Rd.
West Paterson, NJ 07424-3353
973-278-5400
www.berkeleycollege.edu/

Brookdale Community College
765 Newman Springs Rd.
Lincroft, NJ 07738-1597
732-842-1900
www.brookdalecc.edu/

Burlington County College
Route 530
Pemberton, NJ 08068-1599
609-894-9311
www.bcc.edu/

Business Training Institute
365 West Passaic St., 6th Fl.
Rochelle Park, NJ 07662-3017
201-845-9300

Camden County College
PO Box 200
Blackwood, NJ 08012-0200
856-227-7200
www.camdencc.edu/

Capri Institute of Hair Design
268 Brick Blvd.
Brick, NJ 08723
201-920-3600

Capri Institute of Hair Design
615 Winter Ave.
Paramus, NJ 07652
201-599-0880

The Chubb Institute
40 Journal Square, 1st Fl.
Jersey City, NJ 07306
201-656-0330
www.chubbinstitute.com/

The Cittone Institute
160 East Route 4
Paramus, NJ 07652
www.cittone.com

Concorde School of Hair Design–Bloomfield
9-15 Ward St.
Bloomfield, NJ 07003
973-680-0099

County College of Morris
214 Center Grove Rd.
Randolph, NJ 07869-2086
973-328-5000
www.ccm.edu/

Cumberland County College
PO Box 1500, College Dr.
Vineland, NJ 08362-1500
856-691-8600
www.cccnj.edu/

Dover Business College
East 81 Route 4, W
Paramus, NJ 07652
201-843-8500

Empire Beauty School–Lawrenceville
1719 Brunswick Pike
Lawrenceville, NJ 08648
800-223-3271, ext. 2315
www.empirebeauty.com

Essex County College
303 University Ave.
Newark, NJ 07102-1798
973-877-3000
www.essex.edu/

Gibbs College
33 Plymouth St.
Montclair, NJ 07042-2699
973-744-2010
www.njgibbscollege.net/

Gloucester County College
1400 Tanyard Rd.
Sewell, NJ 08080
856-468-5000
www.gccnj.edu/

Gordon Phillips School of Beauty Culture
729 Haddon Ave.
Collingswood, NJ 08108
609-858-1900

Gordon Phillips School of Beauty Culture
1305 Blackwood-Clementon Rd., Commerce Plaza 2
Laurel Springs, NJ 08021
610-352-1776

Harrison Career Institute
1227-31 Main Ave.
Clifton, NJ 07011

Harrison Career Institute
South Orange, NJ

Hudson County Community College
25 Journal Square
Jersey City, NJ 07306
201-656-2020
www.hccc.edu/

Mercer County Community College
1200 Old Trenton Rd.
PO Box B
Trenton, NJ 08690-1004
609-586-4800
www.mccc.edu/

Middlesex County College
2600 Woodbridge Ave.
PO Box 3050
Edison, NJ 08818-3050
732-548-6000
www.middlesexcc.edu/

Monmouth County Vocational School District
255 West End Ave.
Long Branch, NJ 07740
732-229-3019

New Community Workforce Development Center
201 Bergen St.
Newark, NJ 07103
973-824-6484, ext. 102

Ocean County College
College Dr., PO Box 2001
Toms River, NJ 08754-2001
732-255-0400
www.ocean.edu/

Ocean County Vocational Post Secondary Division
137 Bey Lea Rd.
Toms River, NJ 08753-2703
732-473-3128
www.ocvts.org

Omega Institute
7050 Route 38, E
Pennsauken, NJ 08109
609-663-4299

Passaic County Community College
One College Blvd.
Paterson, NJ 07505-1179
973-684-6800
www.pccc.cc.nj.us/

Pennco Tech
99 Erial Rd., PO Box 1427
Blackwood, NJ 08012-9961
856-232-0310
www.penncotech.com/

Raritan Valley Community College
PO Box 3300
Somerville, NJ 08876-1265
908-526-1200
www.raritanval.edu/

Vocational/Career Colleges

Rizzieri Aveda School for Beauty and Wellness
6001 W. Lincoln Dr.
Marlton, NJ 08053
856-988-8600, ext. 200
www.rizzieri.com

Salem Community College
460 Hollywood Ave.
Carneys Point, NJ 08069-2799
856-299-2100
www.salemcc.org/

Sanford-Brown Institute
675 US Route 1, 2nd Fl.
Iselin, NJ 08830
908-634-1131
www.uds-nj.com/

Star Technical Institute
1255 Route 70, Ste. 12, North
Lakewood, NJ 08701-5947
908-901-9710

Star Technical Institute
2 Carnegie Rd.
Lawrenceville, NJ 08648
609-406-1505

Star Technical Institute
43 South White Horse Pike
Stratford, NJ 08084
609-435-7827

Star Technical Institute
1386 South Delsea Dr.
Vineland, NJ 08360
609-696-0500

Star Technical Institute
1000 Main St.
Voorhees, NJ 08043
609-877-2727

Star Technical Institute–Deptford
1450 Clements Bridge Rd.
Deptford, NJ 08096
609-384-2888

Star Technical Institute–Ocean Township Campus
2105 Hwy. 35
Ocean Township, NJ 07712-7201
908-493-1660

Stuart School of Business Administration
2400 Belmar Blvd.
Wall, NJ 07719
800-924-2924
www.stuartschool.com

Sussex County Community College
1 College Hill
Newton, NJ 07860
973-300-2100
www.sussex.edu/

Union County College
1033 Springfield Ave.
Cranford, NJ 07016-1599
908-709-7000
www.ucc.edu/

Warren County Community College
475 Route 57 West
Washington, NJ 07882-4343
908-689-1090
www.warren.edu/

New York

Adirondack Community College
640 Bay Rd.
Queensbury, NY 12804
518-743-2200
www.sunyacc.edu/

Allen School–Brooklyn
188 Montague St.
Brooklyn, NY 11201
212-686-0036

Allen School–Jamaica
163-18 Jamaica Ave.
Jamaica, NY 11432
212-686-0036

American Academy McAllister Institute of Funeral Service
450 West 56th St.
New York, NY 10019-3602
212-757-1190
www.a-a-m-i.org/

American Barber Institute
252 West 29th St.
New York, NY 10001-5271
212-290-2289, ext. 000

Apex Technical School
635 Ave. Of The Americas
New York, NY 10011
212-645-3300
www.apextechnicalschool.com/

The Art Institute of New York City
75 Varick St., 16th Fl.
New York, NY 10013
212-226-5500
www.ainyc.aii.edu/

Berk Trade and Business School
312 West 36th St., 4th Fl.
New York, NY 10018

Berkeley College-New York City Campus
3 East 43rd St.
New York, NY 10017-4604
212-986-4343
www.berkeleycollege.edu/

Berkeley College-Westchester Campus
99 Church St.
White Plains, NY 10601
914-694-1122
www.berkeleycollege.edu/

Borough of Manhattan Community College of the City University of New York
199 Chambers St.
New York, NY 10007-1097
212-346-8000
www.bmcc.cuny.edu/

Bramson ORT College
69-30 Austin St.
Forest Hills, NY 11375-4239
718-261-5800
www.bramsonort.edu/

Bronx Community College of the City University of New York
University Ave. & West 181st St.
Bronx, NY 10453
718-289-5100
www.bcc.cuny.edu/

Broome Community College
PO Box 1017
Binghamton, NY 13902-1017
607-778-5000
www.sunybroome.edu/

Bryant and Stratton College
1259 Central Ave.
Albany, NY 12205-5230
518-437-1802
www.bryantstratton.edu/

Bryant and Stratton College
150 Bellwood Dr.
Rochester, NY 14606
585-720-0660
www.bryantstratton.edu/

Bryant and Stratton College
1225 Jefferson Rd.
Rochester, NY 14623-3136
585-292-5627
www.bryantstratton.edu/

Bryant and Stratton College
953 James St.
Syracuse, NY 13203-2502
315-472-6603
www.bryantstratton.edu/

Bryant and Stratton College, Amherst Campus
Audubon Business Center, 40 Hazelwood Dr.
Amherst, NY 14228
716-691-0012
www.bryantstratton.edu/

Bryant and Stratton College, Buffalo Campus
465 Main St., Ste. 400
Buffalo, NY 14203
716-884-9120
www.bryantstratton.edu/

Bryant and Stratton College, Lackawanna Campus
1214 Abbott Rd.
Lackawanna, NY 14218-1989
716-821-9331
www.bryantstratton.edu/

Bryant and Stratton College, North Campus
8687 Carling Rd.
Liverpool, NY 13090-1315
315-652-6500
www.bryantstratton.edu/

Caliber Training Institute
500 7th Ave., 2nd Fl.
New York, NY 10018
212-564-0500

Part 5: Appendices

Cayuga County Community College
197 Franklin St.
Auburn, NY 13021-3099
315-255-1743
www.cayuga-cc.edu/

Clinton Community College
136 Clinton Point Dr.
Plattsburgh, NY 12901-9573
518-562-4200
clintoncc.suny.edu/

The College of Westchester
325 Central Ave., PO Box 710
White Plains, NY 10602
914-948-4442
www.cw.edu/

Columbia-Greene Community College
4400 Route 23
Hudson, NY 12534-0327
518-828-4181
www.sunycgcc.edu/

Computer Career Center
340 Flatbush Ave. Ext-3rd Fl.
Brooklyn, NY 11201
718-422-1212, ext. 1400
www.ccctraining.edu

Computer Career Center
200 Garden City Plaza
Garden City, NY 11530-3301
516-877-1225
www.ccctraining.net/

Computer Career Center
95-25 Queens Blvd., Ste. 600
Rego Park, NY 11374
718-897-4868

Continental School of Beauty Culture–Jefferson
633 Jefferson Rd.
Rochester, NY 14623
716-272-8060

Corning Community College
One Academic Dr.
Corning, NY 14830-3297
607-962-9011
www.corning-cc.edu/

Dover Technical School
3075 Veterans Memorial Hwy.
Ronkonkoma, NY 11779
516-471-9100

Drake Business School
32-03 Steinway St.
Astoria, NY 11103
718-777-3800

Drake Business School
225 Broadway
New York, NY 10007
212-349-7900

Drake Business School
148 New Durp Lane
Staten Island, NY 10306
718-980-9000

Drake School of the Bronx
2122 White Plains Rd.
Bronx, NY 10462
718-822-8080

Dutchess Community College
53 Pendell Rd.
Poughkeepsie, NY 12601-1595
845-431-8000
www.sunydutchess.edu/

Elmira Business Institute
303 North Main St.
Elmira, NY 14901
607-733-7177
www.ebi-college.com/

Erie 2 Chautauqua-Cattaraugus BOCES
8685 Erie Rd.
Angola, NY 14006
716-549-4454
e2ccboces.wnyric.org

Erie Community College
121 Ellicott St.
Buffalo, NY 14203-2698
716-851-1001
www.ecc.edu/

Eugenio María de Hostos Community College of the City University of New York
500 Grand Concourse
Bronx, NY 10451
718-518-4444
www.hostos.cuny.edu/

Finger Lakes Community College
4355 Lakeshore Dr.
Canandaigua, NY 14424-8395
585-394-3500
www.flcc.edu/

Fiorello H. LaGuardia Community College of the City University of New York
31-10 Thomson Ave.
Long Island City, NY 11101-3071
718-482-7200
www.lagcc.cuny.edu/

Franklin Career Institute
91 North Franklin St.
Hempstead, NY 11550
516-679-1616

French Culinary Institute
462 BRd.way
New York, NY 10013
212-219-8890

Fulton-Montgomery Community College
2805 State Hwy. 67
Johnstown, NY 12095-3790
518-762-4651
www.fmcc.suny.edu/

Genesee Community College
1 College Rd.
Batavia, NY 14020-9704
585-343-0055
www.genesee.suny.edu/

Herkimer County Community College
Reservoir Rd.
Herkimer, NY 13350
315-866-0300
www.herkimer.edu

Hudson Valley Community College
80 Vandenburgh Ave.
Troy, NY 12180-6096
518-629-4822
www.hvcc.edu/

Island Drafting and Technical Institute
128 Broadway
Amityville, NY 11787
631-691-8733
www.idti.edu/

Jamestown Business College
7 Fairmount Ave., Box 429
Jamestown, NY 14702-0429
716-664-5100
www.jbcny.org/

Jamestown Community College
525 Falconer St.
Jamestown, NY 14701-1999
716-665-5220
www.sunyjcc.edu/

Jefferson Community College
1220 Coffeen St.
Watertown, NY 13601
315-786-2200
www.sunyjefferson.edu/

Katharine Gibbs School
320 South Service Rd.
Melville, NY 11747-3785
631-370-3300
www.gibbsmelville.com/

Katharine Gibbs School
200 Park Ave.
New York, NY 10166-0005
212-867-9300
www.katharinegibbs.com/

Kingsborough Community College of the City University of New York
2001 Oriental Blvd,
Manhattan Beach
Brooklyn, NY 11235
718-368-5000
www.kbcc.cuny.edu/

Learning Institute for Beauty Sciences
38-15 BRd.way
Astoria, NY 11103
718-726-8383

Learning Institute for Beauty Sciences
2384 86th St.
Brooklyn, NY 11214
718-373-2400
www.libs.org

Learning Institute for Beauty Sciences
22 West 34th St.
New York, NY 10001
212-967-1717
www.libs.org

Long Island Business Institute
6500 Jericho Turnpike
Commack, NY 11725
631-499-7100
www.libi.edu/commack/index.html

Vocational/Career Colleges

Madison Oneida
  BOCES–Continuing
  Education
4937 Spring Rd.
Verona, NY 13478-0168
315-361-5800
www.moboces.org/
  communityeducation/

Mandl School
254 West 54th St., 9th Fl.
New York, NY 10019
212-247-3434
www.mandlschool.com/

Merkaz Bnos-Business
  School
54 Ave. O
Brooklyn, NY 11204
718-234-4000
www.mbs-career.org

Mohawk Valley Community
  College
1101 Sherman Dr.
Utica, NY 13501-5394
315-792-5400
www.mvcc.edu/

Monroe Community College
1000 East Henrietta Rd.
Rochester, NY 14623-5780
585-292-2000
www.monroecc.edu/

Nassau Community College
1 Education Dr.
Garden City, NY 11530-6793
516-572-7500
www.ncc.edu/

New York Automotive and
  Diesel Institute
33-24 Northern Blvd.
Long Island City, NY 11101
718-361-1300

New York City College of
  Technology of the City
  University of New York
300 Jay St.
Brooklyn, NY 11201-2983
718-260-5000
www.citytech.cuny.edu/

New York International
  Beauty School, Ltd.
210 West 50 St.
New York, NY 10019
212-265-1400

New York School for Medical/
  Dental Assistants
116-16 Queens Blvd.
Forest Hills, NY 11375-2330
718-793-2330

Niagara County Community
  College
3111 Saunders Settlement Rd.
Sanborn, NY 14132-9460
716-614-6222
www.niagaracc.suny.edu/

North Country Community
  College
23 Santanoni Ave., PO Box 89
Saranac Lake, NY 12983-0089
518-891-2915
www.nccc.edu/

Olean Business Institute
301 North Union St.
Olean, NY 14760-2691
716-372-7978
www.obi.edu/

Onondaga Community
  College
4941 Onondaga Rd.
Syracuse, NY 13215-2099
315-498-2622
www.sunyocc.edu/

Orange County Community
  College
115 South St.
Middletown, NY 10940-6437
845-344-6222
www.orange.cc.ny.us/

Phillips Hairstyling Institute
709 East Genesee St.
Syracuse, NY 13210
315-422-9656

Professional Business
  Institute
125 Canal St.
New York, NY 10002-5049
212-226-7300

Queensborough Community
  College of the City
  University of New York
222-05 56th Ave.
Bayside, NY 11364
718-631-6262
www.qcc.cuny.edu/

Ridley-Lowell School of
  Business
26 S. Hamilton St.
Poughkeepsie, NY 12601
845-471-0330
www.ridley.edu

Rochester Business Institute
1630 Portland Ave.
Rochester, NY 14621
716-266-0430
www.rochester-institute.com/

Rockland Community College
145 College Rd.
Suffern, NY 10901-3699
914-574-4000
www.sunyrockland.edu/

Sanford-Brown Institute
711 Stewart Ave., 2nd Fl.
Garden City, NY 11530
516-248-6060
www.uds-longisland.com/

Sanford-Brown Institute
120 East 16th St., 2nd Fl.
New York, NY 10003
212-460-8567
www.ultrasounddiagnostic
  school.com/default.htm

Sanford-Brown Institute
333 Westchester Ave.
White Plains, NY 10604
914-347-6817
www.uds-elmsford.com/
  index.asp

Schenectady County
  Community College
78 Washington Ave.
Schenectady, NY 12305-2294
518-381-1200
www.sunysccc.edu/

Shear Ego International
  School of Hair Design
525 Titus Ave.
Rochester, NY 14617
716-342-0070

State University of New York
  College of Agriculture and
  Technology at Morrisville
PO Box 901
Morrisville, NY 13408-0901
315-684-6000
www.morrisville.edu/

State University of New York
  College of Technology at
  Alfred
Alfred, NY 14802
607-587-4111
www.alfredstate.edu/

State University of New York
  College of Technology at
  Canton
Cornell Dr.
Canton, NY 13617
315-386-7011
www.canton.edu/

State University of New York
  College of Technology at
  Delhi
Main St.
Delhi, NY 13753
607-746-4000
www.delhi.edu/

Suburban Technical School
175 Fulton Ave.
Hempstead, NY 11550
516-481-6660

Suffolk County Community
  College
533 College Rd.
Selden, NY 11784-2899
631-451-4110
www.sunysuffolk.edu/

Sullivan County Community
  College
112 College Rd.
Loch Sheldrake, NY 12759
845-434-5750
www.sullivan.suny.edu/

TCI–The College of
  Technology
320 West 31st St.
New York, NY 10001-2705
212-594-4000
www.tciedu.com/

Tompkins Cortland
  Community College
170 North St., PO Box 139
Dryden, NY 13053-0139
607-844-8211
www.sunytccc.edu/

Trocaire College
360 Choate Ave.
Buffalo, NY 14220-2094
716-826-1200
www.trocaire.edu/

Ulster County Community
    College
Cottekill Rd.
Stone Ridge, NY 12484
914-687-5000
www.sunyulster.edu/

Utica School of Commerce
201 Bleecker St.
Utica, NY 13501-2280
315-733-2307
www.uscny.edu/

Wayne-Finger Lakes BOCES
    School of Practical
    Nursing
131 Drumlin Ct.
Newark, NY 14513-1863
315-332-7400
www.wflboces.org

Westchester Community
    College
75 Grasslands Rd.
Valhalla, NY 10595-1698
914-785-6600
www.sunywcc.edu/

Western Suffolk BOCES
152 Laurel Hill Rd.
Northport, NY 11768-3499
631-261-3600, ext. 201
www.wilsontech.org

Wood Tobe–Coburn School
8 East 40th St.
New York, NY 10016
212-686-9040
www.woodtobecoburn.com/

Pennsylvania

Academy of Medical Arts and
    Business
2301 Academy Dr.
Harrisburg, PA 17112-1012
717-545-4747
www.acadcampus.com/

All-State Career School
501 Seminole St.
Lester, PA 19029-1825
610-521-1818

Allied Medical and Technical
    Careers
166 Slocum St.
Forty Fort, PA 18704-2936
717-288-8400
www.alliedteched.com/

Allied Medical and Technical
    Careers
571 Ash St.
Scranton, PA 18509-2903
717-288-8400

Ambler Beauty Academy
50 East Butler Pike
Ambler, PA 19002
215-643-5994

American Center For
    Technical Arts and
    Sciences
9122 Blue Grass Rd.
Philadelphia, PA 19114
215-969-1300

The Art Institute of
    Philadelphia
1622 Chestnut St.
Philadelphia, PA 19103-5198
215-567-7080
www.aiph.artinstitutes.edu/

Automotive Training Center
114 Pickering Way
Exton, PA 19341
610-363-6716
www.autotraining.com/

Berean Institute
1901 West Girard Ave.
Philadelphia, PA 19130-1599
215-763-4833
www.bereaninstitute.org/

Berks Technical Institute
2205 Ridgewood Rd.
Wyomissing, PA 19610-1168
610-372-1722
www.berkstech.com/

Bidwell Training Center
1815 Metropolitan St.
Pittsburgh, PA 15233-2234
412-323-4000
www.bidwell-training.org/

Bradley Academy for the
    Visual Arts
1409 Williams Rd.
York, PA 17402-9012
717-755-2300
www.bradleyacademy.net/

Bucks County Community
    College
275 Swamp Rd.
Newtown, PA 18940-1525
215-968-8000
www.bucks.edu/

Butler County Community
    College
College Dr., PO Box 1203
Butler, PA 16003-1203
724-287-8711
www.bc3.edu/

Cambria-Rowe Business
    College
422 South 13th St.
Indiana, PA 15701
724-463-0222
www.crbc.net/

Cambria-Rowe Business
    College
221 Central Ave.
Johnstown, PA 15902-2494
814-536-5168
www.crbc.net/

Center For Innovative
    Training and Education
714 Market St., Ste. 433
Philadelphia, PA 19106
215-922-6555

CHI Institute
520 St. Rd.
Southampton, PA 18966-
    3747
215-357-5100
www.chitraining.com/

CHI Institute, RETS Campus
Lawrence Park Shopping
    Center, Rt. 320 &
    Lawrence Rd.
Broomall, PA 19008
610-353-7630
www.chitraining.com/

The Chubb Institute
965 Baltimore Pike
Springfield, PA 19064-3957
215-543-1747

The Cittone Institute
2180 Hornig Rd., Building A
Philadelphia, PA 19116-4202
www.cittone.com

The Cittone Institute
1 Plymouth Meeting Mall
    #300
Plymouth Meeting, PA
    19462-1326

Commonwealth Technical
    Institute
727 Goucher St.
Johnstown, PA 15905-3092
814-255-8200
www.hgac.org/

Community College of
    Allegheny County
800 Allegheny Ave.
Pittsburgh, PA 15233-1894
412-323-2323
www.ccac.edu/

Community College of
    Beaver County
One Campus Dr.
Monaca, PA 15061-2588
724-775-8561
www.ccbc.edu/

Community College of
    Philadelphia
1700 Spring Garden St.
Philadelphia, PA 19130-3991
215-751-8010
www.ccp.edu/

Computer Learning Network
2900 Fairway Dr.
Altoona, PA 16602
814-944-5643
www.clnaltoona.com

Computer Learning Network
1110 Fernwood Ave.
Camp Hill, PA 17011-6996
717-761-1481
www.clntraining.net

Consolidated School of
    Business
1605 Clugston Rd.
York, PA 17404
717-764-9550
www.csb.edu/

Dean Institute of Technology
1501 West Liberty Ave.
Pittsburgh, PA 15226-1103
412-531-4433
www.deantech.edu/

Delaware County Community
    College
901 South Media Line Rd.
Media, PA 19063-1094
610-359-5000
www.dccc.edu/

Vocational/Career Colleges

Douglas Education Center
130 Seventh St.
Monessen, PA 15062
724-684-3684
www.douglas-school.com/

DPT Business School
9122 Blue Grass Rd.
Philadelphia, PA 19114-3202
215-673-2275

DuBois Business College
1 Beaver Dr.
DuBois, PA 15801-2401
814-371-6920
www.dbcollege.com/

Duff's Business Institute
100 Forbes Ave., Ste. 1200
Pittsburgh, PA 15222
412-261-4520
www.duffs-institute.com/

Empire Beauty School
3941 Jonestown Rd.
Harrisburg, PA 17109
717-652-8500

Empire Beauty School
124 West Broad St.
Hazleton, PA 18201
717-429-1800

Empire Beauty School
2302 North 5th St.
Reading, PA 19605
610-372-2777

Empire Beauty School
1634 MacArthur Rd.
Whitehall, PA 18052
610-776-8908

Empire Beauty School
117 South Main St.
Wilkes-Barre, PA 18701
570-823-5987

Empire Beauty School
1101G South Edgar St.
York, PA 17403
717-854-7698

Empire Beauty
School–Philadelphia
2632 S. Broadway
Philadelphia, PA 19145
800-832-3337, ext. 2315
www.empirebeauty.com

Episcopal Hospital–School of
Nursing
100 E. Lehigh Ave.
Philadelphia, PA 19125-1098
215-427-7468
www.templehealth.org/
episcopalnursing

Erie Business Center South
170 Cascade Galleria
New Castle, PA 16101-3950
724-658-9066
www.eriebc.com/

Erie Business Center, Main
246 West Ninth St.
Erie, PA 16501-1392
814-456-7504
www.eriebc.edu/

Erie Institute of Technology
5539 Peach St.
Erie, PA 16509
814-868-9900
www.erieit.org/

Gordon Phillips Beauty
School
The Plaza on Mall Blvd.
Monroeville, PA 15146
412-373-7127

Gordon Phillips Beauty
School
1522 Chestnut St.
Philadelphia, PA 19102
610-352-1776

Gordon Phillips Beauty
School
7248 Frankford Ave.
Philadelphia, PA 19135
215-331-4444

Gordon Phillips Beauty
School
313 West Market St.
West Chester, PA 15382
610-349-7665

Harcum College
750 Montgomery Ave.
Bryn Mawr, PA 19010-3476
610-525-4100
www.harcum.edu/

Harrisburg Area Community
College
1 HACC Dr.
Harrisburg, PA 17110-2999
717-780-2300
www.hacc.edu/

ICM School of Business &
Medical Careers
10 Wood St. at Fort Pitt Blvd.
Pittsburgh, PA 15222-1977
412-261-2647
www.icmschool.com/

Information Computer
Systems Institute
2201 Hangar Place
Allentown, PA 18103-9504
610-264-8029
www.icsinstitute.com/

J. H. Thompson Academies
5100 Peach St.
Erie, PA 16509
814-456-6217

Johnson College
3427 North Main Ave.
Scranton, PA 18508-1495
570-342-6404
www.johnson.edu/

Keystone College
One College Green
La Plume, PA 18440
570-945-5141
www.keystone.edu/

Lackawanna College
501 Vine St.
Scranton, PA 18509
570-961-7810
www.lackawanna.edu/

Lancaster County Career and
Technology Center
1730 Hans Herr Dr.
Willow St., PA 17584
717-464-7065
www.lcctc.org

Lansdale School of Business
201 Church Rd.
North Wales, PA 19454-4148
215-699-5700
www.lsbonline.com/

Laurel Business Institute
11-15 Penn St.
Uniontown, PA 15401
724-439-4900
www.laurelbusiness.net/

Lehigh Carbon Community
College
4525 Education Park Dr.
Schnecksville, PA 18078-2598
610-799-2121
www.lccc.edu/

Lehigh Valley College
2809 East Saucon Valley Rd.
Center Valley, PA 18034
610-791-5100
www.lehighvalley.edu/

Lincoln Technical Institute
5151 Tilghman St.
Allentown, PA 18104-3298
610-398-5300
www.lincolntech.com/

Lincoln Technical Institute
9191 Torresdale Ave.
Philadelphia, PA 19136-1595
215-335-0800
www.lincolntech.com/

Luzerne County Community
College
1333 South Prospect St.
Nanticoke, PA 18634-9804
570-740-0300
www.luzerne.edu/

Manor College
700 Fox Chase Rd.
Jenkintown, PA 19046
215-885-2360
www.manor.edu/

McCann School of Business
& Technology
2650 Woodglen Rd.
Pottsville, PA 17901
570-622-7622
www.mccannschool.com/

Median School of Allied
Health Careers
125 7th St.
Pittsburgh, PA 15222-3400
412-391-7021
www.medianschool.edu/

Montgomery County
Community College
340 DeKalb Pike
Blue Bell, PA 19422-0796
215-641-6300
www.mc3.edu

New Castle School of Trades
New Castle Youngstown Rd.,
Route 422 RD1
Pulaski, PA 16143-9721
724-964-8811
www.ncstrades.com/

Part 5: Appendices

Newport Business Institute
941 West Third St.
Williamsport, PA 17701-5855
570-326-2869
www.newportbusiness.com/

Northampton County Area
  Community College
3835 Green Pond Rd.
Bethlehem, PA 18020-7599
610-861-5300
www.northampton.edu/

Orleans Technical Institute
1330 Rhawn St.
Philadelphia, PA 19111
215-728-4700
www.jevs.org/schools_svs.
  asp

Pace Institute
606 Ct. St.
Reading, PA 19601
610-375-1212
www.paceinstitute.com/

Penn Commercial Business
  and Technical School
242 Oak Spring Rd.
Washington, PA 15301
724-222-5330
www.penncommercial.net/

Pennco Tech
3815 Otter St.
Bristol, PA 19007-3696
215-824-3200
www.penncotech.com/

Pennsylvania Highland
  Community College
PO Box 68
Johnstown, PA 15907-0068
814-532-5300
www.pennhighlands.edu/

Pennsylvania Institute of
  Technology
800 Manchester Ave.
Media, PA 19063-4098
610-892-1500
www.pit.edu/

Pittsburgh Institute of
  Aeronautics
PO Box 10897
Pittsburgh, PA 15236-0897
412-462-9011
www.pia.edu/

Pittsburgh Institute of
  Mortuary Science,
  Incorporated
5808 Baum Blvd.
Pittsburgh, PA 15206-3706
412-362-8500
www.p-i-m-s.com/

Quaker City Institute of
  Aviation
9800 Ashton Rd.
Philadelphia, PA 19114
215-545-7518

Reading Area Community
  College
PO Box 1706
Reading, PA 19603-1706
610-372-4721
www.racc.edu/

Sanford-Brown Institute
3600 Horizon Blvd., Ste. GL1
Bensalem, PA 19020
215-244-4906
www.uds-philadelphia.com/

Schuylkill County Area
  Vocational-Technical
  School
Schuylkill Intermediate Unit
  #29, PO Box 130
Mar Lin, PA 17951-0110
717-544-4748
www.iu29.org/

Schuylkill Institute of
  Business and Technology
171 Red Horse Rd.
Pottsville, PA 17901
570-622-4835
www.sibt.edu/

South Hills School of
  Business & Technology
508 58th St.
Atloona, PA 16602
814-944-6134
www.southhills.edu/

Star Technical Institute
1619 Walnut St., 3rd Fl.
Philadelphia, PA 19103
215-640-0177

Star Technical Institute
9121 Roosevelt Blvd.
Philadelphia, PA 19114
215-969-5877

Star Technical
  Institute–Allentown
2102 Union Blvd.
Allentown, PA 18103
610-434-9963

Star Technical
  Institute–Scranton
  Campus
1636 Nay Aug Ave., Green
  Ridge Plaza
Scranton, PA 18509
570-963-0144
www.startechinstitute.com

Thompson Institute
2593 Philadelphia Ave.
Chambersburg, PA 17201
717-709-9400
www.thompsoninstitute.com

Thompson Institute
5650 Derry St.
Harrisburg, PA 17111-3518
717-564-4112
www.thompson.edu/

Thompson Institute
3440 Market St., 2nd Fl.
Philadelphia, PA 19104
215-387-1530
www.thompsoninstitute.org

Triangle Tech, Inc.–DuBois
  School
PO Box 551
DuBois, PA 15801-0551
814-371-2090
www.triangle-tech.com/

Triangle Tech, Inc.
  –Greensburg School
222 East Pittsburgh St., Ste. A
Greensburg, PA 15601-3304
724-832-1050
www.triangle-tech.com/

Triangle Tech, Inc.–Pittsburgh
  School
1940 Perrysville Ave.
Pittsburgh, PA 15214-3897
412-359-1000
www.triangle-tech.edu/

University of Pittsburgh at
  Titusville
PO Box 287
Titusville, PA 16354
814-827-4400
www.upt.pitt.edu/

Venus Beauty School
1033 Chester Pike
Sharon Hill, PA 19079
610-586-2500

Western School of Health
  and Business Careers
1 Monroeville Center, Ste.
  250, Route 22, 3824
  Northern Pike
Monroeville, PA 15146-2142
412-373-6400
www.westernschool.com/

Western School of Health
  and Business Careers
421 Seventh Ave.
Pittsburgh, PA 15219-1907
412-281-2600
www.westernschool.com/

Westmoreland County
  Community College
400 Armbrust Rd.
Youngwood, PA 15697-1898
724-925-4000
www.wccc-pa.edu/

WyoTech
500 Innovation Dr.
Blairsville, PA 15717
724-459-9500
www.wyotech.com/

York Technical Institute
1405 Williams Rd.
York, PA 17402-9017
717-757-1100
www.yti.edu/

Yorktowne Business Institute
West Seventh Ave.
York, PA 17404
717-846-5000
www.ybi.edu/

Virginia

Applied Career Training, Inc.
1100 Wilson Blvd., Mall Level
Arlington, VA 22209
703-527-6660
www.healthtraining.com

Beta Tech
1610 Forest Ave. - Ste214
Richmond, VA 23229
804-673-7110

Vocational/Career Colleges

Beta Tech
7914 Midlothian Turnpike
Richmond, VA 23235
804-330-0111
www.tidetech.com

Blue Ridge Community College
PO Box 80
Weyers Cave, VA 24486-0080
540-234-9261
www.brcc.edu/

Bryant and Stratton College, Richmond
8141 Hull St. Rd.
Richmond, VA 23235-6411
804-745-2444
www.bryantstratton.edu/

Central Virginia Community College
3506 Wards Rd.
Lynchburg, VA 24502-2498
434-832-7600
www.cvcc.vccs.edu/

Cooper Career Institute
129 North Witchduck Rd.
Virginia Beach, VA 23462
757-519-9500

Dabney S. Lancaster Community College
100 Dabney Dr., PO Box 1000
Clifton Forge, VA 24422
540-863-2800
www.dl.vccs.edu/

Danville Community College
1008 South Main St.
Danville, VA 24541-4088
434-797-2222
www.dcc.vccs.edu/

Eastern Shore Community College
29300 Lankford Hwy.
Melfa, VA 23410-3000
757-789-1789
www.es.cc.va.us/

ECPI College of Technology
5555 Greenwich Rd.
Virginia Beach, VA 23462
757-671-7171
www.ecpi.edu/

ECPI Technical College
800 Moorefield Park Dr.
Richmond, VA 23236
804-330-5533
www.ecpitech.edu/

Germanna Community College
2130 Germanna Hwy.
Locust Grove, VA 22508-2102
540-727-3000
www.gcc.vccs.edu/

J. Sargeant Reynolds Community College
PO Box 85622
Richmond, VA 23285-5622
804-371-3000
www.reynolds.edu

John Tyler Community College
13101 Jefferson Davis Hwy.
Chester, VA 23831-5316
804-796-4000
www.jtcc.edu/

Kee Business College
825 Greenbrier Cr.
Chesapeake, VA 23320
757-361-3900

Kee Business College
803 Diligence Dr.
Newport News, VA 23606
757-873-1111
www.cci.edu/

Lord Fairfax Community College
173 Skirmisher Lane
Middletown, VA 22645
540-868-7000
www.lfcc.edu/

Mountain Empire Community College
PO Drawer 700
Big Stone Gap, VA 24219-0700
540-523-2400
www.me.vccs.edu/

National College of Business & Technology
1813 East Main St.
Salem, VA 24153
540-986-1800
www.ncbt.edu/

New River Community College
PO Box 1127
Dublin, VA 24084-1127
540-674-3600
www.nr.cc.va.us/

Northern Virginia Community College
4001 Wakefield Chapel Rd.
Annandale, VA 22003-3796
703-323-3000
www.nv.cc.va.us/

Patrick Henry Community College
PO Box 5311
Martinsville, VA 24115-5311
276-638-8777
www.ph.vccs.edu/

Paul D. Camp Community College
PO Box 737, 100 North College Dr.
Franklin, VA 23851-0737
757-569-6700
www.pc.vccs.edu/

Piedmont Virginia Community College
501 College Dr.
Charlottesville, VA 22902-7589
434-977-3900
www.pvcc.edu/

Potomac Academy of Hair Design
350 South Washington St.
Falls Church, VA 22046
www.naccas.org/potomacacademy/

Rappahannock Community College
12745 College Dr.
Glenns, VA 23149-2616
804-758-6700
www.rcc.vccs.edu/

Southside Virginia Community College
109 Campus Dr.
Alberta, VA 23821-9719
804-949-1000
www.sv.vccs.edu/

Southwest Virginia Community College
PO Box SVCC
Richlands, VA 24641-1101
276-964-2555
www.sw.edu/

Thomas Nelson Community College
PO Box 9407
Hampton, VA 23670-0407
757-825-2700
www.tncc.vccs.edu/

Tidewater Community College
121 College Place
Norfolk, VA 23510
757-822-1122
www.tcc.edu/

Tidewater Tech
932 Ventures Way
Chesapeake, VA 23320
757-549-2121

Tidewater Tech
7020 North Military Hwy.
Norfolk, VA 23518
757-853-2121

Tidewater Tech
2697 Dean Dr., Ste. 100
Virginia Beach, VA 23452
757-340-2121
www.tidetech.com/

Tidewater Tech
1429 Miller Store Rd.
Virginia Beach, VA 23455
757-363-2121

Tidewater Tech–Newport News Campus
616 Denbigh Blvd.
Newport News, VA 23608
757-874-2121
www.tidetech.com/

Virginia Highlands Community College
PO Box 828
Abingdon, VA 24212-0828
276-739-2400
www.vhcc.edu/

Virginia School of Massage
2008 Morton Dr.
Charlottesville, VA 22903
804-293-4031
www.vasom.com/

Part 5: Appendices

Virginia School of Technology
100 Constitution Dr., Ste. 101
Virginia Beach, VA 23462
757-499-5447

Virginia Western Community
  College
PO Box 14007
Roanoke, VA 24038
540-857-7311
www.virginiawestern.edu/

Wards Corner Beauty
  Academy
216 East Little Creek Rd.
Norfolk, VA 23505
757-583-3300

Woodrow Wilson
  Rehabilitation Center
Route 250
Fishersville, VA 22939-1500
540-332-7265
www.wwrc.net

Wytheville Community
  College
1000 East Main St.
Wytheville, VA 24382-3308
276-223-4700
www.wcc.vccs.edu/

West Virginia

Eastern West Virginia
  Community and Technical
  College
HC 65 Box 402
Moorefield, WV 26836
304-434-8000
www.eastern.wvnet.edu/

Fairmont State Community &
  Technical College
1201 Locust Ave.
Fairmont, WV 26554
304-367-4892
www.fscwv.edu/fsctc/

Garnet Career Center
422 Dickinson St.
Charleston, WV 25301
304-348-6195
kcs.kana.k12.wv.us/garnet/

Huntington Junior College
900 Fifth Ave.
Huntington, WV 25701-2004
304-697-7550
www.huntingtonjunior
  college.com/

Huntington School of Beauty
  Culture–Main Campus
5185 Route 60, East Hills Mall
Huntington, WV 25705-2030
304-736-6289

Mountain State College
1508 Spring St.
Parkersburg, WV 26101-3993
304-485-5487
www.mountainstate.org/

National Institute of
  Technology
5514 Big Tyler Rd.
Cross Lanes, WV 25313-1390
304-776-6290
www.nitschools.com/

Potomac State College of
  West Virginia University
Fort Ave.
Keyser, WV 26726-2698
304-788-6800
www.potomacstatecollege.
  edu/

Southern West Virginia
  Community and Technical
  College
Dempsey Branch Rd.
PO Box 2900
Mount Gay, WV 25637-2900
304-792-7160
www.southern.wvnet.edu/

West Virginia Junior College
1000 Virginia St. East
Charleston, WV 25301-2817
304-345-2820
www.wvjc.com/

West Virginia Northern
  Community College
1704 Market St.
Wheeling, WV 26003-3699
304-233-5900
www.northern.wvnet.edu/

West Virginia University at
  Parkersburg
300 Campus Dr.
Parkersburg, WV 26104-8647
304-424-8000
www.wvup.edu/

SCHOLARSHIPS AND FINANCIAL AID

Delaware

Charles L. Hebner Memorial Scholarship
Award for legal residents of Delaware who plan to enroll full-time at the University of Delaware or Delaware State University. Must pursue their career in humanities or social sciences. Must have combined score of 1350 on the SAT. Full tuition, fees, room, board, and books at the University of Delaware or Delaware State University. Renewable for up to three additional years. One award every year per school. Deadline is March 13. **Academic Fields/Career Goals:** Humanities; Social Sciences. **Award:** Scholarship for use in freshman, sophomore, junior, senior, graduate, or postgraduate years; renewable. **Number:** 1. **Eligibility Requirements:** Applicant must be enrolled or expecting to enroll full-time at a two-year, four-year, or technical institution or university; resident of Delaware and studying in Delaware. Available to U.S. citizens. **Application Requirements:** Application, transcript. **Application deadline:** March 13. **Contact:** Maureen Laffey, Director, Delaware Department of Education, Carvel State Office Building, 820 North French Street, Wilmington, DE 19801. **Phone:** 302-577-5240. **Fax:** 302-577-6765. **E-mail:** dedoe@doe.k12.de.us.

Christa McAuliffe Teacher Scholarship Loan
Award for Delaware residents who are pursuing teaching careers. Must agree to teach in Delaware public schools as repayment of loan. Minimum award is $1000 and is renewable for up to four years. Available only at Delaware colleges. Based on academic merit. Must be ranked in upper half of class, and have a score of 1050 on SAT or 25 on the ACT. **Academic Fields/Career Goals:** Education. **Award:** Forgivable loan for use in freshman, sophomore, junior, or senior years; renewable. **Number:** 1–60. **Amount:** $1000–$5000. **Eligibility Requirements:** Applicant must be enrolled or expecting to enroll full-time at a four-year institution or university; resident of Delaware and studying in Delaware. Applicant must have 2.5 GPA or higher. Available to U.S. citizens. **Application Requirements:** Application, essay, test scores, transcript. **Application deadline:** March 31. **Contact:** Donna Myers, Program Administrator, Delaware Higher Education Commission, 820 North French Street, 5th Floor, Wilmington, DE 19801. **Phone:** 302-577-3240. **Fax:** 302-577-6765. **E-mail:** dmyers@doe.k12.de.us.

Delaware Solid Waste Authority John P. "Pat" Healy Scholarship
Scholarships given to residents of Delaware who are high school seniors or freshmen or sophomores in college. Must be majoring in either environmental engineering or environmental sciences in a Delaware college. Must file the Free Application for Federal Student Aid (FAFSA). Scholarships are automatically renewed for three years if a 3.0 GPA is maintained. Deadline: March 15. **Academic Fields/Career Goals:** Environmental Health. **Award:** Scholarship for use in freshman or sophomore years; renewable. **Number:** 1. **Amount:** $2000. **Eligibility Requirements:** Applicant must be enrolled or expecting to enroll full-time at a two-year or four-year institution or university; resident of Delaware and studying in Delaware. Applicant must have 3.0 GPA or higher. Available to U.S. citizens. **Application Requirements:** Application, financial need analysis, FAFSA. **Application deadline:** March 15. **Contact:** Donna Myers, Program Administrator, Delaware Higher Education Commission, 820 North French Street, 5th Floor, Wilmington, DE 19801. **Phone:** 302-577-3240. **Fax:** 302-577-6765. **E-mail:** dmyers@doe.k12.de.us.

Diamond State Scholarship
Award of $1250 per year and renewable for up to three additional years. Must be a legal residents of Delaware. The deadline is March 31. **Award:** Scholarship for use in freshman, sophomore, junior, or senior years; renewable. **Number:** 50. **Amount:** $1250–$5000. **Eligibility Requirements:** Applicant must be high school student; planning to enroll or expecting to enroll full-time at a two-year, four-year, or technical institution or university and resident of Delaware. Available to U.S. citizens. **Application Requirements:** Application, transcript. **Application deadline:** March 31. **Contact:** Maureen Laffey, Director, Delaware Department of Education, Carvel State Office Building, 820 North French Street, Wilmington, DE 19801. **Phone:** 302-577-5240. **Fax:** 302-577-6765. **E-mail:** dedoe@doe.k12.de.us.

Diamond State Scholarship
Renewable award for Delaware high school seniors enrolling full-time at an accredited college or university. Must be ranked in upper quarter of class and score 1200 on SAT or 27 on the ACT. **Award:** Scholarship for use in freshman year; renewable. **Number:** 50–200. **Amount:** $1250. **Eligibility Requirements:** Applicant must be high school student; planning to enroll or expecting to enroll full-time at a four-year institution or university and resident of Delaware. Applicant must have 3.5 GPA or higher. Available to U.S. citizens. **Application Requirements:** Application, essay, test scores, transcript. **Application deadline:** March 31. **Contact:** Donna Myers, Program Administrator, Delaware Higher Education Commission, 820 North French Street, 5th Floor, Wilmington, DE 19801. **Phone:** 302-577-3240. **Fax:** 302-577-6765. **E-mail:** dmyers@doe.k12.de.us.

Educational Benefits for Children of Deceased Military and State Police

Renewable award for Delaware residents who are children of state or military police who were killed in the line of duty. Must attend a Delaware institution unless program of study is not available. Funds cover tuition and fees at Delaware institutions. The amount varies at non-Delaware institutions. Must submit proof of service and related death. Must be ages 16-24 at time of application. Deadline is three weeks before classes begin. **Award:** Grant for use in freshman, sophomore, junior, or senior years; renewable. **Number:** 1–10. **Amount:** $6255. **Eligibility Requirements:** Applicant must be age 16-24; enrolled or expecting to enroll full-time at a two-year or four-year institution or university and resident of Delaware. Applicant or parent of applicant must have employment or volunteer experience in police/firefighting. Available to U.S. citizens. Applicant or parent must meet one or more of the following requirements: general military experience; retired from active duty; disabled or killed as a result of military service; prisoner of war; or missing in action. **Application Requirements:** Application, verification of service-related death. **Application deadline:** Continuous. **Contact:** Donna Myers, Program Administrator, Delaware Higher Education Commission, 820 North French Street, 5th Floor, Wilmington, DE 19801. **Phone:** 302-577-3240. **Fax:** 302-577-6765. **E-mail:** dmyers@doe.k12.de.us.

Educational Benefits for Children of Deceased Veterans and Others

Award for legal residents of Delaware. Must be a child of deceased U.S. military veterans or state police officers whose cause of death was service related or of military veterans held prisoner of war or declared missing in action. Must be 16 to 24 years old. Must attain full- or part-time undergraduate student admission at a public institution in Delaware. Award must not exceed tuition and fees at a Delaware public institution adjusted for other colleges. **Award:** Grant for use in freshman, sophomore, junior, or senior years; renewable. **Number:** 4. **Eligibility Requirements:** Applicant must be age 16-24; enrolled or expecting to enroll full or part-time at a two-year or four-year institution or university and resident of Delaware. Available to U.S. citizens. Applicant or parent must meet one or more of the following requirements: general military experience; retired from active duty; disabled or killed as a result of military service; prisoner of war; or missing in action. **Application Requirements:** Application, transcript. **Application deadline:** varies. **Contact:** Maureen Laffey, Director, Delaware Department of Education, Carvel State Office Building, 820 North French Street, Wilmington, DE 19801. **Phone:** 302-577-5240. **Fax:** 302-577-6765. **E-mail:** dedoe@doe.k12.de.us.

Governor's Workforce Development Grant

Award for residents of Delaware who are U.S. citizens. Must be employed by a company in Delaware that contributes to the Blue Collar Training Fund Program. Must attend a participating college in Delaware on a part-time basis. Individual income must not exceed $32,417 annually. Full-time students are not eligible. The maximum Governor's Workforce Development Grant for one academic year is $2000 for part-time undergraduate study. Applications are due by the end of the free drop/add period each term. **Award:** Grant for use in freshman, sophomore, junior, or senior years; not renewable. **Number:** 1. **Amount:** $2000. **Eligibility Requirements:** Applicant must be age 18; enrolled or expecting to enroll part-time at a two-year or four-year institution or university; resident of Delaware and studying in Delaware. Available to U.S. citizens. **Application Requirements:** Application, transcript. **Application deadline:** varies. **Contact:** Maureen Laffey, Director, Delaware Department of Education, Carvel State Office Building, 820 North French Street, Wilmington, DE 19801. **Phone:** 302-577-5240. **Fax:** 302-577-6765. **E-mail:** dedoe@doe.k12.de.us.

Legislative Essay Scholarship

Must be a senior in high school and Delaware resident. Submit an essay of 500 to 2000 words on a designated historical topic (changes annually). For more information visit: www.doe.state.de.us/high-ed **Award:** Scholarship for use in freshman year; not renewable. **Number:** 62–65. **Amount:** $750–$7500. **Eligibility Requirements:** Applicant must be high school student; planning to enroll or expecting to enroll full or part-time at a two-year, four-year, or technical institution or university and resident of Delaware. Available to U.S. citizens. **Application Requirements:** Application, applicant must enter a contest, essay. **Application deadline:** varies. **Contact:** Donna Myers, Program Administrator, Delaware Higher Education Commission, 820 North French Street, 5th Floor, Wilmington, DE 19801. **Phone:** 302-577-3240. **Fax:** 302-577-6765. **E-mail:** dmyers@doe.k12.de.us.

Legislative Essay Scholarship

Award for high school seniors from Delaware in public or private schools or in home school programs, who plan to enroll full-time at a nonprofit, regionally accredited college. Must submit an essay of between 500-2000 words. See Web site for essay topic and more information: www.doe.k12.de.us/ Deadline is December 1. Three statewide, nonrenewable awards of $7500, $3750, and $2250. **Award:** Scholarship for use in freshman year; not renewable. **Number:** 3. **Amount:** $2250–$7500. **Eligibility Requirements:** Applicant must be high school student; planning to enroll or expecting to enroll full-time at an institution or university and resident of Delaware. Available to U.S. citizens. **Application Requirements:** Application, essay. **Application deadline:** December 1. **Contact:** Maureen Laffey, Director,

Scholarships and Financial Aid

Delaware Department of Education, Carvel State Office Building, 820 North French Street, Wilmington, DE 19801. **Phone:** 302-577-5240. **Fax:** 302-577-6765. **E-mail:** dedoe@doe.k12.de.us.

Michael C. Ferguson Achievement Award

Merit-based awards for eighth and tenth grade students who demonstrate superior performance on the Delaware Student Testing Program (DSPT) in reading, writing, and mathematics. Annual award of $1,000. **Award:** Scholarship for use in freshman year; not renewable. **Amount:** $1000. **Eligibility Requirements:** Applicant must be enrolled or expecting to enroll at an institution or university and resident of Delaware. Available to U.S. citizens. **Application Requirements:** Application, transcript. **Application deadline:** varies. **Contact:** Tony J. Marchio, Superintendent, Delaware Department of Education, 118 South Sixth Street, PO Box 4010, Odessa, DE 19730-4010.

Robert C. Byrd Honors Scholarship

Federally funded program for high school graduates from Delaware who show academic excellence and the promise of continued postsecondary education. A Byrd Scholar receives $1500 for each academic year for a maximum of four years to be applied toward undergraduate study at any accredited college or university in the United States. The number of scholarships awarded each year is subject to change due to funding. Deadline is March 31. **Award:** Scholarship for use in freshman, sophomore, junior, or senior years; not renewable. **Number:** up to 20. **Amount:** $1500–$6000. **Eligibility Requirements:** Applicant must be high school student and planning to enroll or expecting to enroll full or part-time at a two-year, four-year, or technical institution or university. Available to U.S. citizens. **Application Requirements:** Application, transcript. **Application deadline:** March 31. **Contact:** Maureen Laffey, Director, Delaware Department of Education, Carvel State Office Building, 820 North French Street, Wilmington, DE 19801. **Phone:** 302-577-5240. **Fax:** 302-577-6765. **E-mail:** dedoe@doe.k12.de.us.

Scholarship Incentive Program (ScIP)

Award for legal residents of Delaware who plan to enroll full-time in an undergraduate degree program at a non-profit regionally accredited institution in Delaware or Pennsylvania. Must have a minimum cumulative, unweighted GPA of 2.5. Graduate students attending the University of Delaware or Delaware State University are not eligible. Awards for undergraduate range from $700 to $2200 depending on GPA; award for graduate is $1000. Deadline is April 15. **Award:** Grant for use in freshman, sophomore, junior, or senior years; not renewable. **Number:** up to 2. **Amount:** $700–$2250. **Eligibility Requirements:** Applicant must be enrolled or expecting to enroll full-time at a two-year or four-year institution or university; resident of Delaware and studying in Delaware or Pennsylvania. Applicant must have 2.5 GPA or higher. Available to U.S. citizens. **Application Requirements:** Application, transcript. **Application deadline:** April 15. **Contact:** Maureen Laffey, Director, Delaware Department of Education, Carvel State Office Building, 820 North French Street, Wilmington, DE 19801. **Phone:** 302-577-5240. **Fax:** 302-577-6765. **E-mail:** dedoe@doe.k12.de.us.

Scholarship Incentive Program

One-time award for Delaware residents with financial need. May be used at an institution in Delaware or Pennsylvania, or at another out-of-state institution if a program is not available at a publicly-supported school in Delaware. Must have minimum 2.5 GPA. **Award:** Grant for use in freshman, sophomore, junior, senior, or graduate years; not renewable. **Number:** 1000–1300. **Amount:** $700–$2200. **Eligibility Requirements:** Applicant must be enrolled or expecting to enroll full-time at a two-year or four-year institution or university; resident of Delaware and studying in Delaware or Pennsylvania. Applicant must have 2.5 GPA or higher. Available to U.S. citizens. **Application Requirements:** Application, financial need analysis, transcript. **Application deadline:** April 15. **Contact:** Donna Myers, Program Administrator, Delaware Higher Education Commission, 820 North French Street, 5th Floor, Wilmington, DE 19801. **Phone:** 302-577-3240. **Fax:** 302-577-6765. **E-mail:** dmyers@doe.k12.de.us.

State Tuition Assistance

Award providing tuition assistance for any member of the Air or Army National Guard attending a Delaware two-year or four-year college. Awards are renewable. Applicant's minimum GPA must be 2.0. For full- or part-time study. Amount of award varies. **Award:** Scholarship for use in freshman, sophomore, junior, or senior years; renewable. **Number:** varies. **Amount:** varies. **Eligibility Requirements:** Applicant must be enrolled or expecting to enroll full or part-time at a two-year or four-year institution or university in Delaware. Applicant must have 2.5 GPA or higher. Available to U.S. citizens. Applicant must have served in the Air Force National Guard or Army National Guard. **Application Requirements:** Application, transcript. **Application deadline:** varies. **Contact:** Robert Csizmadia, State Tuition Assistance Manager, Delaware National Guard, 1st Regiment Road, Wilmington, DE 19808-2191. **Phone:** 302-326-7012. **Fax:** 302-326-7029. **E-mail:** robert.csizmadi@de.ngb.army.mil, .

District of Columbia

American Council of the Blind Scholarships

Merit-based award available to undergraduate, graduate, vocational or technical students who are legally blind in both eyes. Submit certificate of legal blindness and proof of acceptance at an accredited postsecondary institution. **Award:** Scholarship for use in freshman, sophomore, junior, senior, or graduate years; renewable. **Number:** 26. **Amount:** $500–$3000. **Eligibility Requirements:** Applicant must be enrolled or expecting to enroll full-time at a four-year, or technical institution or university. Applicant must be visually impaired. Applicant must have 3.5 GPA or higher. Available to U.S. citizens. **Application Requirements:** Application, autobiography, essay, references, transcript, evidence of legal blindness. **Application deadline:** March 1. **Contact:** Terry Pacheco, Affiliate and Membership Services, American Council of the Blind, 1155 15th Street, NW, Suite 1004, Washington, DC 20005. **Phone:** 202-467-5081. **Fax:** 202-467-5085. **E-mail:** info@acb.org.

ANLA National Scholarship Endowment–Usrey Family Scholarship

Award for students accredited undergraduate or graduate landscape horticulture program or related discipline at a two- or four-year institution. The applicant must be a student enrolled in a California state university or college. Preference given to applicants who plan to work within the industry. Must have a minimum 2.5 GPA. **Academic Fields/Career Goals:** Horticulture/Floriculture; Landscape Architecture. **Award:** Scholarship for use in sophomore, junior, senior, graduate, or postgraduate years; not renewable. **Number:** 1. **Amount:** $1000–$1500. **Eligibility Requirements:** Applicant must be enrolled or expecting to enroll full-time at a two-year, four-year, or technical institution or university and studying in California. Applicant must have 2.5 GPA or higher. Available to U.S. and non-U.S. citizens. **Application Requirements:** Application, essay, financial need analysis, references, transcript. **Application deadline:** April 1. **Contact:** Teresa Jodon, Endowment Program Administrator, American Nursery and Landscape Association, 1000 Vermont Avenue, NW, Suite 300, Washington, DC 20005. **Phone:** 202-789-2900 Ext. 3014. **Fax:** 202-789-1893. **E-mail:** hriresearch@anla.org.

Carville M. Akehurst Memorial Scholarship

Scholarship is available to resident of Maryland, Virginia, or West Virginia. Applicant must be enrolled in an accredited undergraduate or graduate landscape/ horticulture program or related discipline at a two- or four-year institution and must have minimum 3.0 GPA. Application deadline April 1. **Academic Fields/Career Goals:** Horticulture/Floriculture; Landscape Architecture. **Award:** Scholarship for use in junior, senior, or graduate years; not renewable. **Number:** 1–2. **Amount:** $1000. **Eligibility Requirements:** Applicant must be enrolled or expecting to enroll full-time at a two-year or four-year institution or university and resident of Maryland, Virginia, or West Virginia. Applicant must have 3.0 GPA or higher. Available to U.S. citizens. **Application Requirements:** Application, essay, financial need analysis, references, transcript. **Application deadline:** April 1. **Contact:** Teresa Jodon, Endowment Program Administrator, American Nursery and Landscape Association, 1000 Vermont Avenue, NW, Suite 300, Washington, DC 20005. **Phone:** 202-789-5980 Ext. 3014. **Fax:** 202-789-1893. **E-mail:** tjodon@anla.org.

DC Leveraging Educational Assistance Partnership Program (LEAP)

Available to Washington, D.C. residents who have financial need. Must also apply for the Federal Pell Grant. Must attend an eligible college at least half time. Contact financial aid office or local library for more information. Proof of residency may be required. Deadline is last Friday in June. **Award:** Grant for use in freshman, sophomore, junior, or senior years; renewable. **Number:** 2274–2300. **Amount:** $250–$1500. **Eligibility Requirements:** Applicant must be enrolled or expecting to enroll full or part-time at a two-year, four-year, or technical institution or university and resident of District of Columbia. Available to U.S. citizens. **Application Requirements:** Application, financial need analysis, transcript, Student Aid Report (SAR), FAFSA. **Application deadline:** June 28. **Contact:** Miss. Carol Talley, District of Columbia State Education Office, 441 4th Street, NW, 350 North, Washington, DC 20001. **Phone:** 202-724-7784.

Robert C. Byrd Honors Scholarship

Federally-funded, state-administered program to recognize exceptionally able high school seniors who show promise of continued excellence in postsecondary education. Must be a U.S. citizen and permanent resident of District of Columbia. **Award:** Scholarship for use in freshman year; renewable. **Number:** 28. **Amount:** $1500–$6000. **Eligibility Requirements:** Applicant must be enrolled or expecting to enroll full-time at a two-year, four-year, or technical institution or university and resident of District of Columbia. Available to U.S. citizens. **Application Requirements:** Application, transcript. **Application deadline:** varies. **Contact:** Michon Peck, Scholarship Coordinator, District of Columbia Public Schools, 825 North Capitol Street, NE, 6th Floor, Room 6077, Washington, DC 20002. **Phone:** 202-442-5110. **Fax:** 202-442-5303. **E-mail:** michon.peck@k12.dc.us.

Spring Meadow Nursery Scholarship

Scholarship for the full-time study of horticulture or landscape architecture students in undergraduate or graduate landscape horticulture program or related discipline at a two- or four-year institution. Applicant must have minimum 2.5 GPA. Application deadline is April 1. **Academic Fields/Career Goals:** Horticulture/

Floriculture; Landscape Architecture. **Award:** Scholarship for use in freshman, sophomore, junior, senior, or graduate years; not renewable. **Number:** 1–2. **Amount:** $1000–$1500. **Eligibility Requirements:** Applicant must be enrolled or expecting to enroll full-time at a two-year, four-year, or technical institution or university. Applicant must have 2.5 GPA or higher. Available to U.S. and Canadian citizens. **Application Requirements:** Application, essay, financial need analysis, references, transcript. **Application deadline:** April 1. **Contact:** Teresa Jodon, Endowment Program Administrator, American Nursery and Landscape Association, 1000 Vermont Avenue, NW, Suite 300, Washington, DC 20005-4914. **Phone:** 202-789-5980 Ext. 3014. **Fax:** 202-789-1893. **E-mail:** tjodon@anla.org.

Maryland

Child Care Provider Program

Forgivable loan provides assistance for Maryland undergraduates attending a Maryland institution and pursuing studies in a child development program or an early childhood education program. Must serve as a professional day care provider in Maryland for one year for each year award received. Must maintain minimum 2.0 GPA. Contact for further information. **Academic Fields/Career Goals:** Education. **Award:** Forgivable loan for use in freshman, sophomore, junior, or senior years; renewable. **Number:** 100–150. **Amount:** $500–$2000. **Eligibility Requirements:** Applicant must be enrolled or expecting to enroll full or part-time at a two-year or four-year institution or university; resident of Maryland and studying in Maryland. Available to U.S. citizens. **Application Requirements:** Application, transcript. **Application deadline:** June 15. **Contact:** Margaret Crutchley, Office of Student Financial Assistance, Maryland Higher Education Commission, 839 Bestgate Road, Suite 400, Annapolis, MD 21401-3013. **Phone:** 410-260-4545. **Fax:** 410-260-3203. **E-mail:** ofsamail@mhec.state.md.us.

Delegate Scholarship Program

Delegate scholarships help Maryland residents attending Maryland degree-granting institutions, certain career schools, or nursing diploma schools. May attend out-of-state institution if Maryland Higher Education Commission deems major to be unique and not offered at a Maryland institution. Free Application for Federal Student Aid may be required. Students interested in this program should apply by contacting their legislative district delegate. **Award:** Scholarship for use in freshman, sophomore, junior, senior, or graduate years; not renewable. **Number:** up to 3500. **Amount:** $200–$7950. **Eligibility Requirements:** Applicant must be enrolled or expecting to enroll full or part-time at a two-year, four-year, or technical institution or university; resident of Maryland and studying in Maryland. Available to U.S. citizens. **Application Requirements:** Application, financial need analysis. **Application deadline:** Continuous. **Contact:** Barbara Fantom, Office of Student Financial Assistance, Maryland Higher Education Commission, 839 Bestgate Road, Suite 400, Annapolis, MD 21401-3013. **Phone:** 410-260-4547. **Fax:** 410-260-3200. **E-mail:** osfamail@mhec.state.md.us.

Distinguished Scholar Award

Renewable award for Maryland students enrolled full-time at Maryland institutions. National Merit Scholar Finalists automatically offered award. Others may qualify for the award in satisfying criteria of a minimum 3.7 GPA or in combination with high test scores, or for Talent in Arts competition in categories of music, drama, dance, or visual arts. Must maintain annual 3.0 GPA in college for award to be renewed. Contact for further details. **Award:** Scholarship for use in freshman, sophomore, junior, or senior years; renewable. **Number:** up to 2000. **Amount:** up to $3000. **Eligibility Requirements:** Applicant must be high school student; planning to enroll or expecting to enroll full-time at a two-year or four-year institution or university; resident of Maryland and studying in Maryland. Available to U.S. citizens. **Application Requirements:** Application, test scores, transcript. **Application deadline:** varies. **Contact:** Monica Tipton, Office of Student Financial Assistance, Maryland Higher Education Commission, 839 Bestgate Road, Suite 400, Annapolis, MD 21401-3013. **Phone:** 410-260-4568. **Fax:** 410-260-3200. **E-mail:** ofsamail@mhec.state.md.us.

Distinguished Scholar-Teacher Education Awards

Up to $3,000 award for Maryland high school seniors who have received the Distinguished Scholar Award. Recipient must enroll as a full-time undergraduate in a Maryland institution and pursue a program of study leading to a Maryland teaching certificate. Must maintain annual 3.0 GPA for renewal. Must teach in a Maryland public school one year for each year award is received. **Academic Fields/Career Goals:** Education. **Award:** Forgivable loan for use in freshman, sophomore, junior, or senior years; renewable. **Number:** 20–80. **Amount:** up to $3000. **Eligibility Requirements:** Applicant must be high school student; planning to enroll or expecting to enroll full-time at a two-year or four-year institution or university; resident of Maryland and studying in Maryland. Applicant must have 3.0 GPA or higher. Available to U.S. citizens. **Application Requirements:** Application, test scores, transcript, must be recipient of the Distinguished Scholar Award. **Application deadline:** July 1. **Contact:** Monica Tipton, Office of Student Financial Assistance, Maryland Higher Education Commission, 839 Bestgate Road, Suite 400, Annapolis, MD 21401-3013. **Phone:** 410-260-4568.

Fax: 410-260-3200. E-mail: ofsamail@mhec.state.md.us.

Educational Assistance Grants

Award for Maryland residents accepted or enrolled in a full-time undergraduate degree or certificate program at a Maryland institution or hospital nursing school. Must submit financial aid form by March 1. Must earn 2.0 GPA in college to maintain award. **Award:** Grant for use in freshman, sophomore, junior, or senior years; renewable. **Number:** 11,000–20,000. **Amount:** $400–$2700. **Eligibility Requirements:** Applicant must be enrolled or expecting to enroll full-time at a two-year or four-year institution or university; resident of Maryland and studying in Maryland. Available to U.S. citizens. **Application Requirements:** Application, financial need analysis. **Application deadline:** March 1. **Contact:** Barbara Fantom, Office of Student Financial Assistance, Maryland Higher Education Commission, 839 Bestgate Road, Suite 400, Annapolis, MD 21401-3013. **Phone:** 410-260-4547. **Fax:** 410-260-3200. **E-mail:** osfamail@mhec.state.md.us.

Edward T. Conroy Memorial Scholarship Program

Scholarship for dependents of deceased or 100% disabled U.S. Armed Forces personnel; the son, daughter, or surviving spouse of a victim of the September 11, 2001, terrorist attacks who died as a result of the attacks on the World Trade Center in New York City, the attack on the Pentagon in Virginia, or the crash of United Airlines Flight 93 in Pennsylvania; a POW/MIA of the Vietnam Conflict or his/her son or daughter; the son, daughter or surviving spouse (who has not remarried), of a state or local public safety employee or volunteer who died in the line of duty; or a state or local public safety employee or volunteer who was 100% disabled in the line of duty. Must be Maryland resident at time of disability. Submit applicable VA certification. Must be at least 16 years of age and attend Maryland institution. **Award:** Scholarship for use in freshman, sophomore, junior, senior, or graduate years; renewable. **Number:** up to 70. **Amount:** $7200–$8550. **Eligibility Requirements:** Applicant must be age 16-24; enrolled or expecting to enroll full or part-time at a two-year or four-year institution or university; resident of Maryland and studying in Maryland. Available to U.S. citizens. Applicant or parent must meet one or more of the following requirements: Army experience; retired from active duty; disabled or killed as a result of military service; prisoner of war; or missing in action. **Application Requirements:** Application, birth and death certificate, and disability papers. **Application deadline:** July 30. **Contact:** Margaret Crutchley, Office of Student Financial Assistance, Maryland Higher Education Commission, 839 Bestgate Road, Suite 400, Annapolis, MD 21401-3013. **Phone:** 410-260-4545. **Fax:** 410-260-3203. **E-mail:** osfamail@mhec.state.md.us.

Firefighter, Ambulance, and Rescue Squad Member Tuition Reimbursement Program

Award intended to reimburse members of rescue organizations serving Maryland communities for tuition costs of course work towards a degree or certificate in fire service or medical technology. Must attend a two- or four-year school in Maryland. Minimum 2.0 GPA. **Academic Fields/Career Goals:** Fire Sciences; Health and Medical Sciences; Trade/Technical Specialties. **Award:** Scholarship for use in freshman, sophomore, junior, or senior years; not renewable. **Number:** 100–300. **Amount:** $200–$4000. **Eligibility Requirements:** Applicant must be enrolled or expecting to enroll full or part-time at a two-year or four-year institution or university; resident of Maryland and studying in Maryland. Applicant or parent of applicant must have employment or volunteer experience in police/firefighting. Available to U.S. citizens. **Application Requirements:** Application, transcript. **Application deadline:** July 1. **Contact:** Gerrie Rogers, Office of Student Financial Assistance, Maryland Higher Education Commission, 839 Bestgate Road, Suite 400, Annapolis, MD 21401-3013. **Phone:** 410-260-4574. **Fax:** 410-260-3203. **E-mail:** ofsamail@mhec.state.md.us.

Graduate and Professional Scholarship Program

Graduate and professional scholarships provide need-based financial assistance to students attending a Maryland school of medicine, dentistry, law, pharmacy, social work, or nursing. Funds are provided to specific Maryland colleges and universities. Students must demonstrate financial need and be Maryland residents. Contact institution financial aid office for more information. **Academic Fields/Career Goals:** Dental Health/Services; Health and Medical Sciences; Law/Legal Services; Nursing; Social Services. **Award:** Scholarship for use in freshman, sophomore, junior, senior, graduate, or postgraduate years; renewable. **Number:** 40–200. **Amount:** $1000–$5000. **Eligibility Requirements:** Applicant must be enrolled or expecting to enroll full or part-time at a four-year institution or university; resident of Maryland and studying in Maryland. Available to U.S. citizens. **Application Requirements:** Application, financial need analysis. **Application deadline:** March 1. **Contact:** institution financial aid office.

Guaranteed Access Grant

Award for Maryland resident enrolling full-time in an undergraduate program at a Maryland institution. Must be under 22 at time of first award and begin college within one year of completing high school in Maryland with a minimum 2.5 GPA. Must have an annual family income less than 130% of the federal poverty level guideline. **Award:** Grant for use in freshman, sophomore, junior, senior, or graduate years; renewable. **Number:** up to 1000. **Amount:** $400–$13,800. **Eligibility

Scholarships and Financial Aid

Requirements: Applicant must be age 21 or under; enrolled or expecting to enroll full-time at a two-year or four-year institution or university; resident of Maryland and studying in Maryland. Applicant must have 2.5 GPA or higher. Available to U.S. citizens. **Application Requirements:** Application, financial need analysis, transcript. **Application deadline:** Continuous. **Contact:** Theresa Lowe, Office of Student Financial Assistance, Maryland Higher Education Commission, 839 Bestgate Road, Suite 400, Annapolis, MD 21401-3013. **Phone:** 410-260-4555. **Fax:** 410-260-3200. **E-mail:** osfamail@mhec.state.md.us.

J.F. Tolbert Memorial Student Grant Program

Available to Maryland residents attending a private career school in Maryland with at least 18 clock hours per week. **Award:** Grant for use in freshman or sophomore years; not renewable. **Number:** 400. **Amount:** up to $400. **Eligibility Requirements:** Applicant must be enrolled or expecting to enroll at a technical institution; resident of Maryland and studying in Maryland. Available to U.S. citizens. **Application Requirements:** Application, financial need analysis. **Application deadline:** Continuous. **Contact:** Carla Rich, Office of Student Financial Assistance, Maryland Higher Education Commission, 839 Bestgate Road, Suite 400, Annapolis, MD 21401-3013. **Phone:** 410-260-4513. **Fax:** 410-260-3200. **E-mail:** osfamail@mhec.state.md.us.

Janet L. Hoffmann Loan Assistance Repayment Program

Provides assistance for repayment of loan debt to Maryland residents working full-time in nonprofit organizations and state or local governments. Must submit Employment Verification Form and Lender Verification Form. **Academic Fields/Career Goals:** Education; Law/Legal Services; Nursing; Social Services; Therapy/Rehabilitation. **Award:** Grant for use in freshman, sophomore, junior, senior, or graduate years; not renewable. **Number:** up to 400. **Amount:** up to $7500. **Eligibility Requirements:** Applicant must be enrolled or expecting to enroll at an institution or university; resident of Maryland and studying in Maryland. Available to U.S. citizens. **Application Requirements:** Application, transcript, IRS 1040 form. **Application deadline:** September 30. **Contact:** Marie Janiszewski, Office of Student Financial Assistance, Maryland Higher Education Commission, 839 Bestgate Road, Suite 400, Annapolis, MD 21401. **Phone:** 410-260-4569. **Fax:** 410-260-3203. **E-mail:** osfamail@mhec.state.md.us.

Maryland State Nursing Scholarship and Living Expenses Grant

Renewable grant for Maryland residents enrolled in a two or four-year Maryland institution nursing degree program. Recipients must agree to serve as a full-time nurse in a Maryland shortage area and must maintain a 3.0 GPA in college. Application deadline is June 30. Submit Free Application for Federal Student Aid. **Academic Fields/Career Goals:** Nursing. **Award:** Forgivable loan for use in freshman, sophomore, junior, senior, or graduate years; renewable. **Number:** up to 600. **Amount:** $200–$3000. **Eligibility Requirements:** Applicant must be enrolled or expecting to enroll full-time at a two-year or four-year institution or university; resident of Maryland and studying in Maryland. Applicant must have 3.0 GPA or higher. Available to U.S. citizens. **Application Requirements:** Application, financial need analysis, transcript, FAFSA. **Application deadline:** June 30. **Contact:** Marie Janiszewski, Office of Student Financial Assistance, Maryland Higher Education Commission, 839 Bestgate Road, Suite 400, Annapolis, MD 21401-3013. **Phone:** 410-260-4569. **Fax:** 410-260-3203. **E-mail:** ofsamail@mhec.state.md.us.

Part-time Grant Program

Funds provided to Maryland colleges and universities. Eligible students must be enrolled on a part-time basis (6-11 credits) in an undergraduate degree program. Must demonstrate financial need and also be Maryland resident. Contact financial aid office at institution for more information. **Award:** Grant for use in freshman, sophomore, junior, or senior years; renewable. **Number:** 1800–9000. **Amount:** $200–$1000. **Eligibility Requirements:** Applicant must be enrolled or expecting to enroll part-time at a two-year or four-year institution or university; resident of Maryland and studying in Maryland. Available to U.S. citizens. **Application Requirements:** Application, financial need analysis. **Application deadline:** March 1. **Contact:** Andrea Mansfield, Director, Maryland Higher Education Commission, 839 Bestgate Road, Suite 400, Annapolis, MD 21401-3013. **Phone:** 410-260-4558. **Fax:** 410-260-3202. **E-mail:** amansfie@mhec.state.md.us.

Physical and Occupational Therapists and Assistants Grant Program

For Maryland residents training as physical, occupational therapists or therapy assistants at Maryland postsecondary institutions. Recipients must provide one year of service for each full, or partial, year of award. Service must be to handicapped children in a Maryland facility that has, or accommodates and provides services to, such children. Minimum 2.0 GPA. **Academic Fields/Career Goals:** Therapy/Rehabilitation. **Award:** Forgivable loan for use in freshman, sophomore, junior, senior, or graduate years; renewable. **Number:** up to 10. **Amount:** up to $2000. **Eligibility Requirements:** Applicant must be enrolled or expecting to enroll full-time at a two-year or four-year institution or university; resident of Maryland and studying in Maryland. Available to U.S. citizens. **Application Requirements:** Application, transcript. **Application

deadline: July 1. **Contact:** Gerrie Rogers, Office of Student Financial Assistance, Maryland Higher Education Commission, 839 Bestgate Road, Suite 400, Annapolis, MD 21401. **Phone:** 410-260-4574. **Fax:** 410-260-3203. **E-mail:** ssamail@mhec.state.md.us.

Robert C. Byrd Honors Scholarship

Scholarship amount changes each year; however, it has ranged from $1000-1500. Amount received by the students is based on the total cost of attendance at each institution of higher education, awarded on merit basis. **Award:** Scholarship for use in freshman, sophomore, junior, or senior years. **Amount:** $1000–$1500. **Eligibility Requirements:** Applicant must be enrolled or expecting to enroll full-time at a two-year, four-year, or technical institution or university. Available to U.S. citizens. **Application Requirements:** Application. **Application deadline:** varies. **Contact:** William Cappe, Maryland State Department of Education, 200 West Baltimore Street, Baltimore, MD 21201. **Phone:** 888-246-0016. **E-mail:** wcappe@msde.state.md.us.

Senatorial Scholarships

Renewable award for Maryland residents attending a Maryland degree-granting institution, nursing diploma school, or certain private career schools. May be used out-of-state only if Maryland Higher Education Commission deems major to be unique and not offered at Maryland institution. **Award:** Scholarship for use in freshman, sophomore, junior, senior, or graduate years; renewable. **Number:** up to 7000. **Amount:** $200–$2000. **Eligibility Requirements:** Applicant must be enrolled or expecting to enroll full or part-time at a two-year, four-year, or technical institution or university; resident of Maryland and studying in Maryland. Available to U.S. citizens. **Application Requirements:** Application, financial need analysis, test scores, application to Legislative District Senator. **Application deadline:** March 1. **Contact:** Barbara Fantom, Office of Student Financial Assistance, Maryland Higher Education Commission, 839 Bestgate Road, Suite 400, Annapolis, MD 21401-3013. **Phone:** 410-260-4547. **Fax:** 410-260-3202. **E-mail:** osfamail@mhec.state.md.us.

Sharon Christa McAuliffe Teacher Education-Critical Shortage Grant Program

Renewable awards for Maryland residents who are college juniors, seniors, or graduate students enrolled in a Maryland teacher education program. Must agree to enter profession in a subject designated as a critical shortage area. Must teach in Maryland for one year for each award year. Renewable for one year. **Academic Fields/Career Goals:** Education. **Award:** Forgivable loan for use in junior, senior, or graduate years; renewable. **Number:** up to 137. **Amount:** $200–$17,000. **Eligibility Requirements:** Applicant must be enrolled or expecting to enroll full or part-time at a four-year institution or university; resident of Maryland and studying in Maryland. Applicant must have 3.0 GPA or higher. Available to U.S. citizens. **Application Requirements:** Application, essay, transcript. **Application deadline:** December 31. **Contact:** Margaret Crutchley, Office of Student Financial Assistance, Maryland Higher Education Commission, 839 Bestgate Road, Suite 400, Annapolis, MD 21401-3013. **Phone:** 410-260-4545. **Fax:** 410-260-3203. **E-mail:** ofsamail@mhec.state.md.us.

Tuition Reduction for Non-Resident Nursing Students

Forgivable loan is available to nonresidents of Maryland who attend a two-year or four-year public institution in Maryland. The loan will be renewed provided student maintains academic requirements designated by institution attended. Loan recipient must agree to serve as a full-time nurse in a hospital or related institution for an equal amount of years as tuition was paid by Maryland Higher Education Commission. Loan recipient will pay tuition of Maryland resident. **Academic Fields/Career Goals:** Nursing. **Award:** Forgivable loan for use in freshman, sophomore, junior, or senior years; renewable. **Number:** 1. **Amount:** varies. **Eligibility Requirements:** Applicant must be enrolled or expecting to enroll full or part-time at a two-year or four-year institution and studying in Maryland. Available to U.S. citizens. **Application Requirements:** Application. **Application deadline:** varies. **Contact:** Financial Aid Office of your school.

Tuition Waiver for Foster Care Recipients

Applicant must be a high school graduate or recipient of a GED under the age of 21. Applicant must either have resided in a foster care home in Maryland at time of high school graduation or GED reception, or until 14th birthday and had been adopted after 14th birthday. Applicant, if status approved, will be exempt from paying tuition and mandatory fees at a public college in Maryland. **Award:** Scholarship for use in freshman, sophomore, junior, senior, or graduate years; renewable. **Number:** 1. **Amount:** varies. **Eligibility Requirements:** Applicant must be age 20 or under; enrolled or expecting to enroll full or part-time at a two-year or four-year institution or university and studying in Maryland. Available to U.S. citizens. **Application Requirements:** Application, financial need analysis. **Application deadline:** March 1. **Contact:** Inquire at financial aid office of your school..

William Donald Schaefer Scholarship

Scholarship for current high school seniors, full-time degree seeking undergraduate and graduate students who are accepted for admission or are currently enrolled at an eligible institution in Maryland that offers courses of study, training, or other educational activities that are designed to prepare individuals for a career in public service. **Academic Fields/Career Goals:** Public Policy and Administration. **Award:** Scholarship for use in freshman, sophomore, junior, senior, or graduate years; renewable. **Amount:** up to $8500. **Eligibility Requirements:** Applicant must be enrolled or expecting to enroll full-time at a two-year or four-year institution or university; resident of Maryland and studying in Maryland. Available to U.S. citizens. **Application Requirements:** Application, financial need analysis, FAFSA. **Application deadline:** March 1. **Contact:** Office of Student Financial Assistance, Maryland Higher Education Commission, 839 Bestgate Road, Suite 400, Annapolis, MD 21401-3013. **Phone:** 410-260-4565. **E-mail:** lasplin@mhec.state.md.us.

William Kapell International Piano Competition and Festival

Quadrennial international piano competition for ages 18-31. $80 application fee. Competition takes place at the Clarice Smith Performing Arts Center at the University of Maryland. Next competition will be in 2007. **Academic Fields/Career Goals:** Performing Arts. **Award:** Prize for use in freshman, sophomore, junior, senior, graduate, or postgraduate years; not renewable. **Number:** up to 12. **Amount:** $1000–$20,000. **Eligibility Requirements:** Applicant must be age 18-31; enrolled or expecting to enroll at an institution or university and must have an interest in music. Available to U.S. and non-U.S. citizens. **Application Requirements:** Application, applicant must enter a contest, autobiography, photo, portfolio, references, CD of performance. **Fee:** $80. **Application deadline:** December 1. **Contact:** Christopher Patton, Coordinator, Clarice Smith Performing Arts Center at Maryland, Suite 3800, University of Maryland, College Park, MD 20742-1625. **Phone:** 301-405-8174. **Fax:** 301-405-5977. **E-mail:** kapell@deans.umd.edu.

New Jersey

Dana Christmas Scholarship for Heroism

Honors young New Jersey residents for acts of heroism. Scholarship is a non-renewable award of up to $10,000 for up to five recipients. This scholarship may be used for undergraduate or graduate study. Deadline: October 1 for Fall and March 1 for Spring. **Award:** Scholarship for use in freshman, sophomore, junior, senior, or graduate years; not renewable. **Number:** up to 5. **Amount:** up to $10,000. **Eligibility Requirements:** Applicant must be age 21 or under; enrolled or expecting to enroll full or part-time at a four-year institution or university and resident of New Jersey. Available to U.S. citizens. **Application Requirements:** Application. **Application deadline:** varies. **Contact:** Gisele Joachim, Director of Financial Aid Services, New Jersey Higher Education Student Assistance Authority, PO Box 540, Trenton, NJ 08625. **Phone:** 800-792-8670. **Fax:** 609-588-7389.

Edward J. Bloustein Distinguished Scholars

Renewable scholarship for students who place in top 10% of their classes and have a minimum combined SAT score of 1260, or are ranked first, second or third in their class as of end of junior year. Must be New Jersey resident. Must attend a New Jersey two-year college, four-year college or university, or approved programs at proprietary institutions. Secondary schools forward to HESAA, names and class standings for all nominees. Deadline: October 1 for Fall and March 1 for Spring. **Award:** Scholarship for use in freshman, sophomore, junior, senior, or graduate years; renewable. **Number:** varies. **Amount:** $1000. **Eligibility Requirements:** Applicant must be high school student; planning to enroll or expecting to enroll full-time at a two-year or four-year institution or university; resident of New Jersey and studying in New Jersey. Available to U.S. citizens. **Application Requirements:** Test scores, nomination by high school. **Application deadline:** varies. **Contact:** Carol Muka, Assistant Director of Grants and Scholarships, New Jersey Higher Education Student Assistance Authority, PO Box 540, Trenton, NJ 08625. **Phone:** 800-792-8670. **Fax:** 609-588-2228.

Law Enforcement Officer Memorial Scholarship

Scholarships for full-time undergraduate study at approved New Jersey institutions for the dependent children of New Jersey law enforcement officers killed in the line of duty. Value of scholarship established annually. **Award:** Scholarship for use in freshman, sophomore, junior, or senior years; renewable. **Number:** 1. **Amount:** varies. **Eligibility Requirements:** Applicant must be enrolled or expecting to enroll full-time at a four-year institution or university; resident of New Jersey and studying in New Jersey. Applicant or parent of applicant must have employment or volunteer experience in police/firefighting. Available to U.S. citizens. **Application Requirements:** Application. **Application deadline:** varies. **Contact:** Carol Muka, Assistant Director of Grants and Scholarships, New Jersey Higher Education Student Assistance Authority, PO Box 540, Trenton, NJ 08625. **Phone:** 800-792-8670. **Fax:** 609-588-2228.

Martin Luther King Physician/Dentist Scholarships

Renewable award available to New Jersey residents enrolled full-time in a medical or dental program. Several scholarships are available. Dollar amount varies. Must be a former or current EOF recipient, a minority or from a disadvantaged background. Applicant must attend a New Jersey institution and apply for financial aid. **Academic Fields/Career Goals:** Dental Health/Services; Health and Medical Sciences. **Award:** Scholarship for use in freshman, sophomore, junior,

Part 5: Appendices

senior, or graduate years; renewable. **Number:** varies. **Amount:** varies. **Eligibility Requirements:** Applicant must be enrolled or expecting to enroll full-time at a four-year institution or university; resident of New Jersey and studying in New Jersey. Available to U.S. citizens. **Application Requirements:** Application, financial need analysis. **Application deadline:** Continuous. **Contact:** Glenn Lang, EOF Executive Director, University of Medicine and Dentistry of NJ School of Osteopathic Medicine, 20 West State Street, 7th Floor, PO Box 542, Trenton, NJ 08625-0542. **Phone:** 609-984-2709. **Fax:** 609-633-8420. **E-mail:** glang@che.state.nj.us.

New Jersey Educational Opportunity Fund Grants

Grants up to $4350 per year. Must be a New Jersey resident for at least twelve consecutive months and attend a New Jersey institution. Must be from a disadvantaged background as defined by EOF guidelines. EOF grant applicants must also apply for financial aid. EOF recipients may qualify for the Martin Luther King Physician/Dentistry Scholarships for graduate study at a professional institution. **Academic Fields/Career Goals:** Dental Health/Services; Health and Medical Sciences. **Award:** Grant for use in freshman, sophomore, junior, senior, or graduate years; renewable. **Number:** varies. **Amount:** $200–$4350. **Eligibility Requirements:** Applicant must be enrolled or expecting to enroll full-time at a four-year institution or university; resident of New Jersey and studying in New Jersey. Available to U.S. citizens. **Application Requirements:** Application, financial need analysis. **Application deadline:** Continuous. **Contact:** Glenn Lang, EOF Executive Director, University of Medicine and Dentistry of NJ School of Osteopathic Medicine, 40 East Laurel Road, Primary Care Center 119, PO Box 542, Trenton, NJ 08625-0542. **Phone:** 609-984-2709. **Fax:** 609-292-7225. **E-mail:** glang@che.state.nj.us.

New Jersey War Orphans Tuition Assistance

Renewable award for New Jersey residents who are high school seniors ages 16-21 and who are children of veterans killed or disabled in duty, missing in action, or prisoner-of-war. For use at a two- or four-year college or university. Write for more information. Deadlines: October 1 for Fall semester and March 1 for Spring semester. **Award:** Scholarship for use in freshman, sophomore, junior, or senior years; renewable. **Number:** varies. **Amount:** $2000–$8000. **Eligibility Requirements:** Applicant must be high school student; age 16-21; planning to enroll or expecting to enroll full-time at a two-year or four-year institution or university and resident of New Jersey. Available to U.S. citizens. Applicant or parent must meet one or more of the following requirements: general military experience; retired from active duty; disabled or killed as a result of military service; prisoner of war; or missing in action. **Application Requirements:** Application, transcript. **Application deadline:** varies. **Contact:** Patricia Richter, Grants Manager, New Jersey Department of Military and Veterans Affairs, PO Box 340, Trenton, NJ 08625-0340. **Phone:** 609-530-6854. **Fax:** 609-530-6970. **E-mail:** patricia.richter@njdmava.state.nj.us.

New Jersey World Trade Center Scholarship

Established by the legislature to aid the dependent children and surviving spouses of NJ residents who were killed in the terrorist attacks, or who are missing and officially presumed dead as a direct result of the attacks; applies to in-state and out-of-state institutions for students seeking undergraduate degrees. Deadline varies: March 1 for Fall, October 1 for Spring. **Award:** Scholarship for use in freshman, sophomore, junior, or senior years; renewable. **Number:** varies. **Amount:** up to $6500. **Eligibility Requirements:** Applicant must be enrolled or expecting to enroll full-time at a four-year institution or university and resident of New Jersey. Available to U.S. citizens. **Application Requirements:** Application. **Application deadline:** varies. **Contact:** Giselle Joachim, Director of Financial Aid Services, New Jersey Higher Education Student Assistance Authority, PO Box 540, Trenton, NJ 08625. **Phone:** 800-792-8670. **Fax:** 609-588-7389.

NJ Student Tuition Assistance Reward Scholarship

Scholarship for students who graduate in the top 20% of their high school class. Recipients may be awarded up to 5 semesters of tuition (up to 15 credits per term) and approved fees at one of New Jersey's 19 county colleges. **Award:** Scholarship for use in freshman or sophomore years; renewable. **Number:** 1. **Eligibility Requirements:** Applicant must be high school student; planning to enroll or expecting to enroll full-time at a two-year institution; resident of New Jersey and studying in New Jersey. Applicant must have 3.0 GPA or higher. Available to U.S. citizens. **Application Requirements:** Application, transcript. **Application deadline:** varies. **Contact:** Carol Muka, Assistant Director of Grants and Scholarships, New Jersey Higher Education Student Assistance Authority, PO Box 540, Trenton, NJ 08625. **Phone:** 800-792-8670. **Fax:** 609-588-2228. **E-mail:** cmuka@hessa.org.

Outstanding Scholar Recruitment Program

Students who meet the eligibility criteria and enrolled as first-time freshmen at participating New Jersey institutions receive annual scholarship awards of $2500 to $7500. The award amounts vary on a sliding scale depending on class rank and combined SAT scores. Must maintain a B average for renewal. Deadline: October 1 for Fall and March 1 for Spring. **Award:** Scholarship for use in freshman,

Scholarships and Financial Aid

sophomore, junior, or senior years; renewable. **Number:** varies. **Amount:** $2500–$7500. **Eligibility Requirements:** Applicant must be enrolled or expecting to enroll at a four-year institution or university; resident of New Jersey and studying in New Jersey. Available to U.S. citizens. **Application Requirements:** Test scores. **Application deadline:** varies. **Contact:** Carol Muka, Assistant Director of Grants and Scholarships, New Jersey Higher Education Student Assistance Authority, PO Box 540, Trenton, NJ 08625. **Phone:** 800-792-8670. **Fax:** 609-588-2228.

Part-time Tuition Aid Grant (TAG) for County Colleges

Provides financial aid to eligible part-time undergraduate students enrolled for 6-11 credits at participating NJ community colleges. Deadline varies: March 1 for Fall, October 1 for Spring. **Award:** Grant for use in freshman, sophomore, junior, or senior years; renewable. **Number:** varies. **Amount:** $116–$375. **Eligibility Requirements:** Applicant must be enrolled or expecting to enroll part-time at a two-year or four-year institution or university; resident of New Jersey and studying in New Jersey. Available to U.S. citizens. **Application Requirements:** Application, financial need analysis. **Application deadline:** varies. **Contact:** Sherri Fox, Acting Director of Grants and Scholarships, New Jersey Higher Education Student Assistance Authority, PO Box 540, Trenton, NJ 08625. **Phone:** 800-792-8670. **Fax:** 609-588-2228.

Richard G. McCormick Prize

Award to the author of an outstanding book on New Jersey history published during the preceding two years. Offered only in odd-numbered years. Nomination form is on the Web site. Must be nominated. **Academic Fields/Career Goals:** History. **Award:** Prize for use in freshman, sophomore, junior, senior, graduate, or postgraduate years; not renewable. **Number:** 1. **Amount:** $1000. **Eligibility Requirements:** Applicant must be enrolled or expecting to enroll at an institution or university. Available to U.S. citizens. **Application Requirements:** Application, nomination, 1 copy of book. **Application deadline:** January 2. **Contact:** Mary Murrin, Director, Grants Program, New Jersey Historical Commission, Attention: Grants and Prizes, 225 W State Street, PO Box 305, Trenton, NJ 08625-0305. **Phone:** 609-984-0954. **Fax:** 609-633-8168. **E-mail:** mary.murrin@sos.state.nj.us.

Survivor Tuition Benefits Program

Program will pay the full tuition for eligible applicants attending two and four-year public colleges and universities as either half-time or full-time students. Eligibility for this program is limited to a period of 8 years from the date of death of the member in the case of a surviving spouse, and 8 years following graduation from high school in the case of a child. Deadline: October 1 for Fall and March 1 for Spring. **Award:** Scholarship for use in freshman, sophomore, junior, or senior years; renewable. **Number:** varies. **Eligibility Requirements:** Applicant must be enrolled or expecting to enroll full or part-time at a two-year or four-year institution or university; resident of New Jersey and studying in New Jersey. Applicant or parent of applicant must have employment or volunteer experience in police/firefighting. Available to U.S. citizens. **Application Requirements:** Application. **Application deadline:** varies. **Contact:** Carol Muka, Scholarship Coordinator, New Jersey Higher Education Student Assistance Authority, PO Box 540, Trenton, NJ 08625. **Phone:** 800-792-8670. **Fax:** 609-588-2228.

Tuition Aid Grant

The Tuition Aid Grant (TAG) program provides financial aid to eligible undergraduate students attending participating in-state institutions. Deadline varies: March 1 for Fall, October 1 for Spring. **Award:** Grant for use in freshman, sophomore, junior, or senior years; renewable. **Number:** varies. **Amount:** $868–$7272. **Eligibility Requirements:** Applicant must be enrolled or expecting to enroll full-time at a two-year or four-year institution or university; resident of New Jersey and studying in New Jersey. Available to U.S. citizens. **Application Requirements:** Application, financial need analysis. **Application deadline:** varies. **Contact:** Sherri Fox, Acting Director of Grants and Scholarships, New Jersey Higher Education Student Assistance Authority, PO Box 540, Trenton, NJ 08625. **Phone:** 800-792-8670. **Fax:** 609-588-2228.

Tuition Assistance for Children of POW/MIAs

Assists children of military service personnel declared missing in action or prisoner-of-war after January 1, 1960. Must be a resident of New Jersey. Renewable grants provide tuition for undergraduate study in New Jersey. Apply by October 1 for fall, March 1 for spring. Must be high school senior to apply. **Award:** Scholarship for use in freshman, sophomore, or junior years; renewable. **Number:** varies. **Amount:** $500. **Eligibility Requirements:** Applicant must be high school student; planning to enroll or expecting to enroll full-time at a two-year or four-year institution or university; resident of New Jersey and studying in New Jersey. Applicant must have 2.5 GPA or higher. Available to U.S. citizens. Applicant or parent must meet one or more of the following requirements: general military experience; retired from active duty; disabled or killed as a result of military service; prisoner of war; or missing in action. **Application Requirements:** Application, transcript. **Application deadline:** varies. **Contact:** Patricia Richter, Grants Manager, New Jersey Department of Military and Veterans Affairs, PO Box 340, Trenton, NJ 08625-0340. **Phone:** 609-530-6854. **Fax:** 609-530-6970. **E-mail:** patricia.richter@njdmava.state.nj.us.

Part 5: Appendices

Urban Scholars

Renewable scholarship to high achieving students attending public secondary schools in the State's urban and economically distressed areas of New Jersey. Students must rank in the top 10% of their class and have a GPA of at least 3.0 at the end of their junior year. Must be New Jersey resident. Must attend a New Jersey two-year college, four-year college or university, or approved programs at proprietary institutions. Students do not apply directly for scholarship consideration. Secondary schools forward to HESAA the names and class standing for all nominees. **Award:** Scholarship for use in freshman, sophomore, junior, or senior years; renewable. **Number:** varies. **Amount:** $1000. **Eligibility Requirements:** Applicant must be high school student; planning to enroll or expecting to enroll full-time at a two-year or four-year institution or university; resident of New Jersey and studying in New Jersey. Applicant must have 3.0 GPA or higher. Available to U.S. citizens. **Application Requirements:** Test scores, nomination by school. **Application deadline:** varies. **Contact:** Carol Muka, Assistant Director of Grants and Scholarships, New Jersey Higher Education Student Assistance Authority, PO Box 540, Trenton, NJ 08625. **Phone:** 800-792-8670. **Fax:** 609-588-2228.

Veterans' Tuition Credit Program

Award for veterans who served in the armed forces between December 31, 1960, and May 7, 1975. Must have been a New Jersey resident at time of induction or discharge or for one year prior to application. Apply by October 1 for fall, March 1 for spring. Renewable award of $200-$400. **Award:** Scholarship for use in freshman, sophomore, junior, or senior years; renewable. **Number:** varies. **Amount:** $200–$400. **Eligibility Requirements:** Applicant must be enrolled or expecting to enroll full or part-time at a two-year, four-year, or technical institution or university. Available to U.S. citizens. Applicant must have general military experience. **Application Requirements:** Application. **Application deadline:** varies. **Contact:** Patricia Richter, Grants Manager, New Jersey Department of Military and Veterans Affairs, PO Box 340, Trenton, NJ 08625-0340. **Phone:** 609-530-6854. **Fax:** 609-530-6970. **E-mail:** patricia.richter@njdmava.state.nj.us.

New York

American-Scandinavian Foundation Translation Prize

Two prizes are awarded for outstanding English translations of poetry, fiction, drama or literary prose originally written in Danish, Finnish, Icelandic, Norwegian or Swedish. One-time award of $2000. **Award:** Prize for use in freshman, sophomore, junior, senior, graduate, or postgraduate years; not renewable. **Number:** 2. **Amount:** $2000. **Eligibility Requirements:** Applicant must be enrolled or expecting to enroll at an institution or university and must have an interest in Scandinavian language. Available to U.S. citizens. **Application Requirements:** Application, applicant must enter a contest. **Application deadline:** June 1. **Contact:** Ellen McKey, Director of Fellowships and Grants, American-Scandinavian Foundation, 58 Park Avenue, New York, NY 10016. **Phone:** 212-879-9779. **Fax:** 212-686-2115. **E-mail:** info@amscan.org.

Broome and Allen Boys Camp and Scholarship Fund

The Broome and Allen Scholarship is awarded to students of Sephardic origin or those working in Sephardic studies. Both graduate and undergraduate degree candidates as well as those doing research projects will be considered. It is awarded for one year and must be renewed for successive years. Enclose copy of tax returns with application. Deadline is May 15. **Award:** Scholarship for use in freshman, sophomore, junior, senior, graduate, or postgraduate years; not renewable. **Number:** 25–60. **Amount:** $500–$2000. **Eligibility Requirements:** Applicant must be Jewish and enrolled or expecting to enroll full or part-time at a two-year, four-year, or technical institution or university. Available to U.S. and non-U.S. citizens. **Application Requirements:** Application, essay, financial need analysis, references, transcript, copy of tax returns. **Application deadline:** May 15. **Contact:** Esme Berg, Director, American Sephardi Foundation, 15 West 16th Street, New York, NY 10011. **Phone:** 212-294-8350. **Fax:** 212-294-8348. **E-mail:** eberg@asf.cjh.org.

New York Aid for Part-time Study (APTS)

Renewable scholarship provides tuition assistance to part-time undergraduate students who are New York residents attending New York accredited institutions. Deadline varies. Must be U.S. citizen. **Award:** Grant for use in freshman, sophomore, junior, or senior years; renewable. **Number:** varies. **Amount:** up to $2000. **Eligibility Requirements:** Applicant must be enrolled or expecting to enroll part-time at a two-year or four-year institution or university; resident of New York and studying in New York. Available to U.S. citizens. **Application Requirements:** Application. **Application deadline:** varies. **Contact:** Student Information, New York State Higher Education Services Corporation, 99 Washington Avenue, Room 1320, Albany, NY 12255. **Phone:** 518-473-3887. **Fax:** 518-474-2839.

New York Lottery Leaders of Tomorrow (LOT) Scholarship

The goal of this program is to reinforce the lottery's education mission by awarding four-year scholarships, $1000 per year for up to four years. One scholarship is available to every New York high school, public or private, that awards a high school diploma. **Award:** Scholarship for use in freshman, sophomore, junior, or

Scholarships and Financial Aid

senior years; renewable. **Number:** varies. **Amount:** $1000. **Eligibility Requirements:** Applicant must be high school student; planning to enroll or expecting to enroll full-time at a two-year, four-year, or technical institution or university; resident of New York and studying in New York. Applicant must have 3.0 GPA or higher. Available to U.S. citizens. **Application Requirements:** Application, essay, transcript. **Application deadline:** March 19. **Contact:** Betsey Morgan, Program Coordinator, CASDA-LOT (Capital Area School Development Association), The University at Albany East Campus, 1 University Place A-409, Rensselaer, NY 12144-3456. **Phone:** 518-525-2788. **Fax:** 518-525-2797. **E-mail:** casdalot@uamail.albany.edu.

New York State Aid to Native Americans

Award for enrolled members of a New York State tribe and their children who are attending or planning to attend a New York State college and who are New York State residents. Award for full-time-students up to $1550 annually; part-time awards approximately $85 per credit hour. Application deadline: July 15 for the Fall semester; December 31 for the Spring semester; and by May 20 for Summer session. **Award:** Scholarship for use in freshman, sophomore, junior, or senior years; not renewable. **Number:** varies. **Amount:** up to $1550. **Eligibility Requirements:** Applicant must be American Indian/Alaska Native; enrolled or expecting to enroll full or part-time at a two-year, four-year, or technical institution or university; resident of New York and studying in New York. Available to U.S. citizens. **Application Requirements:** Application. **Contact:** Native American Education Unit, New York State Education Department, New York State Higher Education Services Corporation, EBA Room 374, Albany, NY 12234. **Phone:** 518-474-0537.

New York State Tuition Assistance Program

Award for New York state residents attending a New York postsecondary institution. Must be full-time student in approved program with tuition over $200 per year. Must show financial need and not be in default in any other state program. Renewable award of $500-$5000. **Award:** Grant for use in freshman, sophomore, junior, or senior years; renewable. **Number:** 350,000–360,000. **Amount:** $500–$5000. **Eligibility Requirements:** Applicant must be enrolled or expecting to enroll full-time at a two-year or four-year institution or university; resident of New York and studying in New York. Available to U.S. citizens. **Application Requirements:** Application, financial need analysis. **Application deadline:** May 1. **Contact:** Student Information, New York State Higher Education Services Corporation, 99 Washington Avenue, Room 1320, Albany, NY 12255.

Regents Professional Opportunity Scholarship

Scholarship for New York residents beginning or already enrolled in an approved degree-bearing program of study in New York that leads to licensure in a particular profession. See the Web site for the list of eligible professions. Must be U.S. citizen or permanent resident. Award recipients must agree to practice upon licensure in their profession in New York for 12 months for each annual payment received. Priority given to economically disadvantaged members of minority groups underrepresented in the professions. **Academic Fields/Career Goals:** Accounting; Architecture; Dental Health/Services; Engineering/Technology; Health and Medical Sciences; Interior Design; Landscape Architecture; Law/Legal Services; Nursing; Pharmacy; Psychology; Social Services. **Award:** Scholarship for use in freshman, sophomore, junior, senior, or graduate years. **Number:** 220. **Amount:** $1000–$5000. **Eligibility Requirements:** Applicant must be enrolled or expecting to enroll full-time at a two-year or four-year institution or university; resident of New York and studying in New York. Available to U.S. citizens. **Application Requirements:** Application. **Application deadline:** May 3. **Contact:** Lewis J. Hall, Coordinator, New York State Education Department, Room 1078 EBA, Albany, NY 12234. **Phone:** 518-486-1319. **Fax:** 518-486-5346.

Regents Professional Opportunity Scholarships

Award for New York State residents pursuing careers in certain licensed professions. Must attend New York State college. Priority given to economically disadvantaged members of minority group underrepresented in chosen profession and graduates of SEEK, College Discovery, EOP, and HEOP. Must work in New York State in chosen profession one year for each annual payment. Scholarships are awarded to undergraduate or graduate students, depending on the program. **Award:** Scholarship for use in freshman, sophomore, junior, senior, or graduate years; not renewable. **Number:** 220. **Amount:** $1000–$5000. **Eligibility Requirements:** Applicant must be enrolled or expecting to enroll full-time at a two-year or four-year institution or university; resident of New York and studying in New York. Available to U.S. citizens. **Application Requirements:** Application. **Application deadline:** May 3. **Contact:** New York State Education Department, Bureau of HEOP/VATEA/Scholarships, New York State Higher Education Services Corporation, Education Building Addition Room 1071, Albany, NY 12234. **Phone:** 518-486-1319.

Scholarship for Academic Excellence

Renewable award for New York residents. Scholarship winners must attend a college or university in New York. 2000 scholarships are for $1500 and 6000 are for $500. The selection criteria used are based on Regents test scores and rank in class. Must be U.S. citizen or permanent resident. **Award:** Scholarship for use in freshman, sophomore, junior, or senior years; renewable. **Number:** up to 8000. **Amount:** $500–$1500. **Eligibility Requirements:** Applicant must be high school student; planning to enroll or expecting to enroll full-time at a two-year or four-year institution or university; resident of New York and studying in New York. Applicant must have 3.5 GPA or higher. Available to U.S. citizens. **Application Requirements:** Application. **Application deadline:** December 19. **Contact:** Lewis J. Hall, Coordinator, New York State Education Department, Room 1078 EBA, Albany, NY 12234. **Phone:** 518-486-1319. **Fax:** 518-486-5346.

World Trade Center Memorial Scholarship
Renewable awards of up to the average cost of attendance at a State University of New York four-year college. Available to the families and financial dependents of victims who died or were severely and permanently disabled as a result of the September 11, 2001 terrorist attacks on the United States and the rescue and recovery efforts. **Award:** Scholarship for use in freshman, sophomore, junior, or senior years; renewable. **Number:** 1. **Amount:** varies. **Eligibility Requirements:** Applicant must be enrolled or expecting to enroll full-time at a two-year or four-year institution or university; resident of New York and studying in New York. Available to U.S. citizens. **Application Requirements:** Application. **Application deadline:** May 1. **Contact:** HESC Scholarship Unit, New York State Higher Education Services Corporation, 99 Washington Avenue, Room 1320, Albany, NY 12255. **Phone:** 518-402-6494.

Pennsylvania

Armed Forces Loan Forgiveness Program
Loan forgiveness for non residents of Pennsylvania who served in Armed Forces in an active duty status between September 11, 2001 and June 30, 2006. Student either left a PA approved institution of postsecondary education due to call to active duty, or was living in PA at time of enlistment, or enlisted in military immediately after attending a PA approved institution of postsecondary education. Must have an eligible, non-default loan. **Award:** Forgivable loan for use in freshman, sophomore, junior, or senior years; not renewable. **Amount:** up to $2500. **Eligibility Requirements:** Applicant must be enrolled or expecting to enroll at a two-year, four-year, or technical institution or university and resident of Pennsylvania. Available to U.S. citizens. Applicant or parent must meet one or more of the following requirements: general military experience; retired from active duty; disabled or killed as a result of military service; prisoner of war; or missing in action. **Application Requirements:** Application. **Application deadline:** December 31. **Contact:** Pennsylvania Higher Education Assistance Agency, AES Lender School Team, PO Box 2461, Harrisburg, PA 17105-2461.

Educational Gratuity Program
This program is for eligible dependents of 100% disabled or deceased veterans whose disability was incurred during a period of war or armed conflict. Must be a Pennsylvania resident attending a Pennsylvania school. Up to $500 per semester may be awarded. **Award:** Grant for use in freshman, sophomore, junior, or senior years; renewable. **Number:** varies. **Amount:** $500. **Eligibility Requirements:** Applicant must be age 16-23; enrolled or expecting to enroll full-time at a two-year, four-year, or technical institution or university; resident of Pennsylvania and studying in Pennsylvania. Available to U.S. citizens. Applicant or parent must meet one or more of the following requirements: general military experience; retired from active duty; disabled or killed as a result of military service; prisoner of war; or missing in action. **Application Requirements:** Application, driver's license, financial need analysis, transcript, birth certificate. **Application deadline:** Continuous. **Contact:** Sophie Matukewicz, Program Manager, Pennsylvania Bureau for Veterans Affairs, Department of Military and Veterans Affairs, Building S-0-47, Ft. Indiantown Gap, Annville, PA 17003-5003. **Phone:** 717-861-8610. **Fax:** 717-861-8589. **E-mail:** smatukewic@state.pa.us.

Loan Forgiveness Program for State Veterans Homes Nurses
Forgivable loans for nursing education. Must have full-time employment as a direct care nurse, within three months of graduation, at one of State Veterans Homes. Applicants must complete qualifying program of study between November 17, 2005 and December 31, 2006 leading to certification as a Licensed Practical Nurse within PA or as a Registered Nurse within PA. **Academic Fields/Career Goals:** Nursing. **Award:** Forgivable loan for use in senior year. **Amount:** up to $10,000. **Eligibility Requirements:** Applicant must be enrolled or expecting to enroll at an institution or university and resident of Pennsylvania. Available to U.S. citizens. **Application Requirements:** Application. **Application deadline:** December 31. **Contact:** Pennsylvania Higher Education Assistance Agency, AES Lender School Team, PO Box 2461, Harrisburg, PA 17105-2461.

New Economy Technology Scholarship (NETS)–SciTech Scholarships duplicate of 92874
Scholarship for undergraduate studying in approved science or technology fields. Recipients of these scholarships must agree to

Scholarships and Financial Aid

work full-time in Pennsylvania following graduation, one year for each year that a scholarship award is received. Funds under this program will be awarded on a first-come, first-served basis. **Academic Fields/Career Goals:** Science, Technology, and Society. **Award:** Scholarship for use in sophomore, junior, or senior years; renewable. **Amount:** up to $3000. **Eligibility Requirements:** Applicant must be enrolled or expecting to enroll full-time at a four-year institution or university; resident of Pennsylvania and studying in Pennsylvania. Applicant must have 3.0 GPA or higher. Available to U.S. citizens. **Application Requirements:** Application. **Application deadline:** varies. **Contact:** Pennsylvania Higher Education Assistance Agency, New Economy Technology Scholarship Program, PHEAA State Grant and Special Programs, 1200 North 7th St, Harrisburg, PA 17102-1444. **Phone:** 800-692-7392.

New Economy Technology Scholarship (NETS)

Scholarships make financial aid available if you are an undergraduate studying in approved science or technology fields. Recipients of these scholarships must agree to work full-time in Pennsylvania following graduation, one year for each year that a scholarship award is received. Funds under this program will be awarded on a first-come, first-served basis. **Academic Fields/Career Goals:** Science, Technology, and Society. **Award:** Scholarship for use in freshman, sophomore, junior, or senior years. **Amount:** up to $1000. **Eligibility Requirements:** Applicant must be enrolled or expecting to enroll full or part-time at a two-year or four-year institution; resident of Pennsylvania and studying in Pennsylvania. Applicant must have 3.0 GPA or higher. Available to U.S. citizens. **Application Requirements:** Application. **Application deadline:** varies. **Contact:** Pennsylvania Higher Education Assistance Agency, New Economy Technology Scholarship Program, PHEAA State Grant and Special Programs, 1200 North 7th St, Harrisburg, PA 17102-1444. **Phone:** 800-692-7392.

Nursing Loan Forgiveness for Healthier Futures Program

Forgivable loans for nursing education. Applicants must pass the Pennsylvania State Board of Nursing examination, and begin full-time employment within three months of graduation as a direct patient care nurse at an approved, participating Pennsylvania facility, or within one year as a nurse educator in an approved participating Pennsylvania postsecondary education program. **Academic Fields/Career Goals:** Nursing. **Award:** Forgivable loan for use in freshman, sophomore, junior, or senior years. **Amount:** up to $12,500. **Eligibility Requirements:** Applicant must be enrolled or expecting to enroll at an institution or university and resident of Pennsylvania. Available to U.S. citizens. **Application Requirements:** Application. **Application deadline:** December 31. **Contact:** Pennsylvania Higher Education Assistance Agency, American Education Services, Nursing Loan Forgiveness for Healthier Futures Program, Lender School Team, PO Box 2461, Harrisburg, PA 17105-2461. **Phone:** 800-859-5442. **Fax:** 717-720-3916.

Pennsylvania State Grants

Award for Pennsylvania residents attending an approved postsecondary institution as undergraduates in a program of at least two years duration. Renewable for up to eight semesters if applicants show continued need and academic progress. Submit Free Application for Federal Student Aid. Deadline is May 1 for renewal applicants and new applicants who plan to enroll in an undergraduate baccalaureate degree and August 1 for new applicants in specific school given in research URL **Award:** Grant for use in freshman, sophomore, junior, or senior years; renewable. **Number:** up to 151,000. **Amount:** $300–$3300. **Eligibility Requirements:** Applicant must be enrolled or expecting to enroll full or part-time at a two-year, four-year, or technical institution or university and resident of Pennsylvania. Available to U.S. and Canadian citizens. **Application Requirements:** Application, financial need analysis. **Application deadline:** varies. **Contact:** Keith New, Director of Communications and Press Office, Pennsylvania Higher Education Assistance Agency, 1200 North Seventh Street, Harrisburg, PA 17102-1444. **Phone:** 717-720-2509. **Fax:** 717-720-3903.

Postsecondary Education Gratuity Program

Waiver of tuition and fees for children of Pennsylvania police officers, firefighters, rescue or ambulance squad members, corrections facility employees, or National Guard members who died in line of duty after January 1, 1976. Child by birth or adoption of a deceased sheriff, deputy sheriff, National Guard member or other individual who was on federal or state active military duty who died since September 11, 2001, as a direct result of performing official duties. **Award:** Grant for use in freshman, sophomore, junior, or senior years; renewable. **Number:** 1. **Amount:** varies. **Eligibility Requirements:** Applicant must be age 25 or under; enrolled or expecting to enroll full-time at a two-year or four-year institution or university; resident of Pennsylvania and studying in Pennsylvania. Available to U.S. citizens. Applicant or parent must meet one or more of the following requirements: general military experience; retired from active duty; disabled or killed as a result of military service; prisoner of war; or missing in action. **Application Requirements:** Application. **Application deadline:** March 31. **Contact:** PHEAA State Grant and Special Programs Division, Pennsylvania Higher Education Assistance Agency, 1200 North Seventh Street, Harrisburg, PA 17102-1444. **Phone:** 800-692-7392.

Part 5: Appendices

Quality Early Education Loan Forgiveness Program

Forgivable loan available to graduates working in Pennsylvania in the field of Early Childhood Education. Applicants must be employed full-time by a Pennsylvania Department of Public Welfare-approved child daycare center or group child daycare home. Applicants cannot have a gross annual income of more than $23,000 from employment in a Pennsylvania Department of Public Welfare-approved child daycare center or group child daycare home. **Academic Fields/Career Goals:** Education. **Award:** Forgivable loan for use in freshman, sophomore, junior, or senior years. **Amount:** up to $3300. **Eligibility Requirements:** Applicant must be enrolled or expecting to enroll at a two-year, four-year, or technical institution or university and resident of Pennsylvania. Available to U.S. citizens. **Application Requirements:** Application. **Contact:** Keith New, Director of Communications and Press Office, Pennsylvania Higher Education Assistance Agency, 1200 North Seventh Street, Harrisburg, PA 17102-1444. **Phone:** 717-720-2509. **Fax:** 717-720-3903. **E-mail:** knew@pheaa.org.

Virginia

College Scholarship Assistance Program

Need-based scholarship for undergraduate study by a Virginia resident at a participating Virginia two- or four-year college or university. Contact financial aid office at the participating institution. **Award:** Grant for use in freshman, sophomore, junior, or senior years; renewable. **Number:** varies. **Amount:** $400–$5000. **Eligibility Requirements:** Applicant must be enrolled or expecting to enroll full or part-time at a two-year or four-year institution or university; resident of Virginia and studying in Virginia. Available to U.S. citizens. **Application Requirements:** Application, financial need analysis, FAFSA. **Contact:** Lee Andes, Assistant Director for Financial Aid, State Council of Higher Education for Virginia, James Monroe Building, 10th Floor, 101 North 14th Street, Richmond, VA 23219. **Phone:** 804-225-2614. **Fax:** 804-225-2604. **E-mail:** leeandes@schev.edu.

Gheens Foundation Scholarship

This scholarship supports students from Louisville, Kentucky, who are enrolled in a HBCU participating school. Please visit Web site for more information: www.uncf.org **Award:** Scholarship for use in freshman, sophomore, junior, senior, or graduate years. **Number:** varies. **Amount:** up to $2000. **Eligibility Requirements:** Applicant must be Black (non-Hispanic); enrolled or expecting to enroll at a four-year institution or university and resident of Kentucky. Applicant must have 2.5 GPA or higher. Available to U.S. citizens. **Application Requirements:** Application, financial need analysis, transcript. **Application deadline:** varies. **Contact:** Rebecca Bennett, Director, Program Services, United Negro College Fund, 8260 Willow Oaks Corporate Drive, Fairfax, VA 22031-8044. **Phone:** 800-331-2244. **E-mail:** rbennett@uncf.org.

Mary Marshall Practical Nursing Scholarships

Award for practical nursing students who are Virginia residents. Must attend a nursing program in Virginia. Recipient must agree to work in Virginia after graduation. Minimum 3.0 GPA required. Recipients may reapply up to three years for an award. **Academic Fields/Career Goals:** Nursing. **Award:** Scholarship for use in freshman, sophomore, junior, or senior years; not renewable. **Number:** varies. **Amount:** $100–$1200. **Eligibility Requirements:** Applicant must be enrolled or expecting to enroll full or part-time at a two-year or technical institution; resident of Virginia and studying in Virginia. Applicant must have 3.0 GPA or higher. Available to U.S. citizens. **Application Requirements:** Application, financial need analysis, references, transcript. **Application deadline:** June 30. **Contact:** Norma Marrin, Business Manager/Policy Analyst, Virginia Department of Health, Office of Health Policy and Planning, PO Box 2448, Richmond, VA 23218-2448. **Phone:** 804-864-7433. **Fax:** 804-864-7440. **E-mail:** norma.marrin@vdh.virginia.gov.

Mary Marshall Registered Nursing Program Scholarships

Award for registered nursing students who are Virginia residents. Must attend a nursing program in Virginia. Recipient must agree to work in Virginia after graduation. Minimum 3.0 GPA required. Recipient may reapply up to three years for an award. **Academic Fields/Career Goals:** Nursing. **Award:** Scholarship for use in freshman, sophomore, junior, or senior years; not renewable. **Number:** 60–100. **Amount:** $100–$1200. **Eligibility Requirements:** Applicant must be enrolled or expecting to enroll full or part-time at a two-year or four-year institution or university; resident of Virginia and studying in Virginia. Applicant must have 3.0 GPA or higher. Available to U.S. citizens. **Application Requirements:** Application, financial need analysis, references, transcript. **Application deadline:** June 30. **Contact:** Norma Marrin, Business Manager/Policy Analyst, Virginia Department of Health, Office of Health Policy and Planning, PO Box 2448, Richmond, VA 23218-2448. **Phone:** 804-864-7433. **Fax:** 804-864-7440. **E-mail:** norma.marrin@vdh.virginia.gov.

Southside Virginia Tobacco Teacher Scholarship/Loan

Need-based scholarship for Southside Virginia natives to pursue a degree in K-12 teacher education in any four-year U.S. institution and then return to the Southside region to live and work. Must teach in Southside Virginia public school for scholarship/loan forgiveness. **Academic Fields/Career Goals:** Education. **Award:** Forgivable loan

Scholarships and Financial Aid

for use in freshman, sophomore, junior, or senior years; renewable. **Number:** varies. **Amount:** up to $4000. **Eligibility Requirements:** Applicant must be enrolled or expecting to enroll full or part-time at a two-year or four-year institution or university and resident of Virginia. Available to U.S. citizens. **Application Requirements:** Application, financial need analysis, FAFSA. **Contact:** Christine Fields, State Council of Higher Education for Virginia, PO Box 1987, Abingdon, VA 24212. **Phone:** 276-619-4376 Ext. 4002.

State Department Federal Credit Union Annual Scholarship Program

Scholarships available to members who are currently enrolled in a degree program and have completed 12 credit hours of coursework at an accredited college or university. Must have an account in good standing in their name with SDFCU, have a minimum 2.5 GPA, submit official cumulative transcripts, and describe need for financial assistance to continue their education. **Award:** Scholarship for use in freshman, sophomore, junior, or senior years; renewable. **Eligibility Requirements:** Applicant must be enrolled or expecting to enroll at a four-year institution or university. Applicant must have 2.5 GPA or higher. Available to U.S. citizens. **Application Requirements:** Application, financial need analysis, transcript. **Application deadline:** April 14. **Contact:** Scholarship Coordinator, State Department Federal Credit Union Annual Scholarship Program, SDFCU, 1630 King Street, Alexandria, VA 22314. **Phone:** 703-706-5019. **E-mail:** marketing@sdfcu.org.

Vice Admiral Robert L. Walters Scholarship

Scholarship for a child, stepchild, ward, or spouse of a Surface Navy Association member. The member must be in their second or subsequent consecutive year of membership. **Award:** Scholarship for use in freshman, sophomore, junior, or senior years; renewable. **Amount:** $2000. **Eligibility Requirements:** Applicant must be enrolled or expecting to enroll at a four-year institution or university. Applicant must have 3.0 GPA or higher. Available to U.S. citizens. **Application Requirements:** Application, essay, references, transcript. **Application deadline:** March 15. **Contact:** Surface Navy Association, 2550 Huntington Avenue, Suite 202, Alexandria, VA 22303.

Virginia Commonwealth Award

Need-based award for undergraduate or graduate study at a Virginia public two- or four-year college or university. Undergraduates must be Virginia residents. The application and awards process are administered by the financial aid office at the Virginia public institution where student is enrolled. Contact financial aid office for application and deadlines. **Award:** Grant for use in freshman, sophomore, junior, senior, or graduate years; renewable. **Number:** varies. **Amount:** varies. **Eligibility Requirements:** Applicant must be enrolled or expecting to enroll full or part-time at a two-year or four-year institution or university; resident of Virginia and studying in Virginia. Available to U.S. citizens. **Application Requirements:** Application, financial need analysis, FAFSA. **Contact:** Lee Andes, Assistant Director for Financial Aid, State Council of Higher Education for Virginia, James Monroe Building, 10th Floor, 101 North 14th Street, Richmond, VA 23219. **Phone:** 804-225-2614. **Fax:** 804-225-2604. **E-mail:** leeandes@schev.edu.

Virginia Guaranteed Assistance Program

Awards to undergraduate students proportional to their need, up to full tuition, fees and book allowance. Must be a graduate of a Virginia high school, not home-schooled. High school GPA of 2.5 required. Must be enrolled full-time in a Virginia 2- or 4-year institution and demonstrate financial need. Contact financial aid office of your institution for application process and deadlines. Must maintain minimum college GPA of 2.0 for renewal awards. **Award:** Scholarship for use in freshman, sophomore, junior, or senior years; renewable. **Number:** varies. **Amount:** varies. **Eligibility Requirements:** Applicant must be enrolled or expecting to enroll full-time at a two-year or four-year institution or university; resident of Virginia and studying in Virginia. Applicant must have 2.5 GPA or higher. Available to U.S. citizens. **Application Requirements:** Application, financial need analysis, transcript, FAFSA. **Contact:** Lee Andes, Assistant Director for Financial Aid, State Council of Higher Education for Virginia, James Monroe Building, 10th Floor, 101 North 14th Street, Richmond, VA 23219. **Phone:** 804-225-2614. **Fax:** 804-225-2604. **E-mail:** leeandes@schev.edu.

Virginia Tuition Assistance Grant Program (Private Institutions)

Renewable awards of approximately $1900-$2500 each for undergraduate, graduate, and first professional degree students attending an approved private, non-profit college within Virginia. Must be a Virginia resident and be enrolled full-time. Not to be used for religious study. Preferred deadline July 31. Others are wait-listed. Information and application available from participating Virginia colleges' financial aid offices. **Award:** Grant for use in freshman, sophomore, junior, senior, or graduate years; renewable. **Number:** 18,600. **Amount:** $1900–$2500. **Eligibility Requirements:** Applicant must be enrolled or expecting to enroll full-time at a four-year institution or university; resident of Virginia and studying in Virginia. Available to U.S. citizens. **Application Requirements:** Application. **Application deadline:** July 31. **Contact:** Lee Andes, Financial Aid Manager, State Council of Higher Education for Virginia, James Monroe Building,

10th Floor, 101 North 14th Street, Richmond, VA 23219. **Phone:** 804-225-2614. **E-mail:** fainfo@schev.edu.

Virginia War Orphans Education Program

Scholarships for postsecondary students between ages 16 and 25 to attend Virginia state supported institutions. Must be child or surviving child of veteran who has either been permanently or totally disabled due to war or other armed conflict; died as a result of war or other armed conflict; or been listed as a POW or MIA. Parent must also meet Virginia residency requirements. Contact for application procedures and deadline. **Award:** Scholarship for use in freshman, sophomore, junior, senior, or graduate years; renewable. **Number:** varies. **Amount:** varies. **Eligibility Requirements:** Applicant must be age 16-25; enrolled or expecting to enroll full-time at a two-year, four-year, or technical institution or university; resident of Virginia and studying in Virginia. Available to U.S. citizens. Applicant or parent must meet one or more of the following requirements: general military experience; retired from active duty; disabled or killed as a result of military service; prisoner of war; or missing in action. **Application Requirements:** Application. **Application deadline:** varies. **Contact:** Doris Marie Sullivan, Coordinator, Virginia Department of Veterans Services, Poff Federal Building, 270 Franklin Road SW, Room 503, Roanoke, VA 24011-2215. **Phone:** 540-857-7101 Ext. 213. **Fax:** 540-857-7573.

Walter Reed Smith Scholarship

Award for full-time female undergraduate student who is a descendant of a Confederate soldier, studying nutrition, home economics, nursing, business administration, or computer science. Must carry a minimum of 12 credit hours each semester and have a minimum 3.0 GPA. Submit letter of endorsement from sponsoring chapter of the United Daughters of the Confederacy. Scholarship amount for the entire academic year will be sent to college/university. **Academic Fields/Career Goals:** Business/Consumer Services; Computer Science/Data Processing; Food Science/Nutrition; Home Economics; Nursing. **Award:** Scholarship for use in freshman, sophomore, junior, or senior years; renewable. **Number:** 1–2. **Amount:** $800–$1000. **Eligibility Requirements:** Applicant must be enrolled or expecting to enroll full-time at a four-year institution or university and female. Applicant or parent of applicant must be member of United Daughters of the Confederacy. Applicant must have 3.0 GPA or higher. Available to U.S. citizens. **Application Requirements:** Application, essay, financial need analysis, photo, references, self-addressed stamped envelope, transcript, confederate ancestor's proof of service. **Application deadline:** March 15. **Contact:** Robert Kraus, Second Vice President General, United Daughters of the Confederacy, 328 North Boulevard, Richmond, VA 23220-4057. **Phone:** 804-355-1636

West Virginia

Higher Education Adult Part-time Student Grant Program

Program to assist needy adult students to continue their education on a part-time basis. Also has a component in which 25% of the funding may be utilized for students enrolled in workforce and skill development programs. Contact institution's financial aid office for more information and deadlines. **Award:** Grant for use in freshman, sophomore, junior, or senior year; not renewable. **Number of awards:** varies. **Eligibility Requirements:** Applicant must be enrolled or expecting to enroll full or part-time at a two-year, four-year, or technical institution or university; resident of West Virginia and studying in West Virginia. Available to U.S. citizens. **Application Requirements:** Application, financial need analysis. **Deadline:** varies. **Contact:** Judy Kee, Financial Aid Manager, West Virginia Higher Education Policy Commission-Office of Financial Aid and Outreach Services, 1018 Kanawha Boulevard East, Suite 700, Charleston, WV 25301. **E-mail:** kee@hepc.wvnet.edu. **Phone:** 304-558-4618. **Fax:** 304-558-4622.

Promise Scholarship

Renewable award for West Virginia residents. Minimum 3.0 GPA, ACT composite of 21, with 19 on each subtest, and combined SAT score of 1000, with no less than 470 verbal and 460 math. Provides full tuition scholarship to a state college or university in West Virginia or an equivalent scholarship to an in-state private college. Financial resources are not a factor. **Award:** Scholarship for use in freshman, sophomore, junior, or senior year; renewable. **Award amount:** $3000. **Number of awards:** 3500. **Eligibility Requirements:** Applicant must be high school student; planning to enroll or expecting to enroll full-time at a two-year or four-year institution or university; resident of West Virginia and studying in West Virginia. Applicant must have 3.0 GPA or higher. Available to U.S. citizens. **Application Requirements:** Application, financial need analysis, test scores, transcript. **Deadline:** January 31. **Contact:** Lisa DeFrank-Cole, Executive Director, West Virginia Higher Education Policy Commission-Office of Financial Aid and Outreach Services, 1018 Kanawha Boulevard East, Suite 700, Charleston, WV 25301. **Phone:** 304-558-4417. **Fax:** 304-558-3264.

Underwood-Smith Teacher Scholarship Program

For West Virginia residents at West Virginia institutions pursuing teaching careers. Must have a 3.25 GPA after completion of two years of course work. Must teach two years in West Virginia public schools for each year the award is received. Recipients will be required to sign an agreement acknowledging an understanding of the program's requirements and their willingness to repay the award if appropriate teaching service is not rendered. **Academic Fields/Career Goals:** Education. **Award:** Scholarship for use in junior, senior, or graduate year; renewable. **Award amount:** $1620–$5000. **Number of awards:** 53. **Eligibility Requirements:** Applicant must be enrolled or expecting to enroll full-time at a four-year institution or university; resident of West Virginia and studying in West Virginia. Available to U.S. citizens. **Application Requirements:** Application, essay, references. **Deadline:** March 1. **Contact:** Michelle Wicks, Scholarship Coordinator, West Virginia Higher Education Policy Commission-Office of Financial Aid and Outreach Services, 1018 Kanawha Boulevard East, Suite 700, Charleston, WV 25301. **E-mail:** wicks@hepc.wvnet.edu. **Phone:** 304-558-4618. **Fax:** 304-558-4622.

West Virginia Division of Veterans' Affairs War Orphans Education Program

Renewable waiver of tuition award for West Virginia residents who are children of deceased veterans. Parent must have died of war-related, service-connected disability. Must be ages 16-23. Minimum 2.0 GPA required. Must attend a state-supported West Virginia postsecondary institution. Deadline: July 1 and December 1. **Award:** Scholarship for use in freshman, sophomore, junior, senior, or graduate year; renewable. **Award amount:** varies. **Number of awards:** varies. **Eligibility Requirements:** Applicant must be age 16-23; enrolled or expecting to enroll full or part-time at a two-year, four-year, or technical institution or university; resident of West Virginia and studying in West Virginia. Available to U.S. citizens. Applicant or parent must meet one or more of the following requirements: general military experience; retired from active duty; disabled or killed as a result of military service; prisoner of war; or missing in action. **Application Requirements:** Application, references. **Deadline:** varies. **Contact:** Ms. Linda Walker, Administrative Secretary, West Virginia Division of Veterans' Affairs, 1321 Plaza East, Suite 101, Charleston, WV 25301-1400. **E-mail:** wvdva@state.wv.us. **Phone:** 304-558-3661. **Fax:** 304-558-3662.

West Virginia Engineering, Science & Technology Scholarship Program

For students attending West Virginia institutions full-time pursuing a career in engineering, science, or technology. Must have a 3.0 GPA on a 4.0 scale. Must work in the fields of engineering, science, or technology in West Virginia one year for each year the award is received. **Academic Fields/Career Goals:** Electrical Engineering/Electronics; Engineering/Technology; Engineering-Related Technologies; Science, Technology, and Society. **Award:** Scholarship for use in freshman, sophomore, junior, or senior year; renewable. **Award amount:** up to $3000. **Number of awards:** 250. **Eligibility Requirements:** Applicant must be enrolled or expecting to enroll full-time at a two-year, four-year, or technical institution or university and studying in West Virginia. Applicant must have 3.0 GPA or higher. Available to U.S. citizens. **Application Requirements:** Application, essay, test scores, transcript. **Deadline:** March 1. **Contact:** Michelle Wicks, Scholarship Coordinator, West Virginia Higher Education Policy Commission-Office of Financial Aid and Outreach Services, 1018 Kanawha Boulevard East, Suite 700, Charleston, WV 25301. **E-mail:** wicks@hepc.wvnet.edu. **Phone:** 304-558-4618. **Fax:** 304-558-4622.

West Virginia Higher Education Grant Program

For West Virginia residents attending an approved nonprofit degree granting college or university in West Virginia or Pennsylvania. Must be enrolled full-time. Based on financial need and academic merit. Award covers tuition and fees. **Award:** Grant for use in freshman, sophomore, junior, or senior year; renewable. **Award amount:** $350–$2846. **Number of awards:** 10,755–11,000. **Eligibility Requirements:** Applicant must be enrolled or expecting to enroll full-time at a two-year or four-year institution or university; resident of West Virginia and studying in Pennsylvania or West Virginia. Available to U.S. citizens. **Application Requirements:** Application, financial need analysis, test scores, transcript. **Deadline:** March 1. **Contact:** Daniel Crockett, Director of Student and Educational Services, West Virginia Higher Education Policy Commission-Office of Financial Aid and Outreach Services, 1018 Kanawha Boulevard East, Suite 700, Charleston, WV 25301-2827. **E-mail:** crockett@hepc.wvnet.edu. **Phone:** 888-825-5707. **Fax:** 304-558-4618.

SUMMER PROGRAMS

District of Columbia

Georgetown University College Prep Program
Washington, DC
General Information: Coed residential and day academic program.
Contact: Ms. Emma Harrington, Special Programs Director, School for Summer and Continuing Education, PO Box 571010, Washington, DC 20057-1010
Phone: 202-687-5719
Fax: 202-687-8954
E-mail: sscespecialprograms@georgetown.edu
Web site: scs.georgetown.edu/sumspec.htm

Georgetown University Gateway to Business Program for High School Juniors
Washington, DC
General Information: Coed residential academic program.
Contact: Ms. Emma Harrington, Special Programs Director, School for Summer and Continuing Education, PO Box 571010, Washington, DC 20057-1010
Phone: 202-687-5719
Fax: 202-687-8954
E-mail: sscespecialprograms@georgetown.edu
Web site: scs.georgetown.edu/sumspec.htm

Georgetown University International Relations Program for High School Students
Washington, DC
General Information: Coed residential and day academic program.
Contact: Ms. Emma Harrington, Special Programs Director, School for Summer and Continuing Education, PO Box 571010, Washington, DC 20057-1010
Phone: 202-687-5719
Fax: 202-687-8954
E-mail: sscespecialprograms@georgetown.edu
Web site: scs.georgetown.edu/sumspec.htm

Georgetown University Summer College for High School Juniors
Washington, DC
General Information: Coed residential academic program.
Contact: Ms. Emma Harrington, Special Programs Director, School for Summer and Continuing Education, PO Box 571010, Washington, DC 20057-1010
Phone: 202-687-5719
Fax: 202-687-8954
E-mail: sscespecialprograms@georgetown.edu
Web site: scs.georgetown.edu/sumspec.htm

George Washington University Summer Scholars Mini-courses
Washington, DC
General Information: Coed residential and day academic program.
Contact: Ms. Georgette Edmondson-Wright, Director, 2100 Foxhall Road, NW, Mount Vernon Campus, Washington, DC 20007
Phone: 202-242-6802
Fax: 202-242-6761
E-mail: scholars@gwu.edu
Web site: www.gwu.edu/summer/scholars

George Washington University Summer Scholars Pre-college Program
Washington, DC
General Information: Coed residential and day academic program.
Contact: Ms. Georgette Edmondson-Wright, Director, 2100 Foxhall Road, NW, Mount Vernon Campus, Washington, DC 20007
Phone: 202-242-6802
Fax: 202-242-6761
E-mail: andriano@gwu.edu
Web site: www.gwu.edu/summer/scholars

iD Tech Camps–Georgetown University
Washington, DC
General Information: Coed residential and day academic program established in 1999.
Contact: Client Service Representatives, 1885 Winchester Boulevard, Suite 201, Campbell, CA 95008
Phone: 888-709-TECH
Fax: 408-871-2228
E-mail: requests@internaldrive.com
Web site: www.internaldrive.com

Junior National Student Leadership Conference
Washington, DC
General Information: Coed residential academic program established in 1989.
Contact: Director of Admissions, 111 West Jackson Boulevard, 7th Floor, Chicago, IL 60604
Phone: 312-322-9999
Fax: 312-765-0081
E-mail: info@nslcleaders.org
Web site: www.jnslcleaders.org

Junior Statesmen Summer School–Georgetown University
Washington, DC
General Information: Coed residential academic program established in 1981.
Contact: Mr. Matt Randazzo, National Summer School Director, 400 South El Camino Real, Suite 300, San Mateo, CA 94402
Phone: 650-347-1600
Fax: 650-347-7200
E-mail: jsa@jsa.org
Web site: summer.jsa.org/summer/georgetown.html

National Student Leadership Conference: Entrepreneurship and Business
Washington, DC
General Information: Coed residential academic program established in 1989.
Contact: Director of Admissions, 111 West Jackson Boulevard, 7th Floor, Chicago, IL 60604
Phone: 312-322-9999
Fax: 312-765-0081
E-mail: info@nslcleaders.org
Web site: www.nslcleaders.org

National Student Leadership Conference: Forensic Science
Washington, DC
General Information: Coed residential academic program established in 1989.
Contact: Director of Admissions, 111 West Jackson Boulevard, 7th Floor, Chicago, IL 60604
Phone: 312-322-9999
Fax: 312-765-0081
E-mail: info@nslcleaders.org
Web site: www.nslcleaders.org

National Student Leadership Conference: Intelligence and National Security
Washington, DC
General Information: Coed residential academic program established in 1989.
Contact: Director of Admissions, 111 West Jackson Boulevard, 7th Floor, Chicago, IL 60604
Phone: 312-322-9999
Fax: 312-765-0081
E-mail: info@nslcleaders.org
Web site: www.nslcleaders.org

National Student Leadership Conference: International Diplomacy
Washington, DC
General Information: Coed residential academic program established in 1989.
Contact: Director of Admissions, 111 West Jackson Boulevard, 7th Floor, Chicago, IL 60604
Phone: 312-322-9999
Fax: 312-765-0081
E-mail: info@nslcleaders.org
Web site: www.nslcleaders.org

National Student Leadership Conference: Law and Advocacy
Washington, DC
General Information: Coed residential academic program established in 1989.
Contact: Director of Admissions, 111 West Jackson Boulevard, 7th Floor, Chicago, IL 60604
Phone: 312-322-9999
Fax: 312-765-0081
E-mail: info@nslcleaders.org
Web site: www.nslcleaders.org

National Student Leadership Conference: U.S. Policy and Politics
Washington, DC
General Information: Coed residential academic program established in 1989.
Contact: Director of Admissions, 111 West Jackson Boulevard, 7th Floor, Chicago, IL 60604
Phone: 312-322-9999
Fax: 312-765-0081
E-mail: info@nslcleaders.org
Web site: www.nslcleaders.org

Maryland

Johns Hopkins University Zanvyl Krieger School of Arts and Sciences Summer Programs
Baltimore, MD
General Information: Coed residential and day academic program.
Contact: Jeff Freedenburg, Enrollment Specialist, 3400 North Charles Street, Suite G1/Wyman Park Building, Baltimore, MD 21218
Phone: 800-548-0548
Fax: 410-516-5585
E-mail: summer@jhu.edu
Web site: www.jhu.edu/summer

National Student Leadership Conference: Engineering
College Park, MD
General Information: Coed residential academic program established in 1989.
Contact: Director of Admissions, 111 West Jackson Boulevard, 7th Floor, Chicago, IL 60604
Phone: 312-322-9999
Fax: 312-765-0081
E-mail: info@nslcleaders.org
Web site: www.nslcleaders.org

National Student Leadership Conference: Mastering Leadership
College Park, MD
General Information: Coed residential academic program established in 1989.
Contact: Director of Admissions, 111 West Jackson Boulevard, 7th Floor, Chicago, IL 60604
Phone: 312-322-9999
Fax: 312-765-0081
E-mail: info@nslcleaders.org
Web site: www.nslcleaders.org

National Student Leadership Conference: Medicine and Health Care
College Park, MD
General Information: Coed residential academic program established in 1989.
Contact: Director of Admissions, 111 West Jackson Boulevard, 7th Floor, Chicago, IL 60604
Phone: 312-322-9999
Fax: 312-765-0081
E-mail: info@nslcleaders.org
Web site: www.nslcleaders.org

University of Maryland Young Scholars Program
College Park, MD
General Information: Coed residential and day academic program established in 2002.
Contact: Ms. Terrie Hruzd, Assistant Director, Office of Extended Studies, College Park, MD 20742
Phone: 301-405-8588
Fax: 301-314-9572
E-mail: hruzd@umd.edu
Web site: www.summer.umd.edu/ysp

University of Maryland Young Scholars Program
College Park, MD
General Information: Coed residential and day arts program established in 2002.
Contact: Ms. Terrie Hruzd, Assistant Director, Office of Extended Studies, College Park, MD 20742Phone: 301-405-8588
Fax: 301-314-9572
E-mail: hruzd@umd.edu
Web site: www.summer.umd.edu/ysp

New Jersey

Appel Farm Summer Arts Camp
Elmer, NJ
General Information: Coed residential arts program established in 1959.
Contact: Ms. Jennie Quinn, Camp Director, PO Box 888, Elmer, NJ 08318-0888
Phone: 856-358-2472
Fax: 856-358-6513
E-mail: appelcamp@aol.com
Web site: www.appelfarm.org

The Hun School of Princeton American Culture and Language Institute
Princeton, NJ
General Information: Coed residential and day academic program established in 1994.
Contact: Ms. Dianne Somers, Director, 176 Edgerstoune Road, Princeton, NJ 08540
Phone: 609-921-7600
Fax: 609-683-4410
E-mail: summer@hunschool.org
Web site: www.hunschool.org

Summer Programs

The Hun School of Princeton–Summer Academic Session
Princeton, NJ
General Information: Coed residential and day academic program established in 1990.
Contact: Ms. LeRhonda Greats, Summer Academic Director, 176 Edgerstoune Road, Princeton, NJ 08540
Phone: 609-921-7600 ext. 2258
Fax: 609-683-4410
E-mail: summer@hunschool.org
Web site: www.hunschool.org

The Hun School of Princeton Summer Theatre Classics
Princeton, NJ
General Information: Coed residential and day arts program established in 1995.
Contact: Ms. Julia Ohm, Summer Programs Office, 176 Edgerstoune Road, Princeton, NJ 08540
Phone: 609-921-7600 ext. 2339
Fax: 609-924-2170
E-mail: summer@hunschool.org
Web site: www.hunschool.org

iD Tech Camps–Princeton University
Princeton, NJ
General Information: Coed residential and day academic program established in 1999.
Contact: Client Service Representatives, 1885 Winchester Boulevard, Suite 201, Campbell, CA 95008
Phone: 888-709-TECH
Fax: 408-871-2228
E-mail: requests@internaldrive.com
Web site: www.internaldrive.com

Junior Statesmen Summer School–Princeton University
Princeton, NJ
General Information: Coed residential academic program established in 1997.
Contact: Matt Randazzo, National Summer School Director, 400 South El Camino Real, Suite 300, San Mateo, CA 94402
Phone: 650-347-1600
Fax: 650-347-7200
E-mail: jsa@jsa.org
Web site: www.jsa.org/summer

Junior Statesmen Symposium on New Jersey State Politics and Government
Princeton, NJ
General Information: Coed residential academic program established in 1996.
Contact: Matt Randazzo, National Summer School Director, 400 South El Camino Real, Suite 300, San Mateo, CA 94402
Phone: 650-347-1600
Fax: 650-347-7200
E-mail: jsa@jsa.org
Web site: summer.jsa.org/symposium/newjersey.html

The New York Film Academy, Princeton University
Princeton, NJ
General Information: Coed residential arts program established in 1992.
Contact: Admissions, 100 East 17th Street, New York, NY 10003
Phone: 212-674-4300
Fax: 212-477-1414
E-mail: film@nyfa.com
Web site: www.nyfa.com

The Summer Institute for the Gifted at Drew University
Madison, NJ
General Information: Coed residential academic program established in 1994.
Contact: Dr. Stephen Gessner, Director, River Plaza, 9 West Broad Street, Stamford, CT 06902-3788
Phone: 866-303-4744
Fax: 203-399-5598
E-mail: sig.info@aifs.com
Web site: www.giftedstudy.com

The Summer Institute for the Gifted at Princeton University
Princeton, NJ
General Information: Coed residential academic program.
Contact: Dr. Stephen Gessner, Director, River Plaza, 9 West Broad Street, Stamford, CT 06902-3788
Phone: 866-303-4744
Fax: 203-399-5598
E-mail: sig.info@aifs.com
Web site: www.giftedstudy.com

New York

Acteen August Academy
New York, NY
General Information: Coed residential and day arts program established in 1978.
Contact: Rita Litton, Acteen Director, 35 West 45th Street, New York, NY 10036
Phone: 212-391-5915
Fax: 212-768-8918
E-mail: rita@acteen.com
Web site: www.acteen.com

Acteen July Academy
New York, NY
General Information: Coed residential and day arts program established in 1978.
Contact: Rita Litton, Acteen Director, 35 West 45th Street, New York, NY 10036
Phone: 212-391-5915
Fax: 212-768-8918
E-mail: rita@acteen.com
Web site: www.acteen.com

Acteen June Academy
New York, NY
General Information: Coed residential and day arts program established in 2004.
Contact: Rita Litton, Director, 35 West 45th Street, New York, NY 10036
Phone: 212-391-5915
Fax: 212-768-8918
E-mail: rita@acteen.com
Web site: www.acteen.com

Adirondack Field Ecology
Lake Placid, NY
General Information: Coed residential academic program established in 2004.
Contact: Chad Jemison, Director, PO Box 187, Lake Placid, NY 12946
Phone: 518-523-9329 ext. 149
Fax: 518-523-4858
E-mail: chad.jemison@nct.org
Web site: www.adkecology.org

Alfred University Summer Institute in Astronomy
Alfred, NY
General Information: Coed residential academic program established in 1998.
Contact: Ms. Melody McLay, Director of Summer Programs, Carnegie Hall, Saxon Drive, Alfred, NY 14802-1205
Phone: 607-871-2612
Fax: 607-871-2045
E-mail: summerpro@alfred.edu
Web site: www.alfred.edu/summer/html/astronomy.html

Alfred University Summer Institute in Entrepreneurial Leadership
Alfred, NY
General Information: Coed residential academic program established in 1998.
Contact: Ms. Melody McLay, Director of Summer Programs, Carnegie Hall, Saxon Drive, Alfred, NY 14802-1205
Phone: 607-871-2612
Fax: 607-871-2045
E-mail: summerpro@alfred.edu
Web site: www.alfred.edu/summer/html/entrepreneurial.html

Part 5: Appendices

Alfred University Summer Institute in Science and Engineering
Alfred, NY
General Information: Coed residential academic program established in 1975.
Contact: Ms. Marlene Wightman, Director of Continuing Education, NYS College of Ceramics at Alfred University, 2 Pine Street, Alfred, NY 14802
Phone: 607-871-2425
Fax: 607-871-2392
E-mail: wightman@alfred.edu
Web site: www.alfred.edu/summer

Alfred University Summer Institute in Writing
Alfred, NY
General Information: Coed residential academic program established in 2000.
Contact: Ms. Melody McLay, Director of Summer Programs, Carnegie Hall, Saxon Drive, Alfred, NY 14802-1205
Phone: 607-871-2612
E-mail: summerpro@alfred.edu
Web site: www.alfred.edu/summer

Barnard's Summer in New York City: A Pre-College Program
New York, NY
General Information: Coed residential and day academic program established in 1985.
Contact: Alexandra Nestoras, Director of Pre-College Programs, Barnard College, 3009 Broadway, New York, NY 10027
Phone: 212-854-8866
Fax: 212-854-8867
E-mail: pcp@barnard.edu
Web site: www.barnard.edu/pcp

Barnard's Summer in New York City: One-Week Humanities Intensive
New York, NY
General Information: Coed residential and day academic program established in 1985.
Contact: Alexandra Nestoras, Director of Pre-College Programs, 3009 Broadway, New York, NY 10027
Phone: 212-854-8866
Fax: 212-854-8867
E-mail: pcp@barnard.edu
Web site: www.barnard.edu/pcp

Career Explorations
New York, NY
General Information: Coed residential academic program established in 2003.
Contact: Josh Flowerman, Director, 18 Exeter Lane, Morristown, NJ 07960
Phone: 973-455-1478
Fax: 973-984-5666
E-mail: jflowerman@ceinternships.com
Web site: www.ceinternships.com

Cornell University Summer College Programs for High School Students
Ithaca, NY
General Information: Coed residential academic program established in 1962.
Contact: Abby H. Eller, Director, B20 Day Hall, Ithaca, NY 14853-2801
Phone: 607-255-6203
Fax: 607-255-6665
E-mail: summer_college@cornell.edu
Web site: www.summercollege.cornell.edu

Dunnabeck at Kildonan
Amenia, NY
General Information: Coed residential and day academic program established in 1955.
Contact: Ronald A. Wilson, Headmaster, 425 Morse Hill Road, Amenia, NY 12501
Phone: 845-373-8111
Fax: 845-373-9793
E-mail: bsattler@kildonan.org
Web site: www.kildonan.org

Environmental Studies Summer Youth Institute
Geneva, NY
General Information: Coed residential academic program established in 1993.
Contact: Prof. Jim MaKinster, Director, ESSYI, 300 Pulteney Street, Geneva, NY 14456
Phone: 315-781-4401
Fax: 315-781-4400
E-mail: essyi@hws.edu
Web site: academic.hws.edu/enviro

FivePoints
Schenectady, NY
General Information: Coed residential academic program established in 2005.
Contact: Michael Dodson, Program Coordinator, Office of Special Events, 807 Union Street, Schenectady, NY 12308
Phone: 800-883-2540
E-mail: fivepoints@union.edu
Web site: www.union.edu/fivepoints

FivePoints
Schenectady, NY
General Information: Coed residential arts program established in 2005.
Contact: Michael Dodson, Program Coordinator, Office of Special Events, 807 Union Street, Schenectady, NY 12308
Phone: 800-883-2540
E-mail: fivepoints@union.edu
Web site: www.union.edu/fivepoints

The Gow School Summer Program
South Wales, NY
General Information: Coed residential and day academic program established in 1990.
Contact: Mr. Robert Garcia, Director of Admissions, 2491 Emery Road, PO Box 85, South Wales, NY 14139
Phone: 716-652-3450
Fax: 716-687-2003
E-mail: summer@gow.org
Web site: www.gow.org

iD Tech Camps–Vassar College
Poughkeepsie, NY
General Information: Coed residential and day academic program established in 1999.
Contact: Client Service Representatives, 1885 Winchester Boulevard, Suite 201, Campbell, CA 95008
Phone: 888-709-TECH
Fax: 408-871-2228
E-mail: requests@internaldrive.com
Web site: www.internaldrive.com

Ithaca College Summer College for High School Students: Session I
Ithaca, NY
General Information: Coed residential academic program established in 1997.
Contact: Mr. E. Kimball Milling, Director of Continuing Education and Summer Sessions, 120 Towers Concourse, Ithaca, NY 14850-7141
Phone: 607-274-3143
Fax: 607-274-1263
E-mail: cess@ithaca.edu
Web site: www.ithaca.edu/summercollege

Ithaca College Summer College for High School Students: Session II
Ithaca, NY
General Information: Coed residential academic program established in 1998.
Contact: Mr. E. Kimball Milling, Director of Continuing Education and Summer Sessions, 120 Towers Concourse, Ithaca, NY 14850-7141
Phone: 607-274-3143
Fax: 607-274-1263
E-mail: cess@ithaca.edu
Web site: www.ithaca.edu/summercollege

Summer Programs

Ithaca College Summer College for High School Students: Minicourses
Ithaca, NY
General Information: Coed residential academic program established in 2002.
Contact: Mr. E. Kimball Milling, Director of Continuing Education and Summer Sessions, 120 Towers Concourse, Ithaca, NY 14850-7141
Phone: 607-274-3143
Fax: 607-274-1263
E-mail: cess@ithaca.edu
Web site: www.ithaca.edu/summercollege

Ithaca College Summer Piano Institute
Ithaca, NY
General Information: Coed residential arts program established in 2000.
Contact: Mr. E. Kimball Milling, Director of Continuing Education and Summer Sessions, 120 Towers Concourse, Ithaca, NY 14850-7141
Phone: 607-274-3143
Fax: 607-274-1263
E-mail: cess@ithaca.edu
Web site: www.ithaca.edu/cess

National Student Leadership Conference: Entrepreneurship and Business
New York, NY
General Information: Coed residential academic program established in 1989.
Contact: Director of Admissions, 111 West Jackson Boulevard, 7th Floor, Chicago, IL 60604
Phone: 312-322-9999
Fax: 312-765-0081
E-mail: info@nslcleaders.org
Web site: www.nslcleaders.org

National Student Leadership Conference: Inside the Arts
New York, NY
General Information: Coed residential academic program established in 1989.
Contact: Director of Admissions, 111 West Jackson Boulevard, 7th Floor, Chicago, IL 60604
Phone: 312-322-9999
Fax: 312-765-0081
E-mail: info@nslcleaders.org
Web site: www.nslcleaders.org

National Student Leadership Conference: Inside the Arts
New York, NY
General Information: Coed residential arts program established in 1989.
Contact: Director of Admissions, 111 West Jackson Boulevard, 7th Floor, Chicago, IL 60604
Phone: 312-322-9999
Fax: 312-765-0081
E-mail: info@nslcleaders.org
Web site: www.nslcleaders.org

National Student Leadership Conference: International Diplomacy
New York, NY
General Information: Coed residential academic program established in 1989.
Contact: Director of Admissions, 111 West Jackson Boulevard, 7th Floor, Chicago, IL 60604
Phone: 312-322-9999
Fax: 312-765-0081
E-mail: info@nslcleaders.org
Web site: www.nslcleaders.org

Power Chord Academy
Jamaica, NY
General Information: Coed residential arts program.
Contact: Elaine Valle, Admissions Director, 7336 Santa Monica Boulevard, #107, Los Angeles, CA 90046
Phone: 800-897-6677
Fax: 775-306-7923
E-mail: info@powerchordacademy.com
Web site: www.powerchordacademy.com

Pratt Institute Summer Pre-College Program for High School Students
Brooklyn, NY
General Information: Coed residential and day academic program.
Contact: Ms. Johndell Wilson, Program Assistant, 200 Willoughby Avenue, ISC Building, Room 205, Brooklyn, NY 11205
Phone: 718-636-3453
Fax: 718-399-4410
E-mail: precollege@pratt.edu
Web site: www.pratt.edu/precollege/

Pratt Institute Summer Pre-College Program for High School Students
Brooklyn, NY
General Information: Coed residential and day arts program.
Contact: Ms. Johndell Wilson, Program Assistant, 200 Willoughby Avenue, ISC Building, Room 205, Brooklyn, NY 11205
Phone: 718-636-3453
Fax: 718-399-4410
E-mail: precollege@pratt.edu
Web site: www.pratt.edu/precollege/

Sarah Lawrence College Summer High School Programs
Bronxville, NY
General Information: Coed residential and day academic program established in 2005.
Contact: Liz Irmiter, Director of Special Programs, 1 Mead Way, Bronxville, NY 10708
Phone: 914-395-2693
Fax: 914-395-2694
E-mail: specialprograms@sarahlawrence.edu
Web site: www.sarahlawrence.edu/summer

Sarah Lawrence College Summer High School Programs
Bronxville, NY
General Information: Coed residential and day arts program established in 2005.
Contact: Liz Irmiter, Director of Special Programs, 1 Mead Way, Bronxville, NY 10708
Phone: 914-395-2693
Fax: 914-395-2694
E-mail: specialprograms@sarahlawrence.edu
Web site: www.sarahlawrence.edu/summer

Skidmore College–Acceleration Program in Art for High School Students
Saratoga Springs, NY
General Information: Coed residential and day arts program established in 1985.
Contact: Ms. Marianne Needham, Coordinator, 815 North Broadway, Saratoga Springs, NY 12866
Phone: 518-580-5052
Fax: 518-580-5029
E-mail: mneedham@skidmore.edu
Web site: www.skidmore.edu/academics/art/summersix/

Skidmore College–Pre-College Program in the Liberal Arts for High School Students
Saratoga Springs, NY
General Information: Coed residential and day academic program established in 1978.
Contact: Dr. James Chansky, Director of Summer Special Programs, 815 North Broadway, Saratoga Springs, NY 12866
Phone: 518-580-5590
Fax: 518-580-5548
E-mail: jchansky@skidmore.edu
Web site: www.skidmore.edu/summer

Part 5: Appendices

The Summer Institute for the Gifted at Vassar College
Poughkeepsie, NY
General Information: Coed residential academic program established in 1992.
Contact: Dr. Stephen Gessner, Director, River Plaza, 9 West Broad Street, Stamford, CT 06902-3788
Phone: 866-303-4744
Fax: 203-399-5598
E-mail: sig.info@aifs.com
Web site: www.giftedstudy.com

Summer Theatre Institute–2007
New York, NY
General Information: Coed residential arts program established in 1989.
Contact: Ms. Allyn Sitjar, Artistic Director, 23 Tomahawk Trail, Sparta, NJ 07871
Phone: 201-415-5329
E-mail: youththeatreallyn@yahoo.com
Web site: www.youththeatre institutes.org

Syracuse University Summer College
Syracuse, NY
General Information: Coed residential and day academic program established in 1961.
Contact: Jolynn Parker, Program Manager, 111 Waverly Avenue, Suite 240, Syracuse, NY 13244-1270
Phone: 315-443-5297
Fax: 315-443-3976
E-mail: sumcoll@syr.edu
Web site: www.summercollege.syr.edu/

Syracuse University Summer College
Syracuse, NY
General Information: Coed residential and day arts program established in 1961.
Contact: Jolynn Parker, Program Manager, 111 Waverly Avenue, Suite 240, Syracuse, NY 13244-1270
Phone: 315-443-5297
Fax: 315-443-3976
E-mail: sumcoll@syr.edu
Web site: www.summercollege.syr.edu/

Tisch School of the Arts–Summer High School Programs
New York, NY
General Information: Coed residential academic program established in 2001.
Contact: Josh Murray, Assistant Director of Recruitment, 721 Broadway, New York, NY 10003
Phone: 212-998-1500
Fax: 212-995-4578
E-mail: tisch.special.info@nyu.edu
Web site: specialprograms.tisch.nyu.edu

Tisch School of the Arts–Summer High School Programs
New York, NY
General Information: Coed residential arts program established in 2001.
Contact: Josh Murray, Assistant Director of Recruitment, 721 Broadway, New York, NY 10003
Phone: 212-998-1500
Fax: 212-995-4578
E-mail: tisch.special.info@nyu.edu
Web site: specialprograms.tisch.nyu.edu

Pennsylvania

Academic Camps at Gettysburg College–Astronomy
Gettysburg, PA
General Information: Coed residential academic program established in 2004.
Contact: Doug Murphy, Director, 300 North Washington Street, Box 2994, Gettysburg, PA 17325
Phone: 800-289-7029
Fax: 718-237-8862
E-mail: academiccamps@gettysburg.edu
Web site: www.gettysburg.edu/homepage/academiccamps/

Academic Camps at Gettysburg College–College Prep & Preview
Gettysburg, PA
General Information: Coed residential academic program established in 2004.
Contact: Doug Murphy, Director, 300 North Washington Street, Box 2994, Gettysburg, PA 17325
Phone: 800-289-7029
E-mail: academiccamps@gettysburg.edu
Web site: www.gettysburg.edu/homepage/academiccamps/

Academic Camps at Gettysburg College–Community Service
Gettysburg, PA
General Information: Coed residential academic program established in 2004.
Contact: Doug Murphy, Director, 300 North Washington Street, Box 2994, Gettysburg, PA 17325
Phone: 800-289-7029
Fax: 718-237-8862
E-mail: academiccamps@gettysburg.edu
Web site: www.gettysburg.edu/homepage/academiccamps/

Academic Camps at Gettysburg College–Foreign Language Study (Spanish)
Gettysburg, PA
General Information: Coed residential academic program established in 2004.
Contact: Doug Murphy, Director, 300 North Washington Street, Box 2994, Gettysburg, PA 17325
Phone: 800-289-7029
Fax: 718-237-8862
E-mail: academiccamps@gettysburg.edu
Web site: www.gettysburg.edu/homepage/academiccamps/

Academic Camps at Gettysburg College–U.S. Civil War
Gettysburg, PA
General Information: Coed residential academic program established in 2004.
Contact: Doug Murphy, Director, 300 North Washington Street, Box 2994, Gettysburg, PA 17325
Phone: 800-289-7029
Fax: 718-237-8862
E-mail: academiccamps@gettysburg.edu
Web site: www.gettysburg.edu/homepage/academiccamps/

Academic Camps at Gettysburg College–Writer's Workshops
Gettysburg, PA
General Information: Coed residential academic program established in 2004.
Contact: Doug Murphy, Director, 300 North Washington Street, Box 2994, Gettysburg, PA 17325
Phone: 800-289-7029
Fax: 718-237-8862
E-mail: academiccamps@gettysburg.edu
Web site: www.gettysburg.edu/homepage/academiccamps/

Carnegie Mellon University Advanced Placement Early Admission
Pittsburgh, PA
General Information: Coed residential and day academic program established in 1974.
Contact: Mr. Joel Ripka, Office of Admission, Pre-College Programs, 5000 Forbes Avenue, Pittsburgh, PA 15213-3890

Phone: 412-268-2082
Fax: 412-268-7838
E-mail: precollege@andrew.cmu.edu
Web site: www.cmu.edu/enrollment/pre-college/

Carnegie Mellon University Pre-College Program in the Fine Arts
Pittsburgh, PA
General Information: Coed residential and day arts program established in 1955.
Contact: Mr. Joel Ripka, Office of Admission, Pre-College Programs, 5000 Forbes Avenue, Pittsburgh, PA 15213-3890
Phone: 412-268-2082
Fax: 412-268-7838
E-mail: precollege@andrew.cmu.edu
Web site: www.cmu.edu/enrollment/pre-college

College Admissions Camps Presented by The Admissions Authority at The Phelps School
Malvern, PA
General Information: Coed residential and day academic program established in 1970.
Contact: Ms. Emily A. Shaker, 583 Sugartown Road, Malvern, PA 19355-0476
Phone: 610-644-1754
Fax: 610-644-6679
E-mail: eshaker@thephelpsschool.org
Web site: www.thephelpsschool.org

Emagination Computer Camps
St. Davids, PA
General Information: Coed residential and day academic program.
Contact: Kathi Rigg, Director, 110 Winn Street, Suite 205, Woburn, MA 01801
Phone: 877-248-0206
Fax: 781-933-0749
E-mail: camp@computercamps.com
Web site: www.computercamps.com

iD Tech Camps–Carnegie Mellon University
Pittsburgh, PA
General Information: Coed residential and day academic program established in 1999.
Contact: Client Service Representatives, 1885 Winchester Boulevard, Suite 201, Campbell, CA 95008
Phone: 888-709-TECH
Fax: 408-871-2228
E-mail: requests@internaldrive.com
Web site: www.internaldrive.com

iD Tech Camps-Villanova University
Villanova, PA
General Information: Coed residential and day academic program established in 1999.
Contact: Client Service Representatives, 1885 Winchester Boulevard, Suite 201, Campbell, CA 95008
Phone: 888-709-TECH
Fax: 408-871-2228
E-mail: requests@internaldrive.com
Web site: www.internaldrive.com

Julian Krinsky Business School at Haverford College
Haverford, PA
General Information: Coed residential and day academic program established in 1995.
Contact: Julian Krinsky, Owner, 610 South Henderson Road, King of Prussia, PA 19406
Phone: 866-TRY-JKCP
E-mail: info@jkcp.com
Web site: www.jkcp.com

Julian Krinsky Business School at Wharton (Leadership in the Business World)
Philadelphia, PA
General Information: Coed residential academic program.
Contact: Julian Krinsky, Owner, 610 South Henderson Road, King of Prussia, PA 19406
Phone: 866-TRY-JKCP
E-mail: info@jkcp.com
Web site: www.jkcp.com

Julian Krinsky Career Builders Summer Internship Program
Philadelphia, PA
General Information: Coed residential academic program established in 2005.
Contact: Julian Krinsky, Owner, 610 South Henderson Road, King of Prussia, PA 19406
Phone: 866-TRY-JKCP
Fax: 610-265-3678
E-mail: info@jkcp.com
Web site: www.jkcp.com

Julian Krinsky Junior Enrichment Camp at Cabrini College
Radnor, PA
General Information: Coed residential and day academic program established in 2003.
Contact: Julian Krinsky, Owner, 610 South Henderson Road, King of Prussia, PA 19406

Phone: 866-TRY-JKCP
E-mail: info@jkcp.com
Web site: www.jkcp.com

Julian Krinsky Management and Technology Summer Institute
Philadelphia, PA
General Information: Coed residential academic program established in 2005.
Contact: Julian Krinsky, Owner, 610 South Henderson Road, King of Prussia, PA 19406
Phone: 866-TRY-JKCP
Fax: 610-265-3678
E-mail: info@jkcp.com
Web site: www.jkcp.com

Julian Krinsky Model UN
Philadelphia, PA
General Information: Coed residential academic program established in 2005.
Contact: Julian Krinsky, Owner, 610 South Henderson Road, King of Prussia, PA 19406
Phone: 866-TRY-JKCP
Fax: 610-265-3678
E-mail: info@jkcp.com
Web site: www.jkcp.com

Julian Krinsky Senior Enrichment Camp at Haverford College
Haverford, PA
General Information: Coed residential and day academic program established in 1991.
Contact: Julian Krinsky, Owner/Director, 610 South Henderson Road, King of Prussia, PA 19406
Phone: 866-TRY-JKCP
Fax: 610-265-3678
E-mail: info@jkcp.com
Web site: www.jkcp.com

Julian Krinsky Senior Enrichment Camp at Haverford College
Haverford, PA
General Information: Coed residential and day arts program established in 1991.
Contact: Julian Krinsky, Owner/Director, 610 South Henderson Road, King of Prussia, PA 19406
Phone: 866-TRY-JKCP
Fax: 610-265-3678
E-mail: info@jkcp.com
Web site: www.jkcp.com

Part 5: Appendices

Julian Krinsky Yesh Shabbat Summer Camp
Glenside, PA
General Information: Coed residential and day academic program established in 2002.
Contact: Julian Krinsky, Owner, 610 South Henderson Road, King of Prussia, PA 19406
Phone: 866-TRY-JKCP
Fax: 610-265-3678
E-mail: info@jkcp.com
Web site: www.jkcp.com

Julian Krinsky Yesh Shabbat Summer Camp
Glenside, PA
General Information: Coed residential and day arts program established in 2002.
Contact: Julian Krinsky, Owner, 610 South Henderson Road, King of Prussia, PA 19406
Phone: 866-TRY-JKCP
Fax: 610-265-3678
E-mail: info@jkcp.com
Web site: www.jkcp.com

National High School Game Academy
Pittsburgh, PA
General Information: Coed residential and day academic program established in 2005.
Contact: Julie Heitzer, Office of Admission, Pre-College Programs, 5000 Forbes Avenue, Pittsburgh, PA 15213-3890
Phone: 412-268-2082
Fax: 412-268-7838
E-mail: precollege@andrew.cmu.edu
Web site: www.etc.cmu.edu/gameacademy

The Performing Arts Institute of Wyoming Seminary
Kingston, PA
General Information: Coed residential and day arts program established in 1998.
Contact: Nancy Sanderson, Director, The Performing Arts Institute of Wyoming Seminary, 201 North Sprague Avenue, Kingston, PA 18704
Phone: 570-270-2186
Fax: 570-270-2198
E-mail: onstage@wyomingseminary.org
Web site: www.wyomingseminary.org/pai

Pre-College Summer Institute, The University of the Arts
Philadelphia, PA
General Information: Coed residential and day arts program established in 1981.
Contact: Erin Elman, Director, Pre-College Programs, 320 South Broad Street, Philadelphia, PA 19102
Phone: 215-717-6430
Fax: 215-717-6433
E-mail: precollege@uarts.edu
Web site: www.uarts.edu/precollege

Summer Academy of Mathematics and Sciences
Pittsburgh, PA
General Information: Coed residential and day academic program established in 2001.
Contact: Office of Admission, 5000 Forbes Avenue, Pittsburgh, PA 15213-3890
Phone: 412-268-2082
Fax: 412-268-7838
E-mail: precollege@andrew.cmu.edu
Web site: www.cmu.edu/enrollment/pre-college/

The Summer Institute for the Gifted at Bryn Mawr College
Bryn Mawr, PA
General Information: Coed residential and day academic program established in 1991.
Contact: Dr. Stephen Gessner, Director, River Plaza, 9 West Broad Street, Stamford, CT 06902-3788
Phone: 866-303-4744
Fax: 203-399-5598
E-mail: sig.info@aifs.com
Web site: www.giftedstudy.com

Summer Study at Penn State
University Park, PA
General Information: Coed residential academic program established in 1991.
Contact: Mr. Bill Cooperman, Executive Director, 900 Walt Whitman Road, Melville, NY 11747
Phone: 800-666-2556
Fax: 631-424-0567
E-mail: precollegeprograms@summerstudy.com
Web site: www.summerstudy.com

University of Pennsylvania–Penn Summer Art Studios: Art and Architecture
Philadelphia, PA
General Information: Coed residential and day arts program established in 2002.
Contact: Ms. Heather Haseley, Youth Programs Coordinator, 3440 Market Street, Suite 100, Philadelphia, PA 19104-3335
Phone: 215-746-6901
Fax: 215-573-2053
E-mail: hsprogs@sas.upenn.edu
Web site: www.upenn.edu/summer

University of Pennsylvania–Penn Summer Science Academy
Philadelphia, PA
General Information: Coed residential and day academic program.
Contact: Ms. Heather Haseley, Youth Programs Coordinator, 3440 Market Street, Suite 100, Philadelphia, PA 19104-3335
Phone: 215-746-6901
Fax: 215-573-2053
E-mail: hsprogs@sas.upenn.edu
Web site: www.upenn.edu/summer

University of Pennsylvania–Penn Summer Theatre Workshop
Philadelphia, PA
General Information: Coed residential and day arts program established in 2005.
Contact: Ms. Heather Haseley, Youth Programs Coordinator, 3440 Market Street, Suite 100, Philadelphia, PA 19104-3335
Phone: 215-746-6901
Fax: 215-573-2053
E-mail: hsprogs@sas.upenn.edu
Web site: www.upenn.edu/summer

University of Pennsylvania–Pre-College
Philadelphia, PA
General Information: Coed residential and day academic program established in 1981.
Contact: Ms. Heather Haseley, Youth Programs Coordinator, 3440 Market Street, Suite 100, Philadelphia, PA 19104-3335
Phone: 215-746-6901
Fax: 215-573-2053
E-mail: hsprogs@sas.upenn.edu
Web site: www.upenn.edu/summer

Summer Programs

Valley Forge Military Academy Summer Band Camp
Wayne, PA
General Information: Coed residential and day arts program established in 1945.
Contact: Maj. Jeffrey Bond, Director of Summer Camps, 1001 Eagle Road, Wayne, PA 19087-3695
Phone: 610-989-1253
Fax: 610-688-1260
E-mail: summercamp@vfmac.edu
Web site: www.vfmac.edu

Wyoming Seminary–Sem Summer 2007
Kingston, PA
General Information: Coed residential and day academic program established in 1991.
Contact: John R. Eidam, Dean of Admissions/Director of International and Summer Programs, Wyoming Seminary, 201 North Sprague Avenue, Kingston, PA 18704
Phone: 570-270-2186
Fax: 570-270-2198
E-mail: summeratsem@wyomingseminary.org
Web site: www.wyomingseminary.org/summer

Virginia

iD Tech Camps–University of Virginia
Charlottesville, VA
General Information: Coed residential and day academic program established in 1999.
Contact: Client Service Representatives, 1885 Winchester Boulevard, Suite 201, Campbell, CA 95008
Phone: 888-709-TECH
Fax: 408-871-2228
E-mail: requests@internaldrive.com
Web site: www.internaldrive.com

iD Tech Camps–College of William and Mary
Williamsburg, VA
General Information: Coed residential and day academic program established in 2006.
Contact: Client Service Representatives, 1885 Winchester Boulevard, Suite 201, Campbell, CA 95008
Phone: 888-709-TECH
Fax: 408-871-2228
E-mail: requests@internaldrive.com
Web site: www.internaldrive.com

Randolph-Macon Academy Summer Programs
Front Royal, VA
General Information: Coed residential and day academic program established in 1966.
Contact: Mrs. Paula Brady, Admissions Coordinator, 200 Academy Drive, Front Royal, VA 22630
Phone: 800-272-1172
Fax: 540-636-5419
E-mail: admissions@rma.edu
Web site: www.rma.edu

NOTES

NOTES

NOTES

NOTES

NOTES

Give Your Admissions Essay an Edge at EssayEdge.com™

FACT:
The essay is the primary tool admissions officers use to decide among hundreds or even thousands of applicants with comparable experience and academic credentials.

FACT:
More than one-third of the time an admissions officer spends on your application will be spent evaluating your essay.

Winning Essays Start at EssayEdge.com

"One of the Best Essay Services on the Internet"
—The Washington Post

"The World's Premier Application Essay Editing Service"
— The New York Times Learning Network

EssayEdge.com's Harvard-educated editors have helped more satisfied applicants create essays that get results than any other company in the world.

Visit EssayEdge.com today to learn how our quick, convenient service can help you take your admissions essay to a new level.

Use this coupon code when ordering an EssayEdge.com service and SAVE 10%

EPGRAD07

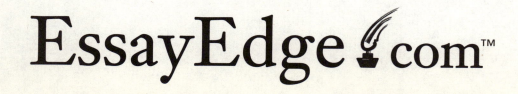

EE2006

Get Matched With an Expert and Get In.

Put an expert in your corner.
Planning for college? Don't get overwhelmed—get in. Peterson's College Consulting matches you with your very own private advisor, trained by America's leading college consultants Howard and Matthew Greene.

- *Top-notch consultants, including former deans of admission*
- *Convenient, one-on-one telephone consultation*
- *Your own in-depth, personalized action plan*
- *Fast, 48-hour service*
- *Satisfaction guaranteed!*

Visit www.petersons.com/pcc1

While you're there, be sure to check out our FREE Chat Series!

PETERSON'S
A nelnet COMPANY